FOR HONEST CITIZEN'S ONLY

Strengthening America's Future
BEYOND POLITICS

By
Charles Patton

FOR HONEST CITIZENS ONLY

Disclaimer

Despite my efforts to be factual and honest, some errors or
omissions may be inevitable. I apologize for any inaccuracies,
misinterpretations, exaggerations, or misremembered details. I
encourage readers to point out any significant flaws so they can
be corrected in future editions.

I used referential terminology (e.g., forefathers, congressman, and
he) when historically accurate while adopting more recent terms
like congresspeople in later years as other genders gained
recognition in these roles. I did not update punctuation to reflect
modern standards or alter historical spellings in quotes or
documents (e.g., *chuse* [sic]).

I relied on recent data for statistical references. While not always
from the current year due to availability, the figures remain valid
and reflect ongoing trends. Although political parties often differ
on key issues, this book presents alternative perspectives without
assigning them to any particular party.

This book is **not** about politics but governance, how societies are
best managed. When offering a position or recommendation, I
have aimed for a fair and balanced interpretation of the facts
rather than political persuasion, though I may argue for particular
alternatives. In the spirit of our founding fathers, I advocate
neither political party but only what I believe is best for
America's citizens. I have sought to be thorough, yet some topics
may be underexplored or omitted, and I sincerely apologize for
any such gaps. Likewise, if I have misrepresented anyone's
views, I extend my apologies.

Short Mystery Press
ISBN: 978-1-963809-36-7

Written for and sponsored by:
Applied Market Solutions, LLC
6045 Lexington Park
Orlando, FL 32819
Editing by: Geoff Patton
Cover by artist: Diogo Leite of Book Design Company through
99Designs.com

Role of Artificial Intelligence (AI) in This Book
As someone with dyslexia, I found OpenAI's ChatGPT and
Google's Bard helpful in refining, simplifying, organizing, and
clarifying my writing, as well as in sourcing and fact-checking.
However, I am solely responsible for selecting topics, structuring
content, crafting prompts, forming opinions, forming proposals,
and writing.

CONTENTS

PREFACE

What happens when the government we trusted no longer serves us? When liberty, justice, and opportunity crack under the weight of division, apathy, and mistrust? A free society depends on citizens who can trust their leaders, protect their freedoms, and uphold a moral, ethical, and just system — yet history reminds us that even the strongest democracies are fragile.

This book explores the forces dividing us, the delicate balance between individual liberty and collective responsibility, and the citizen's role in securing democracy. Rather than prescribing a rigid path, it fosters critical thinking and open dialogue, urging Americans to rise above partisanship and find common ground.

We must confront hard truths as global dynamics shift, and technology accelerates change. Culture and identity are evolving, national borders are shifting, and misinformation spreads faster than ever. While some nations resist these changes, others adapt — but at what cost? Seven world leaders, each driven by ambition, shape the course of peace, climate, and security. Perhaps a more peaceful world would emerge if they could set aside their rivalries.

But change does not begin with governments alone — it starts with us. Who are we? What do we stand for? Are we driven by self-interest or by the greater good? Governance should reflect the lives we aspire to live, yet only an engaged and informed citizenry can ensure this.

Former President Jimmy Carter chose to be called "Citizen" after leaving office, reminding us that a nation's strength lies in its leaders and people. Being a citizen is not passive — it is an active role.

The fate of democracy rests with those who refuse to be silent bystanders. The time to act is now. Let's get to it.

INTRODUCTION

Despite endless communication tools, Americans feel more disconnected than ever. Trust in government has hit historic lows — only 22% of Americans trust the federal government to do what is right "just about always" or "most of the time," according to a June 2024 Pew Research report.

This book is more than an analysis; it is an invitation. Not to observe, but to engage. "The things that unite us, these are far greater than the things that divide us," said John F. Kennedy in 1961. That truth still holds.

It is time to move beyond division, seek understanding, and demand accountability from our leaders. Citizenship is not a spectator sport. Your voice matters. Your role is essential.

Let us begin with open minds and a commitment to unity.

Our Current Evolutionary State

Since 1992, when the Internet became widely available, technology, society, and government have changed at an astonishing speed. Advances in communication, business, healthcare, education, and governance now shape every part of daily life. Meanwhile, wealth is concentrating at an extreme rate in America and worldwide, raising concerns about power and control.

More recently, satellite internet from companies like SpaceX, Amazon, and OneWeb has expanded high-speed access to nearly every corner of the world. This scientific advancement has helped close the digital divide, changing how people live, connect, and understand each other.

At the same time, the political and social landscapes have undergone dramatic changes. For example, the cost of running for political office has skyrocketed, making running for office increasingly exclusive to the wealthy — first millionaires and now billionaires.

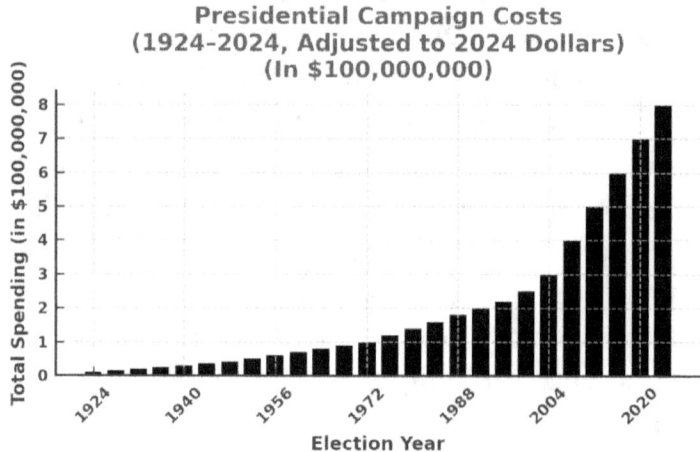

The total expenditure in 2024 for the Federal Elections is estimated at $15.9 billion, about the same as for 2020. With the undoubted consequence of much waste and raises suspicions about <u>why so much money would be spent</u>.[242] More on this later under Campaign Financing Reform.

With the aid of all this increased communication, social issues, such as abortion, voting rights, election security, and diversity, have become profoundly polarizing, fracturing communities and political discourse. Gun violence has also reached alarming levels, threatening the safety and cohesion of communities across the nation.

And, most significantly, over the past two centuries, the degree to which citizens are directly represented by their elected officials has diminished dramatically to the point of ineffectiveness. <u>As you will read below, our ability as citizens to shape the issues that divide us is as obstructed as ever</u>.

As American citizens, we are responsible for ensuring that our government adapts to change directly or through our elected representatives. Ignoring these shifts could push the country toward decline, instability, or irrelevance.

To stay free, we must have a government that answers to the people, the core principle of constitutionalism, and this must be restored.

Despite deep challenges and growing divisions, America's democracy has endured. Its survival depends on engaged citizens who demand accountability, lead when needed, and support candidates who uphold our foundational principles and serve the people. But how much have our needs changed?

How We Changed Since 1787

The United States of America has changed vastly as a country and as a people since our Founding Fathers signed our Constitution on September 17, 1787. Over the years that followed, our Constitution has been amended 27 times. The most recent amendment (the 27th, about congressional compensation) was ratified on May 7, 1992. The one before that, the 26th, allowed 18-year-olds to vote and was ratified on July 1, 1971. The 28th Amendment, the Equal Rights Amendment, has been ratified by the necessary number of states but final confirmation has been held up by various challenges. More on this later.

Because so much has changed in our lives over the last 236 years, and even since 1992, it is reasonable to ask whether our system of governance is keeping pace and if our laws should be updated accordingly. Adjustments become necessary when societal and technological advances outstrip our government's ability to govern effectively. As we consider today's pressing issues, it is imperative to examine the foundational elements of our political system. Let us begin with our system of representation and the qualifications of our leaders.

Representation

Our representation in Congress has been gradually but thoroughly diluted over the years. Without meaningful representation and changes in governance, we risk straying from our founding principles and failing to address most Americans' true needs and desires.

In his Farewell Address (1796), George Washington warned that political factions could lead to division, corruption, and a weakening of national unity. Similarly, John Adams saw political parties as a threat to national stability, fearing they would serve special interests rather than the common good.

Despite the framers' general opposition to factionalism, political parties emerged just four to six years after the Constitution was signed, with the formation of the Federalists and Democratic-Republicans. Washington's concerns proved valid as partisan divisions took hold, shaping American politics ever since.[283]

Citizen-to-House Representative Ratio

One clear example of our diluted representation is that the number of House Representatives has not kept pace with population growth. When the government was founded, there was one representative for every 20,000 citizens, which was later adjusted to 30,000 and then 40,000. After that, Congress stopped making adjustments. If the original ratio still applied today, we would have 8,298 representatives instead of 435, each representing an average of 767,816 citizens. It is impossible for a single representative to truly understand and advocate for the needs of nearly a million diverse people.

Polling a well-designed sample of a million people might offer comparable representation. However, trust in polls has declined, especially after high-profile inaccuracies in the

2016 and 2020 U.S. presidential elections. Many Americans believe polls can be biased by question framing, sampling errors, and shifting response rates. Relying on polling data instead of accurate representation reduces citizens to mere statistics rather than recognizing their unique needs and concerns.

As a result, Congress only nominally represents the people in crafting and passing laws. Voters often support the party that aligns closest to their views, but many do not fully understand where their party stands on all issues. Instead, political choices are shaped by friends, social circles, TV, news, and social media, most biased or driven by specific agendas. Many also vote against the party they oppose, swayed by negative propaganda, media narratives, and partisan rhetoric. The resulting confusion often forces voters to simplify their vote to the lesser of two evils, sometimes going against their values while overlooking critical needs that directly impact on their lives.

Citizen to Senator Ratio

The House of Representatives is not the only case of diluted representation. Since America's founding, the number of states has grown from 13 to 50, and the number of senators from 26 to 100. This structure aligns with John Adams' view that senators represent state interests. However, while a senator in 1787 represented about 25,000 people, today that number exceeds six million. We would need 12,220 senators, or more states, to match the original ratio. Alternatively, states must develop a better system to relay citizens' needs to their senators.

Congress is already distant from the people and heavily influenced by those who can access them — lobbyists and wealthy donors. Kristina Karamo, Michigan's Republican Party chairwoman, admitted, "You are required to do their bidding to get their funds, and so we just wind up destroying the country slower than the Democrats." Meanwhile, the needs of urban and rural America vary widely, what matters in Chicago may not in downstate Illinois.

Political beliefs evolve. Just as religious doctrines shift, like debates over priestly celibacy or women's roles in the clergy, voters reconsider their stances on issues such as population control, stem cell research, and LGBTQ rights. Adjusting political principles is part of personal and societal growth. However, with only two dominant political parties, voters often compromise their values rather than fully align with a candidate. In navigating today's issues, we must focus on core American principles and demand better representation — perhaps even a new representation system.

One possible solution would be a layered system using regional committees to engage citizens via online platforms, mail surveys, and town halls. Findings would inform national referendums.

This system would have two levels of representation:

1. Regional Representatives — One for every 50,000 people, elected from areas not confined by state lines, grouped into 13 districts (West, Midwest, Mideast, and East — each divided into North, Central, and South — plus a district for U.S. territories, Hawaii, Alaska, and D.C.).

2. District Committees — Each district elects one representative to bring regional concerns directly to Congress. These committees advise the House of Representatives, providing non-binding yet strong recommendations to better reflect public interests.

Representatives in this system could serve part-time, meet quarterly, and receive minimal compensation. This approach would decentralize political influence while seamlessly integrating with the existing government structure to strengthen communication between citizens and

Congress. If this model isn't the right fit, a better one can surely be devised.

The Speaker of the House

A third example of questionable citizen representation is that the Speaker of the House, who is third in line for the presidency, is not elected by the public but by members of the House of Representatives. This arrangement differs from the vice president, who is chosen by voters as part of the presidential ticket and serves as president of the Senate. Given the Speaker's place in the presidential line of succession, citizens should have more direct influence over this role.

One possible reform would be to include the Speaker of the House on a party's national ticket alongside the presidential and vice-presidential candidates. This change would require modifications to the political system, likely including a constitutional amendment.

With these changes, people would be more engaged, representation would be fairer, and legislating would be easier.

Who Picks Party's Candidates?

Another concern about representation is the excessive power of political party leadership, which controls candidate selection, debate participation, and funding, significantly influencing election outcomes. A party's national chairperson and committee members are not elected by the public but chosen through internal party processes. The chairperson is typically selected by the party's national committee or the presidential nominee, while committee members come from state party elections, appointments, or automatic inclusion based on party roles.

One way to democratize this process would be to allow all registered party members to vote for the national chairperson and party committee members rather than relying on unelected state party officials or appointments. This reform could increase democratic participation within parties and ensure that leadership more accurately reflects its members' collective will and values.

Lobbyists and Other Influencers

Lobbying is another powerful force influencing congressional representation. While deeply embedded in politics, it remains highly controversial, as it derives from the constitutional right to petition. Lobbying shapes policymaking through frequent interactions between officials and interest groups, yet it often conflicts with public interests.

Despite congressional efforts to enforce ethics, oversight remains weak — akin to a "fox guarding the henhouse." Recent controversies, including those involving Supreme Court justices in 2023, underscore the urgent need for stronger ethical standards across all three branches of government. Reforming lobbying practices to increase transparency and accountability is essential to restoring public trust in the political system.

The Right to Petition and Its Evolution

The constitutional right to petition allows individuals, groups, and corporations to influence government decisions. Rooted in the First Amendment, this right ensures that people can challenge government actions without fear of reprisal. It dates back to medieval England when peasants petitioned the crown for redress.

In early America, lobbying was informal, with individuals directly approaching lawmakers. By the 1800s and early 1900s, businesses and interest groups began hiring professional lobbyists, leading to the first lobbying firms. As lobbying grew more sophisticated in the mid-20th century, lawmakers introduced disclosure laws to increase transparency.

Today, lobbying is a global force, with foreign governments shaping U.S. policy and American lobbyists working abroad. However, not all lobbying is equal — while any citizen can petition their representatives, wealthy special interests hold far more significant influence due to their financial power and insider connections.

The Scale of Lobbying Influence

Lobbying expenditures in the U.S. have soared to $5 billion annually, with firms employing over 12,600 registered lobbyists and 21,750 additional staff. Lobbyists command starting salaries averaging $300,000, reflecting the vast resources corporations, labor unions, and interest groups dedicate to shaping policy.

This financial influence has grown exponentially. Fifty years ago, lobbying spending was only a fraction of today's levels. By the late 1990s, the industry became highly specialized, employing law, government affairs, and public relations experts to shape policy through direct lobbying, grassroots campaigns, and media influence. Today, the Internet and social media have further transformed lobbying, allowing firms to mobilize supporters, craft targeted messages, and track legislation in real-time.

The Cost of Influence on Government

With 535 legislators in Congress, lobbying investments exceed $9 million per legislator annually. On average, 64 people are tasked with influencing each lawmaker. This imbalance raises concerns about whether lobbying aligns with the democratic principles envisioned by the Founding Fathers and whether the government truly represents the people or the highest bidders.

Revolving Door and Conflicts of Interest

The deep financial ties between lobbying and government raise concerns about conflicts of interest. Since leaving office, 427 former members of Congress have taken jobs as lobbyists or senior advisers. Of the 75 members who left the 113th Congress (2015), 64.2% entered the lobbying sector by working for lobbying firms or clients. This revolving door raises questions about whether lawmakers shape policy with future lobbying careers in mind rather than representing public interests.

Concerns Over Transparency and Accountability

Despite efforts to enforce ethical rules, oversight remains weak — often described as "the fox guarding the henhouse." The 2023 Supreme Court ethics controversies further highlight the need for stronger accountability across all branches of government.

Some advocate for stricter lobbying regulations to ensure transparency and fairness, but major groups like the National Rifle Association (NRA) and the American Civil Liberties Union (ACLU) have opposed reforms. The point is that corporate and labor interests wield far more power in Congress than the average citizen.

What Could Be Done?

Several things could be done to strike a more favorable balance for citizen representation and address lobbyists' disproportionate influence on our representatives. One approach involves restricting lobbyists' access to party leaders and legislators to one day per week, coupled with a requirement for comprehensive documentation and public accessibility of all lobbying meetings. This restriction would enhance transparency and allow public scrutiny.

Further, establishing an independent counsel to act as a watchdog over these activities could bolster oversight. This body would ensure that all interactions between lobbyists and lawmakers are transparent. Alternatively, moving away from group lobbying towards a system where a government body processes petitions from individual citizens could improve direct representation. This shift could integrate well with a proposed regional structure aimed at enhancing how citizen concerns are addressed.

In any event, stronger ethics regulations in lobbying, with independent, nonpartisan enforcement to prevent violations effectively, are crucial. Enhancing lobbying disclosure laws would also increase transparency, requiring detailed, real-time reporting of all lobbying activities, including contacts with government officials, campaign contributions, and grassroots efforts.

A more radical proposal would eliminate organized lobbying and replace it with Regional Councils. These councils would become the primary conduit for legislative influence, ensuring that the voices shaping Congress's actions come directly from the citizens, not special interests. Such sweeping reforms would realign legislative influence to favor public interest, potentially revitalizing trust and participation in the democratic process.

The pervasive influence of campaign financing is yet another way in which the representation of ordinary citizens is being eroded.

The Influence of Campaign Financing on American Governance

In modern politics, corporations wield substantial influence through campaign donations as well as lobbying. The *Citizens United v. FEC* decision, which equated corporate spending with free speech, has amplified the role of money in political campaigns, distorting democracy by allowing wealthy corporations and individuals to hold far more sway than the average citizen.

To correct this imbalance, better laws should impose stricter limits on corporate contributions and safeguard elections from the overwhelming financial influence of a privileged few. The goal must be to restore fairness and transparency to the political process, ensuring that every citizen's voice carries equal weight.

Campaign Financing and Political Action Committees (PACs)

Campaign financing has become one of the most powerful influences in American governance. In recent decades, the financial demands of running public offices have skyrocketed, with costs for federal elections now exceeding $16 billion. This staggering sum reflects the high cost of campaign operations — such as advertising, travel, staff, social media marketing, and events — and underscores the increasing reliance on substantial financial backing. We will discuss Campaign Financing Reform later but here the issue is the creation of undue influence on our elected officials to the point where representation of our citizens' needs and views become overshadowed by money influence.

Political Action Committees (PACs) play a pivotal role in this funding system. Initially created to support or oppose political candidates, PACs collect donations from individuals, corporations, unions, and, in the case of Super PACs, even anonymous non-profits (501(c)(4)s). Unlike traditional PACs, Super PACs can raise and spend unlimited funds, although they are legally prohibited from coordinating directly with campaigns. This ability to wield vast sums of money has amplified the influence of well-funded interest groups, often at the expense of average citizens' voices.

Super PACs differ from traditional PACs primarily in their ability to raise and spend unlimited funds independently of candidate campaigns. While they cannot donate directly to candidates or coordinate with their campaigns, they use their financial power for advertising and outreach to influence elections. Super PACs can significantly shape public perceptions and influence elections without being held responsible for the accuracy of their claims. Their funding often comes from a mix of disclosed donors and "dark money" sources, obscuring some contributions' origins and raising concerns about transparency and accountability.

The rise of Super PACs and 501(c)(4) organizations has further expanded money's role in shaping policy and political outcomes. This shift challenges the democratic principle of equal representation, raising critical questions about who ultimately drives American governance and whose interests are prioritized.

The Cost of Elections: $Billions and Rising

The cost of U.S. elections has skyrocketed, with the 2024 cycle projected to reach $16 billion, making it the most expensive in American history. This includes spending on presidential, congressional, and down-ballot races, driven by competitive House and Senate contests, especially those affected by court-ordered redistricting.

Outside spending, particularly from Super PACs, is expected to exceed $5 billion, further shaping election outcomes. Compared to 50 years ago, when campaigns were less costly and sophisticated, today's elections have become high-stakes financial battles. While digital media and connected TV (CTV) now supplement traditional broadcast ads, lowering communication costs, overall spending continues to surge, highlighting the increasing financial intensity of American elections.

The result is a system that often prioritizes donors' interests over those of the general public, as candidates and elected officials are incentivized to cater to the needs of their financial backers to ensure continued support. In this landscape, money's influence on elections creates a cycle where only those with substantial funding can realistically contend for office. This concentration of power in the hands of the wealthy undermines the notion of "one person, one vote," transforming elections into a high-stakes competition driven by financial clout.

The concern for American Citizens is the dramatic increase in the influence of money in elections and the impact of large donations on democratic representation and transparency.

Corruption, Foreign Influence, and Influence Peddling

The vast sums of money in American politics have also opened the door to domestic and foreign corruption. Foreign powers, recognizing the importance of financial influence in the U.S. political system, have sought to impact American elections and policy decisions through covert donations and influence peddling. While U.S. law prohibits direct foreign contributions to political campaigns, foreign entities have exploited legal loopholes, such as contributing through U.S.-

based subsidiaries or super PACs, to influence American elections.[422] This foreign involvement raises concerns about national sovereignty, as policy decisions influenced by foreign interests may not align with the best interests of the American people.

Influence peddling, the practice of using political connections to secure favorable outcomes in exchange for financial or political favors, has become increasingly common. This often takes the form of campaign donations or support for PACs that benefit specific candidates. In some cases, public officials and candidates have been known to trade access, policy support, or regulatory leniency for donations, undermining the integrity of their offices and further eroding public trust in government.

The Expansion of Graft and Indirect Corruption

In recent years, indirect forms of graft have become more prevalent in American politics. This form of corruption often involves funneling funds through properties, companies owned by public officials, or their families. For example, a lobbyist or interest group may book events at a hotel a politician owns, resulting in indirect financial benefits, even though the rule (Not yet a law!) has been that politicians are to turn over their assets to an independent, unrelated manager for the length of their term. Similarly, corporations may contract with companies owned by family members of influential officials to secure favor or leniency on regulatory matters.

Though technically legal, such practices blur the line between public service and personal profit, raising ethical concerns and creating conflicts of interest. They represent a form of legal corruption that allows officials to benefit financially from their positions without facing the same scrutiny as direct bribes. This situation erodes the public's trust in government, as it suggests that financial gain rather than public service often drives decision-making.

Anti-Corruption

Corruption is another force that undermines our representation in government. Trust in government institutions is foundational for societal stability and progress within democratic frameworks, yet public trust in these bodies is at a historic low. The lowest recorded level of trust in the U.S. government occurred in 2024, when only 16% of U.S. adults expressed confidence that the government would act rightly most of the time. This figure represents one of the lowest points in over six decades of polling, underscoring the urgency for robust anti-corruption measures.[284]

Effective strategies to address corruption and improve trust include enforcing transparency and accountability and maintaining high ethical standards across all government levels.

Legislation like the Supreme Court Ethics, Recusal, and Transparency Act of 2022 exemplifies efforts to enhance judicial accountability by establishing a formal code of conduct for Supreme Court justices, though it faces challenges related to judicial independence.

Further efforts in 2023 saw the introduction of the first formal ethics code by the U.S. Supreme Court. Despite being a significant step, the code has been criticized for lacking substantial reforms and an effective enforcement mechanism, reflecting ongoing debates over its adequacy and necessity.

Moreover, in July 2024, the U.S. Senate drafted the Ending Trading and Holdings in Congressional Stocks (ETHICS) Act, a bipartisan initiative to prevent members of Congress and their immediate families from trading individual stocks. The bill was introduced in the Senate in April 2023 and advanced out of the Senate Committee on Homeland Security and Governmental Affairs in July 2024. However, as of February 2025, the Act has not yet passed both chambers of Congress or been signed into law by the President and is therefore not enforceable.

The cumulative efforts in legislation and policy reform aim to restore public confidence and ensure that government actions are guided by fairness and public interest, not personal gain. These initiatives are integral to upholding the integrity of democratic institutions and ensuring they serve the public effectively and justly.

The Path Forward

Strengthening anti-corruption efforts that prioritize ethics, transparency, and accountability and limit special interest influence is key. As citizens, we must support laws and regulations that demand high ethical standards from public officials, ensure government transparency, hold wrongdoers accountable, and curb the power of special interests. By doing so, society can create a more just and trustworthy political system. Reforms such as these can reinforce public confidence in democracy, protect the integrity of institutions, and ensure that government truly serves the people.

Anticipating our Future

As technology continues to advance rapidly, it will dramatically reshape our society and daily experiences. To navigate this changing landscape effectively, it's essential that our representatives in Congress fully understand and address the implications of these technological advancements on its citizens. For example, the integration of Artificial Intelligence (AI) and robotics into everyday life is reshaping everything from mundane chores to complex job roles, raising critical questions about the future role of humans alongside machines.

The proliferation of AI and automation is set to drastically alter the job market, displacing a wide range of roles from manufacturing to administrative tasks and prompting a fundamental shift in global work dynamics.

David Schacht, SVP and CIO for Simon Properties from 1997 to 2020 and industry consultant, warns "our government is paying far too little attention to AI. Considering the concentration of wealth if you go back in time to perhaps the early eighties. America had a strong middle class. That strong middle class has been decimated mostly, by two things. Automation and free trade. AI stands to be at least as impactful if not more so. The societal impact stands to be really big. Bots and algorithms don't pay into social security, pay income taxes, buy houses, cars, or groceries. Those of us who own the companies who will benefit from AI will be OK, those who don't will be further marginalized. Our government is asleep on this issue."

This proliferation's impact is not merely job loss but a complete transformation of economic structures that will require societies to adapt to a new reality where human labor is less central. This shift necessitates a reevaluation of social safety nets and workforce training programs to manage the immediate impact on employment and the broader implications for economic value in a technologically advanced world.

Moreover, demographic changes such as slowing population growth will challenge existing business models that rely on continual consumer and workforce expansion. Technological breakthroughs like quantum computing and 5G are accelerating digital transformation, impacting various sectors, including healthcare, where advances in genetic engineering and telemedicine are promising to extend human lifespans and improve quality of life.

As we face these sweeping changes, our policymakers must be equipped to ensure that technological progress aligns with the foundational principles of equity and human dignity. Ensuring that Congress is fully informed and proactive in addressing these shifts is vital for maintaining societal stability and fostering a future that benefits all citizens.

Protecting Liberty--Our Primary Goal

Over the last 232 years, the concept of liberty embedded in the U.S. Constitution has experienced shifts influenced by societal changes, government policies, and evolving court interpretations. Envisioned by our Founding Fathers as a cornerstone for ensuring personal freedom and limiting governmental overreach, liberty has sometimes been curtailed in the name of security, social order, or public welfare.

Landmark moments such as suspending civil liberties during wartime, expanded government surveillance powers, and laws regulating individual behaviors highlight a balancing act between freedom and control. While liberty has been protected and expanded through amendments like the Bill of Rights and the Civil Rights Movement's legislative successes, recent decades have seen contentious debates over privacy, free speech, and personal autonomy.

Liberty must be reaffirmed as a foundational principle when addressing issues such as strengthening citizen representation in all three branches of government, establishing safeguards for digital privacy, limiting government surveillance powers, and reinforcing protections against laws that infringe on individual rights. Liberty is essential to our freedom but does come with rules – laws necessary to keep people behavior in check.

What To Do About Citizen Representation

Having highlighted the decline in the average citizen's ability to influence our government, it is now essential to revisit and reaffirm our fundamental governing principles. These foundational principles serve as the bedrock of our society and guide us in addressing the issues previously discussed and the others that will be reviewed after the following foundational reminders.

PART I – OUR FOUNDATION

THE ROLE AND PURPOSE OF GOVERNMENT

Power

Government is all about power. The concept of power within governments revolves around control and security, controlling the populace and safeguarding the nation's place in the world. However, critical questions arise about the purpose and beneficiaries of this power.

Purpose of Power

In theory, government power is intended to serve the citizenry, provide safety, order, and facilitate services that allow individuals and communities to flourish. Governments enact laws, levy taxes, and administer services that ideally contribute to a well-functioning society. Yet, the extent to which these measures are genuinely for the public good versus maintaining the status quo or protecting the elite can be a point of contention.

Protection of Way of Life

The protection of a "way of life" can be seen as a justification for a range of government actions, from economic policies that favor specific industries to harsh stances on immigration. This notion assumes that a way of life is static and uniformly valued by all citizens — a perspective that may ignore society's dynamic, diverse nature. Additionally, it raises the question of whose way of life is being protected and at what cost to other ways of life, among various ethnic, religious, gender, sexual orientation, socioeconomic, age, and disability groups, both within and beyond the nation's borders.

Necessity of Protection

The validity of protecting a particular way of life depends on multiple factors, including external threats, internal inequalities, and society's evolving values. Protection might be necessary for genuine threats; however, invoking protection without clear justification can lead to excessive surveillance, reduced freedoms, and a climate of fear and exclusion. This aspect touches on the subject of protecting liberty.

This framework sets the stage for a broader discussion on the role and responsibilities of government in a rapidly changing world. It invites a deeper exploration of how power should be wielded in an era marked by global interconnectivity and swift social changes. The challenge lies in ensuring that governmental power, while robust enough to provide protection, does not become so overpowering that it stifles the very freedoms it aims to safeguard, nor should it impede the freedoms of those in other nations.

Historical and analytical perspectives suggest that wars often serve the interests of the powerful, protecting wealth at the expense of the masses. A.J. Muste noted that war is driven by the government's power to conscript and tax, which are used to safeguard or capture wealth and power, often sidelining the general welfare. Similarly, during the Nuremberg Trials, Hermann Göring revealed how leaders manipulate public sentiment to justify wars, exposing the misuse of government power to serve elite interests while ordinary citizens bear the costs. Starkly put, the wealthy instigate wars for their benefit while the poor die fighting them.

These insights underscore the recurring theme that government power, when unchecked, can lead to conflicts that serve narrow interests under the guise of national security or patriotic duty.[281-282]

Geographical Boundaries

The concept of boundaries, both geographical and political, while integral to current global and national frameworks, may not be as permanent as they appear. These divisions are arbitrary, often drawn during periods of conflict or colonization, without regard to the cultural and historical continuities of the people living within them.

Boundaries define the limits of a government's power. For this reason, those in Power will do whatever is needed to protect their borders and expand them if they can.

The relevance of traditional boundaries may start being questioned as the world becomes increasingly interconnected through advancements in technology, economics, and communication. The growing emphasis on global citizenship, portable translation technology, and multinational cooperation suggests a future where boundaries might become more fluid or even regarded as an arcane relic of a less connected past. This shift could lead to reimagining how communities define themselves and interact globally and, in the distant future, challenging the fixed nature of national and regional lines. Could all of government be replaced by a robust online system? It may come to that.

Geographical boundaries can help organize societies by defining jurisdictions, promoting cultural identity, and managing resources, but they often create divisions that can hinder global cooperation, especially when governments are intertwined with religions. Geographical boundaries also sustain control of natural resources (think hoarding). While arbitrary borders have served historical and political needs, they do not always align with natural, cultural, or economic realities. Ideally, the world could be organized to respect continental or regional identities while fostering collaborative governance models extending beyond strict borders, allowing governments to work effectively at local and broader cooperative scales.

Government Role in Morality and Behavior

A nation should encourage behavior that upholds respect, integrity, and civic responsibility among its citizens, fostering a society where individuals contribute positively to the community and uphold shared values. While allowing personal freedom, the country can still promote principles that discourage harmful vices and reinforce ethical behavior for a more cohesive and resilient society.

How much authority should a government have to enforce morals and behavior if liberty is the goal? And is there a built-in conflict of interest when a government taxes and profits off vices under the questionable motive of using taxes to curb demand (one of the gauges is what does their action do to the health of its citizens)?

Greed

Greed — the intense desire for wealth, power, or status — often drives individuals to seek government leadership for personal gain. Holding office provides access to influential networks and financial opportunities, shifting priorities from public service to self-enrichment. Leaders with legislative and economic control can exploit these powers to benefit themselves and their allies, often at the public's expense.

The impact of greed varies worldwide; strong legal systems can limit its influence, while weak governance fosters corruption and nepotism. Combating greed requires stricter regulations, greater transparency, public accountability, and ethical leadership to reduce corruption and promote integrity in government.

In 1944, then-Vice President Henry A. Wallace wrote an article titled "The Danger of American Fascism," published in *The New York Times* on April 9th. In this piece, Wallace defined a fascist as "one whose lust for money or power is combined with such an intensity of intolerance toward those of other races, parties, classes, religions, cultures, regions or nations as to make him ruthless in his use of deceit or violence to attain his ends." He warned that American fascists would "poison the channels of public information" and "use every opportunity to impugn democracy." Wallace emphasized that their ultimate goal was to "capture political power so that... they may keep the common man in eternal subjection."[325]

So, the driving forces behind those seeking office are Power (Control) and Money (Greed), both bolstered by a healthy dose of Ego.

Fairness

The Fourteenth Amendment guarantees equal protection under the law, ensuring that individuals are treated equally in similar legal circumstances. However, it does not guarantee fairness in every aspect of life. A common misconception is that equal rights and fairness are the same, but the Constitution does not promise fairness as an explicit right. Life's unpredictability naturally leads to inequalities in society, governance, and daily life.

At the same time, many Americans believe in providing support for those who cannot sustain themselves, whether due to circumstances beyond their control or other challenges. This belief underpins the idea that essentials like food, shelter, and healthcare should be accessible to those in need. However, the implementation of such principles varies, shaped by ongoing political, economic, and social debates that influence the structure and effectiveness of assistance programs.

Despite numerous policies and support systems, gaps remain in addressing critical issues such as food insecurity and healthcare access. Child hunger persists despite programs like the Supplemental Nutrition Assistance Program (SNAP) and the National School Lunch Program. According to Feeding America, a nonpartisan nonprofit organization, nearly 14 million children in the U.S. lived in food-insecure households in 2023, meaning about one in five lacked consistent access to sufficient food. Research also confirms that proper nutrition enhances learning, with well-fed students demonstrating better focus and engagement in school.

Similarly, medical expenses remain a significant financial burden for many Americans. A 2019 study in the *American Journal of Public Health* found that medical issues contributed to 66.5% of bankruptcies in the U.S., despite programs like Medicaid and the Affordable Care Act. This suggests that current healthcare policies may not fully address the financial risks associated with medical costs.

These challenges highlight the complexity of policy solutions and the need for informed public engagement. Citizens play a key role in assessing the effectiveness of government policies and advocating for improvements that balance economic sustainability with social support. Addressing these issues requires ongoing discussion and practical solutions that reflect both fiscal responsibility and the well-being of the nation.

Government Purposes

A key challenge in forming a government is choosing wise leaders while keeping their power in check to prevent abuse. History shows that long-term authority often leads to corruption. Many once-popular leaders have changed laws to stay in power, censored the media, and silenced opposition. Lord Acton, a British historian, wrote in 1887 to Bishop Mandell Creighton, "Power tends to corrupt, and absolute power corrupts absolutely. Great men are almost always bad men..."[350] This maxim expresses that a person's sense of morality lessens as their power increases.

The Founding Fathers, including John Adams and Thomas Jefferson, grappled with this dilemma. Drawing on a deep understanding of history, they considered various forms of government, from English aristocracies to the early democracies of Athens. Even after the signing of the Constitution, debates persisted over the merits of monarchies versus representative bodies, the balance between manufacturing and agriculture, and the impact of taxation on individual motivation. Central to these discussions was a fundamental question: What should the government's purpose be?

History and experience show that Governments exist to maintain order, enforce laws, and protect people from harm — both from each other and external threats. Without government, chaos and conflict would dominate. Whether democratic or authoritarian, every government shapes human behavior through rules, consequences, and enforcement.

The fundamental purpose of any government is to control and regulate human behavior, including protecting one from another. The U.S. Constitution was explicitly designed to 'protect the minority from the tyranny of the majority,' a principle attributed to Alexis de Tocqueville from his later work *Democracy in America* (Vol. 1), published in 1835.

This core concept reflects the concerns of Founding Fathers like James Madison and Thomas Jefferson, who advocated for checks and balances and the separation of powers to prevent any single group or entity from gaining excessive control. Unchecked human behavior often tends toward being self-serving and self-centered. To control this tendency, citizens must be willing to surrender some liberty and freedom to maintain order and prevent chaos.

James Madison, in particular, addressed this issue in Federalist No. 10, written in 1787. In it, he argued for a large republic to mitigate the risks of factionalism (groups of citizens whose interests might conflict with the rights of others or the common good) and prevent any single group from dominating others.[288] James Madison and other framers designed our Constitution with checks and balances, federalism, and the separation of powers specifically to protect minority rights and individual liberties from being overridden by majority rule.

While Tocqueville's phrasing came after, the principle was deeply embedded in the Constitution's framework through mechanisms like the Senate's equal representation for states, the Electoral College, and the Bill of Rights. These elements aimed to balance power between the majority and minority groups in society.

The founders of America, with a deep understanding of human nature, sought to minimize the loss of personal liberty required for peaceful coexistence. They meticulously designed a government that would protect individual rights and distribute power across different branches to prevent any one faction from dominating. However, over time, the federal government has taken on roles not initially specified in the Constitution, such as operating a central bank, instituting a permanent income tax, managing large administrative departments, and regulating businesses and industries.

While these expanded roles offer practical benefits, such as ensuring national economic stability, protecting the environment, and creating uniform regulations, it raises the question of whether the federal government is always the best entity for these tasks. Some may argue that large corporations may be better equipped to handle specific business operations, and local governments are more effective at regulating individual behavior due to their closer proximity to the needs of the community.

The primary purposes of the federal government, as outlined in the Constitution, include maintaining order, protecting citizens from internal and external threats, defending the nation's borders, safeguarding individual rights, regulating commerce by managing currency, and establishing treaties and trade relationships with other countries. This is the brief Job Description for our President and Congress. Everything else was intended to fall upon the States to address.

However, following World War II, the U.S. government expanded its role to encompass defending critical external resources not found in quantity in America, promoting democracy abroad through foreign aid, and occasionally intervening in the internal affairs of other nations. One unwritten rule since 9-11 has been to support our allies' battles overseas to keep fights from coming to our shores. Similar central government role expansions have taken place by other major powers, such as Japan, Russia, Germany, and China, resulting in increased competition for vital resources and alliances on the global stage.

Unchecked human behavior often tends toward self-serving and self-centeredness. One of the significant challenges facing the United States today is the excessive concentration of power among a consortium of large businesses, special interest groups, multiple billionaires, and the two dominant political parties. These groups should not dictate the behavior of individual states and their citizens beyond the scope of their respective branch's constitutional role.

In Congress, power is held mainly by a few dozen people, including the 20 House committee chairs, party leaders, the Speaker of the House, the Senate President Pro Tempore, and the Vice President as President of the Senate. This concentration risks undermining the balance of power the founders intended, suggesting that it may be time to reassess how authority is distributed across the political structure.

Property, Ownership and Privacy

Real Estate

The government is key in regulating real estate, a cornerstone of any democratic economy. A primary function is enforcing property rights and ensuring land and buildings have clear, legal ownership. Secure property rights foster economic stability and encourage investment, driving growth and prosperity.

Land ownership supports personal autonomy and economic independence in democracies. By enabling private ownership, governments can promote a fairer distribution of wealth and power, though this depends on policies and regulations. Additionally, governments regulate land use to balance private rights with public needs, including environmental protection, urban planning, and development.

Patents and Other Intellectual Property

The concept of Patents has been around since before 500 BC. The government's role in intellectual property (IP), such as patents, copyrights, and trademarks, is to protect creators' rights. The government incentivizes innovation and creativity by granting exclusive rights to use, sell, or develop an invention or creative work, driving technological advancement and cultural richness. This protection is vital for a knowledge-based economy, where intangible assets increasingly constitute a substantial portion of economic value.

Patents, a crucial form of IP, are granted to inventors as a form of recognition and incentive. They give inventors the right to exclude others from exploiting their inventions for a certain period. This exclusivity allows inventors to recover their investment in research and development, encouraging continuous innovation in various fields.

Land as a Foundation of Democracy

Land ownership is deeply intertwined with the democratic process. Historically, property ownership was linked to voting rights; landowners were considered to have a stake in the community and the wisdom to vote responsibly. While modern democracies have moved beyond property-based suffrage, land still plays a critical role by ensuring that wealth and power are not concentrated solely in the hands of the state or a few individuals. A broad base of property owners helps distribute economic power, fostering a more resilient and participative democracy.

Alternatives to Private Ownership

Consider for a moment that there are alternatives to absolute private ownership that reflect different philosophical and practical approaches. Community land trusts, cooperative ownership, and government-held land for public use prioritize community and public interests over individual property rights. These models can help manage land in a way that promotes accessibility, affordability, and communal benefit, often addressing housing shortages and urban development issues without the speculative pressures of the private market. Government can own land but should they and what happens if they own too much or if a group of wealthy individuals own too much.

Consider that the combined wealth of the world's billionaires is about $14 trillion[289], while the total value of all residential, commercial, and agricultural real estate in America is estimated at $60–$80 trillion[290-292]. At the current growth rate of billionaire wealth (8% annually) compared to the historic real estate appreciation (3%), they could potentially buy all U.S. real estate, excluding what they already own within, 33-34 years, making for them a top and smart global investment. In the lifetime of the average American citizen, the world's billionaires could theoretically "own" America. While this scenario is unlikely for many reasons, it does put in perspective the magnitude of the power shift that is happening.

Privacy and Property Rights

At its core, the concept of property is intertwined with privacy. Ownership confers the right to exclude others, allowing individuals to control their environment and personal information. In the digital age, the intersection of privacy and property becomes particularly relevant in intellectual property, where personal data can be a commodity. Governments, therefore, must navigate the delicate balance of protecting individual privacy rights while fostering an environment conducive to innovation and economic growth.

Individual Liberty vs. Government Authority

Another essential founding principle is that the welfare of the individual takes precedence over the needs of the state, except in matters of international relations, national defense, or situations that pose a danger to many citizens. This principle protects individual rights while allowing the federal government to safeguard collective welfare.

Most Americans believe the government should not interfere in personal choices, which should be left to individual conscience. However, attitudes often shift when it comes to legally permissible actions that some religions consider immoral. While religious institutions may seek to influence personal beliefs, it is questionable whether the government should take on a similar role, aiming to persuade rather than dictate.

Despite efforts by some political groups to regulate personal behavior, citizens must assert that their rights take precedence over societal or political interests. While governments often claim to represent all of society, they typically govern with a mandate from only a portion of the population.

The principle that individual rights should outweigh societal interests has far-reaching implications. For example, should wearing a helmet be a personal choice or a legal requirement? Should women have the autonomy to decide on abortion? These questions expose inconsistencies in how individual rights are interpreted across different issues. They also reinforce the idea that personal independence is essential to liberty and freedom, with government intervention justified only in public safety or national interest matters.

This discussion of liberty, individual rights, and the role of government naturally leads to the historical context and origins of these rights, as enshrined in the Constitution.

THE HISTORICAL CONTEXT

Life in 1775–1787

When the U.S. Constitution was created, American colonial society was quite different from today. Most people lived on farms, growing food and making goods to support their families. Travel and communication were slow, relying on horses, carriages, and ships. People got news from newspapers, pamphlets, or word of mouth.

Society had a clear social order. Wealthy landowners, merchants, and professionals were at the top. Small farmers and artisans comprised the middle, while laborers, indentured servants, and enslaved people were at the bottom. Religion was a big part of daily life, shaping education, laws, and values. Many settlers came to America to escape religious persecution and wanted the freedom to practice their faith without government control. After seeing the dangers of church and state mixing, early leaders prioritized religious freedom, ensuring no one was forced to follow a particular religion.

This environment shaped the founders' priorities and challenges in drafting the Constitution. Their experiences with colonial rule, war, and weak governance highlighted the need for a strong yet balanced system that safeguarded individual rights and prevented tyranny.

Founding our Constitution: Three Critical Steps

The journey toward establishing the U.S. Constitution began with the First Continental Congress in 1774, where delegates from 12 of the 13 colonies gathered to coordinate a response to British actions. Although no constitution was drafted then, this meeting marked the first step toward united colonial governance.

With the outbreak of war with Brittain in 1775, the Second Continental Congress assumed leadership, bravely guiding the colonies through the tumultuous Revolutionary War, declaring independence in 1776. During this period, the Congress drafted Articles of Confederation, the nation's first constitution. However, the Articles soon revealed serious weaknesses, lacking the authority to regulate trade, levy taxes, or enforce laws. By the mid-1780s, issues like interstate disputes, economic instability, and Shays' Rebellion underscored the need for a stronger government. By the way, Shays' Rebellion (1786–1787) was an armed uprising in Western Massachusetts led by Daniel Shays, a former captain in the Continental Army. The Rebellion was fueled by economic hardship and discontent among rural farmers, many of whom were Revolutionary War veterans. These individuals faced crushing debt, high taxes, and the threat of losing their farms due to foreclosures.

In response to the weaknesses of the Articles, the Constitutional Convention convened in Philadelphia on May 25, 1787, to replace the Articles. The result was the U.S. Constitution, which introduced Federalism, establishing a system of checks and balances and protecting individual liberties. Federalism is a system of government in which power is divided between a central authority and constituent political units, such as states or provinces. It was not until June 21, 1788, that the necessary nine states officially ratified it. It went into effect on March 4, 1789. (Nine was the 2/3rds of the 13 states – the requirement at the time).

The subsequent addition of the Bill of Rights on December 15, 1791, ensured these liberties were enshrined, creating the foundation for the nation's governance that endures today.

The Declaration of Independence

The Declaration of Independence was foundational in describing our responsibilities as American citizens. With our Declaration of Independence, more a commitment to ourselves than a message to the King, we announced our separation from Great Britain and their despotic taxes without representation on July 4, 1776.

"We hold these truths to be self-evident, that all men are created equal, that they are endowed by their Creator with certain unalienable Rights, that among these are Life, Liberty and the pursuit of Happiness. — That to secure these rights, Governments are instituted among Men, deriving their just powers from the consent of the governed, — That whenever any Form of Government becomes destructive of these ends, it is the Right of the People to alter or to abolish it, and to institute new Government, laying its foundation on such principles and organizing its powers in such form, as to them shall seem most likely to effect [sic] their Safety and Happiness. Prudence, indeed, will dictate that Governments long established should not be changed for light and transient causes; and accordingly, all experience hath shewn that mankind are more disposed to suffer, while evils are sufferable than to right themselves by abolishing the forms to which they are accustomed. But when a long train of abuses and usurpations, pursuing invariably the same Object evinces a design to reduce them under absolute Despotism, it is their right, it is their duty, to throw off such Government, and to provide new Guards for their future security."

The underlined portions emphasize that our government should not be changed for "light and transient causes." But when faced with "a long train of abuses and usurpations," it becomes our right and duty to replace it and establish new safeguards for our future security. This standard forces us to ask: Are we now at that point, or can the system still be reformed to protect individual liberty?

In the 21st century, we again endure a wide range of taxes and impositions imposed by a Congress over which we have little direct control. It may be time to consider altering aspects of our current government to delay—or even prevent—the need for its full replacement. This consideration cannot happen without serious changes in how citizens are represented.

As an American, do you believe our government is "mostly right"? Can we come together to solve or compromise core issues, perhaps through a few key reforms in Representation and Ethics? If not, are you prepared for either a more autocratic government or a radical overhaul?

To use a car analogy, we don't need a brand-new model, but we have more than a few dents. We may need to overhaul parts of the engine.

Our elections often reflect preferences for a simpler tax code, smaller government, and reduced waste. Yet these changes have not fully materialized. Many challenges still require compromise and consensus—not edict. In this context, gradual reform is preferable; it imposes a lighter toll than abrupt revolution. The events of January 6, 2021, showed that most Americans reject the idea of government overthrow. We must find solutions acceptable to the vast majority.

The Role of Constitutions

A constitution is a foundational document that defines how a government operates, distributing power among branches, outlining government responsibilities, and safeguarding individual rights. It provides a framework for creating laws, selecting leaders, and resolving disputes, thereby ensuring governance is just, balanced, and accountable. Constitutions reflect a society's values, guiding the country and its citizens. Through this legal structure, societies achieve stability, prevent abuses of power, and offer protection from arbitrary or authoritarian rule.

Throughout history, constitutions have taken various forms. Even ancient texts, such as the Ten Commandments, can be viewed as early forms of constitutional principles. While most often religious, they offered a system of rules governing behavior and expectations for leaders and individuals alike.

The U.S. Constitution reflects this tradition, grounding the principles of American democracy in a durable framework based on the wisdom of centuries of great thinkers and doers. While it has guided the nation effectively through generations of change, the rapid pace of modern societal shifts presents new and pressing challenges.

Origins of our Constitution

These foundational documents were influenced by Natural Law and the philosophical ideas of John Locke, a 17th-century English philosopher and political theorist, who formulated principles such as individual liberty, the Social Contract, natural rights of citizens, government by consent, and the separation of powers. John Locke believed that humans live naturally in a state of freedom and equality, but they consent to enter into a Social Contract to avoid the inconveniences and dangers of completely unrestricted freedom.

Before the U.S. Constitution, Natural Law was the foundation of European legal and moral systems, shaping classical legal traditions. It holds that fundamental rights and wrongs, inherent and universally recognizable, form the basis of just laws. This concept profoundly influenced Western legal philosophy and played a key role in shaping constitutional frameworks, including those of the United States and the United Kingdom.

As Cicero explained, natural law is a set of fair and unchanging rules based on reason and nature. It helps people and societies do what is right and good. It teaches that people should live in harmony with nature by using reason and developing good character. It also reminds us that we are not born just for ourselves but to help others and make society better. A government, in turn, should create fair laws that protect everyone, not just a small group of people. This idea connects personal freedom with social responsibility.

The idea of mixed government, which combines democracy, aristocracy, and monarchy, was another important lesson from history. Cicero supported this system, and it influenced how the U.S. government was designed. Ancient thinkers like Plato and Aristotle also wrote about good government and the best ways to run a country.

The Founding Fathers, including James Madison, Thomas Jefferson, and John Adams, studied these ideas in school. They learned about Greek and Roman history, philosophy, and law, which shaped how they thought about government. James Madison went to the College of New Jersey (now Princeton University), where he studied Latin, Greek, and philosophy. His teacher, John Witherspoon, was a respected scholar and a signer of the Declaration of Independence. Madison's education helped him write the U.S. Constitution and the Federalist Papers.

The Federalist Papers are 85 essays written by Alexander Hamilton, James Madison, and John Jay under the name Publius. They were published in newspapers from 1787 to 1788 to explain why the U.S. Constitution was needed. These essays argued for a strong government with fair rules, including separation of powers and checks and balances. Today, they still help us understand what the Founding Fathers wanted for the country.

Our Constitution's Evolution: Key Amendments

The Constitution's adaptability has allowed it to endure centuries of social change. Amendments, like the Bill of Rights addressed fears of government overreach by explicitly protecting freedoms like speech, religion, and fair trials. Later amendments, such as the Reconstruction Amendments (13th, 14th, and 15th), abolished slavery and secured voting rights, reflecting the Constitution's role in promoting justice over time.

Further amendments have responded to evolving social, political, and economic realities, such as the 19th Amendment (1920), which Granted women the right to vote, the 22nd Amendment (1951), which limited presidential terms to two, and the 26th Amendment (1971), which lowered the voting age to 18 to include those in our military.

Contemporary laws often try to chip away at our rights, with the Supreme Court's role being to prevent such attempts.

These amendments show how the Constitution has been updated to reflect the values of each era, addressing injustices and expanding protections to meet societal needs.

GOVERNMENT STRUCTURES

If you think our government is all wrong and want to reformulate our governance, you had best review the possibilities. People use different descriptive terms but so often either misunderstand what the terms mean or misrepresent the meaning of the terms. Our Founding Fathers no doubt considered all of the possibilities and rejected all but one.

Government Systems

Understanding different types of government systems helps us see how societies handle power, rights, and problems, and it lets us compare them to our system. If we want to improve our government, we must know what other systems exist. History and culture shape how governments work, so countries have different ways of ruling. Learning about these systems also helps us understand democratic values like fairness, freedom, and laws that protect people's rights, especially when compared to strict governments that control everything. The following section explains different types of government, though many countries use a mix of these systems. Simply put, government structure can be seen as a line or spectrum moving from left to right.

Overview of Governance Ideologies

Many Americans seem uncertain about the core ideologies of governance, sometimes using terms like democracy, federalism, and liberty in inconsistent or unclear ways. Here is a brief overview:

- **Communism:** A far-left ideology advocating for a classless, stateless society where all property is communally owned, often associated with Marxist-Leninist principles.
- **Socialism:** A system advocating social ownership or control of the means of production, with varying degrees of state involvement, and often aimed at reducing inequality.
- **Liberalism:** A centerish ideology focused on individual rights, democracy, free markets, and the rule of law.
- **Conservatism:** A right-leaning ideology that emphasizes tradition, stability, and limited government intervention in the economy.
- **Fascism:** A far-right authoritarian ideology emphasizing nationalism, centralized control, military supremacy, suppression of dissent, mass media control (for propaganda), protection of corporate power and suppression of labor power, distain for intellectuals and the arts, religion used for power building, rampant sexism, and the subordination of individual freedoms to the state.

The Democratic Party generally favors issues on the left side of the spectrum, while the Republican Party extends to the right. How far to the extreme a candidate or group goes depends on the individual and the context.

Most people do not fit neatly into one category; they often hold different views depending on the issue. For instance, someone might favor conservative economic policies, like balanced budgets, while supporting liberal stances on social issues. Political Parties tend to be less flexible and chose one position on the spectrum even though the rarely can do all they promise or threaten.

Government Dimensions

Governments have at least four dimensions. The primary dimension, running through all forms of government, ranges from citizens making decisions collectively at one extreme to a single individual dictating decisions at the other.

A second dimension is how power is contained, whether by constitutional limits that separate power into branches or by concentrating it in the hands of a few or a single entity. While the first dimension involves the distribution of decision-making authority (from democratic to authoritarian), the second dimension deals with the framework and checks within which that authority is exercised — such as separation of powers, checks and balances, or centralization of authority.

A third dimension considers the economic system, focusing on how a society organizes its economic activities and resources. The options range from capitalist systems, where market forces, supply and demand, and private ownership predominate, to socialist and communist systems, where the state often plays a central role in planning and resource distribution.

A fourth dimension of governmental structure is Liberty -- the degree to which the government is involved in the everyday lives of its citizens. This dimension includes the extent of governmental intervention in personal and economic activities, ranging from minimal interference (laissez-faire) to extensive control (totalitarian).

In more liberal regimes, the state might limit its role to essential functions such as maintaining law and order, enforcing contracts, and protecting property rights. In contrast, more authoritarian governments may impose strict regulations on education, employment, and personal conduct and often justify such measures as necessary for national security or societal welfare. In some countries, the government even dictates the clothes women can wear. This dimension is what critically influences individual freedoms, directly impacting personal choices, privacy, and economic autonomy.

These four dimensions interact but do not necessarily correlate directly; for instance, a country might have a highly centralized form of government where a single party or leader makes all the decisions (authoritarian) but still maintains a separation of powers in theory, or it could be a democracy with weak separation of powers, leading to different challenges. Similarly, an authoritarian regime might adopt capitalist economic principles, while a democratic society might implement extensive social welfare policies typical of socialist systems.

Socialism

Socialism is frequently misunderstood as being the same or similar to democracy, but the two fundamentally differ. Democracy is a system of government where citizens participate in the creation of laws and choose representatives to ensure their voices are heard in decision-making processes. In contrast, Socialism prioritizes the collective good over individual interests, especially regarding economic organization. In its more extreme forms, socialism resembles communism, where the means of production are collectively owned, and individuals contribute to shared goals. Resources, products, and labor are distributed equally in these systems, often eliminating traditional wage structures or implementing uniform compensation for all.[22]

The internet has created a form of collectivism, as socialism element. Millions of people contribute time and creativity by freely sharing valuable content, collaborating on open-source software, and participating in collective decision-making processes. Over the past few decades, collective communities — ranging from small-scale communes in the U.S. to large-scale socialist experiments like the U.S.S.R. — have experienced varying degrees of success. While many have faced significant challenges, others persist, sustained by dedicated members who embrace compromise and shared responsibilities.

Participation in collective communities is often driven, not by a profit motive, but by a search for personal fulfillment, a sense of belonging, or the desire for a simpler, focused lifestyle. These societies thrive on mutual effort, charity, and a minimized focus on transactional exchanges.

The Inuit communities, indigenous people inhabiting the Arctic regions of Canada, Greenland, and Alaska, traditionally exemplify socialistic collectivism through communal sharing of resources and collective decision-making processes. In these societies, community members often share essential resources such as food, shelter, and tools to ensure mutual survival and well-being. This sharing economy is underpinned by strong social norms and cultural practices prioritizing the group's welfare over individual gain. Decisions, particularly those affecting the whole community, are made collectively, often through consensus or in consultation with elders, reflecting a democratic and inclusive approach to governance within the community. Such practices highlight the Inuit's embodiment of socialistic collectivism, where community cohesion and collective welfare are fundamental.

Such communal organizational structures echo the principle popularized by Karl Marx, though predating him: "from each according to his ability, to each according to his needs." However, such communities require a delicate balance, with more individuals contributing than taking. When the number of takers outweigh the contributors, societal stability can unravel. Even in socialist communities, leadership often emerges as individuals seek control for power, status, personal fulfillment or by cultural obligation.

Large-scale socialist societies face additional challenges in ensuring a "fair" distribution of resources. Historically, imbalances in socialist systems — such as the notorious shortages in the U.S.S.R. — have underscored the difficulties of equitable distribution. Although fairness is a central tenet of socialism, it plays a limited formal role in democracies beyond the electoral process. These challenges highlight the complexities and limitations of implementing large-scale socialism effectively.

A fundamental distinction between socialism and democracy is property ownership. In democratic societies, individual property rights are protected, allowing people to accumulate wealth and profit from ownership. In socialist systems, property is collectively owned or managed by the whole. For example, before communism, land in China was mostly controlled by landlords and wealthy elites, while the government heavily taxed farmers, at times claiming up to 60% of agricultural production. In contrast, after the Communist Revolution, the state seized all land, eliminating private ownership and fully controlling agricultural production.

One potential drawback of collective efforts is a lack of personal responsibility. In socialist settings, exceptional contributions are often rewarded with intangible benefits, such as praise or respect, rather than material compensation. This can discourage individual initiative as decision-making processes become homogenized by committees, potentially slowing progress. While democracy carries risks — such as entrenched power networks — personal responsibility and freedom remain central to its structure.

Human societies, like many animal groups, often gravitate toward hierarchical structures where dominant leaders emerge through strength, bravery, intelligence, empathy, decisiveness, resilience, integrity, vision, adaptability or other distinguishing features. This tribal dynamic is evident today in many social and political systems, from family units to larger communities, reflecting our ancestral tendencies. Within these structures, hierarchies and leadership dynamics often form among groups such as castes, tribes, and religious congregations.

It is essential to recognize that democracies and socialist systems can share overlapping elements. Free-market democracies may incorporate socialist principles, such as publicly funded education and healthcare, while socialist societies may allow some private ownership. The boundaries between these systems are not always clear-cut, with many modern states blending various elements of both approaches.

Totalitarianism

Totalitarian governments are regimes where the state or a centralized authority exercises absolute control over all public and private life aspects. While autocracies and authoritarian governments share features such as centralized power and restricted political freedoms, they do not necessarily impose the same level of total control over society that defines totalitarianism. In a totalitarian regime, a single ruling party dominates, employing strict censorship, pervasive propaganda, and the suppression of dissent to maintain complete dominance over the population.[64]

Marxism

Marxism represents the opposite end of the ideological spectrum from capitalism, emphasizing collective ownership and control of the means of production as opposed to individual or private enterprise. It is a doctrine formulated by German philosophers Karl Marx and Friedrich Engels in the mid-1800s and articulated in *The Communist Manifesto in 1848.*

The manifesto's first chapter, as noted by Dictionary.com, argues that "the State throughout history has been a device for the exploitation of the masses by a dominant class, that class struggle has been the main agency of historical change, and that the capitalist system, containing from its inception the seeds of its decay, will inevitably, after a period of dictatorship of the proletariat, be superseded by a socialist order and a classless society."

Marxism gained significant momentum after Marx's death in 1883, especially with the rise of communism in the early 20th century. Its ideas spread across various movements, profoundly shaping the political landscape in countries that embraced Marxist principles as a foundation for revolutionary change and societal transformation.[65]

Marxist Socialism

Marxist socialism refers explicitly to the economic and political strategies within Marxism aimed at replacing capitalism with socialism. This approach involves the working class (proletariat) overthrowing the capitalist system (bourgeoisie) and eventually establishing a state where communal ownership of the means of production is established, leading to a classless, stateless society. Marxist socialism is, therefore, a subset of Marxism focused on the political and economic strategies to achieve the goals laid out by Marxist theory.[276]

A historic example of Marxist socialism is the Russian Revolution of 1917. This revolution saw the Bolsheviks, a vanguard of the proletariat, successfully overthrow the Russian tsarist regime, which embodied the bourgeoisie's control. The Bolsheviks, inspired by Marxist ideology, aimed to eliminate class distinctions by redistributing property and centralizing political power in workers' councils or soviets, setting the stage for the eventual creation of a communist state.

Fascism

Fascism is a far-right ideology built on ultranationalism, authoritarian rule, and the suppression of political opposition. It glorifies a single leader, prioritizes the state above individuals, and enforces strict control through militarism and dictatorship. Fascist regimes reject democracy and pluralism, silencing dissent and targeting marginalized groups as scapegoats.

The Holocaust Museum provides a deep look into fascism, highlighting its core traits and dangers. It shows how fascism thrives on division, propaganda, and control, using fear and scapegoating to maintain power. The Museum's analysis warns against these patterns, offering lessons from history to prevent fascism's return.

Here are the key elements of fascism as identified by the Holocaust Museum:
- Powerful and continuing nationalism
- Disdain for human rights
- Identification of enemies as a unifying cause
- Rampant sexism

- Controlled mass media
- Obsession with national security
- Intertwined religion and government
- Corporate power protected
- Labor power suppressed
- Disdain for intellectuals & the arts (& now the sciences)

Economic Systems

An economic system determines how resources, goods, and services are distributed in society. It includes systems like capitalism and socialism, addressing resource ownership, the balance between markets and government control, and the effects on wealth distribution. Economic ideologies often shape governance and influence how societies function.

Capitalism

Capitalism is an economic and social system where private individuals own and control production assets like land, factories, and technology. Goods, labor, and capital are exchanged in markets, with profits going to owners or being reinvested for growth. It is defined by private property, free markets, wage labor, and competition, which drive innovation and economic progress. However, critics argue that capitalism exploits workers, as owners accumulate wealth by paying wages lower than the value of workers' contributions, maximizing profits at the expense of fair pay.[66]

Capitalism offers several benefits. It creates jobs, fosters innovation, and provides opportunities for personal and economic growth. It allows individuals to earn a living, develop skills, and advance in society. Capitalism supports liberty — not absolute freedom, but the ability to make choices within a system that protects rights and promotes responsibility. This balance of autonomy and accountability is central to its function.

Capitalism can exist under different forms of government, with its structure influenced by government involvement in the economy through regulation, taxation, and public ownership.

Laissez-faire

Laissez-faire is an economic philosophy advocating minimal government intervention. It allows businesses and individuals to operate freely within the market while the government focuses on protecting property rights, enforcing contracts, and maintaining public order.

In a pure laissez-faire capitalist system, the government's role is minimal but essential. It protects property rights, enforces contracts, and maintains a legal framework while letting supply and demand set prices and production. This system may allow monopolies.

However, most modern economies are mixed, blending capitalism with government intervention. Governments regulate industries, provide public services like education and healthcare, and establish social safety nets. The level of intervention varies across countries.

Social Democracies

Social Democracies go further by integrating a market-based economy with a strong welfare state, actively regulating markets, and redistributing wealth to reduce economic inequality. They aim to balance economic growth with social equity. In contrast, state capitalism features a more direct role for the government, which may own or control key industries and resources. This approach is often seen in authoritarian regimes where state control and market practices coexist to achieve strategic goals.

Planned or Command Economies

Planned or command economies, often linked to communist or socialist states, involve extensive government control over production and economic planning. Private ownership and market competition are limited or nonexistent, with the state directing production, pricing, and distribution.

While capitalism is primarily an economic framework, the extent and nature of government involvement determine how it is regulated, managed, or complemented by social programs and services.

Democracy

Democracy is not a one-size-fits-all system; it varies by country and evolves. While some nations emphasize equal rights, democratic practices and structures differ.

Liberal Democracy typically includes political pluralism, where multiple political groups, viewpoints, and interests compete for influence. It also upholds equality before the law, the right to petition officials for grievances, due process, civil liberties, and an independent civil society.

As previously discussed, in the United States, a core democratic principle is the separation of powers, ensuring that the legislative, executive, and judicial branches function independently to prevent the concentration of power. In contrast, the United Kingdom follows the doctrine of parliamentary sovereignty, where Parliament holds supreme legal authority, with its power balanced by an independent judiciary. This difference highlights the diversity in democratic governance structures worldwide.

Over the past century, the success of democratic systems has led to their adoption and adaptation worldwide, reflecting a growing shift toward democratic principles. In the early 1900s, only 10–12 countries were democratic; according to the Democracy Index by the Economist Intelligence Unit, as of 2022, about 75 of 167 countries and territories were classified as either "full" or "flawed" democracies.[59-23]

The exact count depends on how "democracy" is defined. University of Chicago Professors Tom Ginsburg and Aziz Z. Hug in their 2018 book, *How to Save a Constitutional Democracy*, said that a healthy democracy rests on three pillars: free and fair elections, freedom of expression and association, and "the bureaucratic rule of law."[322] Other definitions focus strictly on free and fair elections, while others include broader criteria like civil liberties, political rights, and institutional checks and balances.

As democracy continues to spread, it is significantly influenced and shaped by cultural, historical, and institutional differences, resulting in distinct forms that reflect the unique circumstances of each country.[30-01.]

Democratic Socialism

According to Grassroots Economic Organizing (GEO), a collective that promotes a "solidarity economy" through education, journalism, community ownership, and sustainability, a democratic socialist is not a Marxist or communist. Instead, they seek to curb capitalism's excesses and direct public funds toward creating opportunities for all.

Democratic socialists believe the economy and society should be run democratically to serve public needs rather than maximize profits for a few. They do not seek to eliminate private corporations but advocate for stronger democratic oversight. This oversight could include government regulations and tax incentives to encourage businesses to act in the public interest while restricting harmful practices like outsourcing jobs to low-wage countries and environmental pollution.[276]

Pluralism

Classical pluralism holds that politics and decision-making occur primarily within a governmental framework, while non-governmental groups influence the process by leveraging their resources. As different groups pursue their interests, conflicts shift, leading to a dynamic but gradual change process. This constant "tug-of-war" among interest groups often results in slow, incremental progress as factions block or overturn legislation.

Competition among diverse interests helps maintain a democratic balance, preventing any group from dominating and allowing individuals to pursue their objectives. Reflecting on pluralist principles, Benjamin Franklin observed, "In free governments, the rulers are the servants and the people their superiors and sovereigns," emphasizing citizen sovereignty and the role of competing interests in democracy.

Pluralists stress civil rights, including freedom of expression and association, and the need for an electoral system with at least two competing parties. However, in practice, only a small portion of the population actively participates in governance, while most citizens remain passive after voting. In the 2024 U.S. election, 156 million out of 245 million eligible voters cast their ballots. As a result, 535 elected officials represent a population of about 340 million. This concentration of political power in a small group raises concerns about representation and accountability. While some argue that elected officials must specialize in governance, others worry that limited citizen participation weakens democracy and gives disproportionate influence to political elites.[23]

Individualism, Beliefs and Society

Popularly-elected representatives are unlikely to have the qualifications for managing numerous enterprises and the large sums of public money involved in civic administration. The "health of the state" depends upon the exertions of individuals for their personal benefit.[37]

Republics Support Individual Independence

Republics stress independence and self-reliance. Individualists promote their own goals and desires, while opposing external interference with their choices, whether by society or any other individual, group, or institution. Individualism is apposed to collectivism, which stresses that communal, community, group, societal, or national goals should take priority over individual goals.[37]

In political philosophy, the individualist theory of government holds that the state should protect the liberty of individuals to act as they wish so long as they do not infringe upon the liberties of others. This contrasts with collectivist political theories, where rather than leaving individuals to pursue their own ends, the state ensures that the individual serves the whole society, even by force if necessary.

Individual independence includes the concept of "laissez faire," which means in French "let [the people] do" [for themselves what they know how to do]. This term is commonly associated with a free market system in economics, where individuals and businesses own and control most factors of production. Government interferences are kept to a minimum.[37]

Individualists are chiefly concerned with protecting their civil and economic autonomy against obligations, like taxes and regulations imposed by social institutions such as the state. For example, they oppose any concentration of commercial and industrial enterprise in the hands of the state and the municipality.

Individualism

In one view of individualism, the government is seen to be composed of individuals. Despite democratic governments being elected by popular vote, the fact remains that all activities of government are carried out by the intentions and actions of individuals, not always constrained by the written laws and regulations. Actions approved or taken may not be consistent with what the majority of voters intended. The individualist wishes to highlight the importance of the individual and prevent absorption into a collective.[37]

Adapting comments made by Chris Anderson in the July 2009 *Wired* magazine article "Waste is Good," laws can be oriented either of two ways. In totalitarian regimes, everything is forbidden unless it is permitted, and order is maintained by force. In democracies, everything is permitted unless it is forbidden. In totalitarian regimes, dictates come from the top-down. In democracies, dictates come from the bottom-up.

Laws provide the basis for command and control and keep citizens from getting out of control. Totalitarian regimes are characterized by strict, often repressive control over many aspects of life, including political, economic, and personal freedoms, with little to no tolerance for dissent.[59-08]

Rule by the majority depends on the honesty of the competitive election process. Many supposed democracies maintain power through election fraud, which invalidates their status as a true democracy. The rights of the people to establish or disassemble their government are inviolable.[37] However, this concept of disassemble stems from democratic principles and philosophies like those of John Locke, who advocated for the right of people to change their government should it fail to protect their rights and liberties. However, exercising this right through violent means or outside the framework of the law typically falls into the realm of rebellion or insurrection. <u>So, we have the right, even the obligation, to disassemble our government if it fails to protect our rights, but only if we do so peacefully. Otherwise, it is treason.</u>

Society

For some political individualists, the word "society" can never refer to anything more than a large collection of individuals. Society does not exist above or beyond these individuals and thus cannot be properly said to carry out actions since actions require intentionality, intentionality requires an agent, and society as a whole cannot be properly said to possess agency; only individuals can be agents. The same holds for the government. Government does not have existence beyond the individuals it represents.[37]

Balance of Power

Being a democracy is insufficient in and of itself, if power can gravitate to any portion of the government. Separation of powers is one way America tries to maintain a balanced political system. Like in a sound accounting process, checks and balances are essential to keep power from becoming absolute. As Lord Acton, a British historian and politician, said, "Power tends to corrupt, and absolute power corrupts absolutely. Great men are almost always bad men." [39-03]

Unlike the U.S., the judicial system in the UK is entirely independent of the other branches of the government and from the prime minister, who as their executive is also a member of their legislature. Legislative power must belong to the people directly or through elected representatives. The elite or biased should not be allowed to make the law.[38]

There also needs to be a role for wise people in our government and in the creation of our laws. However, wisdom can be trumped and buried by power.

Our government structure is not perfect, but none are. It is nothing short of a miracle that our forefathers considered all the above options and others to arrive at the form of government they defined for us.

☐ Disparities in state laws create significant challenges in areas such as voting rights, healthcare, and education, where states' autonomy can sometimes hinder national progress.

To address these issues, proposed reforms suggest clarifying the limits of state autonomy, particularly in cases where overarching national interests are at stake. These include ensuring equitable access to voting and healthcare, where consistent standards across states could foster greater unity and effectiveness in addressing these critical issues.

Nationalization

As previously mentioned, the first American political parties emerged in the late 1700s. By 1824, the Federalist Party had largely disappeared from the political landscape, marking the end of its influence in American politics.[24]

Our Founding Fathers had several options when establishing the government, ranging from aristocracy to dictatorship, conservatism to liberalism, republic to representative democracy, pure democracy to socialism, and totalitarianism to communalism. Communism, as a formal ideology, had not yet emerged; it began to take shape around 1829.[39-01].

Ultimately, they opted for a republic with a representative democracy, designed to be flexible enough to shift between conservatism and liberalism as needed to address citizens' evolving needs. They incorporated many essential principles — though not necessarily unique — into the American governmental framework.

Overall, democracy as a system of government can coexist with various ideologies. Liberalism emphasizes individual freedoms, while Conservatism focuses on traditional values. Socialism and Communism, which prioritize collective ownership and social equality, can either complement or challenge democratic principles. Pluralism, the acceptance, and coexistence of diverse ideologies, plays a crucial role in shaping governance and societal structures, highlighting the importance of considering multiple perspectives in political decision-making.[29-03]

The Spectrum of Politics

Political positions are defined by the type of government, its economic policies, and its position on the dimensions described earlier. Uncertainty about where people stand on political issues has become more common, often due to misconceptions. Here is a breakdown of general categories on the spectrum of Left to Right:

Far-left: Advocates for radical equality, often through revolutionary means. This group usually supports dismantling capitalism and traditional structures in favor of collectivist or socialist systems.

Progressive: Pushes for major social reforms, focusing on equity, climate change, and systemic change, but works within democratic systems.

Liberal: Prioritizes individual rights, civil liberties, and social progress, often supporting government intervention to promote fairness and opportunity.

Moderate or Centrist: Takes a balanced approach, mixing ideas from both sides of the spectrum and favoring compromise and practical solutions.

Libertarian: Strongly values individual liberty and personal responsibility. Supports minimal government interference in economic and personal matters, often advocating for free markets and personal freedoms.

Conservative: Values tradition, stability, and smaller government. Conservatives are generally cautious about rapid change and focus on maintaining established systems.

Far-right: Emphasizes strict nationalism and traditional hierarchies. This group rejects liberal democratic norms and may advocate authoritarian measures.

Social Hierarchies and Classes

Social Structure is how societies organize through various strata, affecting individuals' access to resources and opportunities. It may include the impacts of class systems, caste systems, and tribal affiliations on social mobility, education, and healthcare access, as well as how these structures enforce social norms and roles.

Cultural norms and values are the shared beliefs and behaviors that shape social interactions, reinforce societal identity, and promote cultural cohesion. These norms vary, such as individualism in Western cultures and collectivism in Eastern ones, influencing daily life and social change.

Governance, economic systems, and social structures are deeply interconnected, shaping a society's political, economic, and social landscapes from progressive to conservative ideologies. These intersections are vast and made more complex by America's diverse cultural influences worldwide.

THE UNITED STATES GOVERNMENT FRAMEWORK

Freedom of Opportunity

All the freedoms protected by our Constitution are designed to safeguard the environment of opportunity that defines our nation. Freedom of opportunity is deeply ingrained in American culture. Elizabeth Dole captured this sentiment in a 1997 College of the Ozarks speech, saying, "America is about dreams." She reminded us that true democracies are places where dreams can come true and where aspirations can be realized. The nation's founders came to this continent in pursuit of their own — seeking land, sustenance, religious freedom, and the liberty to enjoy the fruits of their labor. The promise of prosperity and the opportunity for self-expression motivated them and continues to inspire Americans today. Throughout history, the nation has upheld a tradition of rewarding creativity, supporting those who seek opportunities, and fostering a spirit of neighborly assistance for those in need.

The foundation of the United States was built on principles that extended beyond economic interests. The Founding Fathers risked their financial security to establish a government prioritizing liberty, justice, and democratic representation. Over time, however, America's focus has increasingly shifted toward economic metrics like GDP Growth, stock market performance, and budget deficits, allowing financial concerns to dominate political discussions and overshadow broader societal values. This shift has reshaped American politics, where campaigns and legislative actions often cater more to corporate sponsors and financial backers than the public good. It has also strayed from the original vision of governance as a duty to the people rather than a means for personal enrichment. Recognizing this shift is essential as we work to realign with the nation's foundational values, ensuring that economic prosperity and the general welfare are balanced and pursued.

The U.S. Is a Republic and a Democracy

America is first and foremost a republic – a government run by an elected or appointed leader, not a hereditary one. Our Constitution also guarantees that states are republics. So, we are a republic of republics as well – because citizens have a role in the control of state governments as well as federal governments, although more directly at the state level. Our Founding Fathers recognized that the separate states had their own personalities, peculiarities, and priorities and that those should be preserved.

In a republic, civil and political rights are fundamental to ensuring individual freedoms and equality under the law. These rights include the protection of people's physical integrity and safety, as well as the guarantee of natural justice, such as procedural fairness in legal matters, the right to a fair trial, due process, and the ability to seek legal remedies. Additionally, they provide protection from discrimination and safeguard individual political freedoms, including freedom of thought, speech, religion, press, and movement. Citizens are also granted the right to participate in civil society and politics, which includes freedom of association, the right to assemble, the right to petition, and the right to vote. These rights collectively form the foundation of a functioning and just republic.

America is also a democracy, meaning that the right to govern is bestowed by the people and exercised through the vote and majority rule, except for inalienable rights.

Democracy is said to have two conditions: "All citizens, not invested with the power to govern, have equal access to power and the second that all citizens enjoy legitimized freedoms and liberties."[36]

Our Founding Principles

The principles embedded in the U.S. Constitution and the structure of the American government were debated long before the Founding Fathers undertook to create a new nation. Influential figures such as John Adams, Thomas Jefferson, George Washington, James Madison, and Alexander Hamilton were deeply educated in the classics and history. Their studies at institutions like the College of William and Mary, King's College (now Columbia University), and the College of New Jersey (now Princeton), as well as private academies, provided a rigorous curriculum that included Latin and Greek grammar, the writings of Cicero and Virgil, and the histories of ancient Greece and Rome.

The Founders drew upon a rich and diverse intellectual background when considering the various forms of government known at the time. Their reflections encompassed not only classical political philosophy but also the principles of governance observed in history. This broad base of knowledge, which included the writings of Cicero and Virgil, and the histories of ancient Greece and Rome, informed the deliberations that shaped America's founding documents.

The process of consolidating these ideas reached its peak between 1776 and 1787, culminating in the drafting of the U.S. Constitution. The Constitutional Convention, tasked with crafting the framework for the new government, included many of the signers and framers of the Declaration of Independence. While John Adams and Thomas Jefferson did not participate directly, both were serving as diplomats in Europe — their contributions to the philosophical foundations of the nation had a profound and lasting impact on the principles that guided the Constitution's creation.

Understanding these foundational ideas is crucial for adequately evaluating the structure and function of the American government today, as it reflects the deliberate choices and intellectual influences that informed the Founding Fathers. The following are examples of ideas they considered.

Roman Law and Natural Justice

The Romans, who embraced the concept of <u>Natural Justice</u>, believed that certain fundamental legal principles are so evident that they should be universally applied without the need for formal laws. This idea is echoed in the United States Declaration of Independence with the phrase, "We hold these truths to be self-evident." Centuries before the founding of the United States, Natural Justice was already an integral part of common law. It is based on the principles that most people are inherently good, that good people should not be harmed, and that one should treat others as one would like to be treated.[21]

Natural Justice encompasses procedural fairness and includes several key principles.[26]

1. **Right to Advance Warning:** Individuals have the right to advance notice of legal charges or proceedings, ensuring they are aware of any accusations or risks of loss they may face.

2. **No Retroactive Contractual Obligations:** Contractual obligations that deprive individuals of their rights should not be applied retroactively.

3. **Adequate Notice for the Accused:** A person accused of a crime or facing potential loss must be given adequate notice about the legal proceedings, including any specific charges against them.

4. **Disclosure of Personal Interests:** Decision-makers, such as judges or juries, should disclose any personal interests or conflicts of interest related to the proceedings to maintain transparency.

5. **Unbiased and Good Faith Decision-Making:** Those making decisions in a legal case must remain impartial, act in good faith, and be free from bias.

6. **Independence of Decision-Makers:** To ensure impartiality, the decision-maker must not be a party to the case or have any personal stake in the outcome.

7. **Fair Conduct of Proceedings:** Legal proceedings should be conducted fairly, ensuring equal treatment and opportunity for all involved.

8. **Opportunity to Challenge Evidence:** Each party has the right to question and dispute the evidence the opposing side presents.

9. **Consideration of Relevant Factors:** Decision-makers should base their rulings on relevant facts and circumstances while disregarding irrelevant considerations.

Ultimately, a community's trust in its legal system depends on the consistent application of these principles to ensure justice is served.

Roman Law and Natural Justice have profoundly shaped the evolution of legal principles everywhere. Still, it is equally important to acknowledge the transformative influence of various cultural and religious texts that have guided society's ethical and legal development.

The Bible

Among these, the Bible holds a pivotal role, particularly in its shift away from the principle of exact retaliation, encapsulated by the "eye for an eye" philosophy. By advocating forgiveness and promoting principles of restorative rather than retributive justice, the teachings of the New Testament, especially those of Jesus, represent a significant shift in moral and legal thought. This transition underscores a broader move towards viewing justice not merely as punishment but as a path to reconciliation and healing, marking a significant evolution in the concept of justice itself.

Magna Carta

Similarly, the Magna Carta stands as a landmark document in the history of law, recognizing subjects' rights and limiting monarchies' power. Its creation was a turning point, laying the foundation for constitutional governance by establishing that everyone, including the king, is subject to the law. This assertion set a precedent for the rule of law and the protection of individual rights.

The establishment of the United States brought further advancements in legal principles, with foundational documents such as the Declaration of Independence, the Bill of Rights, and the U.S. Constitution. These texts collectively laid the groundwork for one of the most democratic republics in history, setting a global standard for the separation of powers, the rule of law, and the safeguarding of individual liberties.

Subsequent American Principles
Original Intentions of Our Founders

The framers of the United States Constitution intended to create a government strong enough to govern effectively while carefully constrained to prevent tyranny. Their federal design emphasized a limited national government that would protect individual rights and maintain order without eroding state autonomy or infringing on personal liberties. However, many Americans today may not fully appreciate these original intentions, instead viewing an expanded role for government as essential. This shift reflects the realities of modern society, where a much larger population, complex global challenges, pandemics, natural disasters, and the rapid evolution of communication and technology demand greater coordination and oversight at the national level.

The Founding Fathers envisioned America as a constitutional republic with a federal structure that balanced power between the national and state governments. While incorporating democratic principles, they were cautious about direct democracy, favoring a system of elected representation to prevent the risks of mob rule. Their design emphasized a government rooted in the consent of the governed, guided by the rule of law, and committed to protecting individual rights. This vision combined elements of federalism, representation, and checks on power to create a stable and just system distinct from monarchies and aristocracies.

Thomas Jefferson's and John Adam's Views

As we consider our future, it is worth reflecting on the philosophies of Thomas Jefferson. Jefferson, who authored the Declaration of Independence and later served as the third president of the United States, had a profound influence on American governance.

Jefferson's Vision for America

Thomas Jefferson, one of the Founding Fathers and the third president of the United States (1801-1809), envisioned America as a democratic republic where power resided with the people, allowing citizens to elect their leaders and participate in government decision-making. Rooted in his Enlightenment-era beliefs, Jefferson was a strong advocate for limited government, emphasizing the protection of individual rights while minimizing government interference in citizens' lives. His ideals of democracy, individual liberty, and self-governance shaped his views on America's future and its Constitution.

Jefferson is best known for drafting the Declaration of Independence, where he asserted that all people are entitled to "life, liberty, and the pursuit of happiness." He supported freedom of speech, religion, and the press and envisioned America as an agrarian society of independent farmers, believing that self-sufficiency would prevent corruption from concentrated wealth. During his presidency, he oversaw the Louisiana Purchase, which doubled the size of the U.S. and offered economic opportunities for Americans to own land.

Education and religious freedom were also key to Jefferson's vision. He founded the University of Virginia and believed that an educated citizenry was essential for democracy. A strong proponent of the separation of church and state, Jefferson famously referred to "a wall of separation" between the two, which became a cornerstone of American governance.

While Jefferson's principles greatly influenced the early republic, his legacy is not without contradictions. His advocacy for liberty clashed with his views on slavery and his policies toward Native Americans. Nonetheless, his core principles continue to shape American political thought.

Jefferson also believed that the Constitution should evolve with the times. He argued that each generation should have the right to amend the Constitution to suit its needs and circumstances, suggesting it be revisited every 19 or 20 years. His forward-thinking view emphasized that the Constitution is not a static document but a living one, designed to adapt to new challenges and ensure the continued happiness of the people.

John Adams' Vision for America

John Adams, one of the Founding Fathers and the second president of the United States (1797-1801), envisioned an independent, self-governing America rooted in republican principles. Like his contemporaries, Adams wanted an America free from British rule and played a critical role in advocating for independence. He was one of the drafters of the Declaration of Independence, which set the foundation for the nation's ideals of freedom and sovereignty.

Adams firmly believed in a republican form of government, where power resided with elected representatives who served the people's interests. He was a strong advocate of a system of checks and balances to prevent any concentration of power. This belief in balanced governance was reflected in his significant role in drafting the Massachusetts Constitution of 1780, which became a model for the U.S. Constitution.

Central to Adams' vision was the need for a strong central government to maintain order and protect the nation's interests, particularly in foreign affairs. He believed in the importance of a society governed by the rule of law, where laws were applied impartially to protect individual rights and liberties. As a diplomat, Adams also understood the value of a strong defense and diplomacy, most notably contributing to the Treaty of Paris in 1783, which ended the Revolutionary War and secured American independence.

Adams also emphasized civic virtue, the commitment of citizens to the common good, as essential for the success of the republic. He saw education as key to fostering civic knowledge and participation, further reinforcing his belief in an informed and engaged citizenry.

Adams recognized that no government could be perfect and believed that the Constitution should be revised over time to adapt to changing circumstances. In *A Defence of the Constitutions of Government of the United States of America* (1787), he noted that "every government will require revision and amendment from time to time, as circumstances shall change or as the opinions of men shall vary." Adams accepted the reality that even the best forms of government may not endure indefinitely. In a letter to David Humphreys in 1819, he wrote, "I do not think that our Republic will last forever. It will last for a long time, but it will not last forever. No government has ever lasted forever."

Adams' belief in the need for periodic revision and adaptation of the Constitution continues to resonate today as we explore how to ensure our governance structures remain relevant and effective in addressing modern challenges. His pragmatic view on governance, coupled with his enduring contributions to the early republic, helped shape the foundation of American democracy.

Comparing Adams and Jefferson

Jefferson's views aligned more closely with what might resemble today's Republican ideology, while Adams' positions shared similarities with modern Democratic principles — but the comparison is not entirely straightforward. Although they were lifelong friends, Jefferson and Adams frequently found themselves on opposite sides of crucial issues, engaging in thoughtful debates about the nature of government, the balance of power, and the role of the people.

Regarding government structure, Adams favored a strong central government with a more centralized federal system, including a powerful executive branch. His role in drafting the Massachusetts Constitution, which established a two-chamber legislature and a governor with significant authority, reflected this belief. In contrast, Jefferson advocated for limited government, states' rights, and a decentralized federal system. He supported a strict interpretation of the Constitution and championed agrarian democracy as the foundation of American society.

Their views on political parties also diverged. As a Federalist, Adams saw political parties as necessary for maintaining order and stability in government. Jefferson, a Democratic-Republican, was more skeptical, viewing political parties as a potential threat to democracy. He preferred a more participatory, populist approach to governance, emphasizing the direct involvement of ordinary citizens in political affairs.

Economic and financial policy was another area of disagreement. Adams supported a robust national economy, advocating for establishing a national bank and protective tariffs to bolster domestic industries. Conversely, Jefferson believed in limiting the federal government's role in economic matters, promoting agrarianism and a laissez-faire approach to economic policy. He saw agriculture as the backbone of the American economy, contrasting Adams' emphasis on manufacturing and commerce.

Their foreign policy priorities also reflected differing visions. Adams focused on maintaining peace with foreign powers and navigating conflicts like the Quasi-War with France. His support for the controversial Alien and Sedition Acts, which restricted immigration and limited free speech during periods of unrest, underscored his concern for stability. Jefferson prioritized territorial expansion, most notably with the Louisiana Purchase, which significantly increased the nation's size and facilitated westward growth.

Finally, their stances on slavery showcased a complex divergence. Adams opposed the expansion of slavery into new territories but did not take a strong early stance against the institution itself. Jefferson, while expressing concerns about slavery, owned enslaved individuals and took no substantial actions to end the practice during his lifetime, reflecting the contradictions and limitations of his views on the issue.

In a letter dated January 21, 1812, Thomas Jefferson acknowledged that, despite having opposing views on some administrative matters, he and John Adams shared common ground regarding the Constitution and the structure of government.

Jefferson and Adams had notable disagreements on several vital issues. Adams supported a strong federal government and advocated for a robust navy, while Jefferson opposed both. They also differed on the balance of federal and state authority, with Adams favoring greater federal power and Jefferson believing that authority should primarily reside with the states. Establishing a national bank was another point of contention, as Adams favored it, whereas Jefferson opposed it. Their economic priorities diverged, with Adams promoting manufacturing growth and Jefferson championing an agrarian economy.[11-12]

Both Adams and Jefferson deeply valued the union. In his response to Jefferson on February 3, 1812, Adams emphasized the need to preserve it, quoting in Latin (translated here): *"Small communities grow great through harmony; great ones fall apart through discord."* This comment reflects the Founding Fathers' strong belief in the Constitution and the necessity of national unity. Today, we should share that same concern, as our nation risks fracturing under political infighting and parties that serve their own interests instead of the people.

Controlling Power in Government

A cornerstone of the Constitution's design is the system of checks and balances, which ensures that power is distributed among the executive, legislative, and judicial branches to prevent any of them from dominating the others. This separation of powers was established to safeguard against tyranny and protect individual freedoms. Each branch has distinct responsibilities and the authority to limit the actions of the others, maintaining a dynamic balance that upholds stability and accountability in governance. Weakening judicial independence, expanding executive powers without oversight, or restricting legislative authority would threaten this equilibrium, increasing the risk of authoritarian rule. Preserving this system is essential to protecting democracy and ensuring the nation's long-term stability.

Representative Democracy

The framers envisioned a representative democracy at the core of government, where citizens would elect leaders to make informed decisions on their behalf. This structure was designed to prevent the risks of direct democracy, where fleeting passions or shifting majorities might sway decisions. Instead, it fostered a more deliberate process that balances diverse interests, ensuring stable governance that protects individual rights and serves the common good.

Balancing State and National Interests

One of the framers' core challenges was designing a government that respected the autonomy of individual states while providing a strong national framework. They recognized that the United States was a federation of diverse states, each with its economy, culture, and priorities. To address this, they established a federal system dividing powers between state and national governments. States would govern their internal affairs, while the federal government handled matters of national concern, such as defense, foreign policy, and interstate commerce.

This balance was formalized in the Tenth Amendment, reserving all powers not explicitly granted to the federal government to the states. Over time, however, population growth, the economy, and technological change have introduced new national challenges that the original framework could not fully anticipate. As a result, the balance between state and federal authority continues to evolve — requiring constant adjustment to preserve local flexibility and national coherence.

The Structure of Congress

The structure of Congress reflects the framers' careful attempt to balance competing interests.

House of Representatives

The House was designed to directly reflect the will of the people, with representation based on population, giving larger states a proportionate voice. Each state is divided into congressional districts, ensuring local areas within states are represented. The House, with its shorter two-year terms, is designed to be the chamber most responsive to shifts in public sentiment, making it the closest institution we have to majority rule.

Senate

On the other hand, the Senate was intended to ensure that smaller states could protect their interests, with equal representation for every state regardless of size. The Senate also provides more stability with its six year terms. This bicameral legislature sought to balance the influence of populous regions against that of less populated areas, ensuring that the needs of individual states were not entirely overridden by the will of the majority. In the Senate, California has the same sway as Rhode Island. The Senate, then, acts as a check on rapid change, emphasizing deliberation and protecting minority interests within the federal system.

Principles vs. Politics: The Federalism Debate

Balancing state interests with national interests involves both principles and politics. Political ideologies significantly influence leaders' views on the roles of states versus the federal government. Some advocate for stronger state rights, arguing that states can better address their citizens' needs without excessive federal oversight. Others support a more powerful federal government, believing that uniform national policies protect rights, facilitate interstate commerce, and provide services that states may struggle to deliver effectively.

The Impact of Social Discourse

Contentious politics have been a hallmark of American life since the nation's founding including on the subject of the balance of power between the nation and its states. The political landscape has continually reshaped the framework set by the framers. In October 2024, Cliff Fleet, President and CEO of Colonial Williamsburg, quoted from a letter Thomas Jefferson wrote to Edward Rutledge, the youngest signer of the Declaration of Independence, on June 24, 1797. Jefferson lamented the decline of civil discourse, noting, "Men who have been intimate all their lives, cross the street to avoid meeting, and turn their heads another way, lest they should be obligated to touch their hat." He observed that "passions are too high at present to be cooled in our day," reflecting deep political divisions.[213]

Landmark court rulings like McCulloch v. Maryland and United States v. Lopez, along with significant legislation and executive orders, have kept the debate over state sovereignty and federal authority alive. This ongoing struggle to define the balance is vital to the nation's governance and was anticipated by the framers as essential to America's enduring success. So, this means that getting political agreement will continue to be a challenge.

Connectivity's impact on Federalism

The evolution of society, driven by technological advancements and increased connectivity, has steadily shifted many issues from the state to the national level. In an era where digital communication and commerce cross state boundaries, what were once local challenges now require national coordination.

The debate over abortion regulation highlights this shift. *Roe v. Wade* had established a national framework for abortion rights, ensuring consistency across states. However, when the Supreme Court overturned it, returning authority to individual states, the result was a patchwork of laws that created confusion and conflict. Some state policies have even led to injuries and deaths. The end of a standardized approach has caused significant upheaval as responsibility shifted to the states.

Similarly, the Affordable Care Act (ACA) was a federal effort to standardize healthcare by aligning state systems with programs like Medicare and Medicaid. The goal was to reduce disparities and ensure more equitable access. Yet, the debate persists: Should healthcare be a federal responsibility to ensure uniformity, or should states control it to reflect local needs better? How different are those local needs from what the national standard has become?

In both cases, the push for national consistency reflects a growing preference for uniform policies. While state autonomy is valuable for addressing localized concerns, the benefits of standardization, especially in critical areas like healthcare, are increasingly difficult to ignore. Balancing these priorities remains a central challenge in federalism today.

Emancipation Proclamation

The Emancipation Proclamation marked another critical milestone, signaling the end of slavery in the United States. This historic decree not only transformed American society but also inspired the world, reinforcing the inherent rights and dignity of every individual.

Each document has played a crucial role in advancing legal principles and promoting societal progress, echoing the foundational themes of Natural Justice and Roman Law. Together, they represent significant milestones on the path toward a more just and equitable world.

The Social Contract

English philosopher John Locke was a leading figure of the Enlightenment and is often called the "Father of Liberalism." His ideas significantly influenced fellow philosopher Jean-Jacques Rousseau, who explored the ideal structure of a political community in his 1762 work The Social Contract. Like Locke, Rousseau believed in the inherent goodness of individuals within a societal framework. Locke's theory proposed that people could collectively establish a government by appointing a neutral arbiter to protect their rights. In contrast, Rousseau argued that <u>a government's legitimacy arises from the consent of the governed</u>, emphasizing the importance of the general will and advocating for direct democracy.

Rousseau's theory of a truly legitimate society is centered around the concept of the 'general will.' He argued that such a society would be governed by the collective will of its citizens, with every individual participating in assemblies to help determine that will. According to Rousseau, for a government to be legitimate, the people themselves — not elected representatives — must directly contribute to shaping the laws. He stressed that citizens must ratify every law directly to ensure that it reflects the general will, as any detachment from this process undermines the legitimacy of the government.[27]

Rousseau's concept of the social contract was a revolutionary idea that inspired political reforms and even fueled European revolutions. It challenged the notion of monarchs' divine right to legislate, asserting instead that the power to make laws belongs solely to the people.

The core idea of the social contract is that each individual places their person and authority under the supreme direction of the general will, with the community recognizing each person as an integral and indivisible part of the whole. In the American context, applying this idea means that while the majority may guide decisions, it cannot infringe upon the natural rights of the minority. This principle safeguards individual freedoms and ensures that the protection of fundamental rights is not subject to the whims of majority rule.[27] This limitation is deliberately designed to prevent majority rule from diminishing, eroding, or abolishing fundamental rights.

Some people believe that majority rule would be better. They fail to understand that while it seems fair, it often is not. History offers glaring examples: the majority once thought slavery was fair. The majority believed voting should be restricted to men because they dominated public life. In the southern states, the majority supported segregation — not just in schools but also in buses, lunch counters, hotels, and restrooms.

Racial prejudice is still evident in parts of America, and its effects are undeniably ugly. When such prejudice reflects the majority's sentiment, justice is absent. Our inalienable rights must serve as foundational protections. Without them, those who advocate for majority rule often aim to sideline certain groups — whether based on race, immigration status, age, or political affiliation.

Biases are not only unnecessary; they also unnecessarily limit our society and economy. There is and has always been room in America for everyone.

Socrates

Jefferson and Adams, well-versed in the classics and history, drew upon past philosophies when shaping the founding principles of the United States. Many of these ideas were derived from influential thinkers like Socrates and Plato. The *New World Encyclopedia* reports that Socrates believed "ideals belong in a world only the wise man can understand, meaning only the philosopher is suited to govern others."[28] In Plato's dialogue, The Republic, Socrates openly criticized the democracy of Athens during his lifetime. He not only scrutinized Athenian democracy but also rejected any form of government that did not align with his ideal of a perfect republic governed by philosopher-kings. During the final years of Socrates' life, Athens experienced continual political upheaval, culminating in the overthrow of democracy by a junta known as the Thirty Tyrants. This regime, led by Plato's relative Critias, a student of Socrates, ruled for about a year before Athenian democracy was restored.[28]

According to Plato's *Apology of Socrates*, Socrates refused to participate in conventional politics, often stating that he could not advise others on how to live when he did not yet understand how to live his own life. He saw himself as a philosopher pursuing truth without claiming to possess it fully. Socrates found the rule of the Thirty Tyrants to be as objectionable as democracy. When ordered by the Tyrants to assist in the arrest of a fellow Athenian, he refused, narrowly escaping death before the regime was overthrown. Despite intense pressure, he remained uncompromising, consistently refusing to act against the laws. His actions suggest that he considered the rule of the Thirty Tyrants less legitimate than the democratic senate that later sentenced him to death. However, he also harbored profound objections to Athenian democracy.

Athenian democracy emerged around 500 BC in the city-state of Athens and was one of the earliest known Direct Democracies. In this system, citizens did not elect representatives to make decisions on their behalf; instead, they voted directly on legislation and executive measures. However, participation was limited to a specific group of citizens, selected without regard to economic status. Direct democracy appears to function most effectively in smaller communities where the number of participants is manageable.[28]

Direct Democracy, also known as pure democracy, involves the assembly of all citizens who choose to participate. Depending on the system, this assembly may pass executive motions, enact laws, elect or dismiss officials, and conduct trials. However, as the number of citizens grows, direct participation can become impractical, prompting the adoption of a different form of governance, Representative Democracy, where elected officials make decisions on behalf of the people.

In representative democracy, sovereignty (i.e., power) is exercised by a subset of the people, usually through elected officials. Countries that follow this system often incorporate limited forms of Direct Democracy, including Initiatives, Referendums ('expressions of will' that may or may not be binding), and Recalls. Referendums may involve voting on whether a specific law should be repealed, effectively giving citizens a veto over government legislation. Recall elections allow citizens to remove elected officials from office before their term ends, providing an additional mechanism for direct public influence on governance.[29]

LOCAL AND STATE GOVERNMENT

Role of Local Government

The 10th Amendment of the Constitution states, "<u>The powers not delegated to the United States by the Constitution, nor prohibited by it to the states, are reserved to the states respectively, or to the people.</u>" This clause gives local governments the primary responsibility for maintaining order, controlling harmful behavior, and protecting individual liberties. Crimes such as murder, manslaughter, robbery, rape, aggravated assault, arson, fraud, weapons violations, vandalism, prostitution, drug possession, vagrancy, and theft typically occur within local communities and thus require appropriate laws and enforcement at the local level. According to the original principles set forth by the Founding Fathers, local authorities should manage these crimes.

However, some crimes extend beyond local jurisdictions and require county or state authorities' oversight. These include corporate fraud, drug trafficking, driving under the influence on state roads, gambling, and kidnapping. Serious crimes like treason, sedition, monopolization, air transportation violations, and other interstate crimes fall under federal jurisdiction and are handled by agencies like the FBI.

The closer governance is to home; the more likely people are to feel a sense of control over their lives and the direction of their leadership. However, there is a growing trend toward centralization, with authority gradually shifting from local to state governments and from states to the federal level. This centralization raises essential questions about the balance of power and the effectiveness of local versus higher-level governance in addressing the needs of communities.

Union of States

Lessons from our nation's early days and the leadership of figures like Abraham Lincoln underscore a key principle: <u>When the actions of individual states threaten the greater good of the Union, the interests of the Union must take precedence.</u> This principle of unity should guide states to avoid actions that obstruct national defense or disrupt essential national services, fostering a sense of common purpose.

At the same time, the federal government must respect the principle that matters falling outside its core mission should be left to the states' discretion. As the Constitution outlines, the federal government's primary mission includes conducting foreign relations, protecting citizens from external threats, defending our rights and national resources, promoting a basic standard of health and welfare, and facilitating interstate commerce, communication, and trade. Beyond these fundamental responsibilities, federal involvement with states and citizens is meant to be limited, reserved for situations of extraordinary necessity — or we should consider amending the Constitution to expand its role?

It is crucial to balance these principles to maintain a functional federal system. This system prioritizes national unity while honoring the autonomy of individual states. By clearly defining the scope of federal authority and recognizing the limits of its reach, we can ensure that the government remains effective in addressing the nation's core needs without encroaching on areas better managed at the state level.

Uniformity vs. Diversity in State Governance

How important is consistency in government processes across all fifty states? As the internet continues to globalize information, some standardization in laws, policies, and ideals seems inevitable. This trend could simplify governance and policy implementation at the national level. However, complete uniformity among states is far from reality. For example, on issues like abortion, differing religious landscapes and the influence of various religious groups continue to shape laws, preventing a standardized approach.

CITIZENS AND THE GOVERNMENT

Citizens' Role in Governing

The role of citizens in governance has been a central question in political philosophy for centuries. Thinkers throughout history have debated who should participate in political decision-making, what qualifications they should have, and what the consequences of broad or restricted participation might be. The perspectives of philosophers like Plato, Aristotle, Rousseau, and John Locke offer distinct views on the responsibilities and rights of citizens in shaping their government.

Plato was one of the earliest to address the question of political participation. He believed that decision-making in governance should be reserved for those best equipped with wisdom and knowledge, whom he referred to as "philosopher-kings." Plato argued that not everyone possesses the capability to make informed and virtuous decisions for the state, suggesting that the general populace might lack the necessary understanding of justice and the common good. In his view, only the most knowledgeable individuals should engage in governance, as their wisdom would ensure that decisions were made in the best interest of society. For Plato, the role of the average citizen was limited, and political power was to be concentrated among the enlightened few.

Aristotle offered a different, yet similarly exclusive, perspective on political participation. He saw the value of citizen involvement in politics, considering it essential for a fulfilling life. However, Aristotle placed limits on who could be considered a citizen. In his ideal society, only free men with leisure time and sufficient education were suited to exercise political rights responsibly. Those without the means or time to deliberate on political matters — such as slaves, women, and laborers — were excluded. For Aristotle, participation in governance required a certain level of virtue, education, and freedom from daily labor, reflecting his belief that not everyone was equally prepared to contribute meaningfully to political decision-making.

Jean-Jacques Rousseau challenged these more restricted views by advocating for the inherent right of all individuals to participate in governance. For Rousseau, sovereignty belonged to the people, and every citizen had a right to express their "general will" through political participation. He viewed voting as a fundamental expression of individual freedom and a crucial element of a legitimate government. Rousseau's emphasis on direct participation placed the power in the hands of the people, suggesting that everyone should have a say in the decisions that affect their lives, regardless of education or social status.

John Locke's philosophy laid the groundwork for modern democratic principles by proposing that all individuals possess natural rights, including life, liberty, and property. Locke argued that government must be based on the consent of the governed, thereby endorsing a more universal approach to political participation. He believed that all people had the right to participate in elections as a means of protecting their natural rights. In Locke's view, the role of citizens was to act as a check on government power, ensuring that it remained just and accountable. His ideas helped shape the foundations of representative democracy, where citizens elect leaders to make decisions on their behalf, while still holding the right to influence the direction of government through voting.

The debate over citizens' roles in governance remains highly relevant today, drawing on the ideas of philosophers like Plato, Aristotle, Rousseau, and Locke. These thinkers offered contrasting views, from limiting political participation to the educated elite to advocating for universal involvement. Whether voting should be a universal right based on equality and autonomy or a privilege requiring specific qualifications continues to shape discussions on voting rights, electoral systems, and fair governance. Understanding these historical perspectives helps inform ongoing debates on balancing inclusivity with responsible decision-making in modern democracies.

What Makes Americans Different?

To truly be effective citizens, we must know who we are, not just how we are perceived but who we really are.

The way Americans are seen — both by themselves and the world — reflects their values, priorities, and aspirations and shapes the vision for constitutional reform. Known for their independence, innovation, and commitment to democratic principles, Americans often view themselves as architects of progress and guardians of liberty. However, these perceptions also carry expectations for addressing inequality, ensuring justice, and adapting governance to modern challenges.

What makes Americans different from citizens in other countries?

Historical View

Historically, critiques of Americans have varied widely, ranging from admiration to disdain. In 1901, Hugo Münsterberg, a German-American psychologist, offered a harsh portrayal, describing Americans as vulgar, money-driven, and corrupt. While his extreme view reflects enduring stereotypes that have persisted over time, it does not fully capture the complexity of American identity, shaped by a mix of ambition, pragmatism, and contradictions.

Since Münsterberg's time, global perceptions of Americans have changed significantly, though they are less frequently discussed. The U.S. may no longer be the focal point of some international conversations, with its global relevance increasingly tied to its role as a marketplace rather than a cultural or moral leader. Still, American influence continues to shape the world, even if its nature is viewed differently than before.[62]

It is difficult to determine how many of these traits are directly attributable to the Constitution. However, the principles of freedom and liberty enshrined in the document have certainly played a significant role in shaping and encouraging these characteristics among American citizens.

Eleven American Traits – Current View

Certain traits are frequently cited globally as uniquely American Traits, reflecting the country's rich history and evolving cultural landscape.

1. Cultural Diversity

A defining characteristic of the U.S. is its cultural diversity, shaped by centuries of immigration. Often described as a "melting pot" or "salad bowl," the country blends various cultures, languages, and traditions. Alongside this diversity is a strong emphasis on individualism, where personal freedom, self-reliance, and autonomy shape social norms, economic practices, and political ideologies. Given that the U.S. has welcomed people from all backgrounds, its Constitution should reflect this diversity.

2. Innovative Spirit

The United States is known for its innovative spirit, reflected in entrepreneurship, technological advancements, and business and scientific research leadership. Much of this innovation stems from the nation's greater wealth than other countries. Nevertheless, this spirit is also driven and sustained by democratic governance, the rule of law, and a system of checks and balances rooted in the Constitution and the Bill of Rights.

3. Strong National Identity and Patriotism

Another defining trait is a deep sense of patriotism and national identity, often linked to historical events like the American Revolution and symbols like the flag. Though the nation has experienced internal conflicts, it has historically united in times of external threats. Younger generations are reshaping this patriotism by incorporating critical historical perspectives, a drive for improvement, and a sense of global responsibility.

4. Optimistic Attitude

Americans also have an optimistic and forward-looking attitude, with a strong belief in progress and positive change. This attitude is reflected in the country's consumer culture, which is defined by high levels of consumption and a focus on material goods.

5. Geographic Diversity

The diverse geographical landscapes, from coastal areas to mountain ranges and plains contribute to varied lifestyles and regional cultures.

6. Strong Global Influence

The United States wields significant global influence culturally, politically, and economically, shaping international perceptions and reinforcing its distinct identity at home and abroad. These traits align with foundational principles like liberty, freedom of speech, the pursuit of happiness, the right to change the government, and the freedom of religion.

7. Defender of Fundamental Freedoms

While different societies have varying approaches to governance, such as theocratic control in some regions or centralized resource management in others, the U.S. is often seen as a defender of significant freedoms. Democracies worldwide strive to uphold human rights but face challenges in achieving unity due to political diversity and historical conflicts.

8. Restrained Until Action Required

Historically, the U.S. has shown caution in engaging in conflicts but has responded decisively when attacked, as seen in Pearl Harbor and 9/11. Its approach to international conflict is shaped by congressional decision-making, balancing restraint, and action.

9. Strong Work Ethic

Countries like China, Russia, Venezuela, Cuba, Iran, and North Korea often limit freedoms and prioritize economic policies that serve the ruling class. In contrast, American culture values creativity, a strong work ethic, and, historically, honoring commitments, such as international treaties.

10. Generosity in times of Need

America has demonstrated extensive generosity in global times of need, providing humanitarian aid, disaster relief, and support for rebuilding efforts across the world. While the U.S. is known for its generosity, this trait is not uniquely American.

11. Military Strength

Outsiders often view America's military strength as a dominant global force capable of projecting power and influence worldwide, but not without criticism. Much of this criticism stems from the United States' frequent interference in the political affairs of other nations, especially in Latin America, where covert operations, regime changes, and economic pressure have left lasting resentment. These actions, combined with America's global prominence and outspoken political culture, have shaped a perception of the U.S. as an influential leader and an overreaching force on the world stage.

These eleven defining traits shape how Americans see themselves and influence how the nation is perceived internationally. They are also the foundation of the United States' future and must be considered in reevaluating our Constitution and the country's direction and role in the world.

THE AMERICAN DREAM AND WEALTH DISTRIBUTION

The American Dream, rooted in the Declaration of Independence's principles of equality and the pursuit of happiness, is the belief that anyone, regardless of background, can achieve success and upward mobility through hard work and perseverance. Traditionally, it has been associated with homeownership, education, and career advancement as symbols of prosperity and stability.

However, achieving the American Dream has become increasingly difficult due to widening economic disparities and the declining accessibility of traditional success markers like homeownership and stable employment. Rising education costs, stagnant wages, inflation, and growing inequality have made upward mobility more elusive for many. Globalization and technological shifts have reshaped job markets, often leaving behind those without access to new skills or education.

As a result, the American Dream may require a reevaluation of what success means today. This shift reflects broader economic trends and ongoing debates about fairness, opportunity, and equality in modern society.

Over the past few decades, the wealth distribution in the United States has shown increasing disparity between the bottom 50% and the top 10% of earners. Here is a summary of how the wealth disparity has evolved:

- **From the 1980s to the 1990s**, wealth growth was evenly distributed across different groups. However, starting in the late 1990s, the wealth of the top 1% began to diverge significantly from that of the bottom 50%.

- **2000s**: The gap widened substantially, with the top 1% experiencing nearly 300% wealth growth by 2019, while the bottom 50% saw virtually no net wealth growth since 1989.
- **2010s to 2020s**: By 2022, the top 10% of earners held about 71% of the nation's wealth, a rise from 61% in 1990. In contrast, the bottom 50% has remained consistently low in wealth accumulation, with the bottom 20% holding only about 3% of total wealth throughout these decades.

The above data reflects significant growth in wealth for the top echelons of earners, primarily driven by investments in stocks and businesses. In contrast, the bottom half of the population has seen minimal increases due to housing costs and minimal stock ownership.[277-279]

It is within the realm of possibilities that real estate values may become stagnant or start to decline as our population begins to decline as is predicted.

POLITICAL SYSTEMS AND REFORM

The form of our government, shaped and affected by politics, is not politics. Politics is a separate animal that, as previously mentioned, did not even exist formally at the beginning of our country.

Origin of Political Parties

Martin Van Buren was pivotal in shaping the modern party system during the 1820s and 1830s. He championed the idea that organized political parties were essential for democracy, helping to formalize party structures, platforms, and the process of selecting candidates. This development laid the groundwork for the political party dynamics and machinations that dominate U.S. politics today.

In our formative years as a country, independent organizations did not decide who would run for office, what they would say, or what rewards would be doled out to the faithful. Giving political parties the power to select the candidates for whom America's citizens will get to vote to represent them in our government was neither contemplated nor provided for in the design of our Constitution.

Two-Party System

America is not obligated to maintain a two-party system. The United States evolved into a two-party system rather than being explicitly designed that way. Political parties were not originally included in the U.S. Constitution but were debated during its drafting. Politics begins with the governing ideologies, economic systems, and social structures including cultural norms and values.

The two-party system in the United States began emerging around 1792 and took clearer shape by the 1796 presidential election, the first in which political parties formally backed candidates. The Federalists, influenced by Alexander Hamilton, supported a strong central government, while the Democratic-Republicans, led by Thomas Jefferson, championed states' rights and a more decentralized government. Though widely admired, George Washington opposed political parties altogether, warning in his farewell address that they would divide the nation and threaten its unity.

The two-party system developed organically over time due to political, historical, and institutional factors rather than foundational laws. This evolution was influenced by the structure of elections, particularly the winner-takes-all system, which favors the dominance of two major parties.

Do party leaders exert too much influence over their members during campaigns and after taking office? Should standardized processes for selecting party leaders be implemented to ensure fairness and accountability? Congressional incumbents often struggle to balance party directives with their duty to represent their constituents. Their reliance on party support — particularly for funding and endorsements — reinforces this dependence. As a result, representatives may feel pressured to prioritize party agendas over their constituents' interests or principles. This reliance on party leadership for electoral success raises serious concerns about whether citizen interests are truly represented in governance.

Do We Need More Than Two Parties?

We could consider multiparty systems. While critics often describe multiparty systems as chaotic and inefficient, they function effectively in many countries. Proponents of the two-party system argue that having only two-parties prevents prolonged elections and simplifies the voting process when no candidate wins a majority — for example if three parties each receive 33% of the vote. However, while multiparty systems may require multiple voting rounds, coalition-building, and interim officeholders, many nations have shown that these challenges can be managed successfully.

Another drawback of introducing a third major party is the risk of vote splitting, where a new party pulls voters from an existing party on the same side of the political spectrum. This risk can lead to a right-leaning party winning despite more overall support for left-leaning candidates or vice versa.

Does a Two-Party System Concentrate Power Too Narrowly?

The dominance of two major political parties raises significant questions about the concentration of power within a small group of individuals, particularly the party leaders. It also may force candidates toward the two extremes of the political categories that were described earlier, while the electorate might prefer more middle-ground positions.

While a two-party system can provide stability and streamline decision-making, it can also create an environment where influence is disproportionately shaped by large donors and lobbyists, often representing powerful business interests. This dynamic has raised concerns that governance is increasingly shaped to serve powerful interests rather than the broader public good. America's economic structure favors large-scale commerce, rewarding billionaires first and the wealthy next, leaving the general workforce, the unemployed, and the poor at the bottom.

As described earlier, compounding these worries is the limited ethical oversight of interactions between lobbyists and unelected party leaders, leaving room for potential conflicts of interest. Understanding the extent of this influence and its implications for democratic governance is critical.

What Do We Need From Our Political Parties?

Political parties are entrenched in our election processes, fundamental to the governance and future trajectory of any country. Once in office, elected officials are held to a set of expectations by their party. Without the following key attributes, political parties risk eroding public trust and failing to meet the demands of a well-informed and active electorate.

Purpose and Priority

To fulfill their purpose effectively, they must prioritize the common good over partisan interests and focus on addressing the needs of the people they represent.

Qualities and Participation

The most important qualities we need from our political parties are integrity, accountability, and a commitment to practical solutions rather than ideological extremes. Political parties must foster collaboration and prioritize policies that advance economic stability, national security, social equity, and environmental sustainability. Without collaboration, a party will drive wedges between them and the other party and polarize our citizens.

Parties should also encourage citizen participation by making the political process transparent, inclusive, and accessible. Ultimately, political parties should serve as vehicles for positive change, uniting rather than dividing the electorate.

Adaptability and Keeping Promises

Additionally, parties must embrace adaptability, recognizing when policies must evolve in response to societal shifts or emerging challenges. Effective governance requires pragmatic problem-solving and focusing on long-term solutions rather than short-term political gains.

A vital element of party obligations is consistency between words and actions. Promises made during campaigns should be accompanied by clear plans and measurable results once in office.

Honesty

Dishonesty in political campaigns has been common throughout history, with notable examples like the 1828 presidential race between Andrew Jackson and John Quincy Adams. Before then, political maneuvering mainly happened behind closed doors, away from public view.

In 1828, the presidential race between Andrew Jackson and John Quincy Adams sank to a new low in American politics. Both sides launched vicious personal attacks — Adams was called corrupt and elitist, while Jackson was painted as violent and unfit. Jackson's wife was accused of bigamy, and she died soon after the election, which Jackson blamed on the smear campaign. It marked the start of modern dirty politics, where character assassination took center stage.

Once elected, representatives must prioritize honesty for effective governance and a strong democracy. Misleading campaign promises, information manipulation, and deceptive legislation weaken trust in democratic institutions. Transparent and truthful leadership fosters public confidence, while dishonesty breeds disillusionment, apathy, and political instability.

In government, honesty ensures responsible use of public funds, integrity in decision-making, and policies that serve the public rather than private interests. It also strengthens the bond between leaders and voters, promoting accountability and informed decision-making. independent oversight, transparent reporting, and a free press help uphold this standard, following the principle of "Trust but Verify," a Russian proverb ("Doveryai, no proveryai") popularized by Reagan. A culture of honesty and transparency strengthens democracy and sets an example of ethical leadership worldwide.

Campaign Contributions Reform

The influence of money in politics has long raised concerns about fairness, transparency, and the balance of power in elections.

Campaign Contributions Issues

The considerable impact of money in politics extends beyond campaign contributions. In the 1952 presidential election featuring Dwight D. Eisenhower and Adlai

Stevenson, the combined spending of both major party candidates amounted to an estimated $19 million (approximately $191 million when adjusted for inflation to 2020 dollars). In the 2020 United States presidential election, including spending by presidential candidates, political parties, various political action committees (PACs), and interest groups, the total expenditure soared to more than $16 billion, marking a staggering 8,800% increase, adjusted for inflation.[89-03]

The pivotal Citizens United case, decided by the Supreme Court in 2010, granted corporations, unions, and specific nonprofit organizations the ability to make unlimited independent expenditures in support of or in opposition to candidates. Notably, this ruling did not alter the ban on direct corporate contributions to candidates but opened the door to heightened spending by external groups. Consequently, this affords organizations a disproportionate level of influence over Congress when compared to individual citizens. This shift of power from citizens to corporations (corporate leaders) has been dramatic.

The Federal Election Campaign Act imposes limits to regulate campaign finance, restricting individual contributions to no more than $2,400 for a specific federal election candidate and $30,400 per year for a political party. The act also prohibits corporations and labor unions from directly contributing to candidates. However, corporations and unions can establish political action committees (PACs), and, as per the 2010 Supreme Court decisions, they can finance advertisements advocating for or against presidential or congressional candidates, provided these ads are produced independently from the candidate's campaign.

The Supreme Court's ruling in *Citizens United v. FEC (2010)* also struck down restrictions on corporations and unions funding independent expenditures, including issue-oriented advertisements, within 30 days of a primary election and 60 days before a general election. While campaign finance laws aim to prevent individuals and organizations from influencing candidates through large contributions in exchange for favors, the ruling permitted unlimited independent spending, arguing that restrictions violated the First Amendment.

On the other hand, "soft money" donations allowed political parties to receive unlimited contributions, ostensibly for "party-building" activities rather than directly supporting candidates. However, much of this funding was used to influence elections indirectly. In the 2000 presidential election cycle, soft money contributions were estimated at nearly $500 million. In 2002, Congress banned these contributions by passing the Bipartisan Campaign Reform Act (McCain-Feingold Act). While parts of the law faced legal challenges, the Supreme Court upheld the soft money ban in McConnell v. FEC (2003). As a result of these dynamics, the representation of the average citizen in the political process has been overshadowed by the financial influence wielded by large corporations and unions.

Campaign Contribution Limits

Campaign contribution limits exist to promote transparency and fairness in political funding, while preventing undue influence and protecting free speech. The rules vary depending on who is giving and who is receiving the money.

Types of donors include individuals, candidate committees, political action committees (PACs), and party committees. PACs can be classified as either *multicandidate* or *non-multicandidate*. Recipients include candidate committees, PACs, and party committees at the national, state, and local levels.

Key Contribution Limits:

- To Candidate Committees:
  - Individuals: up to $3,300 per election
  - Candidate committees: up to $2,000
  - PACs (of any type): up to $5,000 per election
  - State/local party committees: up to $5,000 combined per election
  - National party committees: up to $5,000 per election
- To PACs:
  - Individuals: up to $5,000 per year
  - Candidate and party committees: no limit
- To State, District, and Local Party Committees:
  - Individuals: up to $10,000 per year
  - PACs: up to $5,000 per year
  - Candidate committees and national parties: no limit
- To Additional National Party Committees' Non-Federal Accounts:
  - Individuals: up to $123,300 per year

Transfers between party committees and candidate committees are generally unlimited.[94]

These limits are periodically updated based on changes in the law and regulatory decisions. They may also vary by jurisdiction and the type of election, such as primary, general, special, or runoff. These rules aim to keep political funding fair and transparent while protecting the democratic process.

Campaign funding in the United States comes from several sources, including individual contributions, Political Action Committees (PACs), and candidate self-financing. According to OpenSecrets, contributions to congressional campaigns are divided into small individual donations ($200 or less), large individual donations (over $200), PAC contributions, and self-financing. In the 2022 congressional races, small individual contributions ranged from about 19% to 35% of total funding, while large individual contributions made up the largest share, between 42% and 59%, depending on the party and chamber. PAC contributions varied, making up between 8.9% and 23.4% of funds, and self-financing was generally low, never exceeding 2%.[357]

The reliance on different funding sources differs across parties, but large individual donations consistently play a dominant role. While exact figures on billionaire contributions are limited, reports indicate that in the 2022 midterms, the top one hundred donors, many of whom were billionaires, spent 60% more than all small donors combined.[358]

The influence of wealthy individuals on political campaigns continues to grow.

Campaign Financing Reform

Comprehensive campaign finance reform is necessary to reduce money's influence in politics. One key measure is setting strict donation limits from single sources or affiliated entities to prevent any group from having excessive sway over candidates. Additionally, redesigning campaign finance rules to ensure most donations come from individual citizens or that donations from large organizations do not exceed those from individuals in aggregate would help level the playing field.

Another essential reform involves closing loopholes related to "soft money" in federal elections. Strengthening the Bipartisan Campaign Reform Act with more precise definitions and stricter limits on funds raised and spent by state committees and affiliated entities would help curb indirect influence. Enhancing the Federal Election Commission's resources and authority, increasing penalties for violations, and streamlining the process for investigating and prosecuting infractions would improve enforcement.

Transparency must also be a priority. Requiring full disclosure of all political contributions and expenditures, including those by super PACs, through real-time reporting systems would allow the public to scrutinize campaign finances more effectively.

Public financing systems could further reduce candidates' reliance on large private donations. At a total campaign cost of $16 billion and with 160 million voters, approximately $100 per voter every four years — or about $30 every other year — would be sufficient to fund federal elections. The average taxpayer paid $19,113 in federal income taxes in 2023, so allocating just $33 per year to a public election fund would make this system feasible.

Raising public and political awareness about the need for strong campaign finance laws is also crucial. Educating voters on the effects of unregulated money in politics can build support for reforms. Strengthening oversight by empowering agencies such as the IRS to investigate illegal donations, particularly those funneled through intermediaries, would add another layer of accountability. These measures collectively aim to restore fairness in the electoral process, ensuring that political influence is not merely a commodity for sale to the highest bidder.

The Need for Greater Transparency

A meaningful concern in campaign financing is the lack of transparency in political contributions, particularly involving PACs and Super PACs. While PACs are required to report donations, the actual sources of these funds can be obscured through intermediaries and layered contributions. The rise of "dark money" organizations, such as 501(c)(4) social welfare groups, adds to the challenge. These organizations can receive unlimited contributions and are not required to disclose their donors, allowing individuals and corporations to influence elections and policy without public scrutiny.

Transparency is essential for maintaining public confidence in the electoral process. To achieve this, PACs, Super PACs, and other political organizations should be required to disclose all funding sources in campaign finance reports, with clear documentation of the origins of contributions. Greater transparency would promote accountability, making it harder for hidden donors to shape policy decisions without oversight.

Restoring Integrity to the Political Process

Reducing money's influence in American politics is essential to gaining or sustaining public confidence in the democratic process. Potential reforms include imposing stricter limits on campaign contributions, mainly from corporate and foreign sources, longer-term planning such as multi-year budgeting, strengthening oversight, and disclosure requirements to prevent abuse. Closing loopholes that enable indirect graft and influence peddling should also be a priority.

A stronger legal framework could also prevent public officials from using their positions for financial gain through direct payments, indirect graft, or influence peddling. By increasing transparency, limiting financial influence, and holding elected officials to higher ethical standards, the U.S. can move toward a more equitable and trustworthy political system, ensuring that every citizen's voice has equal weight.

Citizens must prioritize campaign finance reform to safeguard the principles of American democracy from the corrosive effects of unchecked power concentration and financial influence.

Political Reform

Reform proposals often focus on enhancing government transparency, accountability, and public engagement. Suggested measures include requiring agencies to release information unless it poses a clear risk, developing searchable online databases for public records, and hosting virtual town hall meetings to improve communication between officials and the public. Other recommendations seek to strengthen oversight in government contracting and ensure careful evaluations before privatizing public services. These efforts reflect a broader push to modernize government operations in line with technological advances and public expectations.

Critics of the current political system argue for reducing short-term decision-making and rebuilding public trust. Proposed solutions include prioritizing government spending on essential needs, limiting unnecessary taxation, and encouraging innovation and community-based initiatives. However, these reform efforts raise an essential question: why weren't such changes implemented when past leaders had the opportunity? This ongoing debate underscores the challenge of balancing political ideals with the practical realities of governance.[81-85]

Free and Honest Elections

Free and fair elections are absent in dictatorships and fundamental to representative democracies. Without them, true representative democracy cannot exist. To ensure elections are free, every qualified voter must have full access to polling places without facing intimidation or obstruction. Election integrity must also be maintained throughout the counting process, with safeguards against manipulating results before, during, or after the count. Bipartisan or multipartisan supervision at every stage of the counting process is essential to maintaining public trust and ensuring objective outcomes. Ballots must be designed to avoid confusion and ensure that votes are accurately recorded and counted. Poor design or mechanical flaws — such as ambiguous marks or "hanging chads," where a punch-card ballot isn't fully perforated — can lead to uncertainty about voter intent. Such issues became a major point of contention during the disputed 2000 U.S. presidential election. A system that includes a cross-check validation process would be best.

Do We Need a "Truth in Naming Legislative Bills" Bill?

Legislative bills often have titles that suggest noble intentions, but their content may not align with these names. This practice can lead to confusion and manipulation, as lawmakers and the public may misinterpret a bill's true impact based on its title alone. A "Truth in Naming" requirement could help ensure bill titles accurately reflect their purpose and provisions, promoting transparency, accountability, and informed public debate.

For example, at the federal level:

- The USA PATRIOT Act, passed after the September 11, 2001, attacks, invoked patriotism and national security. While it did enhance security measures, it also expanded government surveillance powers, raising concerns about privacy and civil liberties.
- The No Child Left Behind Act (2002) suggested comprehensive educational improvements but instead prioritized standardized testing and accountability, leading to a narrowed curriculum and excessive focus on test scores.

- The Inflation Reduction Act (2022) claimed to address inflation but included provisions for climate change investments, healthcare reforms, and corporate tax measures. Critics argued its title misrepresented the law's broader scope by leveraging public concerns about inflation.

At the state level, misleading titles are also common:
- Florida's Parental Rights in Education Act (2021) was presented as protecting parental rights and classroom discussions, but critics argued it restricted LGBTQ+ topics and diversity conversations.
- Florida's Student Success Act suggested a commitment to improving education but emphasized standardized testing and school choice, which sparked controversy.
- Arizona's Protect the Elderly Act (2017) sounded like a safeguard for seniors but would have made affordable healthcare access more difficult.
- Missouri's Right to Farm Act (2022) appeared to protect farmers but primarily shielded agribusinesses from liability for environmental damage.
- Connecticut's Act Concerning Various Pay Equity and Fairness Matters (2018) claimed to address gender pay equity but mainly limited employers from inquiring about wage history rather than tackling broader compensation issues.

A "Truth in Naming" requirement would help maintain trust and clarity in the lawmaking process, ensuring public discussions and policymaking are based on the actual content and consequences of proposed laws.

RIGHTS AND LIBERTIES

Protection of Rights, Liberty, and Individual Freedoms

In America, the Constitution defines the government's role as "promoting the general welfare," which entails protecting citizens' well-being and safeguarding their rights, including those of vulnerable or minority groups. Alexis de Tocqueville emphasized that an essential function of government is "protecting the inalienable rights of minorities against oppression by the majority." Without such protections, historical injustices like slavery and the denial of voting rights might have persisted.

While the Constitution guarantees certain rights, it has room for strengthening protections in other areas. For instance, amendments could explicitly ensure equal treatment regardless of sexual orientation or gender identity and reevaluate issues like the death penalty, which most other democracies have abolished as inconsistent with modern human rights standards.

Basic Human Rights

While many global declarations and national constitutions affirm fundamental human rights, not all governments recognize or defend them. With its history of championing individual liberties and democratic values, the United States has the potential to set an example. However, this requires ongoing efforts to refine its governance and uphold its foundational principles. By doing so, the U.S. can encourage other nations to strengthen their commitment to human rights.

Other Governments' Human Rights

The United Nations (UN), founded in 1945 to promote peace, security, human rights, and development, shares key principles with the U.S. Constitution. As a founding member, the U.S. played a significant role in shaping the UN's core values, which align with American ideals such as the rule of law, individual rights, and democratic governance. The UN Charter emphasizes sovereign equality, justice, and human rights — paralleling the U.S. Constitution's commitment to individual liberties and accountable government. Both documents support fundamental rights and peaceful conflict resolution, reflecting a shared vision for a just and stable international order.

There are 193 members countries and besides The Holy See and Palestine which hold observer status in the United Nations, allowing them to participate without full membership. Approximately 10 to 12 entities, including Taiwan, Western Sahara, and Kosovo, are not UN members due to disputes over sovereignty and recognition, often stemming from ongoing conflicts or opposition by powerful member states.

Human Rights on a Global Scale

While the U.S. Constitution has guided the nation for over two hundred years, the world lacked a comparable foundational document until the formation of the United Nations. In 1946, the U.N. established a Commission on Human Rights, which worked until December 10, 1948, when the General Assembly adopted the Universal Declaration of Human Rights (UDHR — see link to a summary at the end of this book).

The most comprehensive, legally binding human rights agreements under U.N. oversight are the International Covenant on Civil and Political Rights and the International

Covenant on Economic, Social, and Cultural Rights. Adopted in 1966, they took effect in 1976. While many principles in the U.S. Constitution were not original, their combination was unique and helped create one of the longest-standing stable governments in history.

At the international level, the U.N. Charter reflects ideals in the U.S. Constitution, such as promoting peace, respecting human rights, and encouraging social progress. The U.S. pioneered constitutional democracy, and its Constitution has had a lasting influence on global discussions about governance and human rights.

The Constitution's emphasis on democracy, individual rights, and the rule of law has influenced many nations, though its impact varies. In some regions where religion is central to governance and social norms, these principles sometimes conflict with religious traditions. This conflict has led to resistance from religious leaders who see them as a challenge to their authority.[59-24]

In 2023, international organizations like the United Nations faced growing challenges in upholding human rights and promoting world peace. Conflicts involving "bad actors" disregarding international laws and human rights standards have fueled humanitarian crises and reversed decades of progress.

Why should Americans care about international human rights? In an increasingly interconnected world, human rights violations anywhere can create instability and conflict, threatening global security — including that of the United States.

Defending human rights reflects America's core values of freedom and justice. Promoting these rights abroad is a moral duty and an ethical responsibility.

Should America Care about Other Democracies?

America should care about democracy overseas because the health of democracy worldwide has direct and indirect consequences for our security, economy, and values. Democracies foster greater stability, respect for human rights, and peaceful international relations. Here's why caring matters:

1. **Security**: Democratic nations are less likely to go to war with one another, a phenomenon known as the "Democratic Peace Theory." Supporting democracy reduces the likelihood of conflicts destabilizing regions, creating refugee crises, or drawing America into costly interventions.

2. **Economic Benefits**: Democracies generally have more transparent and stable economic systems, which foster trade, innovation, and mutually beneficial economic partnerships. By promoting democracy, America helps create trading partners and global economic stability, reducing the risk of economic downturns that impact everyone.

3. **Shared Values**: As a nation built on liberty and self-governance, supporting democracy reflects America's ideals. Championing these principles abroad strengthens their legitimacy and influence, countering authoritarianism and ensuring freedom remains a global aspiration.

4. **Global Influence**: Democracies are more likely to align with the U.S. on global issues such as climate change, counterterrorism, and human rights. By fostering democratic systems, America builds alliances that advance shared goals and protect international norms.

5. **Moral Responsibility**: As a global leader, America has a role in supporting the fundamental rights and dignity of all people. Opposing tyranny and championing democracy helps ensure that basic freedoms are not the privilege of a few but the right of all.

Ignoring the promotion of democracy overseas risks empowering authoritarian regimes, spreading instability, and undermining international norms that have long upheld global peace and prosperity.

Furthermore, the resulting global stability and prosperity directly affects U.S. national security and economic interests.[59-09,10]

Promoting and respecting human rights strengthens prosperity by fostering stable, law-abiding societies that support education, economic opportunity, and inclusive growth. Such environments attract investment and enable sustainable development both nationally and globally. Healthy, educated, and empowered populations are key to productivity and long-term progress.

By championing human rights, the U.S. reinforces democratic governance worldwide, helping to create more stable and cooperative international partners. This approach bolsters America's global reputation and influence, vital for broader foreign policy goals. Beyond these practical benefits, there is a fundamental human dimension — empathy and solidarity with those who suffer rights abuses, a cause that should matter to all, including Americans.

Civil Rights and Liberties

Civil rights and liberties are the foundation of democracy, ensuring that all citizens receive equal protection under the law, can express themselves freely, participate in the political process, and live without discrimination. As the nation faces complex issues related to racial and gender equality, LGBTQ+ rights, voting rights, and more, it is essential to examine how these challenges are addressed while upholding fundamental democratic principles.

Debates over civil rights and liberties have long shaped American society, reflecting differing views on protecting individual freedoms and ensuring equality. These discussions often involve constitutional amendments, such as the First Amendment (freedom of speech, religion, and assembly), the Second Amendment (right to bear arms), and the Fifteenth and Nineteenth Amendments (voting rights).

One perspective emphasizes the need for government action to safeguard rights and address systemic inequalities. Advocates support initiatives that expand access to voting, combat discrimination, and protect marginalized groups, including racial minorities, women, and LGBTQ+ individuals. This approach often relies on the Equal Protection Clause of the Fourteenth Amendment, which prohibits states from denying any person equal protection under the law. Supporters argue that proactive measures, such as voting law reforms and policies addressing systemic inequality, are necessary to create a more inclusive society where all individuals can fully exercise their rights.

Another perspective prioritizes limiting government intervention to maximize personal freedoms, including religious liberty, free speech, and economic choice. Supporters of this view often invoke the First Amendment to defend religious and free speech rights, even in cases involving controversial or unpopular viewpoints. They also emphasize the Second Amendment's role in protecting individual liberty. Advocates argue that reducing government regulations and promoting free-market solutions enhance personal and economic freedom, viewing these principles as essential to safeguarding civil liberties.

Both approaches have faced criticism. Opponents of government intervention argue that expanding regulations and programs can infringe on personal freedoms, increase bureaucracy, and overstep constitutional boundaries. On the other hand, critics of the limited-government approach warn that it may fail to protect vulnerable populations and address systemic barriers to equality, such as disparities in access to voting, healthcare, and economic opportunities.

Ultimately, the debate over civil rights and liberties reflects differing interpretations of how constitutional protections should be applied in modern society. These discussions remain crucial in the ongoing effort to build a just and equitable nation guided by the principles of the Constitution.

Liberty

Life, liberty, and the pursuit of happiness are fundamental principles Americans hold dear, with liberty occupying a central role. Liberty is not only vital for the pursuit of happiness but also integral to our way of life.

Liberty refers to the state of being free from oppressive restrictions or control by authority, society, or government. It allows individuals the autonomy to act according to their own will and preferences within the bounds of law and respect for the rights of others. It encompasses freedom from interference (negative liberty) and the ability to pursue one's goals (positive liberty).

Personal Liberty

Therefore, many consider liberty the paramount American principle. The primary function of our government is to protect liberty and prevent any undue influence or factions from undermining the rights of our citizens.[51]

In the government's role of preserving our liberty, all three branches – executive, legislature, and judiciary – operate with the shared objective of maintaining a system of checks and balances.

The American principles of freedom of speech, the right to assemble, and freedom of religion emerged in response to the oppression of monarchial governments and the founders' unwavering commitment to liberty. Our federal government plays a crucial role in safeguarding these three freedoms. Although these rights are not as absolute as liberty, they are intricately connected to and reliant upon it. For instance, freedom of speech has limitations, including the prohibition of causing harm to others or inciting imminent lawless action, as defined by the Supreme Court. Additionally, certain forms of commercial speech are not protected.

Corporate Liberty

The government usually grants corporations similar legal rights as individual citizens, treating them as distinct legal entities with some similarities but not complete equivalence to individuals. However, there are instances where the government intervenes to protect citizens from corporate actions.

The treatment of corporations versus individuals is highlighted through various case studies that show how regulatory measures are implemented to protect the public. The establishment of the federal do-not-call (DNC) list restricts corporate telemarketing practices, shielding individuals from unsolicited marketing calls. Similarly, the Environmental Protection Agency (EPA) enforces laws like the Clean Air Act and Clean Water Act to limit industrial pollution, ensure clean air and water for communities, and prevent environmental harm. In the financial sector, the Consumer Financial Protection Bureau (CFPB) oversees activities such as mortgage lending, credit card offers, and payday loans to promote fair, transparent, and competitive practices, protecting consumers from predatory financial practices and fraud. These examples demonstrate how regulations often impose restrictions on corporate behavior to safeguard individual rights and well-being.

Diversity vs. Homogenization

Society faces an inherent contradiction: It wants to embrace and preserve diversity of cultures, identities, and perspectives while steadily moving toward equal and consistent treatment for all. Homogenization, the melding of cultures, seeks to standardize and unify, often at the cost of unique identities and practices. Think of how McDonald's™ has spread across the world, albeit with some cultural refinements. Everyone eating the same type of food instead of eating their local specialties: German, Japanese, Chinese, Mexican, etc. Equal treatment can mean homogenizing everyone – pushing everyone into wanting to or needing to be the same.

In a broader context, should we prioritize preserving diversity in cultures, viewpoints, and identities? Despite our varying appearances, languages, and culinary preferences, we share common aspirations – the pursuit of freedom, safety, nourishment, shelter, warmth, and, most importantly, meaningful connections with family and friends. As humans, we are not naturally inclined to solitude; instead, our intrinsic purpose is to support one another in various ways. To act otherwise would mean resigning ourselves to isolation, which contradicts our inherent nature. And given current trends in technology and culture, the eventual homogenization of the entire world appears inevitable – some day in the distant future. It is only a matter of how gradually or quickly it happens.[59-11,12]

Discrimination

There is still work to be done regarding discrimination in the U.S. Constitution. Although the Constitution and its amendments, such as the Fourteenth Amendment's Equal Protection Clause, provide a foundation for protecting against discrimination, certain areas remain contentious or lack explicit protections. Several issues warrant consideration for constitutional updates or clarifications:

1. **Explicit Protections for Sexual Orientation and Gender Identity**

   The Constitution does not explicitly prohibit discrimination based on sexual orientation or gender identity. While court decisions, such as the Supreme Court's ruling in *Bostock v. Clayton County* (2020), have interpreted existing civil rights laws to protect LGBTQ+ individuals from workplace discrimination, these protections are not explicitly enshrined in the Constitution. An amendment could be proposed to ensure clear, comprehensive protection against discrimination for LGBTQ+ individuals in various areas, including employment, housing, and public services. Who would it harm?

2. **Equal Rights Amendment (ERA**

   The proposed Equal Rights Amendment (ERA), which aims to guarantee equal legal rights regardless of sex, has not been ratified. The ERA was first proposed by Alice Paul, a prominent women's rights advocate and leader of the National Woman's Party. It read, "Men and women shall have equal rights throughout the United States and every place subject to its jurisdiction." It was introduced to Congress in December 1923 but did not gain significant traction until the women's rights movement (1960s and 1970s). In 1972, Congress approved an updated version of the ERA, but it has yet to be fully ratified into the Constitution.

Though gender equality has gained legal recognition through legislation and court decisions, many advocates argue that the ERA would provide a more robust, constitutional foundation for combating sex-based discrimination. This amendment could offer a clear statement against gender discrimination and solidify protections for women's rights.

3. **Racial Discrimination and Systemic Inequality**

   While the Constitution prohibits racial discrimination, some argue that it does not go far enough in addressing systemic inequality. Issues such as racial disparities in criminal justice, voting rights, and economic opportunity suggest that constitutional changes or an amendment could be considered to strengthen protections and ensure more proactive measures against racial discrimination.

4. **Disability Rights**

   Although federal laws like the Americans with Disabilities Act (ADA) protect against discrimination based on disability, the Constitution does not explicitly address disability rights. An amendment that explicitly recognizes and protects the rights of individuals with disabilities could bolster these protections and ensure they are consistently upheld.

5. **Religious Discrimination and Balancing Free Exercise and Anti-Discrimination**

   The First Amendment protects religious freedom but balancing this right with anti-discrimination principles can be challenging. Constitutional clarifications or amendments could better address the tension between religious liberty and protecting individuals from discrimination, especially in cases involving public services and accommodations.

6. **Age Discrimination**

   While federal laws, such as the Age Discrimination in Employment Act (ADEA), prohibit age-based discrimination for workers aged 40 and older, the U.S. Constitution does not explicitly list age as a protected category. A constitutional amendment could formally ban age discrimination in employment, healthcare, and public services, strengthening protections for individuals of all ages. Age discrimination in hiring remains widespread. A 2023 study by the Society for Human Resource Management (SHRM) found that nearly one-third of HR professionals acknowledged that an applicant's age influenced hiring decisions. Similarly, a 2024 AARP survey reported that six in ten workers aged fifty and older have witnessed or experienced subtle forms of age discrimination in the workplace. While federal contractors must take affirmative action to ensure equal employment opportunities for women and minorities, no similar requirement exists for age. Implementing hiring verification based on applicant proportions across age groups would require new legislation or policy changes. Expanding legal protections could help address ongoing biases and ensure fair treatment for workers of all ages.

Why should any law abiding citizen be treated as less than others based on race, color, national origin, age, disability, sex, sexual characteristics, intersex traits, physical or health conditions, deformities, sexual orientation, gender identity, or sexual stereotypes?

Equal Rights and Equity

According to the U.S. Constitution, Americans are born with equal rights, but their life opportunities may differ due to variations in capabilities, family resources, and societal conditions. This concept is often described as "equal opportunity but not necessarily equal outcomes." This point is not about minority group equality, which involves separate considerations. Each person is born with unique innate capacities for thinking, learning, and thriving, leading to differences in intelligence, skills, and rewards based on individual efforts.

The key distinction is ensuring that society does not create artificial barriers that prevent people from reaching their full potential. When these barriers are absent, it can be considered an acceptable level of equality. The government's role is to protect every individual's right to be different and pursue their paths.

This perspective emphasizes the importance of personal initiative, taking responsibility for one's actions, and securing the benefits of one's labor. At the same time, it acknowledges the need to assist those facing severe circumstances beyond their control, balancing individual rights with social responsibility.

Freedom of speech in the age of social media

Free Expression vs. Misinformation and Hate Speech

Balancing the right to free expression with the need to combat misinformation and hate speech is crucial for maintaining a healthy democratic society. Ensuring that public discourse remains open and informed requires nuanced and targeted approaches that do not infringe upon fundamental freedoms.

The Southern Poverty Law Center (SPLC), an organization focused on tracking hate groups and advocating for civil rights, is often described as left-leaning due to its progressive approach and critiques from conservative circles. In 2023, the SPLC identified 595 hate groups, including white nationalists and neo-Nazis, as well as 835 anti-government groups, such as militias and conspiracy propagandists.[355]

While extremist groups have a presence in the United States, public opinion studies indicate that the vast majority of Americans oppose their ideologies and actions. For instance, a 2022 survey found that 78% of respondents viewed political violence as a problem, with more than half describing it as a "major" problem.[356]

These findings suggest that, despite the activities of extremist groups, most Americans reject political violence and support efforts to address and prevent extremism.

Enhancing Media Literacy

Enhancing media literacy is one of the most effective ways to combat misinformation without infringing on free speech. Educational programs that teach individuals how to evaluate sources critically, understand biases, and verify facts can empower people to make informed decisions about the information they consume and share. Schools, libraries, and community centers can serve as hubs for these educational efforts. AI automated warnings may also be effective in alerting users to deceptive information.

Encouraging Responsible Platform Use

Social media platforms play a pivotal role in the spread of information. Encouraging these platforms to adopt responsible policies that promote transparency and facilitate the identification of reliable content can help reduce the spread of misinformation. This includes improving algorithms to prioritize verified information, labeling unverified or potentially false content, and providing users with easy access to fact-checking resources.

Promoting Open Dialogue

Creating spaces for open dialogue can help bridge divides and reduce the impact of misinformation. Public forums, debates, and workshops that bring together individuals from different backgrounds to discuss and understand varying perspectives can foster a more informed and empathetic community.

Strengthening Fact-Checking Services

Supporting independent fact-checking organizations can provide a crucial service in verifying claims and educating the public about misinformation. These organizations can work in partnership with media outlets and social media platforms to ensure that accurate information is accessible and prominent. Remember this fact, fact-checking does not hurt the Freedom of Speech other than neutralizing lies and leveling exaggeration.

Legislative and Regulatory Approaches

While care must be taken not to infringe on free speech, targeted legislation can address specific types of harmful misinformation without broad censorship. Laws can be crafted to address the most dangerous or egregious forms of misinformation, such as false information about public health or safety, while ensuring that they are narrowly tailored and subject to judicial oversight.

By employing a combination of educational initiatives, platform responsibility, open dialogue, and targeted legislative measures, societies can tackle misinformation effectively while upholding the crucial tenet of free expression. These strategies ensure that the public discourse remains robust and fact-based, thereby strengthening the foundations of democracy.

Media

There was a time when all of America watched the evening news and was able to trust what they were hearing as objective and factual. Those days are gone. The current media landscape is widely perceived as heavily biased.

Media Biases

For those familiar with the term 'Tabloid News,' you will recognize it as referring to those newspapers and magazines found at grocery checkout counters, known for their extreme, exaggerated, and often false inflammatory stories. Now, you probably recognize that almost ALL news is now Tabloid news. Major cable news channels are sometimes accused of not only being inaccurate but also sensationalizing news, with some perceived as leaning significantly towards either the left or the right politically. Various factors influence this perception of bias.

As background, the nature of journalism often involves highlighting social injustices and giving a voice to the marginalized, which can lead to a focus on "underdog" narratives. This focus is sometimes interpreted as a left-leaning bias, as stories about disadvantaged groups' challenges tend to receive more attention. Additionally, negative or shocking stories are often seen as more newsworthy or engaging than positive ones, also influencing the type of content that is more frequently broadcast or published.

That said, to be fair, media outlets do have diverse editorial policies and perspectives, and the perception of bias can vary among audiences, depending on the "the view of the viewer." In the sixties, for example, the two Chicago Daily Newspapers staked out their political turf, with the Chicago Tribune being conservative and the Sun Times being liberal.

Some believe that the perceived leanings of various media reflect the views of the owners of those media. This is a topic often discussed in media studies and political communication. It is generally accepted that the owners of media outlets can influence the editorial stance and content of their publications or broadcasts, although the degree and nature of this influence varies.

For example, consider Rupert Murdoch's News Corporation, which owns various media outlets worldwide, including Fox News in the United States. Murdoch's conservative political views are often seen as reflected in the editorial stance of Fox News, particularly in its opinion programming, which has a reputation for leaning conservative.

Since Jeff Bezos, the founder of Amazon, acquired *The Washington Post*, there have been ongoing discussions about the potential impact of his business interests and personal views on the newspaper's reporting. Historically, *The Washington Post* has aimed to uphold editorial independence. However, during the 2024 presidential campaign, reports suggested Bezos may have influenced its editorial direction. He reportedly urged or directed the paper's editors to break its 44-year tradition of endorsing a presidential candidate, which spanned seventeen elections.

Some television news outlets now lack balance and objectivity. However, many people still seek and value news sources that provide balanced reporting, honesty, and truth — or that align with their political beliefs, consciously or unconsciously.

Propaganda

The Oxford Reference Dictionary defines Propaganda as persuasive mass communication that filters and frames the issues of the day in a way that strongly favors particular interests; usually those of a government or corporation. Also, the intentional manipulation of public opinion through lies, half-truths, and the selective re-telling or omission of history.[39-04]

The increasing concentration or consolidation of media ownership is also an issue, where fewer individuals or organizations control increasingly larger shares of mass media outlets. This can lead to a lack of diversity in perspectives and a single narrative dominating public discourse. Ensuring the independence of the press is crucial for safeguarding all our freedoms.

Such centralization can be seen in companies like Comcast, which owns NBCUniversal, or Disney, which owns ABC, ESPN, and several other media entities, or Paramount Global, which owns TV stations, production companies, and streaming services.

Critics argue that when a few entities control a substantial portion of the media landscape, it can negatively impact democratic processes by limiting the range of viewpoints and information accessible to the public. This concentration can be seen as a threat to freedom of expression and a well-informed citizenry, which are crucial for a healthy democracy.

The increasing inability of many listeners and viewers to distinguish truth from lies — or even to care about the veracity of information presented to them — has become troubling. In today's media-saturated world, the rapid spread of misinformation and disinformation, often amplified by social media algorithms, creates an environment where falsehoods can travel faster and farther than ever. Compounding this issue is the tendency of some individuals to accept information that aligns with their existing beliefs or biases, regardless of its factual accuracy.

This problem is further exacerbated by many audiences' lack of critical thinking skills and growing distrust of traditional sources of true information such as journalism, academia, and science. The lines between opinion, entertainment, and factual reporting are increasingly blurred, leaving audiences vulnerable to manipulation by those who seek to exploit this confusion.

Equally concerning is "truth apathy," where individuals prioritize emotional resonance, ideological alignment, or entertainment value over the accuracy of the information they consume. In such cases, lies are not just tolerated, they are embraced if they serve a preferred narrative or evoke a desired response.

Addressing this issue requires a multifaceted approach, including promoting media literacy, encouraging critical thinking, and fostering a culture that values truth and evidence-based reasoning. Without these efforts, the ability to discern truth from lies risks further erosion, with significant consequences for informed decision-making and the health of democratic societies.

However, the rise of digital social media and the Internet has introduced new platforms and voices, such as X.com and Bsky.social, countering the effects of traditional media concentration. Recently, though, the acquisition and control of online media by entities like Meta (Facebook), X (Twitter),

Instagram, and others is becoming a new area of consolidation and concern.

Should there be a size limitation on media, not unlike our laws about monopolies? Perhaps something like no more than 15-20% market share? Should there be a standard for truth-telling, i.e., fact-checking?

The Role of Propaganda

Should our laws extend the use of libel laws to include political claims about opponents? Should we as a people require truth in campaigning?

Our goal should be to eliminate or at least "call out" propaganda – information intended to deceive, especially of a biased or misleading nature, used to promote a political cause or point of view. It often involves the dissemination of selected facts, arguments, rumors, half-truths, or lies to influence public opinion or obscure the truth.

There is a well-known saying, often paraphrased as:
"A lie told often enough becomes the truth." This phrase is frequently attributed to Joseph Goebbels, the Nazi propaganda minister, though there is no direct evidence he said it. The sentiment reflects the "illusory truth effect" in psychology, where repeated exposure to a false statement can make it seem more believable over time.

Propaganda can be found in various forms such as TV and Cable broadcasts, social media, online blogs and articles, public statements, educational materials, and even entertainment.[39-05]

Important Constitutional Principles

It is vital to recognize the enduring principles that have sustained the nation's stability and must continue to do so, at least for the foreseeable future. These core elements form the bedrock of the republic, safeguarding individual liberties and ensuring the proper functioning of government.

Reform is not about abandoning the Constitution's core values but adapting its provisions, only if necessary, to meet today's and tomorrow's demands, ensuring a just and sustainable future for all. The following are fundamental principles that should remain unchanged.

On Church and State

Figures like James Madison and Thomas Paine were steadfast in their belief that religious institutions should be kept separate from government to avoid the kinds of conflicts that had plagued Europe for centuries. James Madison famously stated, "The purpose of the separation of church and state is to keep forever from these shores the ceaseless strife that has soaked the soil of Europe with blood." Paine was equally critical, describing organized religion as a tool used to control and exploit society.

The United States was founded on principles of religious freedom, as enshrined in the First Amendment. While Christianity has undeniably influenced the nation's history, the Constitution remains neutral, ensuring that no religion — or lack thereof — is favored. It is essential to recognize that while morals, often shaped by religious beliefs, play a significant role in shaping personal conduct and societal values, the law must remain secular, providing an impartial framework that protects the rights of all citizens, regardless of belief. Any legal changes should uphold this commitment to religious liberty and maintain the clear distinction between moral beliefs and legal governance, ensuring that America continues to be a nation where all beliefs are respected and protected equally.

Jefferson on Religion and Government

Thomas Jefferson strongly advocated for the separation of church and state and promoted religious freedom, principles that shaped his political and legal contributions. His 1777 Virginia Statute for Religious Freedom laid the groundwork for the First Amendment, emphasizing that an individual's religious beliefs should be private and free from state interference.

Jefferson's religious views were unconventional for his time. Identifying as a Deist, he rejected traditional religious teachings in favor of a belief in a creator who does not intervene in human affairs. He criticized institutional Christianity and believed strongly in secularism, once stating, "Christianity neither is nor ever was a part of the common law." As we contemplate constitutional changes today, Jefferson's ideas remain relevant, particularly his emphasis on personal freedoms and his cautious approach to the intertwining of religion and government. His legacy underscores the importance of maintaining a clear distinction between church and state in any future constitutional revisions.

The Judiciary

In Federalist Paper #78, Hamilton wrote: "According to the plan of the convention, all judges who may be appointed by the United States are to hold their offices *during good behavior...*" He also wrote "The judiciary, on the contrary, [to the executive and congress] has no influence over the sword or the purse; no direction either of the strength or of the wealth of the society; and can take no active resolution whatever. It may truly be said to have neither FORCE nor WILL, but merely judgment and must ultimately depend upon the aid of the executive arm even for the efficacy of its judgments." More importantly, he wrote:

"It equally proves that though individual oppression may now and then proceed from the courts of justice, the general liberty of the people can never be endangered from that quarter; I mean so long as the judiciary remains truly distinct from both the legislature and the Executive. For I agree, <u>that 'there is no liberty, if the power of judging be not separated from the legislature and the executive powers.</u>' And it proves, in the last place, that as liberty can have nothing to fear from the judiciary alone, but would have everything to fear from its union with either of the other departments..."

The Right to a Fair Trial

The right to a fair and speedy trial by an impartial jury is a foundational pillar of the American legal system. As Martin Luther King Jr. wrote in *Letter from Birmingham Jail*, "Justice too long delayed is justice denied."[423] This essential protection ensures that no individual is unjustly deprived of life, liberty, or property without the full benefit of due process. Undermining these rights — whether by restricting access to jury trials or eroding "due process" protections — would strike at the very core of justice and fairness in the United States.

Ensuring a fair and timely prosecution is also a cornerstone of constitutional justice and a societal necessity. This principle prevents judicial procedures from being unduly delayed or manipulated, reinforcing public trust in the legal system. Excessive delays in prosecutions, sometimes extending beyond four years, can severely undermine public confidence. Judicial rules must be structured to avoid such procedural delays, facilitating swift justice that respects the accused's rights while serving society's broader interests. Striking the right balance between protecting defendants' rights and conducting timely legal proceedings is crucial for maintaining the justice system's integrity. The constitutional right to a timely prosecution guards against indefinite delays, safeguarding the interests of the defendant and society. This balance is vital, ensuring fairness and protecting the rights of the accused without compromising the swift administration of justice.

The Bill of Rights

The first ten amendments to the U.S. Constitution, the Bill of Rights, form the cornerstone of American individual liberties. These amendments guarantee fundamental freedoms such as speech, religion, and the press, as well as the rights to assemble, petition the government, and bear arms. They also protect against unreasonable searches and seizures and ensure due process under the law. These rights are not just legal formalities but are essential to preserving the freedoms that define the American way of life. Any attempt to weaken these protections would undermine the government's primary role: safeguarding its citizens' liberties. Even the often-debated Second Amendment, which protects the right to bear arms, plays a crucial role in national defense by serving as a deterrent to potential threats from foreign and domestic adversaries.

Equal Representation in the Senate

The system of providing two senators for each state, regardless of population, ensures that smaller states maintain an equal voice in the legislative process. This principle of equal representation safeguards the interests of less populous states, preventing larger states from dominating the legislative agenda and ensuring a more balanced consideration of regional concerns. Altering this structure would disrupt the equilibrium between the states, potentially concentrating legislative power in more densely populated areas and marginalizing smaller states. Preserving this balance is essential to maintaining the federal nature of the U.S. government and protecting the diverse interests of all states.

The Amendment Process

The Amendment Process must be retained, protected, and kept as difficult to pass as it is now. The Constitution wisely allows for its amendment through a rigorous and deliberate process, ensuring that changes are made only when there is broad consensus and thoughtful consideration. This process safeguards against hasty or impulsive alterations to the nation's fundamental law. The careful balance between flexibility and stability must be preserved.

While the country will continue to evolve, the core principles that have sustained American democracy — individual liberty, equality before the law, and the prevention of tyranny — should never be compromised. These foundational values are essential to the nation's strength and must endure. Any constitutional amendments should focus on addressing modern challenges while upholding these essential protections that have guided the country throughout its history.

COMPARING CONSTITUTIONS

How Our Constitution Compares

For a frame of reference, consider how our Constitution compares to Canada's and the equivalent structures in England (U.K.). The U.S. Constitution, Canada's Constitution Act, and the U.K.'s constitutional framework share some similarities but exhibit significant differences in structure, legal authority, and amendment processes.

The U.S. Constitution is a fully codified, written document established in 1787 and ratified in 1788. In contrast, Canada's Constitution is a combination of written and unwritten elements, primarily stemming from the Constitution Act of 1867 (formerly known as the British North America Act) and the Constitution Act of 1982, which added the Charter of Rights and Freedoms. The United Kingdom, on the other hand, operates under an unwritten constitution based on statutes, conventions, legal documents such as the Magna Carta (1215) and the U.K. Bill of Rights (1689), and long-standing traditions, evolving over centuries.

Amending these constitutions differs across the three countries. The U.S. Constitution requires a formal process involving a supermajority in Congress and ratification by the states. Canada's amendment process is also formal but allows some flexibility, especially in cases where provincial consent is needed. The U.K., with its principle of parliamentary sovereignty, can change constitutional law through a simple majority in Parliament.

Regarding rights protections, the U.S. Constitution includes the Bill of Rights (first ten amendments) and additional amendments to safeguard individual freedoms.

Canada's Charter of Rights and Freedoms, part of the Constitution Act of 1982, provides similar protections but allows Parliament to use the "notwithstanding clause" to override certain rights. The "notwithstanding clause" is a provision in the Canadian Constitution — specifically Section 33 of the Canadian Charter of Rights and Freedoms — that allows federal or provincial governments to override certain rights and freedoms guaranteed by the Charter for a limited period. In the U.K., human rights are protected through various laws, such as the Human Rights Act of 1998, but Parliament retains the authority to change these protections.

The roles of the head of state and head of government also differ. In the U.S., the President serves both roles and is elected. As a constitutional monarchy, Canada has the monarch as the head of state, represented by the Governor General, while the Prime Minister is the head of government. The U.K. similarly has a monarch as the head of state and a Prime Minister as the head of government.

Regarding the division of powers, the U.S. operates under a federal system, clearly dividing responsibilities between federal and state governments. Canada also has a federal system that allows power-sharing between federal and provincial governments. However, the U.K. uses a unitary system with devolved powers to regions like Scotland, Wales, and Northern Ireland, but ultimately, Parliament remains sovereign.

Judicial review is robust in the U.S., where the Supreme Court can overturn laws that are deemed unconstitutional. Judicial review exists in Canada, but Parliament can override certain court decisions using "the notwithstanding clause." In the U.K., although courts conduct judicial reviews, Parliament's sovereignty means it has the final say on legal matters.

Parliamentary sovereignty plays different roles in each country. In the U.S., the Constitution is the supreme law, with no concept of parliamentary sovereignty. Parliament's sovereignty is present in Canada but limited by the Charter and constitutional framework. The U.K.'s Constitution places parliamentary sovereignty at its core, making Parliament the ultimate legal authority.

The use of conventions varies. While the U.S. relies on codified rules, Canada and the U.K. heavily incorporate conventions, which play a significant role in interpreting constitutional rules but are not necessarily legally binding. In the U.K., conventions are fundamental, with many constitutional practices based on long-standing traditions rather than written law.

Each country's ultimate legal authority differs: the U.S. has a rigid, codified Constitution; Canada blends written laws with conventions; and the U.K. relies on statutes, conventions, and historical documents, reflecting distinct approaches to governance and constitutional structure.

ADAPTING TO A DECLINING POPULATION

The decline in the global population, coupled with aging demographics, will profoundly impact modern economics and society. Countries like Japan, Italy, and Germany are already navigating these shifts. Japan's population decreased from 128 million in 2010 to around 125 million in 2020, with a significant increase in the elderly demographic, representing about 28% of the population. Italy is expected to see its population drop from sixty-one million in 2020 to 54 million by 2050, with an increase in the median age from 45.7 years to 50.7 years. Similarly, Germany's population could decrease to between 65 and 70 million by 2060, down from eighty-three million in 2020, with a growing proportion of the population over 67 years old.

These trends are causing labor shortages and increased healthcare costs, impacting economic productivity and social security systems.

The United States is also experiencing demographic shifts, although the patterns are somewhat different from those in countries like Japan, Italy, and Germany due to higher immigration rates. The U.S. population is aging, but the effects are mitigated by a steady influx of younger immigrants, which helps somewhat balance the age distribution.

The median age in the U.S. has been rising; it was approximately 38 years in 2020, up from 35 years in 2000. The percentage of the population aged 65 and older is also increasing, projected to grow from 16% in 2020 to over 20% by 2030. This aging trend suggests increasing healthcare demands, potential labor shortages in specific sectors, and greater fiscal pressures on social security and pension systems.

However, the U.S. population continues to grow, albeit at a slower rate than in previous decades, partly due to lower birth rates among the general population and partly due to immigration, which adds both to the population size and to the workforce. The challenge for the U.S. will be in managing these demographic changes effectively, ensuring economic stability, adapting policies to the needs of an older population, and integrating and leveraging the contributions of immigrants.

The End of Market Growth: A New Economic Paradigm

For centuries, population expansion has driven economic growth, which has fueled demand for goods and services, provided a growing labor force, and supported larger tax bases. As population growth levels off or declines, economies will need to find new ways to achieve growth without relying on ever-increasing consumer markets. This may involve a shift towards sustainable development, technological innovation, and increased productivity rather than expanding consumption.

Employment

While it might be surprising to some, the proportion of the U.S. Population employed is 60%, down 4.7%-points from before Covid, but still recovering. The other 40% include retirees, students, unemployed, stay-at-home parents, and those with health problems.

As economies transition, some sectors are likely to contract, leading to fewer jobs in traditional industries. This could result in higher unemployment or underemployment, especially for younger generations. Societies may need to rethink how people contribute to and benefit from economic life. For instance, there may be a growing need for policies that support individuals who are not working, whether through social safety nets, universal basic income, or other forms of economic support. This evolution should occur gradually but rapidly enough to occur in a single lifespan.

Potential Impacts of Declining Job Growth

The shift away from a growth-based economy could affect our laws in several ways.

Economic Rights and Social Safety Nets

As job opportunities diminish, there may be growing pressure to expand social safety nets and provide more robust support for individuals who are unemployed or choose non-traditional paths. This shift could spark debates about whether our laws should explicitly guarantee economic rights, such as the right to a basic standard of living. Currently, our laws leave policies like unemployment benefits and social security to federal and state legislatures.

The idea of laws ensuring economic protections — such as universal basic income, affordable healthcare, or housing rights — might gain traction. Adopting such measures would represent a shift toward a more social-democratic model, where the state is tasked with ensuring the material well-being of its citizens. Here are some possible changes.

Jobs-Do People Need Them?

If society reaches a point where traditional notions of meaningful work are substantially replaced by automation and technological advances, it will necessitate a significant cultural and economic shift. This scenario prompts a reevaluation of what constitutes "meaningful" work and how individuals derive purpose and fulfillment. The necessity of traditional jobs is being challenged by economic, psychological, and societal shifts. Historically, jobs have been crucial for economic survival and social identity, providing income for basic needs and a sense of purpose vital for mental health. However, with the rise of automation and AI, many tasks once done by humans are being automated, leading some experts to foresee a future where employment is not directly tied to survival. This societal change could require universal basic income (UBI), allowing individuals to pursue work for personal fulfillment rather than economic necessity, fundamentally redefining the role of work in society.

As traditional jobs decline, potential increases in leisure time could lead to increased time wasted on trivial activities. However, such a shift may also present opportunities for enriching personal and societal engagement in education, arts, and community service. Such activities could replace traditional employment roles, provided society adapts with supportive policies and social structures.

In a future where meaningful work is redefined by technology, there may be a greater emphasis on human exploration and creativity. Freed from conventional roles, people could explore new territories, from space travel to innovative arts, offering fresh challenges and opportunities for fulfillment. This shift would require significant cultural and economic adjustments to redefine meaningful engagement in a highly automated world.

Reimagining the Right to Work

A shrinking job market may mean fewer traditional jobs, so society may need to broaden its definition of valuable contributions, including caregiving, volunteerism, and artistic pursuits.

Taxation and Public Funding

A shrinking workforce could strain public services funding, as income, consumption, and property tax revenues may decrease. This may render the current tax system inadequate for an economy with fewer workers and consumers, requiring a reevaluation of revenue-generating methods.

Legislators may need to introduce alternative taxation strategies, such as wealth taxes, financial transaction taxes, or resource usage taxes, to sustain essential public services.

Supporting a Growing Non-Working Population

As the proportion of non-working individuals grows, society may need to support a larger population that is not directly contributing to the traditional economy. This could include more retirees, people engaged in non-market activities, and those who choose not to work for lifestyle or personal reasons. If the social contract evolves to accommodate many non-working individuals, the government's role in providing social support may need to expand.

Universal Basic Income (UBI)

The concept of Universal Basic Income (UBI) has gained significant attention as a potential solution to economic instability caused by declining job availability. UBI would provide a guaranteed income to all citizens, regardless of employment status, ensuring individuals have the means to support themselves even if they are not part of the traditional workforce. Beyond stabilizing the economy, UBI could serve as a foundational measure for addressing economic inequality.

Reassessing Social Security and Retirement Policies

Social Security, a cornerstone of retirement security for millions of Americans, faces significant financial challenges. According to the Social Security Administration's 2023 report, the trust funds that support Social Security are projected to be depleted by 2035. At that point, the program can only pay about 80% of scheduled benefits due to insufficient funds. This shortfall is primarily due to an aging population, with a higher ratio of beneficiaries to working contributors.

In 2020, approximately 2.8 workers for each beneficiary were expected to decline to about 2.3 by 2035. This demographic shift places increased pressure on the financing of Social Security. The "retirement bubble" caused by the Baby Boomer generation is expected to wane by the late 2030s as this demographic group ages, which could help stabilize the ratio of workers to beneficiaries. However, this change alone will make it unlikely that the program will be returned to a fully sustainable level without additional reforms. Policy options such as increasing the payroll tax rate, raising the cap on taxable earnings, or altering benefits are being debated to address these challenges and ensure long-term stability for this vital program.

The annual shortfall for Social Security post-2035 is estimated at $200 billion. The $200 billion annual shortfall for Social Security represents approximately 0.81% of the U.S. Gross National Product (GNP) and about 3.33% of the federal budget. Therefore, the government could choose to fund this shortfall until the demographic shift stabilizes around 2040. The total funding required would be approximately $1 trillion over five years.

Potential Social and Cultural Shifts

A shrinking population may also bring about social and cultural changes that impact how Americans perceive rights, responsibilities, and the role of government. Individual self-reliance, central to American identity, may need to be reinterpreted in a society where work is no longer the primary means of contributing to the common good.

Redefining the Social Contract

The social contract in America has traditionally been based on the idea that individuals work to support themselves and their families while contributing to the nation's prosperity. As work becomes less central to daily life, the expectations of what citizens owe to each other and the state may change. This could lead to a reevaluation of rights and responsibilities.

Freedom, Leisure, and the Pursuit of Happiness

Our Constitution emphasizes the pursuit of happiness as a fundamental right, but this has historically been tied to economic productivity and work. As more people spend time outside the workforce, there may be a cultural shift towards valuing leisure, personal development, and non-economic forms of fulfillment.

As the economy moves away from reliance on growth, our laws must adapt to changes in economic participation, social support, and work definitions. Overcoming divisive issues will facilitate this legal adaptation, ensuring that American values of freedom, equality, and opportunity persist in a world where traditional employment is less central. Balancing economic conditions with individual rights and social responsibilities will be crucial for this transition.

New States and State Boundaries

Throughout American history, there have been several proposals to rearrange state boundaries or create new states driven by cultural, economic, political, or geographical differences. Notable examples include the successful creation of West Virginia during the Civil War, multiple proposals to split California into up to six states, and discussions about dividing Texas into five separate states as allowed by its annexation agreement.

Additionally, there's the ongoing movement to establish the State of Jefferson from parts of northern California and southern Oregon and advocate for statehood for Puerto Rico and the District of Columbia. Proposals to split New York into separate states for New York City and its suburbs versus the rural upstate regions also reflect regional differences. In addition to splitting some states, combining some states (e.g., North and South Dakota or North and South Carolina) might also be considered. While delineating states based on political leanings could heighten divisiveness, such restructuring could enhance representation, improve governance efficiency, and strengthen cultural identities, albeit alongside significant economic implications. These proposals face substantial hurdles, including legal requirements, the need for legislative approval at both state and federal levels, and often a referendum by the affected populations.

More recently, unconventional ideas such as annexing Canada, acquiring Greenland, and reclaiming control over the Panama Canal have surfaced. However, such ideas will involve diplomatic and legal challenges.

Canada

Canada has a population of approximately 39,943,610 as of January 2025.[302] If they agreed, and had a House Representative for each 767,816 citizens, as the U.S. has, they would qualify for 52 House Members. In a recent survey, 64% of Canadian respondents indicated they would prefer Kamala Harris over Donald Trump if they could vote in the U.S. election.[303] This ratio might flip the House control to Democrats.

Acquiring Greenland

Based on its natural resources, strategic value, and land usability, its 836,330,000 acres should be worth about $3,500 per acre or $3Trillion in total. Assuming America would not take it by force, which could lead to severe international condemnation, economic sanctions, potential military conflict with Denmark and its allies, a breakdown of NATO relations, and long-term geopolitical instability in the Arctic, we must consider other uses for $3 trillion, such as funding Social Security.

Taking the Panama Canal Back

Reassuming control of the Panama Canal would involve significant geopolitical, financial, and operational implications for the United States. The canal handles 5-6% of world trade with 2024 net income of about $3.5 billion. Strategically, this move could enhance U.S. influence over a critical global shipping route, strengthening national security and global trade positioning.

However, it would also likely provoke international tension, particularly with China, which has invested heavily in the region and regards the canal as a key component of its Belt and Road Initiative. The Belt and Road Initiative is China's global infrastructure and investment strategy, launched in 2013, to expand trade routes and economic influence by funding major projects across Asia, Africa, and Europe.[424] Financially, the cost of maintaining and upgrading the canal to handle modern mega-ships could run into billions of dollars, considering the recent expansion project completed in 2016 cost over $5 billion. Additionally, substantial operational costs would be associated with staffing, security, and environmental management. The reacquisition could lead to diplomatic repercussions, necessitating careful negotiation to manage international relationships while asserting U.S. interests.

PRESERVE THE FOUNDATION, EMBRACE CHANGE

The Constitution's endurance can be credited to its foundational principles—such as the division of powers, the rule of law, individual rights, and government accountability—and its ability to adapt through amendments and interpretation when needed.

Division of Powers

A large portion of Americans have growing concerns regarding the division of powers within the U.S. government, particularly the expanded role of the president in shaping laws through executive orders and policy directives. This shift, which has accelerated in recent decades, contravenes the original intent behind the separation of powers envisioned by the nation's founders. It diverts power away from Congress, the primary legislative body that effectively represents the people's will, to the executive branch. Partisanship compounds the challenges in rectifying this imbalance; when one party holds the executive office and Congress, there's little incentive to alter the status quo. Conversely, a divided government struggles to enact significant changes. Ultimately, restoring the balance of power may hinge on enhancing the representativeness and effectiveness of Congress, reaffirming its role as a cornerstone of governance by the people.

Executive Administration

Concerns about the Executive Branch

The president's position is NOT intended to wield power like the CEO of a company. He is NOT the sole person in charge! Neither is Congress nor the Supreme Court.

Our forefathers designed our government to be balanced, with a built-in system of checks and balances to prevent any branch from exercising unchecked power. No branch was intended to operate independently of the others' oversight. As head of the executive branch and commander-in-chief, the president is responsible for managing the military, overseeing treaty negotiations, and proposing the annual budget.

The branches of government were also not meant to be influenced by any external "faction," particularly religious groups. Through the First Amendment, the Constitution establishes a clear separation of church and state to prevent the government from endorsing or establishing any religion. This separation reflects the diversity of religious beliefs among Americans and aims to ensure that no single group's religious values dominate government policy. While many early settlers came to America seeking religious freedom, the Founding Fathers instituted these constitutional safeguards to protect individual liberties and prevent government entanglement with religious institutions or doctrines.

What America Needs in an Executive

Commonsense and historical precedent indicate that America needs an Executive who embodies inclusive leadership with a clear and inspiring vision for the nation's future. Effective leadership, as demonstrated by figures such as Abraham Lincoln, Franklin D. Roosevelt, and Dwight D. Eisenhower, requires addressing immediate challenges while upholding foundational values. Political theorists, including Aristotle and James Madison, have long emphasized the need for leaders who balance pragmatism with vision, ensuring stability while fostering national progress.

America's leader must prioritize unity, bridging political, cultural, and socioeconomic divides through dialogue and collaboration. This principle echoes George Washington's warnings in his farewell address against excessive partisanship, recognizing that division undermines national stability. Successful Presidents, from Theodore Roosevelt's "Square Deal" to Lyndon B. Johnson's "Great Society," have understood the importance of coalition-building to achieve meaningful reform.

Competence and strategic thinking are critical, requiring deep policy knowledge and the ability to make informed decisions under pressure. In *The Federalist Papers No. 70*, Alexander Hamilton argued that an energetic executive is essential to effective governance, requiring both decisiveness and a deep understanding of policy. In modern leadership studies, scholars like James MacGregor Burns have highlighted the necessity of strategic vision in transformative leadership.

Strong communication skills are equally vital. From Lincoln's Gettysburg Address to Reagan's ability to connect with the American public, history has shown that a President's capacity to convey ideas, inspire trust, and motivate action is essential for national unity and policy success.

Integrity and accountability are cornerstones of democratic leadership. The Founding Fathers structured the Constitution to ensure that power would be wielded with responsibility. John Adams warned that "facts are stubborn things," emphasizing the necessity of truth in leadership. Leaders who prioritize ethical governance, from Harry

Truman's blunt honesty to Jimmy Carter's commitment to transparency, set enduring examples of accountability.

Global awareness is indispensable in today's interconnected world. Successful leaders, including Franklin D. Roosevelt during World War II and George H.W. Bush in the post-Cold War era, navigated complex international relationships by appreciating cultural diversity and strategic diplomacy. Contemporary challenges, from cybersecurity to climate policy, demand a President capable of balancing national interests with global cooperation.

Adaptability and resilience are necessary traits for leadership, particularly in times of crisis. Lincoln's ability to evolve his stance on slavery and Franklin D. Roosevelt's New Deal response to the Great Depression illustrates the importance of leaders who can pivot strategies while maintaining national confidence. These qualities remain essential in an era of rapid technological change, economic shifts, and social upheavals.

Empathy and emotional intelligence distinguish great leaders, allowing them to understand and address the concerns of a diverse populace. From John F. Kennedy's advocacy for civil rights to George W. Bush's response to 9/11 attacks, Presidents who demonstrate compassion and fairness build stronger national cohesion.

A dedication to institutional integrity ensures the preservation of democracy. The principles of checks and balances, as outlined in *The Federalist Papers*, are designed to prevent the erosion of democratic institutions. Leaders who uphold the Constitution reinforce the legitimacy of governance rather than seeking to circumvent it.

Finally, a focus on sustainability and innovation is crucial for national progress. The ability to balance economic growth with environmental responsibility, technological advancements, and infrastructure improvements has defined effective governance in the modern era. From

Eisenhower's interstate highway system to recent investments in clean energy, innovation has consistently driven American leadership.

History, political theory, and contemporary governance studies affirm that <u>America's ideal Executive Administrator is a leader who fosters unity, integrity, and innovation while addressing national challenges</u>. The above qualities are not speculative ideals but demonstrated necessities for effective governance, supported by centuries of political thought and practical leadership. The strength of democracy rests not only on institutions but on the caliber of those entrusted to lead them.

Limits and Role of Executive Orders

Executive orders allow the U.S. president to manage federal operations, but their power is carefully constrained. Constitutionally, executive orders cannot create laws, allocate funds, or exceed powers reserved for Congress. They must align with existing laws and constitutional provisions, and they are subject to judicial review and legislative oversight. Courts, as seen in Youngstown Sheet & Tube Co. v. Sawyer, have invalidated executive orders that overreach, such as when President Truman's attempt to seize steel mills was struck down.

While Congress can counter an executive order through legislation, overcoming a presidential veto poses significant challenges. Public scrutiny also acts as an informal check on their use. Executive orders are confined to the executive branch and lack authority over the legislative or judicial branches, only indirectly impacting state governments through federal funding or regulations.

In recent years, some executive orders have stretched the traditional understanding of executive power, raising concerns about the balance of authority between branches of government. These orders remain in force until reversed by the sitting president, overridden by Congress, or invalidated by the courts, and future presidents retain the power to rescind or modify their predecessors' orders.

Congress

Congress's primary responsibilities are to create and pass federal laws, control government spending and taxation, provide oversight of the executive branch, declare war, and represent the interests of the American people.

Concerns about Congress

Over the past two decades, public perception of Congress has steadily declined, with approval ratings frequently hitting historic lows. A 2023 Gallup poll reported Congress's approval rating at just 19%, consistent with a long-term trend of disapproval that has persisted since the early 2000s. This skepticism stems mainly from widespread perceptions of partisan gridlock, where intense divisions between parties stall legislative progress and foster a sense of dysfunction. For instance, a 2022 Pew Research Center study found that 72% of Americans believed members of Congress prioritized their political agendas over the needs of the public.

The consequences of this gridlock are tangible. Key issues like immigration reform, climate change legislation, and healthcare policy have been left unresolved for years, exacerbating frustration among voters. Furthermore, a 2021 report by the Congressional Management Foundation revealed that 67% of constituents felt disconnected from their representatives, citing a lack of meaningful engagement on pressing issues. This combination of legislative inaction and perceived self-interest has eroded trust in Congress as an institution, leaving many Americans skeptical of its ability to govern effectively and represent their interests.

High-profile government shutdowns, contentious debates on critical issues like healthcare, budget deficits, immigration, and perceived inefficiency have exacerbated this distrust. Additionally, a growing concern about the influence of special interest groups and lobbying has led to the widespread belief that Congress is more responsive to corporate interests than the public's needs. Though some individuals and moments have briefly restored confidence, such as in times of crisis or significant legislative achievements, Congress as an institution struggles to maintain public faith in its role as a functional and representative branch of government.

Most current issues plaguing our government, such as the insufficient funding of social security, inefficiencies in Medicare, and economic problems, can be traced back to the decisions, or lack thereof, made by Congress.

What America Needs in a Congressperson

America needs Congresspersons with integrity, vision, and a commitment to public service who prioritize constituents' needs while addressing national challenges. They must uphold democratic principles and defend the Constitution, foster bipartisanship, and balance long-term solutions with practical governance to unite diverse voices and drive progress.

Predominance of Lawyers

This situation is further complicated by what some consider the overrepresentation of lawyers in Congress, which some critics argue skews legislative priorities and decision-making. According to the American Bar

Association, the U.S. has about 1,150,000 lawyers—roughly one for every three hundred Americans. This high ratio suggests an oversupply of attorneys, far exceeding what would be needed for everyday legal matters.[181-08]

The primary concern may lie in Congress, specifically in that 77% of the Senate and 71% of the House consists of lawyers. Additionally, numerous senior positions within the government are held by individuals with legal backgrounds, although specific statistics on this matter are not readily accessible.

While legal expertise can be valuable for crafting and interpreting laws, the predominance of legal professionals has led to perceptions that Congress may disproportionately favor the interests of the legal profession, their clients, and other well-connected sectors. Critics suggest this dynamic can contribute to a focus on self-preservation, catering to financial backers, potential post-congressional employers, and the professional networks legislators are part of rather than prioritizing the well-being of American citizens.

For example, debates over tort reform highlight concerns about potential conflicts of interest. Tort reform seeks to modify the legal system to reduce frivolous lawsuits, limit excessive damages, and lower litigation costs, aiming to create a fairer balance between plaintiffs and defendants. Proponents argue it fosters economic growth by reducing business liability, while critics warn it may restrict access to justice for those with legitimate claims.

Some argue that lawmakers may be hesitant to pass comprehensive reforms to limit lawsuits because such changes could affect the legal profession, a field many members of Congress come from or might return to after their tenure. Similarly, issues like preserving generous congressional medical and retirement benefits or lobbying reform reflect broader concerns that legislative decisions may be influenced by personal or professional self-interest, undermining public trust in Congress.

Political Party Control Issues

The party not in control blames the party in control and vice versa. As we previously mentioned, having political parties is not something specified by the Constitution. They came along later, built in power struggles, and created division that might not be there otherwise.

Positive Results

Although many current challenges have roots in decisions made by Congress in the past, it is also true that Congress has been instrumental in positive developments, like enacting anti-discrimination laws, aiding disabled people, and establishing national parks. Yet, over the last two centuries, the evolving political and social landscape appears to have caused some confusion among members of Congress about their primary roles and duties.

Over Regulation

The continuous creation of new laws has led to an overly extensive and burdensome legal system that many believe is increasingly encroaching on individual liberty. There is a concern that Congress has strayed from the foundational principles set by the Founding Fathers, instead becoming overly influenced by big business, greed, and special interests. This is nothing new. Bethany Hughes, a member of the Choctaw Nation of Oklahoma, and assistant professor at the University of Michigan's department of Native American studies was quoted on Dec. 3, 2024 in a BBC article by Lucy Sherriff: "A desire for wealth and power in the form of land ownership, chattel slavery, the drive for unending growth and profit, and the commodification of natural resources is the reason for the intense overhunting of bison and the political and physical attacks on indigenous nationhood and humanity over five centuries." Greed is behind a loss of trust in our Congress.

This loss of trust demands that Congress realign itself with the foundational values established by the nation's founders and commit to representing the broader citizenry, not just select groups.

At the federal level, Congress has enacted over 30,000 statutes since 1789, with each biennial term producing 200 to 600 new laws.[234]

These statutes are codified in the United States Code, which, as of 2018, spanned 54 volumes and approximately 60,000 pages. The Code of Federal Regulations, which compiles these rules, contained about 188,000 pages across 200 volumes as of 2021.[235]

Additionally, each of the fifty states, along with countless local jurisdictions, enacts its own laws and regulations, further expanding the legal landscape.

We have hundreds of thousands of laws; we do not need to keep creating more, except in areas where entirely new ideas require new regulations. With fewer lawyers in Congress, making way for more regular citizens, the pace may slow.

Congressional Reforms

The so-called Congressional Reform Act of 2010, seen repeatedly on social media, is a widely circulated proposal that suggests sweeping reforms to address perceived inequities and inefficiencies in Congress. Among its ideas were term limits for members of Congress, elimination of congressional pensions, requiring Congress to participate in the same healthcare programs as American Citizens and Social Security consolidating their retirement funds into the Social Security Trust Fund, prohibiting members from exempting themselves from laws they impose on others, and mandating that all laws apply equally to citizens and legislators. Despite its popularity as a viral concept, this "Act" was never formally introduced or codified as legislation. Its circulation reflects widespread frustration with the perceived privileges of lawmakers and the desire for greater accountability. It remains a symbolic expression of public sentiment rather than a legislative reality.

The Judiciary

The Supreme Court of the United States (SCOTUS) is the nation's highest court, tasked with interpreting the Constitution, ensuring federal law is applied consistently, and resolving disputes involving constitutional issues, federal statutes, and conflicts between states or the federal government. Through judicial review, established in *Marbury v. Madison* (1803), it can invalidate laws or actions that violate the Constitution. As the final appellate court, SCOTUS ensures equal justice under the law and has original jurisdiction in limited cases, such as disputes between states or involving foreign diplomats.

The American judiciary, a cornerstone of democracy, has increasingly become a battleground for distinct ideological views. A central divide in judicial philosophy shapes this tension. Some advocate for a progressive interpretation of the Constitution, supporting judges who adapt its principles to modern societal values and evolving civil liberties. Others favor a conservative, originalist approach, endorsing judges who interpret the Constitution according to its original text and intent. This philosophical divide profoundly influences the selection and confirmation of judges, particularly

Supreme Court justices, and shapes American legal precedents.

The political influence on the Supreme Court became especially evident during President Franklin D. Roosevelt's New Deal in the 1930s when the Court's makeup profoundly affected national policy direction. Since then, the ideological leanings of judicial appointments and rulings have often reflected those of the prevailing President and Senate. This trend has intensified with recent political polarization, heightening scrutiny of the judiciary's impact on critical issues like reproductive rights, voting laws, and gun control. In high-profile cases, the conservative majority's originalist interpretation of the Constitution continues to shape societal norms and values.

In the mid-20th century, the judiciary's role in social policy expanded, particularly in civil rights and free speech areas. This growth intensified the political stakes of judicial appointments. Lifetime appointments for Supreme Court justices mean that each nomination represents a long-term investment in a specific vision of the law, further embedding judicial appointments as a critical aspect of political strategy. The ability to shape the judiciary in line with ideological preferences has become a powerful tool, impacting the course of American law and politics for generations.

This period also witnessed landmark Supreme Court rulings that brought profound shifts in American society, with their influence enduring into the 21st century. As the Court continues to tackle issues central to American life, the enduring impact of these decisions underscores the judiciary's significant role in interpreting and shaping the nation's laws and values. Here are the profound Supreme Court Rulings in recent years:

- **Brown v. Board of Education (1954)**: This decision declared that state laws establishing separate public schools for black and white students were unconstitutional, overturning the "separate but equal" doctrine of Plessy v. Ferguson. It marked a crucial step in the civil rights movement, leading to the desegregation of schools.
- **Miranda v. Arizona (1966)**: This ruling established "Miranda rights" for detained criminal suspects, including the right to remain silent and the right to an attorney. This decision significantly transformed police interrogation practices and reinforced the rights of the accused.
- **Loving v. Virginia (1967)**: This decision struck down state laws banning interracial marriage in the United States, ending all race-based legal restrictions on marriage and advancing civil rights.
- **Roe v. Wade (1973), Overturned in the Dobbs v. Jackson (2022)** (Women's Health Organization Case, June 24, 2022): This landmark decision legalized abortion nationwide, ruling that the Constitution protects a pregnant woman's liberty to choose to have an abortion without excessive federal government restriction. It was a pivotal moment in the reproductive rights movement. It was overturned after the addition of three justices appointed by President Donald Trump: Neil Gorsuch in 2017, Brett Kavanaugh in 2018, and Amy Coney Barrett in 2020.

The cases mentioned previously tended to align with certain principles until the Supreme Court's decision overturned *Roe v. Wade*. This decision did not address the morality of Abortion; instead, it ruled that the Constitution does not explicitly grant a right to Abortion, effectively returning the authority to regulate Abortion to individual states. This shift has resulted in a diverse range of state laws, with some states imposing strict restrictions and others protecting abortion rights. The court's ruling focused solely on constitutional interpretation.

However, the ruling has led to notable consequences. Women in states with restrictive abortion laws face significant challenges in accessing services. They may need to travel long distances to states with more permissive laws, navigate complex legal requirements, and deal with financial and logistical hurdles. Critics argue that these difficulties disproportionately impact women from lower socioeconomic backgrounds, those with limited access to transportation or healthcare, and younger or more vulnerable populations.

The transfer of abortion regulation to state control has created a patchwork of laws across the United States, leading to significant disparities in access based on geographic location. This shift has also spurred legal battles and heightened political divisions around reproductive rights. (See the section on Abortion for further discussion.)

Concerns about Judiciary

The lifetime tenure of Supreme Court justices raises concerns about an aging judiciary potentially disconnected from evolving societal values, as justices often serve well beyond typical retirement age. This extended tenure can lead to judicial decisions that may not resonate with contemporary issues, affecting public confidence in the Court's adaptability. Judicial philosophies, such as judicial activism versus originalism, further shape landmark rulings on civil rights to privacy, reflecting the Court's role in balancing foundational intent with current societal needs.

Composition of the Supreme Court

Following the nomination and subsequent congressional confirmation between 2017 and 2020 of three new justices with conservative leanings, concerns have been raised about the politicization of the selection process for the Supreme Court. These appointments, made during a Republican presidency, contributed to a shift in the court's ideological balance.

This was not the first time in American history that this occurred:

The History of the Supreme Court Composition

1789: The Judiciary Act established the court with six justices.

1801: The Judiciary Act of 1801 reduced the number to five, to take effect upon the next vacancy. However, this act was quickly repealed by the Judiciary Act of 1802 before any reduction took place, and the number returned to six.

1807: The number of justices was increased to seven under the Jefferson administration to accommodate the expansion of the nation.

1837: During Andrew Jackson's presidency, the number was raised to nine to reflect the growing number of federal judicial circuits.

1863: During the Civil War, the number rose to ten under the Abraham Lincoln administration, again to align with the number of circuits.

1866: Post-Civil War, Congress passed the Judicial Circuits Act, which reduced the number to seven, to prevent President Andrew Johnson from making any appointments. This reduction was to occur as seats became vacant.

1869: The Judiciary Act of 1869, signed by President Ulysses S. Grant, set the number of justices at nine, where it has remained ever since.

What America Needs in a Supreme Court Justice

America needs Supreme Court justices who demonstrate unwavering integrity, a deep understanding of the Constitution, and a commitment to impartiality. Justices must interpret the law based on its text, history, and principles while remaining open to evolving societal contexts without succumbing to political or ideological pressures. They should possess exceptional legal expertise, strong analytical skills, and the ability to navigate complex legal issues fairly and clearly. Equally important is humility and respect for precedent, ensuring stability in the legal system while recognizing when change is necessary to uphold justice. Above all, America needs justices who prioritize the public good and maintain the Court's role as an impartial guardian of the Constitution and the rule of law.

Perception of Supreme Court Bias Is Not New

The Supreme Court has historically engaged in decisions widely perceived as politically motivated, often reflecting the prevailing ideologies of the justices rather than strict legal interpretation. In *Dred Scott v. Sandford* (1857), the Court ruled that African Americans could not be citizens, a decision that exacerbated tensions leading to the Civil War and aligned with pro-slavery interests. Similarly, during the New Deal era, the Court struck down several key pieces of President Franklin D. Roosevelt's legislation in cases like *Schechter Poultry Corp. v. United States* (1935), reflecting conservative opposition to expansive federal power. In *Bush v. Gore* (2000), the Court effectively determined the presidential election's outcome, with its majority split along ideological lines. More recently, the overturning of *Roe v. Wade* reignited debates about the politicization of the judiciary, as the decision reflected a significant shift in the Court's ideological makeup and overturned nearly 50 years of precedent on abortion rights. These examples highlight moments when the Court's role as an impartial arbiter has been questioned due to decisions aligning with broader political or ideological goals.

History of Contentious Decisions

This process is designed to allow federal judges to make impartial and fair decisions based on the law. However, it is essential to note that this ideal is not always realized. Cases with political overtones have occurred throughout the Supreme Court's history.

These politically charged cases have included instances when the court ruled that it had the authority to declare acts of Congress unconstitutional, denied citizenship to African Americans, and declared the Missouri Compromise unconstitutional, exacerbating tensions leading up to the Civil War. Other examples include when the court upheld racial segregation, endorsing the "separate but equal" doctrine, and declared state laws establishing as unconstitutional separate public schools for black and white students. The court's involvement in the 2000 presidential election, ending the recount in Florida and resulting in George W. Bush becoming president, was another highly political case.

The Supreme Court has not always been perfect in providing "checks and balances" against the executive and congressional branches of government. This is why more must be done to ensure the absence of political bias and the presence of the purest rule of law.

Supreme Court Ethics

Public concerns also include perceived ethics issues, as seen in reports of justices receiving benefits considered unethical for elected officials and not recusing themselves from cases involving benefactors or family members with conflicts of interest.

Pace of Justice

Delays in the federal court system, with cases often stalled for months or years, further highlight the need for reforms to strengthen judicial integrity and maintain public trust. The way a person is appointed to the Supreme Court attempts to limit political influence through the process that has not changed since Jefferson's and Adams' day.

Justice Approval Process

The process for appointing federal judges, including Supreme Court justices, begins with a nomination by the president of the United States. Candidates are chosen based on qualifications, legal expertise, sometimes their history and stated positions on current issues, and other relevant factors, with many coming from state courts where they may have been previously elected or appointed.

Once nominated, the candidate undergoes a confirmation process in the U.S. Senate, beginning with hearings by the Senate Judiciary Committee. During these hearings, committee members assess the nominee's qualifications and probe their judicial philosophy and legal views.

After the committee review, the full Senate votes on the nomination, typically requiring a simple majority for confirmation. If confirmed, the nominee assumes a federal judgeship. Federal judges, including Supreme Court justices, receive lifetime appointments, allowing them to serve indefinitely unless they choose to retire or are impeached and removed by Congress for "high crimes and misdemeanors." [or *Bad Behavior*, as Hamilton said, "...all judges who may be appointed by the United States are to hold their offices *during good behavior*..."] This lifetime tenure is intended to protect judges from political pressures and uphold their independence in judiciary. A possible Constitutional Amendment solution would be to require 60% or higher percent confirmation.

TERM LIMITS

A practical approach to limiting the concentration of power is to impose term limits on elected officials. By Term Limits we mean the number of times a Congressperson can be reelected. This would help encourage qualified citizens to participate in public service rather than allowing professional politicians to dominate the political landscape. Such a change would uphold a fundamental principle of government: balancing capable leadership with accountability.

U.S. senators serve six-year terms <u>with no term limits</u>, while House representatives serve two-year terms, and Supreme Court Justices serve <u>for Life</u> without term limits.

The debate over term limits for senators, congresspeople, and Supreme Court justices involves carefully weighing the benefits and drawbacks.

Forefathers' Views on Term Limits

Our forefathers did not envision membership of Congress to even be a full-time commitment, let alone a lifelong job. The early congressmen all had professions and returned to their "day jobs" when they were not in session. We should return to this approach. Career Politicians can become out of touch with their constituents or forget who they represent. The U.S. Senate is scheduled to be in session for approximately 149 days, while the House of Representatives plans to be in session for about 112 days. This time in session means senators have around 216 days and representatives about 253 days allocated for constituent work, district activities, and personal time. With less time in session, Congress has less time to create more laws, which some would see as a good thing.

Term limits are essential for breaking control of power.

Thomas Jefferson notably wrote in 1789 that "Whenever a man has cast a longing eye on offices, a rottenness begins in his conduct,"[233]

With term limits in place, the potential for special interests to influence legislators is lessened, allowing for a greater focus on the needs and concerns of regular citizens.

Several notable figures, including Senator Ted Cruz, Representative Ralph Norman, and Representative Ro Khanna, have proposed constitutional amendments to cap congressional terms. Such measures typically limit senators to two terms and House members to three or four terms, though such measures have yet to gain the necessary legislative support for enactment.

In 2002, law professors Paul Carrington (Duke University) and Roger Cramton (Cornell University) proposed a plan for reforming the Supreme Court that included term limits for justices. Their proposal, which called for staggered 18-year terms, helped to spark a modern debate on the topic. More recently, academics and politicians have been proposing 20-year terms for Supreme Court justices.

Pros of Changing Term Limits

A significant advantage of shorter-term limits is the increased turnover, which can diminish the influence of incumbency and bring fresh perspectives to the legislative process. This turnover helps prevent the entrenchment of career politicians, promoting a more diverse and dynamic pool of elected officials. Term limits also aid in balancing power by limiting the accumulation of influence over time, aligning with democratic principles of fair representation. Moreover, they enhance accountability, as more frequent elections compel politicians to stay responsive to the needs and concerns of their constituents.

Cons of Changing Term Limits

On the other hand, shorter term limits can lead to a loss of valuable experience, as seasoned lawmakers with deep knowledge of the legislative process and governance are forced to leave office. This loss can hinder the ability to address complex issues effectively and pursue long-term policy objectives, potentially disrupting the legislative process. Additionally, in their final terms, officials may experience reduced accountability, as they are no longer seeking reelection and may feel less obligated to respond to constituents' needs. There is also a risk of increased political polarization, with frequent elections incentivizing politicians to focus on short-term, populist measures rather than tackling long-term challenges.

Congress

The length of terms for senators (six years with one-third each two years) and congresspeople (two years) seems appropriate. However, the number of times they can be reelected if no more than twice for senators (12 years total) and no more than three times for congresspeople (six years), we avoid becoming led by a cabal of professional politicians. This change was scheduled to be proposed as a Constitutional Amendment in 2025.

Supreme Court Limits

Currently, Supreme Court Justices hold lifetime appointments. However, proposals such as the Supreme Court Tenure Establishment and Retirement Modernization

(TERM) Act, introduced to Congress in September 2023, suggest changing this to staggered 18-year terms. This act, backed by Democrat senators including Cory Booker and Sheldon Whitehouse, mandates that justices, upon completing their terms, assume a senior status while maintaining life tenure and compensation. The proposed legislation envisions appointing a new justice every two years in line with this term structure.

The motivation behind the TERM Act and similar initiatives is to restore balance, legitimacy, and fairness to the Supreme Court by mitigating partisan influences and ensuring ongoing judicial competence, especially in the face of health or age-related cognitive decline. Critics argue that term limits could compromise judicial independence, which lifetime appointments aim to protect by insulating justices from political pressures and promoting impartial decision-making.

Currently, the TERM Act remains in the "Introduced" stage. It was referred to the Senate Committee on Homeland Security and Governmental Affairs on the day it was introduced (November 15, 2023) and has not advanced further in the legislative process.

Term limits should be considered for all lower-level federal judges appointed on a partisan basis to support judicial fairness further and reduce political bias in the judiciary. These legislative efforts reflect a deeply partisan debate, with Democrats generally in favor and Republicans typically opposed.

State Interference vs. Local Control

The autonomy of local governments to pass laws appropriate to their own local citizens should be preserved. States should not interfere with the governance of counties and cities (or counties if consolidated). If Harrison, AR, wants to remain a dry county, they should be able to do so. If California wants to legalize marijuana, even though science shows the drug suppresses initiative and drive, it should have the right to do so. If Orange County, FL, wants to ban further commercial development or limit building densities, that right should not be overridden by state edict.

Privacy and Technology

In an era of mass surveillance, big data, and constant connectivity, traditional notions of privacy, free speech, and due process face unprecedented challenges. The Fourth Amendment's protections against unreasonable searches and seizures were conceived when personal property was physical and tangible. Today, much of our "personal property" is digital, stored across cloud servers and online platforms, and frequently subject to collection by private companies and the government. New laws may be needed to explicitly safeguard digital privacy rights, ensuring they are protected with the same rigor as physical property rights, adapting to the realities of the digital age.

Government Accountability

The Constitution is the source of government accountability in the United States, structuring a system where power is divided and checked to prevent abuse and ensure transparency. It establishes clear roles and responsibilities for each branch of government — executive, legislative, and judicial — while mandating mechanisms such as checks and balances and regular elections to hold leaders answerable to the people. The Constitution enforces a standard of responsibility by requiring adherence to the rule of law and empowering institutions like Congress and the courts to investigate, oversee, and correct misconduct. The Supreme Court interprets constitutional provisions to address overreach or violations, ensuring that governmental actions align with democratic principles and maintain the public's trust.

Power versus Rights

It is essential to recognize that protecting citizens' rights is a delicate balancing act, and the more exceptions the government introduces, the greater the potential for erosion of those rights. Power begets the desire for more power. And, as John Dalberg-Acton, 1st Baron Acton, said in April 1887 in a letter to ecclesiastic scholar Mandell Creighton about why monarchs and popes are not above judgment by their subjects, "Power tends to corrupt, and absolute power corrupts absolutely." What many seldom hear is the comments that follow that statement, "Great men are almost always bad men, even when they exercise influence and not authority: still more when you superadd the tendency or certainty of corruption by full authority. There is no worse heresy than the fact that the office sanctifies the holder of it."[55]

Just as Jefferson had hoped, our Constitution has set an example for the rest of the world and has, along with principles from other countries, influenced the United Nations to define for the entire world a set of human rights.

☐

Shifting Power Dynamics

The balance of power between the federal government and the states and among the three branches of government may need to be revisited to reflect modern realities. The original system was designed with checks and balances to prevent any entity from becoming too powerful. However, today's increasingly complex challenges often require coordinated federal actions that strain the limits of states' rights and individual liberties. Additionally, expanding executive powers, primarily during crises, has raised concerns that the presidency may overshadow Congress and the judiciary. Clarifying the distribution of powers more precisely could strengthen democracy by ensuring that no branch can avoid its constitutional duties or overstep its authority.

The Dangers of Concentrated Wealth

The combined wealth of the world's billionaires ($14T) is growing 8% annually, outpacing the 3% annual growth of U.S. residential, commercial, and agricultural real estate ($60-80T). To put this wealth into perspective, if these trends continue, billionaires could feasibly own all U.S. property in 33 years, accounting for inflation and the $3-4 Trillion in real estate they already control. This scenario highlights the accelerating concentration of wealth and raises questions about economic equity and the future distribution of global assets.

Throughout history, thinkers and leaders have warned about the dangers of wealth consolidating into the hands of a few. Theodore Roosevelt famously took aim at the Robber Barons of his time, stating that "a small class of enormously wealthy and economically powerful men, whose chief object is to hold and increase their power," posed a threat to democracy.[304] Similarly, Justice Louis Brandeis cautioned, "We can have democracy in this country, or we can have great wealth concentrated in the hands of a few, but we cannot have both."[305] Mark Twain said, "Nothing incites to money-crimes like great poverty or great wealth."[306]

These warnings resonate today as the rapid accumulation of wealth among billionaires mirrors the economic disparities of the Gilded Age, raising concerns about the balance of power, opportunity, and equity in modern society.

"Taking Back Control"

Americans have often railed against being controlled by big business, politicians doing the bidding of their billionaire backers, and too little representation. Excessive wealth accumulation is dangerous for American democracy. As discussed above, all citizens must demand certain actions of their representatives.

Preventing excessive wealth accumulation requires progressive income taxation as a cornerstone, with higher rates on the ultra-wealthy and eliminating loopholes that favor certain types of income, like lower taxes on capital gains. Wealth taxes on high-net-worth individuals, targeting assets such as investments and luxury properties, can directly address extreme concentrations of wealth. Inheritance and estate taxes also play a vital role, curbing the growth of dynastic wealth by taxing large transfers and closing loopholes that allow wealth to be shielded.

Reforming corporate taxes is equally important, ensuring companies pay their fair share by eliminating offshore tax shelters and penalizing practices like stock buybacks that disproportionately benefit executives. Strengthening antitrust laws to break up monopolies and promote competition prevents economic power from concentrating excessively in a few hands.

Additionally, universal access to public goods like education, healthcare, and housing can reduce reliance on personal wealth for basic needs, leveling the playing field. Policies encouraging fair wages, bolstering labor unions, and reforming capital gains taxation can further curb speculative wealth accumulation. International cooperation is essential to limit tax havens and enforce financial transparency on a global scale. Together, these measures are the best ways to prevent the consolidation of dangerous wealth while promoting a fairer and more sustainable economy.

The concentration of wealth in the hands of a few poses a significant threat to democracy by consolidating power in a few. When a small group of individuals controls vast financial resources, they gain disproportionate influence over political processes, often shaping policies and decisions in their favor. This influence can manifest in the form of large campaign contributions, lobbying efforts, and control of media narratives, which drown out the voices of ordinary citizens and skew public policy away from the common good. These steps lead toward autocratic leadership.

Such wealth-driven influence creates a system where economic power translates directly into political power, eroding trust in democratic institutions. The resulting policies may favor the wealthy, perpetuating inequality and marginalizing the majority. This cycle risks creating an oligarchy, where governance serves the elite rather than the people.

Implementing measures such as robust campaign finance reform, greater transparency in political donations, and limits on corporate influence, alongside policies that reduce wealth concentration, is critical. Without these safeguards, the ideals of democratic representation and equality risk being replaced by a system of governance that prioritizes the interests of a privileged few.

One important step would be publicly financed elections, so billionaires will not own our leaders! Limits on lobbying would help curtail undue influence. Stricter laws on accepting gifts in all three branches of our government would further curtail undue influence, with no anonymous donors and no more Political Action Committees (PACs**)**.

PART II – TODAY'S ISSUES

ARTIFICIAL INTELLIGENCE & PROTECTIONS

As artificial intelligence (AI) becomes more integrated into society, it poses new risks to privacy, autonomy, and even democracy itself. The rapid development and deployment of AI technologies, from surveillance systems to decision-making algorithms, raises serious concerns about how these tools can be used — and potentially misused — without clear legal boundaries. Legal protections are needed to ensure that AI is developed and applied in ways that respect fundamental rights and freedoms.

AI

The onset of Artificial Intelligence (AI) is analogous to the invention of dynamite. The world would have been better if dynamite had never been invented, but it did a lot of good too. The same can be said about AI; it will so radically change the world that we may regret its invention, but at the same time, a lot of good will also result.

AI provides the ability to standardize, automate, and optimize processes across countless industries, making systems more efficient, reducing human error, and unlocking innovations in fields like healthcare, education, and logistics. It can organize, calculate, and edit better than people.

However, like dynamite, its potential for harm is profound. AI can be weaponized, used for mass surveillance, or displace millions of jobs, creating vast social and economic upheaval. This duality underscores the need for legislation to address AI's ethical and regulatory challenges. Safeguards must ensure that AI development and use are transparent, accountable, and protective of intellectual property while aligning with core values such as human rights, privacy, liberty, and equality. AI risks destabilizing societal structures in unforeseen and uncontrollable ways without such legal limits.

Top AI Applications

Medicine

AI analyzes medical imaging, predicts disease outbreaks, and personalizes treatment plans.

Fraud Detection

Systems like FICO's Falcon Fraud Manager predict and prevent credit card fraud.

Automobile Control

AI enhances vehicle safety with autonomous driving and driver-assistance systems.

Internet Search Engines

AI optimizes search results and improves user experience across platforms.

Transportation

AI manages systems like Norfolk Southern's train network for efficiency and safety.

Customer Service

AI chatbots and virtual assistants streamline customer support, providing instant, personalized responses.

Finance

AI models enhance stock market predictions, optimize investment portfolios, and detect insider trading activities.

Manufacturing

AI systems monitor production lines, predict equipment failures, and improve supply chain logistics.

Education

AI-driven platforms offer personalized learning experiences, adapting to individual student needs and progress.

Cybersecurity

AI identifies and mitigates cyber threats by analyzing vast amounts of data in real-time to detect vulnerabilities and intrusions.

Privacy

AI's ability to collect, analyze, and use vast amounts of personal data can undermine privacy and liberty making it crucial to establish safeguards against intrusive surveillance. Without explicit legal protections, individuals risk being subjected to constant monitoring or automated profiling, which could lead to discrimination or unfair treatment. Ensuring that AI technologies are transparent, accountable, and subject to oversight would help prevent abuses and reinforce personal freedoms.

Intellectual Property

Creative arts are among the most vulnerable sectors, facing challenges from financial instability, technological disruption, and intellectual property concerns. Artists, musicians, writers, and other creatives often struggle with inconsistent income, relying on gig work, grants, or fluctuating sales.

The rise of digital technology has brought both opportunities and risks. While streaming platforms and social media provide broader audiences, they also reduce traditional revenue streams. Music and film industries, for instance, have faced declining physical sales and increasing concerns over fair compensation from digital distribution. Additionally, generative AI has raised debates about copyright protection and the ethical use of artists' work in training datasets.

Piracy remains a persistent issue, affecting everything from books to software and diminishing creators' earnings. Meanwhile, corporate consolidation in the publishing, film, and music industries has led to fewer opportunities for independent artists to thrive, as large companies prioritize mass-market content over niche or experimental works.

Despite these vulnerabilities, creative industries continue to evolve, with many artists leveraging crowdfunding, direct-to-consumer sales, and decentralized platforms to maintain control over their work and income. However, ensuring fair compensation and protection for artists in the digital age remains a key challenge for policymakers and industry leaders.

Social Media and Government Control

Corporate Power

The increasing dominance of a few major companies in artificial intelligence (AI) and digital platforms raises concerns about fairness, competition, and the broader impact on democracy. These corporations wield significant influence over the information people access, their conversations, and even their decision-making processes. This power becomes especially problematic when AI tools and search engines are perceived to reflect political bias, potentially distorting search results and eroding trust in what should be neutral information systems.

Some critics argue that AI models like OpenAI's ChatGPT limit discussions on sensitive topics such as politics and religion, interpreting these restrictions as violating free speech principles. However, freedom of speech — mainly as defined by the First Amendment in the United States — protects individuals from government censorship but does not require private companies to permit unrestricted communication on their platforms. AI content moderation policies are generally designed to prevent misinformation, comply with ethical and legal standards, and reduce the spread of harmful or offensive material.

The challenge lies in balancing responsible AI governance with the need for open discourse. While safeguards are essential to prevent abuse and misinformation, concerns about potential bias or overreach highlight the importance of transparency and accountability in AI development. As AI systems shape public discourse, ongoing discussions about regulation, ethical standards, and corporate responsibility will be crucial in maintaining trust and fairness in digital spaces.

Spread of False Information

At the same time, foreign and domestic actors are deliberately spreading false information online to mislead voters and interfere with elections. This manipulation undermines democracy by eroding trust in the information people rely on to make informed decisions.

Compounding this issue, some governments are advocating for "digital sovereignty," seeking greater control over the internet within their borders. While this may be framed as a measure to protect national interests, it often results in censorship, political manipulation, and fragmented global communication. Instead of strengthening democracy, any restrictions can limit free expression, suppress dissent, and reduce access to diverse perspectives, weakening democratic principles.

Political Favoritism

Political favoritism toward some companies while targeting others worsens the problem, increasing the risk of collusion between governments and tech giants. Researchers attempting to uncover these issues often face systemic barriers, including academic censorship, defunded research programs, government investigations, and pressure from powerful corporations. These obstacles weaken oversight and accountability, making it harder to address the growing concentration of power in digital spaces.

As corporations' and governments' influence over the digital landscape becomes more intertwined, ensuring that technology serves the public good — rather than the interests of a select few — may require action. A clear and fair digital policy is essential to preserving transparency, competition, and democratic values. Without safeguards, unchecked power in the digital realm could continue to erode trust, fairness, and the proper functioning of democracy.[236]

Reliance of Artificial Intelligence (AI)

The increasing reliance on AI in criminal justice, hiring, and healthcare areas highlights the need for clear legal standards to prevent bias and protect against unjust outcomes. Establishing safeguards would help ensure that automated systems do not infringe on human rights or reinforce existing inequalities. Legal frameworks could define the limits of AI decision-making, requiring transparency, accountability, and human oversight to maintain fairness. Immediately strengthening these protections would help balance technological advancements with preserving individual rights, ensuring that AI serves society equitably rather than undermining democratic values.

Embedded Spyware

A related concern is the infiltration of spyware into processing chips. When combined with AI, spyware embedded in chip technology seriously threatens national security, individual privacy, and economic stability. Malicious software can be covertly installed during manufacturing, granting unauthorized access to sensitive data, critical infrastructure, and personal devices. Such intrusions compromise privacy, weaken government and business security, and enable widespread surveillance, intellectual property theft, and devastating cyberattacks.

To address this threat, a law should prohibit the integration of spyware into hardware or software at any stage of production. Implementing stringent oversight and accountability measures for technology manufacturers would help ensure that security and individual rights are prioritized over corporate interests or geopolitical pressures. Additionally, establishing clear legal consequences for violations would deter exploitation and reinforce protection for digital sovereignty, safeguarding national and economic interests in an increasingly interconnected world.

The Rise of Robotics:

Implications

Robotics is rapidly expanding beyond factories and specialized industries into everyday life, bringing significant benefits and legal challenges. Robots now serve roles ranging from household assistants and delivery drones to healthcare aides and autonomous vehicles. As this technology advances, its impact will extend even further, potentially transforming entire sectors such as law enforcement, where robots could be used for surveillance, crowd control, or even direct intervention in criminal activities.

Integrating robotics into people's lives raises constitutional and legal questions about privacy, liability, and regulation. Data collection, decision-making authority, and accountability for robotic actions must be addressed to prevent misuse, particularly in sensitive healthcare and law enforcement areas. Establishing clear legal frameworks will ensure that robotics enhances society while protecting individual rights, maintaining transparency, and upholding ethical standards.

Robotics in Daily Life

The growing presence of robots in daily life offers unprecedented convenience and efficiency, with applications in cleaning, caregiving, and logistics. Advanced AI-powered robotics can perform complex tasks autonomously, improving quality of life, assisting individuals with disabilities, and addressing labor shortages in essential industries. However, their increasing use raises important concerns about privacy, safety, and accountability.

For example, determining liability becomes complex if a hospital robot provides incorrect medication instructions due to a malfunction. Should responsibility fall on the manufacturer, the programmers, the AI system, or the healthcare facility that deployed it? These uncertainties highlight the need for clear policies to establish accountability, ensure safety, and regulate the ethical use of robotics. Addressing these challenges will be crucial as automation continues to shape various aspects of society.

Potential Role in Law Enforcement

Robotics could fundamentally transform law enforcement operations. Robots are already being used for high-risk tasks such as bomb disposal, handling hazardous materials, military weapon delivery, and conducting surveillance in dangerous environments. In the future, autonomous drones or robotic units may take on roles in patrolling, suspect apprehension, and even use-of-force scenarios. While these technologies can potentially improve officer safety and operational efficiency, they also raise significant constitutional concerns related to civil rights liberties, accountability, and the appropriate use of force.

Legal Implications of Robots

Deploying robots in law enforcement and other public roles presents potential conflicts with existing constitutional rights. The Fourth Amendment's protection against unreasonable searches and seizures may need reinterpretation in light of robotic surveillance capabilities. For instance, can a drone legally monitor a person in their backyard, or would that constitute an invasion of privacy? Can a robot be sued for false arrest?

As these technologies become more widespread, more explicit legal standards will be needed to define the boundaries of permissible surveillance.

The use of robotic force may also raises concerns regarding the Eighth Amendment, which prohibits cruel and unusual punishment. Autonomous systems programmed to use force must be governed by strict guidelines to prevent excessive or arbitrary actions. Additionally, the risk of AI bias in robotic decision-making could result in discriminatory outcomes, potentially violating the constitutional guarantee of equal protection under the law.

Economics under AI

When contemplating a future where most work is automated and humans are primarily freed from traditional labor, several economic models and implications arise.

Service and Creative Industries Expansion

Even with high levels of automation, there will likely be increased opportunities in inherently human-centric sectors, such as the arts, culture, leisure, and human-focused services like therapy, eldercare, and personalized education. These areas may become the new frontiers for employment, emphasizing creativity, empathy, and interpersonal skills.

Economic Restructuring

The economy might shift towards more collaborative and shared economic models, such as cooperative businesses and peer-to-peer services that leverage community resources and capabilities. This restructuring could foster a more community-oriented economy that values contribution in various forms beyond conventional employment.

Redistribution of Wealth and Ownership

As AI-driven automation increases productivity and reshapes industries, wealth accumulates among technology owners and capital investors. This concentration of economic gains could widen inequality, necessitating mechanisms to distribute AI-driven prosperity more equitably. Potential solutions include progressive taxation on AI-generated profits, employee equity in AI-powered enterprises, or state participation in key automated sectors to ensure the benefits of AI integration extend across the broader economy.

Continued Role of Humans in AI

Humans might focus on roles involving complex decision-making, automated system oversight, and innovation in new technologies and services. There would likely be a continuing need for human skills in areas that require judgment, moral considerations, and high-level strategy.

Lifelong Learning and Re-skilling

Education systems might evolve to emphasize lifelong learning, helping individuals adapt to an ever-changing job market. This system could involve continuous skill development in emerging fields and re-skilling for industries that require more human interaction or higher levels of creativity.

Challenges to Traditional Economic Measures

Standard measures of economic health, such as GDP and employment rates, may become less relevant in a highly automated economy. New metrics that better reflect well-being, environmental sustainability, and social equity might be developed to measure societal progress.

Political and Ethical Considerations

The transition to a highly automated economy involves significant political and ethical considerations, including who controls the technology, how privacy is protected, and how the benefits of automation are distributed. Robust public debates and policy development will likely aim to manage these issues responsibly.

In summary, the economy of a post-labor world would likely involve a combination of basic income schemes, shifts towards service and creative industries, wealth redistribution, and a greater emphasis on social and ethical dimensions of economic activity. The path there would require careful planning, policy innovation, and ongoing adjustments to new realities.

The Path Forward

As robotics advance and integrate into daily life, laws may need updates to protect fundamental rights and ensure these technologies serve the public good. Proactive measures could include enacting laws to govern the deployment of robots, such as banning invasive surveillance in public spaces and requiring transparency in law enforcement applications. Oversight mechanisms, like independent review boards or warrant permission, could monitor their use in sensitive areas to prevent abuse. At the same time, mandatory ethical standards for developers and manufacturers would ensure accountability for harm caused by autonomous systems. These steps would protect democratic principles, uphold public trust, and ensure that innovation enhances, rather than undermines, individual rights and freedoms.

BALANCE OF POWER AND CONTROL

Power and control are related concepts, but they are not the same thing. Each has distinct characteristics and functions, although they often interact in meaningful ways.

Power: Power generally refers to the ability or capacity to influence, direct, or shape outcomes, events, or the behavior of others. It is the underlying force or resource that allows a person, organization, or entity to enact change or exert influence. Power can come in many forms — political, social, economic, intellectual, or physical. It can be used positively to empower others and create constructive change, or negatively to dominate, coerce, or manipulate.

Control: On the other hand, Control involves active exercise or application of power to manage, regulate, or direct something or someone. It is the process of using power to maintain authority, enforce rules, or ensure that specific outcomes are achieved. Control focuses more on the mechanisms and strategies employed to maintain influence and keep certain behaviors, processes, or systems within desired parameters.

The following is not a political statement but simply a logical progression: The wealthy seek to protect and grow their wealth because it grants them power. They then use that power to influence the government, a process that inevitably subjugates or further marginalizes the non-wealthy.

Key Differences

Power is the potential, while control is the action. Power is the capacity to influence, while control is the deliberate effort to guide or manage that influence. For example, a manager may have the power to make decisions in a company, but they exercise control when they implement policies or supervise employees.

Power can be passive, while control is active. One can possess power without necessarily exerting it. Control, by definition, involves taking active steps to direct or manage situations.

Power often involves broader influence, while control focuses on specifics. Power may enable someone to influence a wide range of outcomes, whereas control is typically concerned with regulating particular behaviors, people, or systems.

Power can be shared, while control often implies exclusivity. Power can be distributed across a group, empowering multiple people to effect change. Control, however, typically suggests that one person or group exerts authority over another.

Interaction Between Power and Control

Power and control frequently overlap, as the possession of power often enables one to exert control. For instance, a government has the power to enact laws, while law enforcement agencies control the enforcement of those laws. However, one can have power without exerting control (e.g., a wealthy individual who chooses not to influence politics), and one can attempt to control without sufficient power (e.g., a manager who struggles to enforce rules due to lack of authority).

In essence, while power is about having the capability to influence or effect change, control is about the application of that capability to achieve specific goals.

BANKING AND FINANCIAL CONTROL

The Fed

The debate about having a central bank or not has raged since the beginning of our country but most seriously since Andrew Jackson.

The Second Bank of the United States was chartered for twenty years during James Madison's presidency in 1816. It was given responsibilities similar to those of the First Bank, serving as a central repository for federal funds and the government's fiscal agent. The Bank was also responsible for regulating state banks and promoting a stable currency.[59-30]

When Andrew Jackson became president, he worked to rescind the bank's federal charter. In Jackson's veto message, the bank needed to be abolished because it concentrated the nation's financial strength in a single institution, exposed the government to control by foreign interests, served mainly to make the rich richer, exercised too much control over members of Congress, and favored northeastern states over southern and western states.

"As did Thomas Jefferson, Jackson supported an 'agricultural republic' and felt the bank improved the fortunes of an 'elite circle' of commercial and industrial entrepreneurs at the expense of farmers and laborers. After a titanic struggle, Jackson succeeded in destroying the bank by vetoing its 1832 re-charter by Congress and by withdrawing U.S. funds in 1833."[181-03] In closing the Second National Bank of the United States, Jackson moved the government's money and the role of lending to small banks that supported agriculture. This stimulated an expansion of credit and speculation, which led first to inflation (banknotes were not backed by "specie" – gold or silver) and then economic instability. Then Jackson required banknotes to become backed by "specie," but it was too limited in supply. This instability led to the collapse of the banks, the Panic of 1837, and a deep economic depression.[181-03]

The concept of a national bank continued to be debated and ebbed and flowed through the succeeding presidents until the Independent Treasury Act of 1846 was passed. This put government money into the treasury, reducing hard money circulation and therefore tightening credit, which restricted trade.[181-05] In the ensuing years, a variety of national banks were tried until 1913, when the Federal Reserve System, known as the Fed, was created.

Ron Paul, the libertarian Republican congressman, published a book, *End the Fed*,[181-04] that makes a case for doing away with the Fed and returning to the gold standard. His arguments fall short, according to his critics, because the existence of a gold standard in the past did not prevent the total collapse of the stock market and runs on banks which cause many to lose their life savings – not once but at least twice.

The Fed exists to create and regulate the money supply, safeguard against banking crises, and manage monetary policy through instruments like interest rates and reserve requirements. Its decisions do not have to be ratified by the president or anyone else in the executive or legislative branches of government. However, it is subject to oversight by Congress, which can amend the Federal Reserve Act of 1913.

Many support government involvement in the economy, particularly when jobs and broader economic stability are at risk. They argue that strategic interventions, such as bailouts during financial crises, can preserve jobs, protect the economy, and maintain critical industries. For instance, the failure of a large company like General Motors (GM) might be viewed not just as a market outcome but as a situation with far-reaching repercussions for workers, communities, and the overall economy — one that may warrant government action to prevent collapse. This perspective aligns with the belief that intervention can be necessary to stabilize key industries and safeguard livelihoods.

On the other hand, many others believe in the primacy of market freedom, self-regulation, and minimal interference in business operations, viewing government bailouts as a distortion of natural market dynamics that can lead to inefficiencies. From this standpoint, businesses should succeed or fail based on their competitiveness and market forces; if a company like GM becomes unsustainable due to high labor costs, it is argued that the market should determine its fate, allowing more efficient competitors to step in. However, the consideration of saving jobs is a factor that often weighs heavily in such discussions.

Bank control can be seen as a necessary compromise. Ironically, Americans often tolerate more controls imposed by their neighborhood homeowners' associations than they would from their federal government. Similarly, during times of crisis, there is a pattern of yielding to government pressures to relinquish some liberties, as seen with the enactment of the Patriot Act following 9/11. A real or perceived crisis often catalyzes consolidating more power and authority in the executive branch, sometimes centralizing it in the hands of a single individual, which could be a significant risk. Having one person make all the decisions for a $29 Trillion organization (America) is not what our founders intended.

The SEC

The Securities and Exchange Commission (SEC) protects investors and ensures fair markets. Despite its resources and enforcement powers, the agency has faced criticism over its effectiveness. High-profile failures, such as the Bernard Madoff scandal, have raised concerns about its oversight, particularly of Wall Street. Internal issues, including whistleblower support and document management, have also drawn scrutiny. In response, the SEC introduced a whistleblower rewards program to encourage reporting of financial misconduct and strengthen oversight.

The SEC enforces transparency, accountability, and fairness to maintain a stable financial system. The SEC aims to protect investors and market integrity by addressing fraud, insider trading, and other unethical practices. The agency has also expanded its focus to modern concerns, such as Environmental, Social, and Governance (ESG) standards, which push corporations to address climate change and social responsibility. This growing role in regulating markets is in response to public expectations.

Balancing regulation with economic growth remains a challenge. The SEC works to protect investors and ensure compliance while avoiding unnecessary rules that could slow market activity. Ongoing debates focus on how much regulation is needed to maintain stability without stifling economic progress. Some discussions involve revisiting post-2008 financial crisis laws, such as parts of the Dodd-Frank Act, with proposals to ease restrictions on smaller banks and create a more flexible business environment.

Strong oversight and balanced regulation remain essential for a resilient financial system as the SEC evolves, especially considering broader government controls, such as federal oversight of banks, which will be explored in the next section.

Wall Street and Financial Institutions

Wall Street is a pivotal marketplace for capital investment and plays a crucial role in the global financial system. While it facilitates essential services like raising capital and trading securities, it also faces ethical challenges related to speculative activities. Charlie Munger, the vice chairman of Berkshire Hathaway once said that Wall Street is "like a denizen of thieves, and they'll sell you what they can sell you."[59-26]

Managing client investments is a common practice in financial institutions, but it also creates opportunities for misuse. This laxity has led to ongoing discussions about oversight and reform, particularly concerning speculative practices that may not benefit clients or the broader economy. Ethical investment strategies, such as Environmental, Social, and Governance (ESG) investing, have gained attention for integrating social responsibility into financial decisions. Supporters argue that ESG helps address risks related to climate change and social equity, while critics question its impact on economic priorities.

The role of financial institutions in sustainable investing, regulatory compliance, and transparency is central to current monetary policy debates. Some policymakers warn that restricting ESG practices could limit shareholder input and reduce investor access to key information about investment risks. Others argue that financial institutions should prioritize traditional business fundamentals and risk management over emerging social concerns.

Calls for regulatory modernization continue in response to economic challenges, including the risks of volatile assets like cryptocurrency and climate-related financial instability. Advocates for stronger oversight argue that reforms are necessary to protect financial stability and address emerging threats. Efforts to reverse deregulation, strengthen safeguards, and update compliance standards reflect a broader push for a more resilient and equitable financial system.

Concerns about excessive speculation and the power of large financial institutions fuel debates over the "too big to fail" issue. Policies like the Dodd-Frank Act and the Volcker Rule aim to prevent banks from engaging in risky trading that could threaten the financial system. Proposals to expand these regulations seek to separate traditional banking from high-risk investments and hold financial executives accountable for reckless practices. Additionally, there is strong support for improving access to credit and strengthening banking regulations to ensure fair and equitable financial services.

Large financial institutions play a crucial role in global transactions and economic stability, yet their size and influence pose systemic risks. Balancing financial stability with responsible investment practices requires measured oversight, which raises further questions about the extent of federal control over banks and the regulatory frameworks needed to manage these risks effectively.

Financial Control

One concept is for Congress to restructure large banks into more specialized entities, with each group focusing on distinct aspects such as retail banking, investment banking, or international finance. This aims to enhance their efficiency and expertise in specific financial sectors. At the same time, reducing their overall size would mitigate the risks associated with large financial institutions. This restructuring would require careful regulatory planning and consultation with banking and financial experts. Here are four ways to better control Wall Street.

- ### *Stricter Regulation of High-Frequency Trading (HFT)*

    High-frequency trading (HFT) relies on complex algorithms to execute large numbers of orders at extremely high speeds. While proponents argue that it enhances market efficiency, critics contend that it can lead to instability and provide an unfair advantage to firms with the resources to develop and use these technologies. To mitigate these issues, regulators could impose tighter controls on HFT, such as limiting the speed of trades or implementing a small transaction tax on each trade to discourage excessive speculative activity.

- ### *Enhanced Transparency in Derivatives Trading*

    Derivatives, including futures and options, play a crucial role in financial markets but can pose significant risks if not adequately managed. A lack of transparency in these transactions contributed to the 2007-2008 financial crisis. Increasing oversight by requiring centralized clearinghouses or more stringent reporting requirements could reduce systemic risks. Ensuring market participants have better visibility into derivatives trading would make financial markets more stable and less vulnerable to sudden shocks.

- ### *Reforming Credit Rating Systems*

    The 2007-2008 financial crisis exposed serious flaws in the credit rating system. Rating agencies failed to provide accurate assessments of financial products, partly due to conflicts of interest. Reforming this system could involve establishing more independent and accountable rating agencies, potentially supported by a public or mixed public-private framework. By reducing reliance on agencies with vested interests, such reforms would improve the reliability of credit ratings and promote financial stability.

- ### *Separation between Investment and Commercial Banking*

  Historically, the Glass-Steagall Act of 1933 separated commercial banking from investment banking to prevent conflicts of interest and protect depositors' funds. However, its repeal of the Glass-Steagall Act in 1999 allowed banks to engage in riskier speculative activities, contributing to financial instability. Restoring a stronger separation between these two banking functions would help prevent excessive risk-taking with consumer deposits and reduce the likelihood of financial crises caused by speculative investment activities.

The Mint and Currency

The future of U.S. currency faces multifaceted challenges, including counterfeiting operations conducted by various countries, such as China, Russia, and North Korea. These nations have developed sophisticated methods that threaten the integrity of U.S. paper currency. Despite ongoing efforts to enhance security features, counterfeiters continuously adapt, necessitating constant advancements in anti-counterfeiting technology.

In addition to counterfeiting concerns, the rise of electronic currencies — such as credit cards, digital payment platforms like Venmo, and cryptocurrencies like Bitcoin — present possible alternatives to traditional paper money. The convenience, potential for higher security, and efficiency of electronic transactions, combined with the global shift toward digital financial systems, suggest that paper currency may eventually be phased out. However, this transition is not without obstacles. Privacy concerns, cybersecurity risks, and regulatory challenges remain significant hurdles to widespread adoption.

A major security issue that must be addressed is the vulnerability of cyber-based financial systems. Until computers can effectively prevent spam, phishing, hacking, ransomware, cryptocurrency theft, and tax evasion, cryptocurrencies may not be the most reliable alternative to other forms of electronic payments. These challenges highlight the need for robust digital security measures before electronic currencies can fully replace traditional cash in the U.S. and global financial systems.

Anti-Corruption

Legislation addressing ethics and transparency in government should be expanded to cover all "meaningful contact" between private individuals and government officials and should be enacted into law. The Executive Branch Reform Act, H.R. 984, of 2007, proposed requiring more than 8,000 executive branch officials to report any "significant contact" from a "private party" — defined as anyone who is not a government official — into a public database. The bill defined "significant contact" as any oral, written, or electronic communication in which a private party seeks to influence or garner support for official action by an executive branch officer or employee. This bill should be revisited and passed.

BUSINESS

The government plays a vital role in business by setting regulations, ensuring fair competition, and balancing economic growth with consumer and worker protections.

International Competition

The U.S. could take stronger measures to counter the EU's restrictions on American companies, aiming to balance fair trade with safeguarding innovation and economic growth. Prioritizing the protection of creativity and industry competitiveness would help ensure a fair and sustainable economic relationship. Experts, such as the Brooking Institute, Senator Tom Cotton (R), and Senator Amy Klobuchar (D), have put forth a number of proposals for improving anti-trust laws:

1. **Modernizing Antitrust Laws**: Update antitrust laws to better address the realities of today's digital economy. This would involve refining definitions and standards for anti-competitive practices to accommodate the nuances of digital markets and platforms.
2. **Bipartisan Commission on Antitrust**: Establish a bipartisan commission or task force to study current market dynamics and make recommendations. This commission would include economics, law, technology, and consumer rights experts, ensuring a balanced perspective.
3. **Enhanced Merger Guidelines**: Update merger guidelines to assess the long-term competitive impacts of corporate mergers and acquisitions more effectively, especially in rapidly evolving sectors like technology and pharmaceuticals.

4. **Balanced Enforcement**: Advocate for consistent and balanced enforcement of existing antitrust laws, avoiding overreach and under-enforcement. This would ensure that the antitrust divisions of the DOJ and the FTC are adequately resourced.

5. **Promoting Competition and Innovation**: Introduce policies that support small businesses and startups, reduce barriers to market entry, and encourage open markets.

6. **Consumer Welfare Focus**: Maintain a focus on consumer welfare, not just in terms of prices but also quality, choice, and innovation. This approach recognizes that consumer interests may not always align with those of competitors in the market.

7. **Global Coordination**: Coordinate with international regulatory bodies to address global antitrust concerns, especially with the rise of multinational corporations and digital platforms that operate across borders.

8. **Regular Review and Adaptation**: Implement a mechanism for regularly reviewing antitrust policies and their effectiveness, allowing for adaptations as market conditions and technologies evolve.

Equal Opportunities for Businesses

Businesses should compete based on efficiency and value rather than securing exclusive supplier deals that limit competition. While economies of scale are a natural advantage for larger companies, smaller businesses face challenges when preferential pricing or access creates barriers to entry. Policies should promote fair supplier access without interfering in market dynamics, ensuring competition is based on quality, service, and innovation rather than supply chain dominance.

Media Group Size Control

We need a renewed commitment to mental health that emphasizes personal resilience and access to diverse perspectives. The concentration of media ownership among a few large corporations influences public discourse, limits competition, and reduces the variety of viewpoints available to consumers. A more competitive media landscape would support local journalism, encourage independent voices, and enhance consumer choice.

While businesses should be free to grow, excessive media consolidation risks undermining a healthy marketplace of ideas. Introducing reasonable ownership limits, such as capping market share at 15% to 20%, could prevent monopolistic control while maintaining a dynamic industry. Balanced media regulations should protect free speech, journalistic integrity, and public trust without overreach, ensuring news and entertainment reflect a broad range of perspectives rather than the interests of a few dominant players.

Antitrust

Antitrust refers to laws and regulations that promote fair competition and prevent monopolies or practices that restrain trade and harm consumers.

Competition

Competition is assumed to be American and supported by the Constitution under its various freedoms. Competition is a form of checks and balances. If a business creates a highly desirable and successful product, other businesses will form to pick up that idea, hopefully improve it and thereby give consumers alternatives.

Once upon a time, the American automobile industry thought that "planned obsolescence" was a smart move to sustain their businesses, until the Japanese car industry began building cars that would last much longer. As a result, competition took a large piece of car buying market share.

Fair Competition

While the United States has been actively pursuing antitrust cases against various industries, including technology, since the Sherman Act of 1890 and the Clayton Act of 1914, some politicians think the U.S. has not done enough, especially against large companies. The European Union (EU) has also been notable for its stringent regulatory actions against some of America's largest companies, particularly in the tech sector. The goal of antitrust actions is to ensure competition and address monopolistic practices in the market. Another motive is to constrain big tech companies from gaining overwhelming control of global communications and commerce. Once more, this objective is about averting excessive concentration of power.

The EU's strict antitrust regulations aim to promote fair competition, protect consumers, and maintain a balanced digital market, including implementing the Digital Markets Act. These measures stem from concerns that large tech companies could dominate key digital economy areas, shaping economic and social dynamics. By addressing market concentration, the EU seeks to create an open and competitive digital marketplace while ensuring that excessive corporate influence does not undermine innovation and consumer choice.[39-09]

European countries have subsidized consortium companies to compete with U.S. firms, particularly in the technology, aerospace, and energy industries. These subsidies are often considered necessary to drive innovation, maintain strategic independence, and protect critical sectors from foreign influence.

While this approach bolsters Europe's global competitiveness, it raises concerns about fairness, especially given the EU's strict antitrust policies within its markets. This incongruity reflects a complex balance — enforcing competition rules domestically while supporting national and regional champions internationally. The effectiveness, impact, and fairness of these subsidies remain topics of ongoing debate.

European Union Enforcement

The European Union (EU) has taken significant antitrust actions against major U.S. technology companies, citing concerns over market dominance and anti-competitive behavior. Google has been fined multiple times for allegedly favoring its services in search and advertising while limiting competitors' access. Apple has faced scrutiny over its App Store policies, particularly regarding its in-app payment system and whether its apps receive an unfair advantage. These cases reflect the EU's broader efforts to address what it sees as imbalances in the technology sector.

Meta Platforms, formerly Facebook, has also come under EU scrutiny for its data handling practices and acquisitions. Regulators are examining whether these activities unfairly reinforce its market dominance and create barriers to competition. These concerns reflect broader debates over the influence of major technology firms. However, the outcomes of such investigations continue to evolve, potentially reshaping the regulatory landscape.

These cases underscore the differing regulatory approaches of the U.S. and the EU. The EU often focuses on market structure and long-term competition, while the U.S. traditionally emphasizes consumer welfare and pricing effects. The EU's proactive stance has influenced global discussions on digital markets, competition, and consumer protection. For the U.S., the challenge is finding a balance between supporting corporate growth and ensuring fair global competition while protecting consumers, fostering innovation, and maintaining strong trade and diplomatic relationships.

Patented Monopoly

Patents can either promote or restrict competition, depending on how they are applied and how competitors respond to the temporary monopoly they create. The history of patents in America began with colonial-era state patents before the U.S. Constitution established a national system in 1787 to promote innovation. The first federal Patent Act in 1790 created a review process, later simplified by the 1793 Act. The establishment of the Patent Office in 1836 formalized examinations and led to a surge in patent filings, particularly during the Civil War era. The 20th century introduced international treaties and major reforms, culminating in the 2011 America Invents Act, which transitioned the U.S. to a "first-to-file" system to align with global standards.

U.S. Antitrust Enforcement

U.S. antitrust authorities have recently intensified efforts to address competition concerns across various industries. The Department of Justice (DOJ) has been investigating Live Nation's dominance in the live music industry following its merger with Ticketmaster, as well as Apple's control over its App Store and mobile operating system, which critics argue harms developers and consumers. Other DOJ inquiries include RealPage's alleged role in coordinating rental price fixing, Visa's potential exclusion of rival payment networks, and UnitedHealthcare's acquisitions, such as Amedisys, for their potential impact on competition in healthcare.

The Federal Trade Commission (FTC) is reviewing Amazon's acquisition of iRobot to determine whether it could unfairly favor Roomba products after quashing the merger of grocery giants Kroger and Albertsons, which would have created the largest grocery chain in the U.S. The energy sector is also under scrutiny, with Exxon Mobil's acquisition of Pioneer Natural Resources and Chevron's purchase of Hess Corp being assessed for their competitive impact. Other FTC investigations include Roark Capital's acquisition of Subway, given its ownership of competing restaurant chains, and Qualcomm's purchase of Autotalks, a key player in autonomous vehicle technology.

These cases highlight the DOJ and FTC's ongoing efforts to maintain competitive markets across key industries, ensuring that mergers and business practices do not unfairly restrict competition or harm consumers.

Market Regulation

The antitrust debate centers on how to regulate markets, particularly large technology companies. One perspective favors a free-market approach with minimal government intervention, arguing that excessive regulation could slow innovation and weaken U.S. firms in global competition, especially against Chinese tech companies.

On the other hand, advocates for stricter antitrust enforcement argue that major tech firms in social media, e-commerce, and digital advertising have too much power, which harms consumers and small businesses by raising prices, reducing choices, and stifling innovation. This view supports updating antitrust laws to address the complexities of the digital economy. Some argue that when a product or service becomes essential, such as internet access, the principles of laissez-faire economics may no longer apply.

Effectively enforcing antitrust laws requires addressing several structural challenges within the current legal framework. Under the Clayton Act, the government must initiate antitrust lawsuits within four years of when the violation occurred or was reasonably discovered. Given the complexity of modern markets and corporate strategies, this limited timeframe can make enforcement difficult. Lengthy investigations, limited resources, and corporate legal tactics can delay action, making it harder to meet the statute of limitations. Extending this timeframe could give regulators more time to investigate and prosecute anti-competitive practices.

Legislative proposals such as the Competition and Antitrust Law Enforcement Reform Act (CALERA), introduced by Senator Amy Klobuchar, have backed efforts to strengthen antitrust enforcement. CALERA calls for increased funding and staffing for agencies like the Federal Trade Commission (FTC) and the Department of Justice's DOJ's Antitrust Division to handle complex cases better. It also aims to modernize legal standards to address the realities of the digital economy and close loopholes that corporations exploit.

Recent executive actions have also promoted greater collaboration between state and federal agencies to improve oversight. These initiatives emphasize increasing transparency in mergers and acquisitions and strengthening whistleblower protections to help regulators detect anti-competitive practices earlier. Along with extending the statute of limitations and modernizing legal frameworks, these measures could significantly improve the enforcement of antitrust laws, ensuring that markets remain competitive while balancing innovation and regulation.

Price Gouging

Should all businesses use the same markup formula, or should pricing strategies differ based on the industry? Some sectors, like restaurants, often use a standardized markup, such as a 40% food cost formula, making uniform pricing models feasible in some instances. However, applying the same markup across industries — such as grocery stores or manufacturing — would be impractical, given cost structure differences, supply chain, and competition.

Preventing price gouging would require oversight at multiple points in the supply chain, but enforcing such regulations presents challenges. Businesses adjust prices based on energy costs, labor, and supply fluctuations. When costs rise, delaying price increases can lead to losses, while when costs fall, some businesses may hesitate to lower prices immediately, often to recover previous losses.

Advancements in AI and automation have improved price tracking, allowing businesses to adjust prices more efficiently based on real-time cost changes. This capability could reduce delays in price adjustments, making pricing more dynamic and responsive. However, balancing market flexibility and consumer protection remains a key consideration, as excessive regulation could hinder competition. At the same time, unchecked pricing practices might lead to unfair costs for consumers.

Consumer Protection and Corporations

The U.S. government's involvement in consumer protection has deep roots, evolving to address the complexities of modern commerce and safeguard citizens from unfair, deceptive, or harmful business practices. The development began with pivotal legislation such as the Pure Food and Drug Act of 1906, which set foundational safety standards, and the Federal Trade Commission Act of 1914, which created the Federal Trade Commission (FTC) to combat unfair business practices.

Over time, additional significant milestones included the establishment of the Consumer Product Safety Commission (CPSC) in 1972, aimed at protecting the public from dangerous products, and the formation of the Consumer Financial Protection Bureau (CFPB) in 2010 in response to the 2007-2008 financial crisis, designed to regulate financial products and services more rigorously.

While these agencies and laws underscore the government's commitment to consumer protection, ongoing debates highlight the tension between safeguarding consumer interests and fostering a competitive, innovation-friendly market. At the same time, fraud, phishing, ransomware, and other confidence schemes are at an all-time high. The 2024 global cybercrime costs reached USD 9.5 trillion, projected to hit $10.5 trillion annually by 2025.[359]

Phishing attacks have surged, with 493.2 million incidents recorded in the third quarter of 2023 alone, up from 180.4 million the previous quarter.[360] Ransomware attacks have also escalated, with the average ransom payment increasing from $812,380 in 2022 to $1,542,333 in 2023.[361] These trends highlight the growing sophistication and frequency of cyber threats, underscoring the need for enhanced security measures and awareness.

Additional laws should reinforce the legitimacy of agencies like the FTC, CPSC, and CFPB, providing a constitutional basis for their regulatory powers and ensuring that any oversight remains focused on upholding these core principles.

Enhanced enforcement is vital to safeguard the public from fraud and con artists. Prioritizing perpetrators operating across state lines as federal targets is crucial. States should allocate more resources to investigation and enforcement efforts, while stricter penalties are needed to deter fraudulent activities.

CITIZENSHIP, IMMIGRATION, AND ENFORCEMENT

Immigration is a major issue for Americans, most of whom are descendants of immigrants – all except Native Americans, of course, and some even believe they came across a land bridge from Asia. The issue is the "legality" of how immigrants have entered or are entering our country. Of course, entry into the country was not restricted until around 1882, when a law passed by President Chester A. Arthur only restricted lunatics, paupers, and criminals – and then Congress amended it to add Chinese for 10 years, later making the restriction permanent.[121] Every ancestor of Americans that arrived before that date arrived in the same manner as every "illegal alien" who arrived in the U.S. this year. They just showed up at one of our entry ports and were let through, had a visa that they "over-stayed," or snuck through where we do not have entry points.

Hiroshi Motomura, University of North Carolina law professor and nationally recognized expert on citizenship and immigration, has identified three approaches America has taken to the legal status of immigrants (considering only legal immigrants) in his book *Americans in Waiting: The Lost Story of Immigration and Citizenship in the United States*:

1. The first [approach], dominant in the 19th century, treated immigrants as in transition – that is, as prospective citizens. As soon as people declared their intention to become citizens, and before the five-year wait was over, they received multiple low-cost benefits, including eligibility for free homesteads (in the Homestead Act of 1869), and in many states the

right to vote. The goal was to make America attractive so large numbers of farmers and skilled craftsmen would settle new lands.

2. By the 1880s, a second approach took over, treating newcomers as "immigrants by contract." An implicit deal existed whereby immigrants who were literate and could earn their own living were permitted in restricted numbers (except for Asians). Once in the United States, they would have limited legal rights but were not allowed to vote until they became citizens and would not be eligible for the New Deal government benefits available in the 1930s.

3. The third more recent policy is "immigration by affiliation," Motomura argues, whereby the treatment in part depends on how deeply rooted people have become in America. An immigrant who applies for citizenship as soon as permitted, has a long history of working in the United States, and has significant family ties (such as American-born children), is more deeply affiliated and can expect better treatment.[120]

The Debate

The contemporary debate on immigration in the United States reflects a mix of historical, legal, and ethical considerations. On the one hand, the United States, a nation primarily built by immigrants, should maintain an inclusive and welcoming stance towards new arrivals, recognizing their contributions to the societal fabric. However, this prompts discussion around the importance of lawful entry and adherence to established immigration processes and raises concerns over national security and resource allocation. This debate also touches on the sensitive issue of birthright citizenship and the rights of children born in the U.S. to non-citizen parents.

The current discourse is not just about the adequacy of existing laws but also about defining what it means to be American, whether through birth, lineage, or legally pledging allegiance to the country. As a democracy, the United States continually evolves its policies.

Immigration

A unified framework for immigration reform could aim to balance national security with the values of inclusivity and cultural integration. Policies that strengthen border security and lawful entry would reflect the nation's commitment to managing immigration to protect its sovereignty while addressing economic and humanitarian considerations.

Key measures could include enhancing entry and exit tracking systems and ensuring that immigration authorities have the necessary resources and technology to enforce border security effectively. A universal employment verification system could promote workplace accountability, discourage hiring unauthorized workers, and create a fairer labor market for immigrants and citizens.

At the same time, immigration policies could support the successful integration of legally present immigrants, fostering a cohesive society. Prioritizing education in U.S. History, Civics and Cultural Integration programs would help immigrants participate fully in American civic life. Policies that promote language proficiency and access to employment opportunities could further strengthen their contributions to communities and the economy.

The nation could also reaffirm its tradition of welcoming refugees by establishing clear, enforceable guidelines for humanitarian protection. Recognizing individuals who have supported American interests abroad and prioritizing those fleeing political oppression and conflict would allow the U.S.

to uphold its humanitarian commitments while ensuring national security considerations remain in focus.

These reforms could provide a structured and balanced approach to immigration policy — strengthening border security, supporting lawful integration, and maintaining the U.S.'s identity as a diverse and welcoming nation.[124-126]

Why Not Open Our Borders?

Permanently opening our borders could profoundly impact economies, societies, and governance worldwide. Economically, it could address labor shortages, foster innovation, and stimulate growth, but it might also depress wages in specific industries and strain public services in unprepared regions. Socially, increased migration would enhance cultural exchange but could lead to urban overcrowding, additional homelessness, inequality, and integration challenges. Politically, open borders could challenge national sovereignty and risk fueling populist movements while requiring unprecedented global coordination. Humanitarian benefits include better opportunities for those fleeing conflict or poverty, though environmental strain and resource disparities could intensify without proper planning. Success would depend on equitable policies and international cooperation.

Consequently, controlling immigration is necessary to balance economic needs, social stability, security, and fairness for everyone involved.

H-1B

The H-1B visa program, a temporary visa allowing foreign workers with specialized skills and at least a bachelor's degree to fill roles in industries like technology and engineering, exemplifies the contradictions in U.S. immigration policy. While it is celebrated for addressing domestic skill shortages and fostering innovation, it prioritizes corporate interests by offering businesses a controlled, often lower-cost labor force. Critics point out that these roles could be filled by training Americans and reducing dependency on foreign workers. At the same time, undocumented immigrants who perform labor-intensive, essential jobs — often under exploitative conditions and for low wages — face relentless deportation threats. This disparity highlights a system that values certain types of labor over others despite both groups making vital contributions to the economy.

Critics of the H-1B visa program argue that some companies exploit loopholes to prioritize cost savings over hiring equally skilled American workers. Although the program is intended to address labor shortages in specialized fields, it is often used to replace or undercut American employees in similar positions. While employers are required to pay H-1B workers the "prevailing wage," these wages are frequently set at the lower end of the market rate.

A 2020 Economic Policy Institute (EPI) report found that 60% of all H-1B jobs were assigned wage levels well below the local median wage confirming that many foreign workers are paid significantly less than their U.S. counterparts for similar work. For example, the median salary for H-1B workers is $118,000, comparable to the U.S. Bureau of Labor Statistics (BLS) figures for high-paying fields such as software development, where the median annual wage was $120,730 in 2022. However, critics emphasize that this median figure obscures the prevalence of lower-wage roles, particularly in outsourcing and contract-based positions, where companies take advantage of permissible wage levels. This practice creates wage compression, disadvantaging American workers who might otherwise command higher pay or better benefits.

EB-5

The EB-5 Immigrant Investor Program grants U.S. residency to individuals who invest substantial capital — typically $1.05 million, or $800,000 in designated high-unemployment or rural areas — into a business expected to create or preserve at least 10 full-time jobs. Supporters argue that the program boosts economic growth, funds job creation, and attracts global entrepreneurs. However, critics question its value, noting that it primarily benefits wealthy investors with little personal connection to the U.S. beyond financial interests while offering uncertain benefits to communities. Concerns about fraud, lack of transparency, and fairness in the immigration system further fuel debate over whether the program truly serves the national interest or merely provides a shortcut for affluent individuals to bypass standard immigration processes. In early 2025, President Donald Trump has proposed a "gold card" visa program that would grant wealthy foreign investors a pathway to U.S. citizenship in exchange for a $5 million investment, replacing the existing EB-5 visa program.

Who Can Be American?

How do we determine who is an "official" American, an American Citizen? One approach could be to issue certified Americans with identification cards. Such an approach would likely invite bribery and forgery. Alternatively, we could respect individual privacy and manage this through government approval processes, such as currently done when claiming entitlements like social security or applying for a passport.

When should a person who lives in America, contributes to its development, swears to defend it, works, and pays taxes – and has done so for an extended period – be afforded some or all the protections of the Constitution?

When can an illegal entrant to America be permitted to remain and apply for citizenship, if ever? Is it enough if they have been registered for five years, contributed to society, paid taxes, raised a family, and sworn allegiance?

Our country's definition of who can claim to be an American is not absolute; it has changed over time and may further evolve in the future.

All Americans are born equal – equal to everyone else in the world, not just equal to others born in America. Everyone living in America, citizens or not, is born with certain inalienable rights. Our Declaration of Independence says so: "We hold these truths to be self-evident, that all Men are created equal, that they are endowed by their Creator with certain unalienable Rights, that among these are Life, Liberty and the pursuit of Happiness. ... That to secure these rights, Governments are instituted among Men, deriving their just powers from the consent of the governed." Of course, since this was written, our laws have been clarified to expand the meaning of Men to include all Americans.

Hopefully, one day, citizens worldwide will enjoy the same inalienable rights and opportunities as Americans do, including access to education, employment, voting, sustenance, healthcare, and all the other freedoms Americans cherish and Europe mostly does. In the meantime, America must uphold and defend the rights afforded by its democracy while welcoming others to join us whenever possible.

Identifying Illegal Aliens

E-Verify is a federal system used to confirm employment eligibility by comparing employee information with government records, but it has been frequently circumvented through identity fraud, including the use of stolen Social Security numbers or forged documents. Despite its intent, the system struggles to detect such fraud, limiting its effectiveness in preventing unauthorized employment. According to a study by Westat, approximately 54% of unauthorized workers screened by E-Verify were incorrectly found to be employment authorized, primarily due to identity fraud. This conclusion means that unauthorized workers were able to pass through the system by using someone else's valid information. To combat this, the Department of Homeland Security introduced the "Self Lock" feature, allowing individuals to lock their Social Security numbers in E-Verify to prevent misuse. However, this measure requires proactive participation and does not address the broader issue of systemic vulnerabilities.[425]

One approach to gaining better control over this problem may involve issuing a government "non-surveillable," blockchain controlled citizenship identity (ID) card, complete with a person's photograph, facial recognition, and contact information securely stored in a government database accessible only to authorized public officials and, with the given individual's permission, employers. Procedures would be needed for those whose identity is not confirmed. It may be time for all citizens to endorse the idea of a national ID card. The government already knows who most of us are, where we live, and where we work through social security, income tax reporting, Medicare, state driver's licenses, passports, TSA, Medicaid, and other databases. This proposal should be advanced in a non-partisan way if it is going to work. The ID must be identity-theft-proof, if possible.

Understanding how to identify illegal aliens is one aspect of examining societal dynamics, but a broader view of social structure reveals deeper divisions. Examining societal classes provides insight into how economic, political, and legal systems shape opportunities, influence mobility, and define group boundaries.

The Cycle of Class

One reason that there are classes or a hierarchy of roles in society is so that those below can serve those above. Societal classes and hierarchies are structured to serve those in higher positions, enabling the upper tiers to benefit from the labor and support of those below. While often justified as necessary for organizing labor or maintaining order, these hierarchies frequently reinforce the power and privileges of those at the top. Classes tend to be self-perpetuating as those in power exploit those in lower tiers. If you are among the top class, how do you keep the lower classes in their places? Keep them poor and dependent. You do this through low wages, high prices, and demanding jobs. When one struggles to survive, you will accept whatever job and income you can find. Class plays into the perspective of who qualifies for citizenship.

Variations in intellect, education, skills, and motivation contribute to the formation of social classes. While differences in ability and ambition can influence who attains positions of influence or wealth, the extent to which this process is genuinely meritocratic is debatable. In many cases, success is shaped not only by talent and effort but also by access to resources, education, and social connections. Systems often reinforce existing advantages, making it easier for those already in power to maintain their status while limiting opportunities for others.

Even when hierarchies are justified as necessary for governance or economic stability, they frequently concentrate wealth and decision-making authority at the top, creating a cycle where resources and influence flow upward. As the English poet observed, "The rich have become richer, and the poor have become poorer." Similarly, the Parable of the Talents (Matthew 25:29) states: "For to everyone who has, more will be given, and they will have an abundance. But from the one who has not, even what they have will be taken away."

Citizenship

A U.S. citizen is someone who has full citizenship rights in the United States. These include the right to vote, the right to live and work in the U.S., and the right to receive assistance from U.S. embassies and consulates while abroad. U.S. citizens can be either born in the United States, born abroad to U.S. citizen parents, or become naturalized citizens after meeting certain requirements. A U.S. national includes all U.S. citizens and certain individuals who are not citizens but owe their allegiance to the United States. The most common examples of U.S. nationals who are not citizens are people born in American Samoa or certain former citizens of the Trust Territory of the Pacific Islands. U.S. nationals who are not citizens have most of the rights of U.S. citizens, including the right to enter and live in the United States. However, they cannot vote in federal elections and are not eligible for specific government jobs.

Most Americans are unfamiliar with the rules around what constitutes citizenship. We all know that if you are born in America to American parents, you are automatically a citizen. Many people believe that citizenship in America gives them certain rights over those who are in America but not born here.

Birthright citizenship, a principle stating that any child born in the U.S. automatically becomes a citizen, subject to certain exceptions, is hotly debated. Some are claiming that the President has the right to modify this practice through executive order because it is not explicitly detailed in the Constitution. This stance challenges the precedent established by the Supreme Court's 1898 decision in United States v. Wong Kim Ark, which is considered "settled law" and affirms birthright citizenship for most children born on U.S. soil, regardless of their parents' citizenship status.

Volunteering for U.S. military service can provide a path to citizenship: lawful permanent residents may apply after one year of honorable service in peacetime; during designated periods of conflict, even non–green card holders may qualify; and all applicants must still meet requirements like good moral character, English proficiency, and civics knowledge.[426]

Naturalization

When does a person who lives in a country but was not born there become a citizen? This question is addressed in a variety of ways across different countries. Can a person become a citizen simply by asking for citizenship, passing a test, or by taking an oath? Under which conditions should a person be allowed to become a citizen? How much importance is placed on how a person came to be in the country?

As mentioned above, citizens by birth normally have full privileges. On the other hand, naturalized citizens, depending on the country to which they emigrated, may or may not be allowed full privileges. They may or may not be permitted to run for office, hold specific government jobs, or vote. These rights may change through marriage to a national. Some countries will grant citizenship if the person is willing to make a large capital investment in the country with long-lasting benefits as described above for the U.S. under EB-5.[39] A broader concept is an "earned right" – to become a citizen by fulfilling certain obligations, such as contributing one's money, time or labor.[40] Volunteering for military service

Limitations placed on naturalized citizens may affect their ability to hold higher public office.

To do so, in the United States, requires meeting specific constitutional eligibility criteria around age and residency; the president must be a "natural-born citizen." This requirement, however, does not imply that where you were born is directly linked to your loyalty to the country. The assumption that non-native-born individuals might inherently have divided loyalties is subjective and not a legal or universally acknowledged standard in U.S. governance. Those wishing to be employed in the public sector, particularly in sensitive roles within national security or intelligence agencies, must undergo stringent background checks and security clearances assessing various factors, including potential foreign ties. These checks are comprehensive and do not solely focus on the individual's place of birth; naturalized citizens who meet the security requirements may hold sensitive positions in the government. For most public jobs in the U.S., the primary requirement is legal citizenship or residency status, ensuring the individual's legal right to work in the country, rather than their place of birth.

Immigration

As a nation that values self-determination, the United States faces complex decisions about its immigration policies. Those with voting rights, representing the American populace, indirectly influence these policies through democratic processes. While established paths to citizenship exist, there is ongoing debate about whether these rules adequately or appropriately address current challenges.

It is reasonable to assert that, given America's size and global standing, structured immigration rules are necessary. However, managing these rules requires a careful balance between maintaining national security and upholding America's long-standing tradition of welcoming immigrants.

Concerns about unregulated immigration include the potential for criminal elements or security threats to enter the country. It is crucial to address these concerns with evidence-based policies that accurately assess and mitigate risks without unfairly stigmatizing entire groups of immigrants.

The vast majority of immigrants are motivated by the pursuit of a better life. While many arrive with limited resources, immigrants, particularly the younger generation, have the potential to contribute a wide and diverse range of benefits to our society, including through paying taxes that help to fund Social Security and other public programs, and filling jobs left open by our aging and shrinking population.

Immigration Impact

Immigration significantly influences U.S. population growth, presenting both opportunities and challenges. In 2023, the U.S. immigrant population increased by approximately 1.6 million, marking the largest single-year rise since 2000.[221]

Projections indicate that if immigration continues at a rate of 1.3 million to 2 million per year until 2050, the U.S. population could reach 439 million, compared to 345 million without such immigration levels.[222]

This growth may place additional demands on infrastructure, including housing, food production, water supplies, job markets, and government services. However, immigrants also contribute to economic growth by filling essential roles in the labor market and driving innovation.[223]

Balancing these factors is crucial for developing policies that manage population growth while leveraging immigration benefits.

Illegal Immigration

Illegal immigration remains an ongoing, complex issue in America without a straightforward solution. Given the vastness of our borders, extensive coastlines, and the openness of our society, curtailing illegal immigration without compromising personal privacy or security presents significant challenges.

It might seem hypocritical to refuse contemporary immigrants the same opportunities that were once available to earlier generations, many of whom are the ancestors of current citizens. This stance questions the fairness of those who arrived earlier or were born to families with deep American roots having a more legitimate claim to residency and citizenship than recent arrivals. It challenges us to consider the evolving nature of immigration and whether the principles that guided past policies should still hold true in a changing global context. This argument invites a reexamination of what it means to be an American and whether the rights and privileges associated with this identity should be equally accessible to all who seek them, regardless of their origin or date of arrival.

A national identity e-card may be seen by some as an unacceptable intrusion into their lives. Although logically you should only be concerned if you are doing something illegal. However, there could be the potential for abuse of power by law enforcement authorities, including depending on how the country addresses the illegal immigrants already residing in the country.

Official Rules of Citizenship

There are three main ways to become a citizen.

First: Birth within the United States

The Supreme Court has never explicitly ruled on whether children born in the United States to illegal immigrant parents are entitled to birthright citizenship via the Fourteenth Amendment, although it has generally been assumed that they are. A birth certificate issued by a U.S. state or territorial government is evidence of citizenship and is usually accepted as proof of citizenship.

In the case of United States v. Wong Kim Ark, 169 U.S. 649 (1898), the Supreme Court ruled that a person becomes a citizen of the United States at the time of birth, by virtue of the first clause of the Fourteenth Amendment of the Constitution, if that person:

- is born in the United States;
- has parents that are subjects of a foreign power, but not in any diplomatic or official capacity of that foreign power;
- has parents that have permanent domicile and residence in the United States; or
- has parents that are in the United States for business.

Second: Through Birth Abroad to Two United States Citizens

A child is automatically granted citizenship in the following cases:

- Both parents were U.S. citizens at the time of the child's birth.

- At least one parent lived in the United States prior to the child's birth.

The Immigration and Nationality Act (INA), the primary body of U.S. immigration law. It was enacted in 1952 and has since been amended multiple times. INA 301(c) and INA 301(a) (3) state, "and one of whom has had a residence." The FAM (Foreign Affairs Manual) states "no amount of time specified."

A person's record of birth abroad, if registered with a U.S. consulate or embassy, is proof of citizenship. They may also apply for a passport or a Certificate of Citizenship to have their citizenship recognized.

Third: Through Birth Abroad to One United States Citizen

A person born on or after November 14, 1986, is a U.S. citizen if all the following are true:

1. One of the person's parents was a U.S. citizen when the person in question was born.
2. The citizen parent lived at least five years in the United States before the child's birth.
3. A minimum of two of these five years in the United States were after the citizen parent's 14th birthday.

INA 301(g) provides additional ways to meet the physical presence requirement for U.S. citizenship by including time spent abroad in "honorable service in the Armed Forces of the United States" or employment with the U.S. government or an international organization. It also allows time spent abroad as the "dependent unmarried son or daughter and a member of the household" of someone in these roles to be counted toward the requirement.

A person born abroad can prove U.S. citizenship if their birth was registered with a U.S. consulate or embassy. They may also apply for a passport or a Certificate of Citizenship as official documentation, which can serve as proof of citizenship when an American birth certificate is unavailable.

Different rules apply to individuals born abroad to one U.S. citizen before November 14, 1986. U.S. laws on this subject changed multiple times throughout the 20th century, and the applicable law is the one in effect at the time of the person's birth.

Non-Citizens

As a country, we need to decide what rights non-citizens enjoy when on America's soil. Visitors should be protected as far as their inalienable rights, including being protected from discrimination, supported by the rule of law (U.S. law), and given basic emergency healthcare if needed.

If necessary to settle this issue, we should have a national referendum on the rules defining naturalization, and those, if any, that should be applied to "illegal" immigrants who have been living and working in America for an extended time.

DOMESTIC AFFAIRS

"Domestic affairs" refers to the governance and management of a nation's internal policies and priorities— issues that unfold within its borders and directly affect its citizens' daily lives. This broad domain encompasses law and order, public health, education, infrastructure, economic policy, social welfare, and disaster preparedness. The quality of a nation's domestic affairs often defines the lived experience of its people, shaping opportunities, freedoms, and general well-being.

Public debate over domestic policy frequently centers on the proper role of government. One prominent view favors an active government that addresses social and economic disparities, ensures access to essential services, and regulates industries in the public interest. Proponents of this approach support expanded healthcare access through mechanisms such as public insurance or universal coverage. They advocate increased investment in public education and relief from student debt, and they view progressive taxation as a way to fund social programs while reducing inequality. They emphasize strong regulation to combat pollution and climate change in environmental matters. This view holds that when used wisely, government can be a powerful tool for promoting fairness, social progress, and shared prosperity.

In contrast, a competing philosophy emphasizes limited government, individual liberty, and market-based solutions. Supporters of this approach generally seek to reduce taxes and scale back public spending, arguing that excessive government intervention weakens personal responsibility and slows economic growth. They often favor privatized alternatives to public services and minimal regulation of businesses, believing that free-market competition delivers better outcomes than bureaucracy. In education, they champion school choice and voucher programs, while in environmental policy, they stress energy independence and economic flexibility over federal mandates. This perspective sees the government's main role as protecting individual rights, enforcing the rule of law, and otherwise staying out of the way.

These diverging viewpoints reflect more profound philosophical questions: Should government be a proactive agent for social change or merely a neutral protector of rights? Should the scope of federal power be more clearly defined to prevent constant policy shifts when leadership changes hands? Or should the government retain the flexibility to adapt as society evolves, even if that means periodically reversing course? These are not abstract questions—they influence the laws we pass, the budgets we approve, and the social contract we uphold.

Domestic Aid and General Welfare

Domestic aid and general welfare policies aim to raise the standard of living and improve the quality of life for all citizens, particularly those facing hardship. These policies manifest in systems of support that include healthcare access, public education, retirement and disability income, affordable housing, and emergency relief. Programs such as Medicare, Medicaid, Social Security, and nutritional assistance have become pillars of the modern welfare state, seeking to ensure that citizens do not fall through the cracks of a complex economy.

These services are designed to protect the vulnerable and strengthen the nation by promoting social stability, economic productivity, and public health. They offer a safety net during times of crisis, a foundation for personal development, and a measure of dignity for the elderly and disabled. While critics caution that these programs can become fiscally unsustainable or foster dependency, supporters argue that they represent an essential investment in the nation's strength and unity.

Infrastructure Investment

Infrastructure investment is a cornerstone of domestic policy, influencing everything from safety and commerce to education and digital access. It includes maintaining and modernizing roads, bridges, transit systems, airports, utilities, and other public assets. Investment also increasingly extends to digital infrastructure, such as broadband internet, and institutional facilities like schools and hospitals.

Advocates for infrastructure spending argue that it enhances public safety, boosts economic competitiveness, and creates jobs. Economists often point out that every dollar spent on infrastructure can yield significant returns in productivity and efficiency. Yet critics raise valid concerns over mismanagement, inflated costs, and the accumulation of national debt. These debates intensify around large-scale federal initiatives such as the 2021 Infrastructure Investment and Jobs Act, which allocated over a trillion dollars to various infrastructure priorities. Implementation of such programs requires long-term planning, cross-sector cooperation, and sustained public oversight.

Disaster Response and Recovery

Effective disaster response and recovery depend on coordination among federal, state, and local governments and collaboration with private industry and nonprofit organizations. The nature of a disaster often determines the appropriate level of response. Local and state authorities typically take the lead when emergencies are contained within their jurisdiction. However, when a crisis overwhelms local resources—as seen in hurricanes, wildfires, or pandemics—the federal government is called upon to provide logistical support, financial aid, and technical expertise.

Recovery efforts go beyond the immediate aftermath. They involve rebuilding infrastructure, restoring services, and supporting communities as they return to normalcy. Successful recovery plans require foresight, clear communication, and a balance between environmental responsibility and regulatory efficiency. The COVID-19 pandemic, for instance, exposed gaps in national readiness and underscored the importance of clearly defined roles among agencies and levels of government. As climate change increases the frequency and severity of natural disasters, investing in resilience and preparedness has become a wise policy and a national imperative.

Domestic Security

The resilience of a nation's critical infrastructure is an essential component of its domestic security. Modern societies depend on complex systems of energy, water, transportation, and communication that must be robust and protected. Increasingly, experts advocate for burying utility lines underground to shield them from storms, fires, and sabotage. At the same time, concerns about emerging threats, such as electromagnetic pulse (EMP) attacks, have led policymakers to emphasize grid security and cyber defense.

Recognizing the vulnerabilities in existing infrastructure, Executive Order 13865, issued in 2019, directed the Department of Homeland Security to develop resilience and security standards to protect the U.S. electric grid from EMP threats. While the directive acknowledged the urgency of hardening national infrastructure, progress on implementation has been slow, and funding remains inconsistent. As global tensions and environmental threats rise, ensuring the integrity of power systems, communications networks, and emergency response capabilities is not merely a matter of efficiency but national survival.

ECONOMIC JUSTICE

The U.S. Constitution defines our governance structure, individual rights, and the distribution of federal powers. However, it does not specifically address economic justice challenges like wealth inequality, poverty, and corporate influence, leaving notable gaps in these areas. The lack of explicit economic guidance means that economic justice issues are left to be resolved through evolving legal interpretations (aka precedents).

Government Size

In the coming years, the government will likely reduce operational costs by leveraging artificial intelligence (AI) to automate tax auditing, data entry, customer service, and financial tracking tasks. To oversee and integrate these technological advancements effectively, establishing a Cabinet-level Secretary for Technology and Artificial Intelligence should be considered. This role would coordinate the integration of AI technologies across government functions, ensuring efficiency and innovation in public services.

Corporate Influence in Politics

The interplay between corporations and government has become a defining issue in modern American democracy. The controversial concept of corporate personhood, which grants corporations certain constitutional rights, has intensified debates around the limits of corporate power. Judicial decisions, such as *Citizens United v. FEC*, have empowered corporations to wield substantial influence in elections, allowing unrestricted political contributions under the claim of free speech. This has arguably led to a democratic system in which wealth equates to political power, sidelining the voices of everyday citizens.

Corporate influence affects policymaking on issues ranging from tax regulations to environmental protections and workers' rights. When corporate entities contribute millions to political campaigns, they effectively gain leverage over the elected officials whose campaigns they support. This dynamic raises ethical questions: Are these officials genuinely serving their constituents, or are they beholden to corporate interests? Aren't government officials supposed to corral corporations that are becoming monopolies? Critics argue that this erosion of democracy, fueled by corporate interests, distorts representation and enables legislation that favors profit over public welfare. In such an environment, the interests of working citizens, those whose labor fuels the economy, often take a back seat to the priorities of corporations and their shareholders.

Corporation Rights

Congress should better define the rights of corporations to ensure they are distinct and more limited than those of individuals. Equating corporate rights with those of individuals raises legal and ethical concerns, often leading to imbalances and gaps in the legal and economic systems. A thorough legal review by experts will be necessary to identify areas where corporate rights differ significantly from individual rights. This review would aim to establish clear legal distinctions, particularly in corporate speech, political contributions, and liability. The goal is to craft a legal framework that appropriately limits corporate rights, recognizing their unique role while protecting the rights and interests of individuals. The objective would be to align current law with the original intention of the Constitution, which did not anticipate extending citizen-like rights to corporate entities.

Corporate Influence

Efforts to address corporate influence and economic inequality have become a focal point in discussions on economic policy, with calls for reforms aimed at balancing corporate power, strengthening labor rights, and enhancing economic protections. One key area of debate is corporate personhood, with proposals to clarify that constitutional rights apply solely to individuals rather than corporate entities. Advocates argue that limiting corporate influence in political campaigns would help ensure elected officials remain accountable to the public rather than financial contributors.

Beyond political influence, labor rights remain central to economic policy discussions. Proposals emphasize fair wages, safe working conditions, and the right to collective bargaining to support workers and promote economic stability. Strengthening these protections could provide a counterbalance to corporate interests, fostering a more competitive and sustainable economy.

Efforts to reduce systemic poverty, establish a living wage, and promote economic mobility strive to create opportunities for all citizens, regardless of background. These initiatives reflect an ongoing discussion about economic fairness and the role of policy in shaping a more inclusive and balanced economic system.

From a different perspective, some argue that fostering economic mobility is best achieved through free-market solutions, reduced regulation, and incentivizing business growth. Excessive government intervention can stifle innovation, discourage job creation, and burden taxpayers. Instead, policies that lower taxes, reduce bureaucratic hurdles, and encourage personal responsibility are seen as more effective ways to expand opportunities and drive long-term prosperity.

Toward Greater Economic Oversight

As the nation navigates the complexities of modern economics and the growing divide between wealthier individuals and the broader population, the role of government intervention remains a key issue. Effective financial regulation, including oversight of banks and financial institutions, is critical in maintaining economic stability and preventing systemic risks. While corporations exert significant influence in policymaking, the federal government has historically implemented banking regulations to curb abuses and protect the economy. Examining the government's role in financial oversight reveals how regulatory frameworks intersect with economic policy and explores whether banking regulations can promote broader economic stability and fairness.

ECONOMIC OPTIONS

Self-sufficiency

Encouraging the return of manufacturing and other industries to the U.S. can be supported through advancements in automation, robotics (where Japan currently leads), and innovation. Protecting intellectual property through continuous technological progress is also essential. Reintroducing key domestic manufacturing sectors, such as steel production, as seen in the recent decision to block the sale of U.S. Steel to a Japanese company, and expanding computerized machine tooling capabilities could enhance self-sufficiency, particularly during a major military conflict.

Strengthening protections for U.S. companies' intellectual property remains a priority, especially with global competitors like China.

Democracy and Economic Systems

The Chicago School

This set of economic principles has been developed, studied, tested, and endorsed by the University of Chicago's Department of Economics members over the past century. These principles have influenced multiple presidential administrations through the Council of Economic Advisers and have shaped the perspectives of many economists working in federal financial agencies and on Wall Street. Economists from this tradition have collectively been associated with 34 Nobel Prizes in Economic Sciences and 12 John Bates Clark Awards, given to an American economist under 40 who has significantly contributed to economic thought and knowledge — more than any other university or group of economists worldwide.

The Chicago School is rooted in neoclassical price theory and strongly advocates for laissez-faire economics, emphasizing free markets, lower taxation, private sector regulation, and government-managed monetary policy. Their work is grounded in empirical studies and has historically aligned more closely with Republican economic perspectives than Democratic ones.

However, historical experience suggests that in some situations, a modified approach incorporating elements of Keynesian economics, which supports government intervention, has been effective. This approach has been more commonly associated with Democratic administrations.

Keynesian Economics

According to Investopedia, Keynesian economic theory argues that active government intervention in the marketplace and monetary policy is the most effective way to promote economic growth and stability. Supporters of Keynesian economics believe that the government should manage economic fluctuations by increasing spending and providing tax breaks during downturns to stimulate growth while reducing spending and raising taxes in strong economic periods to control inflation.

During the 2007-2008 financial crisis, the government intervened but did not implement broad tax cuts; instead, it adopted a mixed economic strategy. This approach aligns more closely with Democratic economic policies than Republican ones.

The Chicago School's economic approach is not inherently opposed to Democratic policies. In practice, measures such as rebates and stimulus checks can function similarly to temporary tax cuts, demonstrating that elements of both economic approaches can be used in different situations.

Recent Global Trends

A complex mix of global economic trends, technological advancements, shifts in trade policies, the impact of the COVID-19 pandemic, geopolitical tensions, environmental challenges, and socio-political changes has shaped our economy in recent years. While some aspects have adjusted naturally, consistent with the Chicago School's emphasis on market self-correction, other areas have required ongoing oversight and, at times, intervention to address persistent challenges and emerging issues, such as the wars in Ukraine and Palestine. Economic dynamics remain highly complex, requiring careful assessment and adaptive strategies.

Society of the Future and Economics

We can anticipate a future where traditional borders, though physically intact, become increasingly blurred conceptually. While physical borders remain important for national security, strengthening them efficiently requires modern approaches rather than outdated, impractical solutions.

The U.S. faces the challenge of managing over 7,479 miles of land, lake, and river borders, and 11,323 miles of coastline.[414] Even with extensive physical barriers, complete border security is impossible. A hypothetical scenario of placing guards every six feet along the border, requiring millions of personnel and hundreds of billions of dollars annually, underscores the impracticality of relying solely on labor or walls for security.

A more effective long-term solution to illegal immigration lies in addressing its root causes. Many migrants seek better economic opportunities in the U.S. because wages, even for low-paying jobs, exceed what they can earn in their home countries despite higher living costs here. Strengthening economic conditions abroad, particularly in Mexico, Central America, and South America, could reduce the pressure driving migration. Fewer would feel compelled to leave if people had viable opportunities at home.

Beyond physical borders, the boundaries of ideas and governance are evolving. Advances in communication and globalization have connected people in unprecedented ways, raising questions about the future of governance. If people worldwide shared common principles, technology could enable more interconnected, cooperative global governance. However, such an idea would face significant resistance from established power structures, national interests, and diverse ideological and religious perspectives.

The rule of law and law enforcement would remain critical concerns in a world where governance transcends borders. A major challenge would be nations where religious institutions or authoritarian regimes control government policy. The fundamental question is whether people, regardless of geography, should have the right to determine how they are governed. While global cooperation continues to grow, the feasibility of a unified system of governance remains a matter of debate.

2007-2008 Financial Crisis

Over the years, Neoclassical and Keynesian economic theories guided America's economic policy. Neoclassical economics emphasizes market efficiency with minimal regulatory interference, allowing markets to find their level.

In contrast, Keynesian economics advocates active government intervention to stabilize the economy during downturns and to boost employment.

The 2007-2008 financial crisis highlighted the limitations of both theories. Triggered by a housing market collapse and exacerbated by risky lending and complex financial products like mortgage-backed securities, the crisis showed the shortcomings of relying solely on market self-correction, as assumed by neoclassical economics. It also pointed out the need for more robust regulatory frameworks than what Keynesian policy had implemented at the time.

In response, the Dodd-Frank Wall Street Reform and Consumer Protection Act of 2010 was passed to increase oversight of the U.S. financial industry, including stricter capital requirements and better consumer protections. Basel III standards were introduced globally to strengthen bank capital requirements and risk management, a departure from prior economic policy, focusing on preventing the financial instability that led to the 2008 crisis. The Basel III standards enhance bank capital requirements, introducing a higher ratio of core equity capital to risk-weighted assets, a non-risk-based leverage ratio to curtail excessive leverage, and two key liquidity ratios — the Liquidity Coverage Ratio (LCR) and the Net Stable Funding Ratio (NSFR) to ensure banks maintain sufficient liquid assets and stable funding. These regulations aim to bolster the banking sector's robustness and risk management practices.

The Dodd-Frank Wall Street Reform and Consumer Protection Act is still in effect as of 2025. However, its regulatory strength has been diluted since its enactment. The Economic Growth, Regulatory Relief, and Consumer Protection Act of 2018 amended and weakened some aspects of Dodd-Frank, particularly affecting provisions related to bank stress tests and other regulatory requirements. Despite these changes, key elements of the Dodd-Frank Act continue to be enforced, aiming to oversee and regulate the financial industry to prevent the types of crises seen in 2007-2008. These reforms need to be protected to assure stability in our financial markets.

Inflation

Inflation is widely disliked due to its broad adverse effects. It reduces the purchasing power of money, creates economic uncertainty, disproportionately impacts fixed-income earners, distorts relative prices, leads to higher interest rates, erodes the value of savings and investments, and weakens international competitiveness. Additionally, inflation can create opportunities for price gouging, where businesses take advantage of rising costs to impose unfair price increases. Gouging can include tactics such as shrinking product sizes while maintaining prices ("shrinkflation"), raising prices faster than inflation justifies, keeping prices high even after inflation subsides, adding excessive fees, and obscuring profit-driven price hikes through hidden charges.

Responses to inflation often reflect differing economic philosophies. Some favor tighter monetary policies, such as raising interest rates and reducing the money supply, to curb inflationary pressures. Others support fiscal measures, including targeted government spending and tax policies, to lessen the burden on lower-income individuals and vulnerable communities. The debate over these approaches continues as policymakers seek to balance economic stability with growth and consumer well-being.

Rule of Law - Future

How might the rule of law function across borders? While achieving complete global legal uniformity is unrealistic due to cultural, political, and ideological differences, greater international cooperation in legal frameworks could enhance stability. Establishing universally accepted laws would require extensive negotiation, but enforcement would remain a significant challenge.

The larger the jurisdiction, the more complex and costly enforcement becomes. A practical approach may involve aligning broad legal principles, such as human rights protections, trade regulations, and environmental standards, while allowing local adaptation to account for national differences. While international agreements like the United Nations' Universal Declaration of Human Rights set aspirational goals, compliance and enforcement vary widely among nations. Some governments lack the resources to enforce laws effectively, while others choose to ignore or reinterpret global standards to fit their agendas.

One of the most significant challenges to international legal consistency is the role of sovereignty — each country retains the right to govern itself. Additionally, religious influence on governance, election integrity, and protections for freedoms like speech and assembly differ drastically worldwide. While democratic nations may favor greater transparency and citizen participation, authoritarian regimes are unlikely to accept external legal oversight. This reality limits the possibility of a truly unified global legal system.

Economic globalization has, in some ways, contributed to greater international cooperation, but it has not necessarily led to stronger democratic governance. While the U.S. has engaged in policies that expand global markets and trade, this has primarily been driven by economic interests rather than a deliberate effort to "level the playing field" in the name of democracy. Many nations engage in globalization for strategic and economic gain, not as a step toward global governance.

Is a fully unified system of governance possible in the foreseeable future? Given current geopolitical realities, probably not. However, increasing legal cooperation on specific global challenges, such as cybersecurity, climate change, and international crime, could be a realistic step toward a more connected and stable world.

The idea of a borderless legal system is intriguing but requires overcoming deeply entrenched national, ideological, and economic divisions. If a single global government is inevitable, far in the future, a practical interim approach would involve strengthening international legal agreements while respecting national autonomy. The challenge is not simply governance without borders but governance with cooperation, a goal that, while challenging, remains worth pursuing.

Administrative Government

Foreign Policy

It is to our benefit to help our strategic partners and our allies, of course. For a stronger world, we should help poor countries to develop as much as we can spare. We should consider economic protectionism only when defending against unfair trade practices (i.e., monopolies) and preserving critical natural resources. When other governments help their manufacturing companies, which then bid against American firms, our firms are at a disadvantage unless we help them to the same degree.

For example, Germany, France, Spain, and the UK were known for subsidizing Airbus. The World Trade

Organization (WTO) found that these EU member states provided subsidized loans for developing new aircraft, such as the Airbus A380 and A350. These subsidies were part of a longstanding dispute between the EU and the U.S. regarding unfair advantages in the aerospace industry.[59-06]

When to help our own citizens and when to be altruistic to the world is an ongoing challenge.

Globalization

Some nations, such as China, Russia, Venezuela, Iran, Vietnam, and North Korea, blend capitalist business practices with strict political control, often under the guise of socialism or communism. While they hold elections, these processes frequently lack transparency. Their governments are known for detaining individuals without fair trials, holding political prisoners, and suppressing dissent through censorship and secret police forces. Despite these governance concerns, the U.S. continues engaging with many nations in business and diplomacy.

U.S. trade and economic policies balance growth, national security, and ethical considerations. Globalization advocates stress fair trade, strong labor and environmental protections, and measures to shield American industries from unfair competition. Intellectual property protection, cybersecurity, and participation in international agreements help shape globalization to align with national interests.

Globalization also raises concerns about sovereignty, as some see international agreements as limiting national autonomy. Policymakers weigh the benefits of global cooperation against the need for independent decision-making.

Regulatory oversight, particularly by institutions like the Securities and Exchange Commission (SEC), helps maintain financial stability and integrity. As global markets evolve, legal frameworks may need updates to ensure international engagement benefits U.S. interests.

A strategic global presence remains crucial for national security and access to critical resources. Calls for more reciprocal terms in foreign aid and trade highlight the importance of clear agreements that protect long-term U.S. interests.

The Budget

While political parties often emphasize fiscal responsibility, budget balancing, and reducing national debt, these goals face significant challenges in practice. Frequent shifts in political power and long-term financial obligations, such as military spending and entitlement programs, make it difficult to maintain fiscal discipline and ensure long-term financial stability.

The budgetary process itself has also been criticized for lacking transparency and effectiveness. Since the enactment of the Budget Act of 1974, the federal government has operated under a complex system that some argue has worsened spending issues. The shift from the previous method of annual appropriation bills — where spending was debated with clearer oversight — to the current system has contributed to the rise of large omnibus spending bills. This approach can make controlling government growth and implementing meaningful fiscal reforms harder.[124]

A significant challenge in fiscal policy is that essential budget processes and financial management reforms remain difficult even when one party holds legislative power for an extended period. The complexities of the entrenched budgetary system often limit efforts to enhance transparency and establish greater control over government spending.

Each new administration inherits its predecessors' successes and challenges, navigating economic conditions shaped by previous policies and external events. For example, in 2008, the incoming administration faced the global financial crisis triggered by the collapse of the housing market and failures in major financial institutions. In response, the administration prioritized stimulus measures, including the American Recovery and Reinvestment Act of 2009, which allocated funds for infrastructure, education, healthcare, and renewable energy, as well as tax cuts and direct aid to struggling industries. This approach reflects the Keynesian economic theory that government spending during downturns can help stabilize the economy and encourage growth.

These dynamics highlight the difficulty of enacting lasting fiscal reforms, regardless of who is in power. The challenge of balancing competing economic forces is longstanding. Since the nation's founding, policymakers have struggled with tensions between self-interest and community, markets and governance, wealth concentration and economic opportunity, and the ongoing need for fiscal responsibility and public investment.[127]

No references have been found in documents authored by the Founding Fathers that directly address wealth concentration as a primary concern; their focus was mainly on preventing the concentration of political power — though excessive wealth could influence governance. However, the Constitution's structure, particularly its system of checks and balances and separation of powers, was designed to prevent any single entity, including economic interests, from overpowering the government.

U.S. political platforms often express a commitment to fiscal responsibility and economic stability, though their approaches reflect different priorities. One perspective emphasizes maintaining fiscal discipline to avoid burdening future generations with debt while investing in key areas such as infrastructure, education , and research to promote long-term economic growth. This approach supports a balanced tax code, stabilizing housing markets to prevent widespread foreclosures and fostering personal savings to ensure financial security and retirement stability.

Another perspective prioritizes minimizing high tax rates, arguing that they discourage savings and reduce investment returns. This view promotes policies that incentivize personal savings, encourage entrepreneurship, and reward self-reliance, hard work, and charitable initiatives. Proponents see economic freedom as a path to prosperity and a means for individuals and families to maintain independence, uphold personal values, and build self-sustaining communities.

These differing viewpoints reflect ongoing debates about how best to balance fiscal responsibility with investment in national priorities and how to empower individuals through economic policy.

Expenses

The largest expenses of the U.S. government, aside from administrative costs, are the entitlement programs, which include Social Security, Medicare, Medicaid, and broader healthcare services. These programs were initially designed to be funded by yearly revenue. However, in recent years and projections for the future, expenditures have outpaced income.

A significant factor contributing to this shortfall is the demographic shift caused by the aging "baby boomer" generation, leading to a surge in demand for these programs. When these entitlement programs were created, such a dramatic increase in beneficiaries was not anticipated. Compounding this issue, Congress did not take proactive measures to address the growing strain despite demographic warnings that have been evident since the late 1940s. Additionally, life expectancy has increased substantially, from 68 years in 1950 to 79 years in 2024, following a recovery from the temporary decline caused by the COVID-19 pandemic. This extended lifespan has amplified the financial pressures on entitlement programs, contributing to the gap between revenue and expenses.[59-21,22]

At this point, if you are a proponent of a balanced budget, action is needed – whether that is reducing benefits, changing the qualifying criteria, or increasing the population (i.e., number of people contributing) through increased immigration or absorption of illegal immigrants.

Debt

The difference between income and expenditure for the U.S. government results in a surplus or deficit, with deficits being more common historically. In the 237 years since our Constitution was signed, our government only ran a surplus budget in 14 years.

Budget Surplus Years by Party[56]					
Year	President	Party	House	Senate	Surplus
1791	Washington	Federalist	Federalist	Federalist	$ 1,949,926
1836	Jackson	Democratic	Whig	Whig	$ 39,430,255
1837	Van Buren	Democratic	Whig	Whig	$ 6,492,969
1846	Polk	Democratic	Whig	Whig	$ 5,546,619
1880	Hayes	Republican	Democratic	Democratic	$ 47,335,653
1881	Garfield	Republican	Republican	Republican	$ 81,690,473
1882	Arthur	Republican	Republican	Republican	$ 145,723,269
1907	T. Roosevelt	Republican	Republican	Republican	$ 89,015,565
1947	Truman	Democratic	Republican	Republican	$ 31,797,512,449
1948	Truman	Democratic	Republican	Republican	$ 11,705,000,000
1998	Clinton	Democratic	Republican	Republican	$ 69,000,000,000
1999	Clinton	Democratic	Republican	Republican	$124,000,000,000
2000	Clinton	Democratic	Republican	Republican	$230,000,000,000
2001	G. W. Bush	Republican	Republican	Republican	$128,000,000,000

The U.S. federal budget deficit has experienced significant fluctuations in recent years. In fiscal year (FY) 2020, the deficit reached approximately $3.1 trillion, primarily due to extensive pandemic-related spending on economic stimulus measures and public health responses during the COVID-19 crisis. The following year, FY 2021, saw a decrease in the deficit to $2.8 trillion, followed by a further reduction to $1.375 trillion in FY 2022. However, in FY 2023, the deficit increased to $1.7 trillion. The most recent data indicates that for FY 2024, which ended on September 30, the deficit grew to $1.8 trillion, marking the third-largest federal deficit in U.S. history outside the pandemic era.[362]
An analysis of fiscal performance over these years suggests neither political party can claim consistent superiority in budget management. The capacity to control the budget is influenced less by party-specific policies and more by prevailing economic conditions and significant external events, such as global conflicts and public health emergencies, which play a dominant role in shaping fiscal outcomes. Ultimately, repeated annual deficits contribute cumulatively to the nation's total debt, underscoring the complex challenges of long-term fiscal sustainability.

Growing Debt

Can the U.S. continue to sustain its growing debt? The real issue is not just the debt's size but its long-term sustainability. A key metric to consider is the gross domestic product (GDP) ratio to national debt. When this ratio exceeds 100%, the country owes more than it produces in a year through economic activities. Such a scenario can raise concerns among creditors (bondholders). Persistent, large deficits without a credible reduction plan can result in serious financial repercussions, including inflation, reduced investor confidence, and higher interest rates.

Higher interest rates, in turn, compound the problem by increasing the cost of servicing the debt, which places a greater burden on the national budget. This escalating financial obligation can restrict funding for crucial domestic programs and infrastructure projects, ultimately impacting economic growth and stability. Addressing these challenges requires strategic fiscal planning to ensure that the national debt remains manageable and does not stifle future economic potential.[101]

In January 2009, the United States faced a significant fiscal challenge, with the federal deficit for fiscal year 2009 reaching a record $1.4 trillion. This surge was driven mainly by the global financial crisis, which led to substantial government interventions, including stimulus spending and financial sector bailouts. At the time, the deficit relative to the economy was the highest since World War II, reflecting a bipartisan effort to stabilize and recover from the economic downturn.

Policymakers proposed pay-as-you-go budgeting rules to address these fiscal challenges, requiring that new spending or tax changes not increase the deficit. Strategies to uphold these rules included winding down U.S. military involvement in Iraq, reducing inefficiencies in government programs, generating revenue through carbon pricing, and closing tax loopholes benefiting special interests and high-income earners. These measures were intended to promote fiscal responsibility while supporting economic recovery and long-term stability.

For years, political parties have pledged to eliminate waste in government programs, yet this often results in one party discontinuing a previous administration's initiatives while introducing new programs that ultimately cost the same or more. The steadily increasing national debt supports this observation.

Radical budget restructuring is difficult unless one party controls the White House, the House, and the Senate. Even then, neither party has significantly reduced government spending. Both advocate for transparency and efficiency, but competing priorities and policy differences often block reform.

Party positions on budgeting, taxation, income redistribution, and national debt shape social programs and economic policy, yet external events—like security threats or recessions—frequently disrupt plans. Achieving a balance between growth, fiscal discipline, and social investment remains a persistent challenge.

A classic economic concept, the "Guns vs. Butter" model, illustrates the trade-off between military and civilian spending. "Guns" represent defense; "Butter" refers to programs such as education, healthcare, and food. Because national resources are limited, governments must choose how to allocate funds.

Increased military spending often reduces resources for domestic programs, especially during times of conflict. Understanding this balance is essential for evaluating national economic policy and long-term priorities.

ENTITLEMENTS

Social Security Outlook

According to the Social Security Administration's 2024 Trustees Report, the Old Age and Survivors Insurance (OASI) Trust Fund reserves are projected to be depleted by 2033. At that point, income would be sufficient to pay only 79% of scheduled benefits.[364]

With reasonable changes to its funding and temporary subsidization for a few years, Social Security, funded through dedicated payroll taxes separate from regular income taxes, should be sustainable. It provides crucial financial support through retirement, disability, and survivor benefits. As of early 2024, the Social Security Trust Fund, which includes the Old-Age and Survivors Insurance (OASI) and Disability Insurance (DI) Trust Funds, held accumulated reserves of approximately $2.8 trillion. These funds have been built up from the many years when payroll tax revenues exceeded the costs of the programs. In fiscal year 2024, which ended on September 30, 2024, the Social Security Trust Funds received approximately $1.404 trillion in total income. This income comprised net payroll tax contributions of $1.283 trillion, taxation of benefits amounting to $53.7 billion, and interest and other income totaling $67.4 billion. During the same period, total expenditure was about $1.461 trillion, resulting in a net decrease in asset reserves.[363]

This financial setup ensures sufficient funds to cover future benefits, with the reserves invested primarily in special issue U.S. Treasury securities to earn interest and grow the fund over time.[309-311]

The Social Security Board of Trustees forecasts that, without program adjustments, the Social Security Trust Fund will be depleted by 2035. This projection indicates that by then, Social Security will begin paying out more in benefits than it collects in taxes and interest, marking a critical shift that could impact millions of beneficiaries. To provide context for this impending shortfall, projected Social Security costs over the next 40 years are as follows:

- **2023**: $1.2 trillion
- **2033**: $2.2 trillion
- **2043**: $3.2 trillion
- **2053**: $4.2 trillion
- **2063**: $5.2 trillion

These projections assume an annual economic growth rate of 2.1%, an unemployment rate averaging 4.7%, and an inflation rate of 2.3%, below the historical average inflation rate of 3%. Additionally, the trustees assume that the average life expectancy will continue to rise, a demographic factor that further influences Social Security's solvency as it lengthens the period that beneficiaries receive payments. However, as projections, these figures could fluctuate based on unforeseen changes in economic and demographic trends.[59-16, 17, 18]

Options to Address the Shortfall

To address the projected shortfall in the Social Security Trust Fund, we must pursue practical, citizen-focused reforms that strengthen the program without compromising its core purpose. First, we need to increase the number of contributors by reversing our shrinking working population. Expanding our population means encouraging immigration policies that welcome younger workers and investing in job creation, especially to offset expected job losses from automation and AI. We should prioritize bringing in energetic, productive workers — not billionaires who contribute little to the system. Second, as life expectancy rises, gradually raising the eligibility age for benefits is a sensible adjustment. Third, eliminating the income cap on Social Security payroll taxes would ensure high earners contribute on all their income, just as lower-income workers do. Fourth, 100% of the federal income taxes collected on Social Security benefits should be directed to the Trust Funds rather than allowing a large portion to flow into the general fund for unrelated expenses. Redirecting this revenue could extend the program's life by up to $100 billion annually. Finally, we must reject any proposal to privatize Social Security or turn it over to Wall Street. The program was built to be stable and reliable, not subject to market risk. These reforms are bipartisan, reasonable, fair, and urgently needed.

Each option comes with trade-offs, including economic impacts on the general fund, potential changes in retirement security, and varied effects on different demographics within the program.

The Impact of Demographic Shifts on Social Security

A significant demographic shift is affecting Social Security's financial health. As the baby boomer generation retires, the number of beneficiaries is increasing faster than the growth of the workforce contributing to the system. According to the Social Security Administration's 2024 Trustees Report, the Old Age and Survivors Insurance (OASI) Trust Fund reserves are projected to be depleted by 2033. At that point, income would be sufficient to pay only 79% of scheduled benefits.[364]

Medicare and Medicaid

The challenges faced by entitlement programs have increasingly become a focus of concern, spurring discussions on ensuring their long-term sustainability and effectiveness. While both major political parties acknowledge the urgent issues within these programs, there is a shared interest in bolstering personal pension plans as a complementary strategy for financial security in retirement. Personal investment accounts have been proposed to empower individuals to take a more proactive role in their retirement savings. However, the success of this approach hinges on individuals' ability to save consistently, manage investment portfolios effectively, and handle the complexities associated with financial markets.

Medicare and Medicaid, which will be covered later, are two of the most extensive and expensive federal programs. They face similar pressures from demographic changes and escalating healthcare costs. Addressing these challenges involves reducing costs through greater efficiency, negotiating drug prices, and promoting market competition to lower expenses. Proposed healthcare reforms focus on improving access and affordability, potentially through adjustments to the Affordable Care Act, introducing a public option, or expanding Medicare coverage. Other key reform priorities include modernizing healthcare infrastructure, expanding mental health and substance abuse treatment, and enhancing pandemic preparedness.

As the workforce-to-retiree ratio is projected to decline from 3.3 workers per retiree to just 2.1 by 2034, revitalizing Medicare and Medicaid to ensure their long-term resilience has become increasingly important. Proposed measures to achieve this include incentivizing high-quality care, fostering competition among healthcare providers, and enhancing public health through adaptable partnerships with state programs. This approach highlights a shared responsibility between federal and state governments, promoting innovative healthcare delivery models that respond to shifting demographic needs.

The balance between government support and personal responsibility remains a central theme. While there is broad support for ensuring the government provides fundamental protections, many also believe individuals should bear responsibility for their basic needs and lifestyle choices, including retirement, healthcare, and everyday expenses. As these discussions continue, the future of entitlement programs will likely reflect a blend of public and private solutions designed to adapt to the country's changing demographic and economic landscape.

Current Statistics on Medicaid:

As of October 2024, approximately 72 million individuals were enrolled in Medicaid, with an additional 7.2 million children covered under the Children's Health Insurance Program (CHIP). These programs provided health coverage to over 79 million people across the United States.[365] In 2023, Medicaid spending grew 7.9% to $871.7 billion, accounting for 18% of national health expenditures.[366]

Medicaid's role in the U.S. healthcare system highlights the importance of ongoing discussions about its sustainability and effectiveness.

The Affordable Care Act (ACA)

The ACA, enacted in 2010, has significantly influenced the U.S. healthcare landscape by expanding access to insurance and implementing consumer protections. As of early 2024, over 45 million individuals were enrolled in ACA-related coverage, including both Marketplace plans and

Medicaid expansion, marking the highest enrollment to date.[367]

During the 2024 Open Enrollment Period, a record 21.3 million people selected Marketplace health plans, with approximately 5 million being new enrollees.[368]

Despite these gains, the ACA faces ongoing challenges. The enhanced premium subsidies, which have made coverage more affordable for many, are set to expire at the end of 2025 unless extended by Congress. If these subsidies lapse, millions could see significant increases in insurance costs, potentially leading to a rise in the uninsured population.[369]

The ACA's future remains a subject of political debate, with discussions focusing on balancing accessibility, affordability, and the extent of government involvement in healthcare. As the law enters its second decade, its impact on reducing the uninsured rate and expanding coverage continues to be a pivotal aspect of U.S. healthcare policy.

EDUCATION

It seems reasonable to observe that a nation as wealthy as the United States ought to provide its people with the basics: access to education, healthcare, food, and shelter— whether through well-paying jobs or a functioning safety net. These aren't just ideals tied to political leanings; they echo the broader American values of fairness, opportunity, and the pursuit of happiness. While some emphasize the government's role in guaranteeing a minimum standard of living, others highlight the importance of personal effort and responsibility. Both views can coexist. For instance, it's hard to argue against the idea that every child deserves a solid education and that no one should go without basic healthcare in a country with our resources. Still, people should be expected to carry their share once those foundational needs are covered. Rewarding effort, allowing wealth to accumulate within fair limits, and encouraging independence are not in conflict with decency but rather part of it. And for those who fall through the cracks or are unable to work, targeted support programs should step in, not to foster dependence, but to help people get back on their feet.

Remarkably, neither the U.S. Constitution nor the Bill of Rights guarantees the right to an education. In a nation where education is the foundation of personal success and national prosperity, this gap has led to disparities based on geography, income, and other factors. While public education exists in all states, its quality and effectiveness vary widely.

Students should be allowed to pursue a traditional academic education, a trade school, or other path compatible with their interests and skills. High schools should provide a well-rounded curriculum that includes arts, shop classes, physical education, music, theater, civics, classical literature,

Latin, foreign languages, and geography. Exposing students to various disciplines early on allows them to explore their interests before choosing a specialized career or educational path after high school.

A balanced approach to these issues is essential. While government ensures that basic opportunities are available to all, individuals must also take responsibility for their own lives. The ongoing challenge is to balance guaranteeing access to essential services and maintaining incentives for self-reliance and economic growth.

Public Education

The great equalizer! Public education is one of the longest-standing American "implied rights." Despite this Constitutional oversight, it has played a crucial role in distinguishing America globally, serving as one of the greatest opportunities for class equalization. Public education, typically encompassing primary and secondary levels (grade school and high school), is managed at the state and local levels rather than federally. States can also certify private schools and establish standards for homeschooling, while higher education often benefits from government subsidies and oversight.

The origins of public education trace back to medieval schools for the poor, which were introduced to America through religious institutions such as those established by the Puritans and Quakers. This early model gradually evolved, becoming institutionalized by the mid-1800s.

The first public schools resembling today's system were established in Massachusetts in the 1850s. Notably, literacy levels were already high in parts of colonial America; for instance, Connecticut had modern levels of literacy before the Revolutionary War. Public education in New Orleans dates back to the 1830s and remained independent until the

20th century, even after the Reconstruction era saw state-wide public school initiatives in the late 1860s.[116]

The significance of education has been recognized throughout American history. However, the Constitution did not formalize federal involvement, leaving the development and management of schooling mainly to state and local authorities. Over time, federal funding and policies have become essential to the functioning of public education, with current expenditures exceeding $25 billion annually. This funding helps close educational access and quality gaps, supports students with special needs and low-income backgrounds, and advances national priorities such as STEM education and school safety.

Thomas Jefferson was a noteworthy historical advocate for public education who recognized its critical role in sustaining a democratic society. He tried establishing free public schools in Virginia, underscoring the importance of accessible education. However, his efforts were unsuccessful due to the legislature's reluctance to levy school taxes. This early attempt highlights the complex relationship between government support, local control, and funding in shaping the landscape of American education. The debate over public education funding, including concerns about programs like school vouchers and their constitutional implications, continues to reflect broader issues surrounding the balance between state, local, and federal oversight.

Censorship

Initially, schools operated with minimal oversight from federal and state governments, emphasizing local control over education funding, primarily supported through local property taxes. Over time, state and federal involvement increased, with significant federal expansion occurring in the

20th century, notably marked by the establishment of the Department of Education in 1979 and the passing of various educational laws.

Efforts to restrict sexually-graphic books in schools were initially seen as measures to protect children, aligning with the principle of "protecting the welfare and safety of all citizens." However, a potential contradiction emerges when similar justifications are used to advocate for gun restrictions in the name of public safety, underscoring the complexities of balancing protection with constitutional rights.

Curriculum Censorship Versus Guns

The debate over banning books (censorship) and regulating guns involves two constitutional rights: the First Amendment's protection of free speech and the Second Amendment's right to bear arms. Courts interpret these rights differently based on legal precedents, public interest, and historical context, leading to debates over their application.

Under the First Amendment, the right to access information is not absolute. Courts allow schools to set content guidelines to ensure age-appropriate material aligns with educational goals. However, disputes arise when book restrictions are seen as excessive censorship or politically motivated decisions rather than educational choices.

Similarly, the Second Amendment protects gun ownership but allows for regulations. The U.S. Supreme Court has ruled that gun rights are not unlimited and can be subject to reasonable restrictions. The scope of these regulations remains a point of ongoing debate, balancing public safety with constitutional protections.

The differences in how these rights are applied stem from varying legal standards and societal values. Courts weigh individual rights against public welfare, and interpretations evolve as societal norms shift.

In education, debates over curriculum content and censorship highlight differences in views on free speech, academic freedom, and parental rights. Some argue that exposing students to diverse viewpoints fosters critical thinking, while others emphasize parental involvement in shaping curricula to reflect community values. The politicization of education has intensified debates on how schools address topics such as gender identity, historical narratives, and cultural perspectives.

Balancing academic freedom with an inclusive curriculum that reflects historical accuracy and diverse viewpoints is challenging. Local governments and school boards play a central role in these discussions, requiring careful dialogue to ensure education prepares students for an increasingly complex world.

Much of the debate centers on <u>when</u> students should be introduced to complex topics, rather than <u>whether</u> they should learn about them. In today's digital world, students are often exposed to different perspectives through online media before parents or schools address them. Ethical reasoning and moral values can be taught in secular education through principles such as fairness, empathy, and civic responsibility.

Project HeadStart

As mentioned above, public education is considered a vital societal equalizer and holds a special place in the American ethos. While the U.S. Constitution does not explicitly guarantee the right to education, the federal government has promoted equitable access through initiatives like Project Head Start. Launched in 1965 under President Lyndon B. Johnson, Head Start aims to support children from low-income families by providing comprehensive education, health, nutrition, and parental engagement services. The program operates by awarding grants directly to local public, private non-profit, and for-profit agencies, thereby reducing bureaucratic inefficiencies associated with additional state administrative layers.

The federal government's involvement in education, health, and social services is often justified through the General Welfare Clause (Article I, Section 8) of the Constitution, which empowers Congress to promote the common welfare. Over the years, Project Head Start has experienced fluctuations in enrollment. During 2022–2023, the program served approximately 799,901 children and pregnant women. However, workforce shortages have impacted the program's ability to operate at full capacity, decreasing funded enrollment from 827,572 in the 2022–2023 program year to 778,420 in the 2023–2024 program year. These staffing challenges have prompted many programs to develop action plans to address or mitigate under-enrollment.[370-371]

In fiscal year 2024, Head Start received approximately $12.27 billion in federal funding, providing all grant recipients with a 2.35% cost-of-living adjustment. This funding equates to an average expenditure of about $12,270 per child. While this figure may seem substantial, research by Nobel laureate James Heckman indicates that high-quality early childhood education programs can yield a return of $7 to $10 for every dollar invested, primarily through higher lifetime earnings and reduced crime and incarceration rates.[372-374]

Despite its benefits, Project Head Start faces significant challenges, particularly in retaining and recruiting qualified teachers. Many educators leave for better-paying jobs in other sectors, leading to classroom closures and under-enrollment. To combat this, the Office of Head Start has implemented the Full Enrollment Initiative, targeting significantly under-enrolled programs. Proposed measures to improve recruitment and retention include increasing wages for Head Start staff to make positions more competitive.

Children from impoverished and disadvantaged backgrounds often start public education at a substantial disadvantage. Their families may lack resources such as education, childcare, transportation, and funds for school-related expenses. Early education should commence as early as age two to give these children a fair opportunity. Without this early intervention, they may continually lag behind their more privileged peers, who benefit from supportive home environments, proper nutrition, and broader learning opportunities.

To better prepare all children for academic success and support family development from an early age, Project Head Start should be revitalized to enhance its effectiveness and expand its use. Encourage parents to enroll their infants and toddlers in Early Head Start, which serves children from birth to age three. This program precedes the main Head Start program for children aged three to five. Both provide early childhood education, health services, and family support.

Trade Skills vs Critical Thinking Skills

The debate between focusing education on trade skill training versus fostering critical thinking skills is significant, reflecting differing perspectives on the primary goals of education. Proponents of trade skill training argue that the education system should equip students with specific skills that prepare them directly for the workforce, potentially leading to immediate employment after graduation. This view is often driven by concerns over job readiness and the desire to meet the immediate needs of industries that require specific technical competencies. Trade skills are seen as a direct investment in the economy, providing a skilled workforce that can fulfill current labor demands, thereby supporting individual career success and broader economic growth.

On the other hand, advocates focused on critical thinking argue that education should cultivate well-rounded individuals who can think independently, reason logically, and approach problems with creativity and adaptability. From this perspective, education is not merely about job preparation but about developing the intellectual flexibility needed to thrive in a complex, rapidly changing world. This approach emphasizes the importance of the arts, humanities, and social sciences—disciplines that teach students to question assumptions, analyze multiple perspectives, and synthesize information across contexts. Supporters maintain that critical thinking skills are essential for personal growth and sustaining a healthy democracy, fostering innovation, and navigating emerging challenges such as misinformation, global conflict, and ethical dilemmas in technology. While vocational training prepares students for specific careers, critical thinking–centered education equips them with the broader skills to adapt, lead, and contribute meaningfully to any field.

Both approaches have merits, and some educational theorists suggest that the most effective education systems might find a balance between the two. These systems integrate skill-specific training with a strong foundation in critical thinking to prepare students for immediate employment and long-term career success. This blended approach can offer students the practical skills they need to enter the workforce while providing the critical thinking abilities necessary to navigate complex life and work environments effectively.

Art in Secondary Schools

The inclusion of art education in secondary schools, often a subject of political debate, plays a crucial role in well-rounded academic development. Art fosters creativity, enables students to express themselves in new ways, and develops transferable skills applicable to science, technology, and business. Additionally, studying art enhances cultural and historical awareness by exposing students to diverse perspectives and forms of expression. Analyzing and interpreting artwork sharpens critical thinking, a skill valuable in both professional and personal contexts.

As of 2024, recent reports indicate a concerning trend: approximately 55% of school districts have either cut or significantly reduced funding for arts programs, leading to their diminished presence or complete elimination in some areas.[375]

This reduction in funding has resulted in only 69% of middle school students and 47% of high school students having art education integrated into their studies, leaving over two million students nationwide without any access to arts instruction.[376]

Art education also strengthens communication skills, helping students articulate complex thoughts and emotions through visual and verbal expression. Beyond cognitive and expressive benefits, engaging in artistic activities supports emotional intelligence by fostering empathy and mental well-being. The physical act of creating art improves fine motor skills and hand-eye coordination, while the discipline required for artistic projects teaches perseverance and focus. Completing creative work instills a sense of accomplishment and boosts confidence, contributing to overall personal growth.

Art education provides essential foundational skills and knowledge for students interested in creative careers. It also ensures a balanced curriculum, complementing analytical subjects and supporting holistic development. As artificial intelligence plays a growing role in visual and auditory arts, proficiency in digital art tools is becoming increasingly crucial for future career opportunities. Art education remains vital to cultivating creative, adaptable individuals with a broad range of critical life skills.

Private Education

Faith-Based Schools and the Constitution

Faith-based schools occupy a unique place in American education, raising essential questions about the relationship between religion and the Constitution. The First Amendment guarantees the free exercise of religion and prohibits the establishment of religion, shaping the legal framework for these institutions. Faith-based schools reflect the free exercise clause, allowing religious communities to establish educational institutions that align with their beliefs and values. At the same time, their interaction with public funding and policy brings the Establishment Clause into focus, which prohibits government actions that promote or favor a specific religion, reinforcing the separation of church and state.

A key constitutional issue surrounding faith-based schools is public funding. Supreme Court rulings such as Everson v. Board of Education (1947) and Espinoza v. Montana Department of Revenue (2020) have established that public funds can, under certain conditions, be used to support faith-based schools if they are part of a neutral program that does not favor or exclude specific religions. For example, school voucher programs and tuition tax credits have been upheld when they offer parents a choice between secular and religious schools. However, these rulings remain controversial, and legal challenges will shape how these policies evolve.

Faith-based schools also play a central role in debates over curriculum and admissions policies. Unlike public schools, they are exempt from many government regulations, allowing them to integrate religious instruction and set faith-based admissions criteria. This autonomy is protected under the First Amendment, but it must be balanced against anti-discrimination laws and the rights of employees and students. Cases such as Our Lady of Guadalupe School v. Morrissey-Berru (2020) have reinforced the ministerial exception, which gives religious schools greater leeway in employment decisions, particularly regarding teachers involved in religious instruction. However, this has sparked ongoing debate about where constitutional protections end and whether such exemptions could lead to unfair treatment of employees.

As legal precedents continue to develop, the role of faith-based schools in American education remains a complex and evolving issue, balancing religious freedom, government neutrality, and civil rights.

Religions and Taxation

Another constitutional issue surrounding faith-based schools is the tax-exempt status of religious institutions, including churches and affiliated schools. Under Section 501(c)(3) of the Internal Revenue Code, these institutions are exempt from property and income taxes, a policy rooted in the First Amendment's free exercise and establishment clauses. Supporters argue that this exemption protects religious freedom by allowing faith-based organizations to operate independently of government influence. They contend that taxing these institutions could lead to government entanglement in religious affairs, potentially violating the separation of church and state.

Critics, however, question this arrangement's financial and equity implications, particularly regarding the significant wealth accumulated by some religious organizations. Large churches, especially mega-churches, often hold extensive property and investments and receive substantial donations, all of which remain untaxed despite their considerable economic influence. Opponents argue that some institutions amass wealth far beyond what is necessary for religious or charitable purposes, allowing them to function similarly to commercial enterprises while benefiting from tax exemptions. This technique reduces the overall tax base, shifting financial burdens onto other taxpayers, particularly in communities where religious organizations own large amounts of property. Some critics argue that these exemptions create an uneven playing field, giving faith-based schools and organizations financial advantages that secular private entities do not always receive.

Under the Internal Revenue Code, Section 501(c)(3) organizations, which include churches and religious institutions, are strictly prohibited from directly or indirectly participating in political campaigns on behalf of or in opposition to any candidate for public office. This prohibition encompasses contributing to political campaign funds or issuing public statements endorsing or opposing candidates. Violations of this rule can lead to the revocation of tax-exempt status and the imposition of certain excise taxes.[377]

Despite these regulations, there have been instances where churches, including some mega-churches, have engaged in political activities that may cross the line into prohibited territory. For example, reports have highlighted cases where churches have made political endorsements or engaged in activities that could be interpreted as political campaign intervention.[377]

Enforcement of these prohibitions by the Internal Revenue Service (IRS) has been inconsistent. While the law restricts political campaign intervention by 501(c)(3) organizations, the IRS has been criticized for not consistently enforcing these rules, leading to ongoing debates about the appropriate role of religious organizations in political processes.[378]

While mega-churches and other religious organizations are legally barred from contributing to political campaigns, there has been documented political involvement, sometimes leading to legal challenges and debates over enforcement. This controversy highlights the broader challenge of balancing religious liberty with tax fairness and public accountability. As concerns grow over the wealth and influence of certain religious institutions, the non-taxation of faith-based schools and churches remains a contested issue at the intersection of constitutional law and economic policy.

What Education Needs

Education in America faces growing demands but often lacks a clear, unified vision for meeting them. The system needs more than funding to prepare students for a rapidly changing world—it requires thoughtful leadership, relevant curriculum expansion, and stronger connections between communities and classrooms. Local school boards play a crucial role in shaping educational priorities yet often operate under outdated frameworks or political pressure. A modern approach to education must balance foundational skills with broader critical thinking, civic understanding, and real-world readiness, ensuring that all students are equipped to thrive, not just graduate.

Local Education Boards

Local governments should promote greater citizen engagement in school boards to help safeguard classrooms from political or religious bias. The primary focus of education should remain on cultivating critical thinking, foundational knowledge, and the open-mindedness essential for lifelong success. Since school boards are often the front lines of debates over curriculum and censorship, active community involvement is vital to ensuring balanced, inclusive, and practical education policies.

Expanding School Curriculum

Strengthen school curricula by incorporating broader lessons in morals, manners, ethics, values, laws, civics, and financial literacy. These additions will help equip students to navigate an increasingly competitive world and understand and support the principles of our form of government.

ENERGY POLICY AND ENVIRONMENTAL STEWARDSHIP

The role of energy in a nation's economy is essential, whether the country is a producer or consumer. Equally significant is energy's impact on the environment. Many forms of energy production contribute to carbon emissions, which scientists widely recognize as a key factor in global warming. However, debates continue over the extent of human impact, the best policy responses, and how to balance economic and environmental priorities.

The oil and coal industries, which have long been central to the energy sector, often advocate policies that support their continued viability while resisting regulations that could increase costs. At the same time, other companies are investing in alternative energy sources, recognizing both economic opportunities and environmental benefits. Some industry groups and political organizations have challenged aspects of climate science or policy proposals, contributing to public debate over energy priorities and environmental regulations.

As fossil fuel reserves are finite and being consumed rapidly, long-term energy security remains an important issue, but raises key questions: Are current energy consumption patterns sustainable? Would it be more strategic to prioritize domestic conservation while utilizing surplus oil from countries with abundant reserves? Such an approach could extend resources for future needs while maintaining energy stability. However, any strategy must also involve continued investment in alternative energy to ensure a balanced and sustainable future.

Energy

With unchecked growth, the world faces increasing pressure on vital resources such as food, fuel, and potable water. While technological advancements have mitigated some challenges, the Earth's finite resources cannot sustain indefinite growth or even a static population forever without proper management. For example, oil, natural gas, and rare minerals, including helium — a critical resource for medical imaging, scientific research, and space exploration — are non-renewable. Once depleted or, in helium's case, released into the atmosphere, they cannot be replaced within a human timescale.

Fortunately, global population growth is beginning to slow. The annual growth rate, which peaked at 2.2% in 1963, is projected to decline to approximately 0.85% by 2025, mainly due to declining fertility rates and improved access to education and healthcare.[337] However, if the world fails to manage its population and consumption responsibly, critical resources will be rapidly depleted, leading to widespread resource scarcity and potentially severe consequences, including famine.

To ensure long-term sustainability, we must adopt a comprehensive "Forever Plan" that prioritizes conserving resources, reducing waste, and transitioning to renewable energy. This plan must account for the economic implications of decoupling growth from population increases, focusing instead on innovation and efficiency as primary drivers of progress.

Transitioning away from gasoline and diesel-fueled vehicles is crucial to this effort. By setting achievable targets, such as phasing out the sale of new gasoline-powered cars by 2030, we align with global climate objectives like the Paris Agreement. This timeline gives industries the lead time to adapt, invest in alternative energy technologies, and expand infrastructure. However, the target year must remain flexible, accounting for technological advancements and market readiness to ensure a realistic and practical transition.

On an individual level, we can contribute by cutting energy usage and reducing light pollution. For instance, motion-activated streetlights that shine downward could significantly lower electricity consumption and help urban residents rediscover the beauty of a star-filled night sky.

By addressing these challenges proactively, we can protect the Earth's resources and create a sustainable future for generations that follow.

Stockpiles

We should stockpile enough oil, munitions, and other critical raw materials to fight two global wars at the same time if necessary. We need to find the underlying cause of oil supply shortages and fluctuating prices. Speculators can contribute to fluctuations in the price per barrel of oil and price per gallon of fuel oil and gasoline, irrespective of actual supply and demand dynamics.

We need an independent panel of non-partisan experts to assess the severity of carbon pollution and validate the reality of Global Warming, ensuring unbiased dissemination and widespread promotion of their findings without political influence or industry bias.

The U.S. should leave as much oil in the ground as possible because it is a depleting resource, and the day will come when the oil supply around the world will run out. We will need our reserves to continue life as we know it.

Reality Check on Drilling

Many voters in 2024 complained that "energy costs are spiraling upward, food prices continue to rise, and as a result, our entire economy suffers." Of course, inflation since Covid (5.3% overall) has impacted on all prices, including food and gasoline. Perspective is important.

Many older Americans can remember 1950 when gasoline (leaded) was $0.27 per gallon. Adjusted for inflation, which is equivalent to $3.32 today. Surprisingly: the average U.S. price of gas on February 14, 2025, was $3.17[79].

The price of a barrel of oil (using Illinois Sweet – one of the industry standards) has risen from $53.79 per barrel in 1974 to $69.70 as of February 2023 when adjusted for inflation. That is a 29% increase over 49 years. This increase of 0.6% per year has been more than offset by the greater efficiency of our oil-using products (like how many miles the cars of today get per gallon compared to the 1970s). Our Oil consumption is also up, having increased from 16.7 million barrels per day (MBPD) in 1974 to 20.6 MBPD in February 2023, which is a 23% increase, mainly due to increased population demand.

On a short-term basis, oil prices fluctuate wildly at times; but over the long-term it does not appear to be spiraling out of control.[129]

It is interesting to note that <u>the United States exports more in finished oil products (gasoline, diesel fuel) than it imports</u>. Here is a breakdown of U.S. Oil Imports and Exports:[129-02]

US Oil Imports and Exports

- The U.S. produces 10 million barrels of crude oil per day.
- The U.S. consumes 8 million barrels of crude oil per day.
- The U.S. refines 12 million barrels of crude oil per day.
- The U.S. exports 4 million barrels of refined products per day.

The point of this reality check on U.S. energy production is that gas prices are determined by business decisions rather than political ones. And we produce more oil than we consume, so foreign sourced oil is an economic decision, not a necessity. Producing more oil and gas in the U.S. is unlikely to lower the price of gas at the pump.

You cannot talk about energy without talking about energy independence and the environment, as extracting energy from our multitude of potential sources has varying impacts on our air, water, the global climate, and land.

Energy Independence

Energy independence is often emphasized for its significant impact on national security, economic stability, and autonomy policy. It reduces a nation's vulnerability to external disruptions like embargoes or conflicts that can affect energy supplies, historically illustrated by the 1970s oil crises that significantly disrupted economies reliant on Middle Eastern oil.

Securing a stable and predictable energy supply helps countries mitigate the volatility of international energy prices, which fluctuate due to global conflicts, trade policies, and market dynamics. Additionally, investing in domestic energy sources, including renewables, allows nations to establish environmental standards and implement energy policies that align with national priorities.

While complete energy independence may not be feasible or economically practical for all countries, particularly those with limited resources, enhancing energy security and diversifying energy sources can provide many of the same benefits. This approach balances self-sufficiency with strategic participation in international energy markets.

In the United States, energy security efforts have focused on increasing domestic production and expanding the energy mix. These initiatives reduce reliance on imports while maintaining engagement in global energy trade, where it remains beneficial.

Policy

Energy policy is crucial to economic prosperity, national security, and environmental sustainability. With rapid technological advancements and the increasing urgency of climate action, updating U.S. energy policies can help address current and future challenges. Modernizing these policies can support economic growth, strengthen national security by reducing reliance on imported energy, and promote environmental sustainability through cleaner energy sources.

Economic and Security Implications

Energy is fundamental to economic growth and national security. High energy costs strain families and small businesses, diverting resources from other critical areas such as education and healthcare. Dependence on foreign oil leads to significant economic outflows and, in some cases, indirect support for regimes with differing political ideologies. Increasing domestic energy production and diversifying energy sources can mitigate these challenges, strengthening the economy and national security.

Energy dependency has far-reaching economic implications. The ongoing transfer of wealth to oil-exporting nations highlights the urgency of reducing reliance on foreign energy sources. Shifting toward domestic production is not just about energy security, it also retains economic value within the country, fosters job creation, and promotes long-term stability.

Updating U.S. energy policy could significantly enhance the national energy strategy. Recognizing energy security as a priority would enable proactive measures to promote energy diversity and support technologies that strengthen domestic energy supplies, including fossil fuels, nuclear power, natural gas, and renewables such as solar, wind, and hydropower. Encouraging a balanced energy portfolio could drive legislative initiatives to develop a sustainable and reliable energy grid.

A strong commitment to technological innovation could support policies that advance cleaner energy solutions through tax incentives and public-private partnerships. Prioritizing energy efficiency could improve building standards, power grids, and automotive technologies, contributing to environmental sustainability and economic competitiveness. Streamlining regulatory processes could accelerate energy project development while balancing environmental considerations with responsible resource management.

The U.S. has set a target of achieving 100% carbon pollution-free electricity by 2035, which reflects a growing emphasis on renewable energy investment. Supporters argue that this initiative could boost private sector confidence, drive job creation, and position the U.S. as a leader in clean energy. Critics, however, caution that the transition must be balanced with economic feasibility, grid reliability, and energy affordability. The long-term success of such policies will likely depend on technological advancements, market developments, and broader energy security considerations.

Strategic Stockpile

In parallel with energy security, strategic preparedness for public health emergencies remains vital to national resilience. The U.S. Strategic National Stockpile (SNS) was designed to serve as a safeguard, housing critical medical supplies and equipment for use during major crises such as pandemics, bioterrorism, or natural disasters. This reserve includes pharmaceuticals, vaccines, ventilators, and personal protective gear intended to supplement strained local resources. However, recent events have exposed gaps in the stockpile's readiness—ranging from outdated inventory to insufficient surge capacity. Strengthening the SNS through modern inventory management, clearer distribution protocols, and sustained federal investment would enhance the nation's ability to respond swiftly and effectively to future health threats. As energy strategy requires foresight and coordination, so does public health readiness.

Addressing Energy Access and Affordability

Energy policy should also account for the social impact of energy costs. Rising prices disproportionately affect lower-income families, making targeted assistance a vital consideration. Federal programs could help ensure equitable access to energy and support efficiency initiatives that reduce costs for vulnerable households. Potential measures include increased funding for low-income heating assistance and investments in weatherization projects to improve energy efficiency and affordability. While some advocate for constitutional provisions mandating such programs, others argue that energy assistance should be addressed through legislative or market-based solutions rather than constitutional requirements.

Conservation and Strategic Energy Use

Conservation and efficient energy use are essential components of a strong energy policy. Policies promoting energy-saving technologies, such as smart thermostats, telecommuting infrastructure, and improved recycling programs, could help reduce energy demand and support long-term sustainability. While some advocate for a constitutional approach to incentivizing conservation efforts, others argue that legislative and market-driven solutions may be more adaptable and effective in promoting energy efficiency.

National Security and Energy Independence

From a strategic standpoint, reducing reliance on imported oil strengthens national security. Supporting domestic oil, gas, and renewable energy development can balance immediate needs with the transition to low-carbon alternatives. Expanding flexible fuel, electric, and natural gas vehicles are practical steps to reduce oil dependence and emissions, though debate continues over policy-driven versus market-driven approaches.

ENVIRONMENTAL STEWARDSHIP

Energy policy and the environment are closely connected. Expanding domestic energy production without considering environmental impact may bring short-term economic benefits but could lead to long-term harm. The country's natural beauty is also an asset, both ecologically and economically, making conservation an essential factor.

Global warming presents challenges like wildfires, floods, rising sea levels, and food shortages. Addressing climate change requires balancing economic stability, national security, and environmental sustainability.

Scientists agree that carbon emissions from burning coal, oil, and natural gas primarily cause global warming. However, debates continue over the best policies to reduce emissions while maintaining energy reliability and economic growth. A mix of new technology, policy changes, and market-driven solutions will likely be needed.

Global Warming

Causes

The main cause of global warming is greenhouse gases (GHGs). The United States is the second-largest emitter of GHGs, contributing about 15% to global emissions. China is the largest producer, at 26%.[79-03,04]

Population

Population growth is a main driver behind the increasing GHGs through increasing demand for energy and food, leading to higher emissions of greenhouse gases as societies expand and consume more natural resources. The world population has increased by another 70,200,000 in 2024 to reach a total of 8,162,000,000 by the end of 2024.[89-02] Good news is that at the declining rate of growth, global population is on track to level out in roughly fifteen years.

Burning Coal

Coal accounts for approximately 40% of global CO_2 emissions, making it the largest single source, primarily due to its electricity generation and industry use. Oil contributes around 33%, driven by transportation and industrial processes, while natural gas adds about 22%, used in power generation and heating. Industrial processes and waste account for the remaining 5% of emissions.[330]

China is the largest consumer of coal, using 4,990 million metric tons annually, which accounts for approximately 50.5% of global coal consumption. This degree of consumption makes China responsible for 56.7% of global CO_2 emissions from coal combustion, releasing 8,550 million metric tons of CO_2 each year, almost a quarter of the entire world's carbon emission problem.

India is the second-largest coal consumer, using 1,110 million metric tons of coal annually (11.2% of global consumption) and emitting 2,030 million metric tons of CO_2 (13.5% of total coal-related emissions).

The United States ranks third, consuming 731 million metric tons of coal (7.4% of global coal consumption) and emitting 1,100 million metric tons of CO_2 (7.3% of total coal emissions).

Other major contributors include Germany (2.6% of global consumption, 1.6% of total emissions), Russia (2.3% consumption, 4.1% emissions), Japan (2.1% consumption, 3.2% emissions), South Africa (2.0% consumption, 3.1% emissions), and South Korea (1.6% consumption, 2.3%

emissions). Together, these eight countries account for the majority of coal consumption and associated CO_2 emissions worldwide, underscoring their critical role in global energy and climate policies.[330]

Burning Oil Resources

As of the end of 2023, the world's proven oil reserves were estimated to be 1.755 trillion barrels.[79-01] It's important to note that "proven" refers to the quantity of oil resources that are known and recoverable under current economic and operational conditions. At the current rate of world consumption, this amount will last 47.3 years.

Of course, this estimate is subject to change for several reasons. Firstly, discoveries can increase the total known reserves. Technological advancements in extraction methods can make previously inaccessible reserves available. Economic factors, such as fluctuations in oil prices, significantly influence the feasibility of extracting certain reserves.

Geopolitical factors are also pivotal; political shifts and policy decisions in oil-rich countries can alter the reported size of their reserves. And global efforts towards sustainability and reducing carbon emissions are increasingly impacting decisions related to the exploration and exploitation of oil reserves, with a growing emphasis on transitioning to cleaner energy sources. On the other side of the ledger, the increase in energy consumption to improve standards of living in developing countries and the growing world's population (0.9% annually but declining) will consume more oil in the years ahead.

Besides fuel, we depend on oil for plastics, synthetic fibers, pharmaceuticals, fertilizers, asphalt, and a wide range of petrochemical-based goods such as detergents, solvents, and adhesives. The reality is that our supply of oil is not unlimited. If the likelihood is that we will run out of economically available oil in less than 100 years, wouldn't it make sense to conserve what we have for these other uses, beginning now?

Transportation Impact

Passenger vehicles in the United States significantly contribute to the country's carbon dioxide (CO_2) emissions. As of April 2023, on average, a typical passenger vehicle emits about 4.6 metric tons of carbon dioxide annually. This figure is based on the average gasoline vehicle having a fuel economy of approximately 22.0 miles per gallon and covering around 11,500 miles per year. Each gallon of gasoline burned creates about 8,887 grams of CO_2. However, the total emissions can vary depending on the vehicle's fuel type, fuel economy, and the miles driven.[77]

Airline travel is more efficient than car travel when comparing per-person fuel consumption. A long-range flight on an airplane that is 75% full can achieve approximately 52 miles per gallon per person. In contrast, a car with only one occupant averages about 20 miles per gallon. Adjusting for the average car occupancy of 1.67 people, the per-person mileage improves to 33.4 miles per gallon. This comparison indicates that, on a per-person basis, cars consume more fuel than airplanes.[79-02,181-10]

As mentioned above, the Intergovernmental Panel on Climate Change (IPCC) has warned of severe consequences if global warming exceeds 1.5°C above pre-industrial levels. In response, the U.S. has committed to reducing its greenhouse gas emissions by 50-52% by 2030 and achieving net-zero by 2050. However, the nation faces substantial economic damage from climate change before 2050, projected to cost annually $100 billion from extreme weather events, $50 billion from loss of agricultural productivity, another $50 billion from rising sea levels, and $20 billion from negative health impacts.

A 2021 study by Columbia University's Center on Global Energy Policy suggests that implementing a federal carbon tax in the U.S. could reduce greenhouse gas emissions by 26% by 2030, create 2.4 million jobs, and add $1.8 trillion to the economy.[78]

Trade, Emissions, and the Push for Domestic Manufacturing

The United States' carbon emissions challenges are closely tied to the relocation of labor- and pollution-intensive manufacturing to countries with lower production costs, such as China, India, Vietnam, Mexico, and Thailand. These shifts transfer emissions overseas and exacerbate the U.S. trade deficit, as many of these goods are re-imported. While countries like China import select American products, including agricultural goods and specific technology, the trade imbalance remains heavily skewed, compounded by China's growing capabilities in manufacturing, including renewable energy technologies and electric vehicles. Recent U.S. efforts to address emissions and strengthen domestic production include major investments in semiconductor manufacturing, such as Intel's $20 billion project in Ohio and Taiwan Semiconductor Manufacturing Company's $12 billion facility in Arizona, aiming to reduce reliance on foreign supply chains. However, the situation is further complicated by intellectual property theft and limited reciprocal demand for American goods, presenting a multifaceted challenge in balancing trade, emissions, and global competitiveness.

CO_2 Trajectory

Over the past five decades, global carbon dioxide (CO_2) emissions have experienced a significant upward trajectory. In 1970, annual emissions were approximately 15.5 billion metric tons. By 1990, this figure had risen to around 22 billion metric tons, marking a nearly 42% increase over two decades. The upward trend continued into the 21st century.

Despite international efforts to mitigate climate change, CO_2 emissions have continued to rise, with 2024 global carbon dioxide (CO_2) emissions reaching a record high of approximately 41.6 billion metric tons, an increase from 40.6 billion tons in 2023.[329-01]

This persistent increase underscores the challenges in reducing global reliance on fossil fuels and highlights the urgency for more effective climate policies and sustainable energy solutions. The increase needs to be stopped and reversed quickly.

Energy Demand

Global energy demand has risen significantly over recent decades, driven by population growth, urbanization, and economic development, particularly in emerging economies. Between 1990 and 2020, global energy consumption increased by nearly 60%, with much of this growth fueled by industrialization in countries like China and India. During the same period, the United States saw a 30% increase in energy demand, driven by expanded commercial and residential energy use and growing reliance on digital technology.[331] Despite the widespread adoption of energy-efficient technologies like LED lightbulbs and low-energy appliances, overall energy consumption in the United States continues to rise. This increase is driven by the growing use of data centers, the proliferation of electric vehicles, and greater electricity use in homes and businesses for heating and transportation. The U.S. Energy Information Administration (EIA) projects that electricity demand will reach record highs of 4,179 billion kilowatt-hours (kWh) in 2025 and 4,239 billion kWh in 2026, up from 4,082 billion kWh in 2024.[379]

Rapid urbanization has expanded infrastructure, increased transportation needs, and higher electricity usage, particularly for residential and commercial buildings. The proliferation of technology and digital services has further boosted electricity demand, with data centers and digital devices accounting for a growing share of energy use. Despite efforts to transition to renewables, fossil fuels, especially coal and natural gas — dominate the energy supply, contributing to rising greenhouse gas emissions. This sustained growth in energy demand underscores the urgent need for energy efficiency measures and accelerated adoption of sustainable energy sources to balance development with environmental goals.

Climate Change's Far-Reaching Impact

Climate change, driven primarily by increased carbon emissions from human activities, poses significant threats to environmental and global stability. Recent data show that global temperatures have risen by about 1.1 degrees Celsius since the late 19th century, leading to extreme weather events, rising sea levels, and significant biodiversity loss. According to the Intergovernmental Panel on Climate Change (IPCC), if warming exceeds 1.5 degrees Celsius, it could result in catastrophic environmental and economic impacts worldwide. What is projected to happen?

Rising sea levels will flood coastal regions without extensive intervention, displacing millions and creating waves of climate refugees. Warmer temperatures and altered precipitation patterns are projected to reduce agricultural productivity, leading to food shortages, increased conflict, and higher levels of poverty and disease. By 2050, some estimates suggest that over 250 million people could be displaced due to famine and water scarcity, heightening instability in volatile regions.

Like many nations, the United States faces its own set of challenges. Coastal erosion, severe storms, forest fires, and prolonged droughts risk urban and rural communities, impacting economies, infrastructures, and overall quality of life. This makes climate change not just an environmental issue but a pressing national security concern. So, are we making any progress?

In 2023, global renewable energy capacity experienced a significant increase, with an estimated 507 gigawatts (GW) added, marking a nearly 50% increase from the previous year. This surge in capacity was driven largely by expansions in solar photovoltaic (PV) and wind energy, which together accounted for 96% of all new renewable capacity. Notably, solar PV and wind are projected to become the largest sources of electricity generation globally by early 2025, overtaking coal. This growth is supported by strong policy backing in over 130 countries and reflects a global trend towards cleaner energy sources.[243,244]

The growth rates of global CO_2 emissions in recent years indicate a slowing trend. From 2020 to 2021, emissions increased by approximately 4.8%, reflecting a rebound from pandemic-related declines. However, growth slowed in subsequent years, rising 1.3% from 2021 to 2022 and 1.1% from 2022 to 2023. Projections for 2024 suggest a further decline in growth, with emissions expected to increase by only 0.8%, keeping total emissions at approximately 37.4 billion metric tons.

The average annual growth rate of 2.25% from 2021 to 2024 highlights progress in curbing emissions increases. While this trend indicates movement toward climate stability, further efforts will be necessary to achieve net reductions and effectively address climate change.[330-01,02]

Current Strategies

Recognizing the need for action on climate change has led the U.S. to implement various strategies, including increased investment in clean technologies (solar and wind power), which reduce emissions but also enhance energy independence. For instance, in 2023 alone, investments in renewable energy technologies in the United States reached $92.9 billion.

R&D Investment

Supporting research and development in advanced technologies like biofuels and carbon capture is also critical to these efforts. Additionally, the U.S. Department of Energy has allocated $97 billion from expanded federal investments in clean energy infrastructure, aiming to achieve carbon-free electricity by 2035 and a net-zero economy by 2050. This investment included $11 billion specifically targeted to advance clean energy across rural America, representing the most significant investment in rural electrification since the 1930s.[245-247]

Cap-and-Trade

Market-driven policies, such as cap-and-trade systems, have been proposed as effective mechanisms for reducing emissions. Cap-and-trade is a market-based system where governments set a limit (cap) on total emissions, and companies can buy, sell, or trade allowances to emit within that cap, incentivizing overall reductions. These systems create economic incentives for businesses to innovate and align their operations with environmental objectives, helping prevent catastrophic climate change changes.

The application of cap-and-trade systems to address climate change has been gaining traction in the United States, though it varies significantly by state. California, Massachusetts, and several Northeast states participating in the Regional Greenhouse Gas Initiative (RGGI) have established cap-and-trade programs to reduce carbon emissions in specific sectors like power generation. Additionally, states like Washington and Oregon have recently implemented or are developing cap-and-invest programs, which aim to reduce emissions through a market-based approach. New York is also considering its state-wide carbon market, which is expected to start by 2025. These programs reflect a growing trend toward using financial mechanisms to incentivize reductions in greenhouse gas emissions while fostering economic opportunities within cleaner industries.[248-250]

Nonetheless, its implementation faces hurdles, including political opposition, concerns about its impact on low-income communities, and whether the scheme can be designed to work effectively in practice. Given the high costs of inaction on climate change, the urgency and significance of implementing a cap-and-trade system in the U.S. seems evident. Further research is required to detail such a system's specific economic costs and benefits.

Energy Design Technologies

Improving energy efficiency in buildings and transportation systems offers immediate benefits. Policies promoting innovative building designs, energy-saving technologies, and grants for early adopters can facilitate the widespread adoption of efficient practices that cut emissions and reduce energy costs for consumers and businesses alike.

Global Cooperation

Global collaboration is essential since climate change is inherently a global issue. Engaging with major carbon-emitting nations to establish agreements with binding commitments to emission reductions ensures that efforts are comprehensive and equitable. This kind of international cooperation is crucial for effectively managing global carbon levels.

Environment

Challenges and the Need for Balance

Balancing environmental goals with economic growth is an ongoing challenge. Effective policies must ensure that efforts to combat climate change do not inadvertently stifle economic opportunity or force undue sacrifices on families and communities. Recognizing the role of technological and market-driven solutions is vital for achieving these goals without compromising the aspirations and way of life that define American society.

1. **Private Stewardship and Public Policy**: Both public and private initiatives play a role in managing natural resources effectively. Historically, private landowners have contributed to environmental stewardship through responsible land management. Encouraging public-private partnerships can enhance conservation efforts by combining government oversight with the innovation and efficiency of private enterprises, leading to more sustainable outcomes.

2. **Flexibility in Energy Sources**: Combating climate change requires a balanced mix of traditional and alternative energy sources. Zero-emission technologies like nuclear power, which generate no greenhouse

gases during electricity production, play a critical role in ensuring both reliability and sustainability in the energy supply. At the same time, natural gas, a cleaner-burning fossil fuel, can act as a transitional energy source, reducing reliance on coal while the energy grid shifts toward renewables.

Pollution and Quality of Life

Humans are undeniably harming the Earth. While there is no question about our environmental impact, we have made significant progress in recent decades through recycling, reducing plastic use, and adopting energy-efficient appliances.

Light pollution, a consequence of industrial civilization and urban development, has grown significantly over the past century, obscuring our view of the night sky and disrupting ecosystems. The effects of light pollution extend beyond merely hindering our ability to observe the stars; it also has profound implications for wildlife, particularly nocturnal species, by altering natural behaviors, migration patterns, and even predator-prey dynamics. Moreover, the excessive use of artificial lighting contributes to energy wastage and carbon footprint.

In large urban areas, the dual challenges of noise and air pollution significantly affect the quality of life and environmental health. Addressing these issues is crucial for creating more livable, sustainable urban spaces.

Plastic litter poses a significant environmental threat due to its non-biodegradable nature and tendency to break down into microplastics, infiltrating food chains and ecosystems. At least 267 marine species have been found with microplastic contamination, impacting 44% of bird species, 43% of mammal species, and 86% of turtle species.[418] Humans are also exposed to and consume an estimated

78,000 to 211,000 microplastic particles annually through food, water, and air.[419] These particles can carry chemical pollutants at concentrations up to a million times higher than their surroundings, posing potential health risks.[420] Biodegradable plastics need to become the standard to address this growing issue. Standards such as ASTM D6400 and EN 13432 require that at least 90% of biodegradable plastics decompose within six months under industrial composting conditions.[421] Ensuring these materials are widely adopted and properly regulated is crucial to reducing plastic pollution and preventing further environmental and health damage.

Protection and Sustainability

The framers of the Constitution lived in a world where the environment seemed boundless and indestructible. Today, with the realities of climate change, pollution, and resource depletion, we face environmental challenges that directly affect public health and future generations.

Urban Sprawl

Urban sprawl in the United States has been an issue since the 1920's and deserves to continue to be a significant concern, as evidenced by the 14% increase in urban land area between 2000 and 2020.[323]

Despite a slight decrease in the annual rate of urbanization — from 2.2% in 2020 to 1.7% in 2023 — the expansion persists, with urban land projected to more than double by 2060.[324]

This ongoing trend contributes to environmental challenges, such as increased air pollution and loss of open spaces. It reduces tillable land and poses sustainability issues.

Food Production and the Environment

Food production profoundly impacts the environment, influencing ecosystems, water resources, and global carbon emissions. Agriculture accounts for approximately 25% of global greenhouse gas emissions, driven by deforestation, livestock methane emissions, rice cultivation, and synthetic fertilizer use. Deforestation, particularly in tropical regions, is often linked to expanding farmland for crops like soy, palm oil, and cattle grazing, leading to biodiversity loss and a decline in carbon sequestration.[332]

Water usage in agriculture is another major concern, as it consumes about 70% of global freshwater resources.[333] Crops like rice, wheat, and sugarcane are especially water-intensive, and inefficient irrigation systems exacerbate water scarcity in vulnerable regions. Additionally, runoff from fertilizers and pesticides pollutes rivers, lakes, and oceans, contributing to issues like algal blooms and dead zones, such as the hypoxic area in the Gulf of Mexico.

Livestock farming, particularly beef and dairy production, contributes to environmental degradation. It requires vast amounts of land and water and produces substantial methane emissions — a greenhouse gas far more potent than CO_2 over short periods. Studies show that livestock alone contributes approximately 14.5% of global greenhouse gas emissions.[334]

Food waste also plays a critical role in environmental impact. An estimated 30-40% of global food is wasted, leading to unnecessary resource use and additional emissions.[335] The energy, water, and land used to produce discarded food and emissions from decomposition in landfills exacerbate the food system's environmental footprint.[336]

Sustainable practices are essential to mitigate these impacts. Innovations such as precision agriculture, alternative proteins (like plant-based or lab-grown meat), and regenerative farming methods can reduce emissions and resource use while maintaining or increasing food production. Efforts to minimize food waste through better supply chains, consumer education, and food recovery programs are equally crucial. Addressing the environmental effects of food production is essential for ensuring food security in the face of climate change and population growth.

A Path Forward

Addressing global warming and ensuring environmental sustainability requires a multifaceted strategy that combines technological innovation, market incentives, international cooperation, and legislative action. These efforts can help the United States mitigate climate risks while fostering long-term sustainability and economic growth.[129-03]

FOREIGN RELATIONS

It is striking that some leaders view the world as an interconnected system where humanity's survival depends on cooperation, while others perceive it as a fragmented collection of entities, each needing to protect itself from perceived threats and encroachments of others. The latter mindset often reflects a grandiose sense of self-importance and a distorted understanding of what is truly important for the long-term well-being of humanity. These leaders prioritize their power and control over fostering peace and unity, contributing to global instability and risking humanity's future.

Why do we divide the world into friends and enemies? Why do the countries we label as "Axis of Evil" hate us? Do they think we are doing things wrong and if so, what? Can those divides be bridged? Perhaps we need to take a closer look at our behaviors, our morals, and our selfishness? Are we as good as we could be? Or could we do better?

Our relationships with foreign powers, whether in relation to international air travel, trade, warfare, peace initiatives, or military affairs, shape the political landscape of the United States. Our political parties have different visions of the nation's role on the global stage.

America's Responsibility to the World

What does America owe to the rest of the world? Throughout history, U.S. innovations have significantly impacted global progress, contributing to advancements in technology, scientific research, and space exploration. The nation has also defended and supported allies in times of need. While America's natural resource abundance provided an early advantage that contributed to high standards of living, freedoms, and wealth, the spirit of innovation maximized these benefits and fueled economic growth.

There are differing views on America's role in global support. One perspective argues that, as a prosperous nation, the U.S. has a moral duty to use its resources to alleviate global poverty and promote equitable living standards. This view emphasizes humanitarian responsibility and the belief that wealthier nations should assist those in need.

Another perspective cautions against extensive resource allocation for global aid, highlighting the risk of depleting national assets and potentially compromising American interests. This viewpoint stresses prioritizing domestic needs, warning that excessive aid could strain resources and contribute to economic imbalances.

Both perspectives reflect ongoing debates about balancing humanitarian efforts with national priorities, weighing the benefits of international assistance against the need for domestic stability.

Addressing these competing views requires a balanced strategy. A critical step is enhancing conservation efforts to manage natural resources better, such as promoting energy efficiency and reducing emissions through sustainable domestic practices like limiting non-essential transportation. Additionally, the U.S. may seek a careful balance between protecting national interests and fulfilling its moral responsibility for international humanitarian aid. Such a strategy depends on the formation of strategic economic partnerships.

Self-Interest vs. Global Perspective

A fundamental question facing America today is whether to adopt an isolationist stance or embrace the role of a global citizen. Should we share or horde? Should we prioritize national interests above all else or recognize that our increasingly interconnected world requires cooperation and mutual support? Our Earth, after all, is a finite and fragile space shared by all humanity. The choice between sharing resources and knowledge or hoarding them for national gain has profound implications for global stability and prosperity.

Isolationism Versus Global Citizenship

While isolationism may sound appealing, especially when framed to safeguard national resources and interests, its practical application often reveals significant limitations. Isolationism involves withdrawing from other nations' political and economic affairs, focusing exclusively on domestic concerns. This approach can create a sense of security and self-reliance, reinforcing the belief that national interests are best protected by limiting foreign entanglements.

However, this perspective overlooks the realities of modern interconnectedness. The consequences of isolationism extend beyond missed diplomatic opportunities and economic stagnation; they include weakened global influence and diminished capacity to address transnational challenges, such as climate change, pandemics, military threats, and international terrorism. These issues do not respect borders and require cooperative, cross-national efforts.

The Ethical Balance: Sustaining the "Haves" and "Have-Nots"

A purely self-focused policy may sustain the "haves" at the expense of the "have-nots," fostering global inequalities and potentially destabilizing international relations. It has been argued that excessive wealth imbalances between nations are a major driver of large-scale immigration, as people seek better opportunities where resources and stability appear more accessible. Should wealthier nations, like the United States, bear the responsibility of supporting less developed countries to create more equitable global living standards? The answer may lie in balancing protecting national interests with promoting global progress. Some other countries may desire what we have, leaving us with the choice to share or risk facing their attempts to take it by force, though what we possess would likely be destroyed in the process. Sharing seems to be the better option.

Sharing resources and expertise does not have to mean undermining domestic well-being. By carefully managing resources and developing comprehensive strategies for conservation and sustainability, the U.S. can lead by example — demonstrating that aiding global development and maintaining national prosperity are not mutually exclusive. Investments in international aid and partnerships can support geopolitical stability, open new markets, and reinforce economic and trade alliances that ultimately benefit both the donor and recipient countries.

A Balanced Approach to Global Engagement
The most effective strategy is to blend national self-preservation with thoughtful global engagement. Policies should be designed to ensure responsible use of resources at home while fulfilling a moral and strategic commitment to aid those in need abroad. Such a balanced approach acknowledges the interconnectedness of modern societies and the reality that long-term national interests are often best served by contributing to a stable and cooperative global environment.

In summary, while isolationism may appear attractive in its simplicity, it fails to address our era's complex web of global interdependence. Embracing a perspective that values national strength and responsible global stewardship can sustain prosperity at home while promoting peace, stability, and shared progress worldwide.

Pros and Cons

Pros

1. **Preservation of Sovereignty**: Isolationism can help preserve a nation's sovereignty by avoiding entanglements in foreign affairs or alliances that may compromise its independence or autonomy. It allows a nation to prioritize its own interests and decisions without external interference.

2. **Avoidance of Foreign Conflicts**: By staying out of international conflicts or wars, isolationist countries can save lives and resources that would otherwise be expended in military engagements. This approach may reduce the risk of casualties and the financial burden of maintaining a large military presence abroad. For example, Costa Rico has had no standing army since 1949.

3. **Focus on Domestic Priorities**: Isolationism allows a nation to focus its resources, attention, and efforts on addressing domestic issues such as economic development, infrastructure improvement, social welfare, and education. By prioritizing internal stability and prosperity, isolationist policies aim to strengthen the nation from within. However, it may hinder innovation and progress.

4. **Reduced Dependency on Foreign Entities**: Isolationism can reduce a nation's dependency on foreign trade, resources, or alliances. By limiting engagement with other countries, a nation may seek to

become more self-sufficient in terms of economic production, energy resources, and national security.

5. **Avoidance of Cultural Homogenization**: Isolationism may help preserve a nation's unique cultural identity, traditions, and values by limiting exposure to external influences. It can support cultural diversity globally and help safeguard traditional practices from being overshadowed by dominant global trends. However, preserving culture doesn't always require isolation, and thoughtful engagement with the world can also strengthen national identity.

6. **Protectionism and Economic Security**: Isolationist policies can include protectionist measures such as tariffs, quotas, or subsidies to shield domestic industries from foreign competition. While controversial, such measures aim to protect jobs, industries, and economic stability within the nation.

7. **Cost Savings**: By reducing or eliminating foreign aid expenditures, isolationist policies can lead to immediate cost savings for the government. These savings can be redirected towards domestic priorities such as infrastructure development, education, healthcare, or tax cuts.

Cons

1. **Economic Impact**: Isolationism can lead to reduced international trade and investment opportunities. By limiting engagement with other countries, a nation may miss potential economic benefits derived from trade partnerships and foreign investments.

2. **Political Isolation**: Isolationist policies can strain diplomatic relations with other nations, leading to increased tension and potential conflicts. Lack of engagement in international forums and agreements may

also diminish a country's influence and ability to address global challenges collaboratively.

3. **Technological and Cultural Stagnation**: Isolationism can impede the flow of ideas, innovation, and cultural exchange. Limiting interaction with other countries may reduce access to new technologies, advancements, and diverse perspectives, ultimately hindering progress and development.

4. **National Security Risks**: Isolationism may weaken alliances and cooperative defense mechanisms, leaving a nation more vulnerable to security threats. By isolating itself from international security arrangements, a country could find itself less prepared to respond to emerging security challenges and threats.

5. **Humanitarian Concerns**: Isolationism may hinder efforts to address global humanitarian crises and promote human rights internationally. By withdrawing from global engagements, a nation may neglect its moral responsibility to support vulnerable populations and uphold humanitarian principles.

6. **Erosion of Soft Power**: Isolationism can diminish a nation's soft power, which is its ability to influence others through cultural, ideological, and diplomatic means. By withdrawing from international dialogue and cooperation, a country may lose credibility and influence in shaping global norms and perceptions.

Successful diplomacy requires skilled leadership that integrates a range of essential competencies, including effective communication, negotiation, cultural awareness, analytical thinking, emotional intelligence, adaptability, networking, conflict resolution, understanding of diplomatic protocols, and language proficiency. Historical examples of such adept leadership include Franklin D. Roosevelt and

George H. W. Bush. Franklin D. Roosevelt (FDR)'s strategic guidance during World War II and his pivotal role in establishing the United Nations highlight his diplomatic mastery and vision for international collaboration. Similarly, George H. W. Bush demonstrated remarkable diplomatic finesse through his management of the Cold War's conclusion, the peaceful reunification of Germany, and the coalition-building effort during the Gulf War. These examples underscore the importance of multifaceted leadership in navigating complex global challenges and fostering global stability.

Foreign Relations with Muslim Countries

Before 9/11, the U.S. engaged in the Middle East to secure oil supply, maintain alliances, and prevent conflicts, while extremists saw these actions as foreign interference, occupation, and support for oppressive regimes. After 9/11, the U.S. shifted from maintaining regional stability to actively combating terrorism, launching wars in Afghanistan and Iraq, while extremists saw this as further occupation and justification for more attacks. The core historical grievances stem from perceived Western interference in Muslim lands, including colonialism, military interventions, political alliances with authoritarian regimes, and the creation of Israel, which many see as a loss of Muslim land. Some also view Western cultural influence as morally corrupt and a threat to Islamic values.

Strengthening U.S. relations with Muslim-majority countries should be a strategic priority, guided by cultural awareness and mutual learning. Key efforts include diplomatic dialogue, economic partnerships, and educational exchanges to foster understanding. Cooperation on global issues like climate change, public health, and regional conflicts is crucial, alongside addressing

Islamophobia and promoting human rights. Public diplomacy and media outreach can improve perceptions, while a formal agreement, similar to the Geneva Convention, could help reduce conflicts with extremist factions. Economic development and expanded cultural exchanges can further strengthen long-term partnerships.

Foreign Relations with China

U.S.-China relations are marked by deep economic interdependencies and ongoing tensions across various fronts, including trade and intellectual property rights. The relationship is particularly strained over issues of intellectual property, where there are frequent instances of unauthorized replication of American music, videos, movies, and other creative content by Chinese entities and military/industrial spying.

The piracy of U.S. companies' intellectual property (IP) is a particular concern, significantly impacting our companies' financial stability, innovation potential, and global competitiveness. The top three countries for IP piracy are China, Russia, and India. In these countries, the logistics of legally enforcing IP rights is challenging, leading to widespread unauthorized reproduction and distribution of U.S. products. This problem results in considerable economic losses for American businesses and can dampen their incentive to invest in new research and development. Furthermore, the issue strains trade relations and poses risks to consumers who may unknowingly purchase substandard or unsafe pirated products.

China poses significant national security threats beyond intellectual property theft. These include cyber espionage targeting U.S. government agencies, critical infrastructure, and private communications networks. Chinese state-backed actors have been linked to attempts to infiltrate power grids, water systems, and transportation networks—raising the risk of disruption in times of conflict or crisis. There are growing concerns about election interference through disinformation campaigns, data harvesting via social media platforms, and efforts to undermine public trust in democratic institutions. These actions reflect a broader strategy to weaken U.S. resilience and global influence. This strategy is not the behavior of a trusted trading partner.

Harmonize with the World

We could set a timeline for harmonizing our human rights policies with other democracies while respecting national differences. As part of this effort, we could launch a global campaign highlighting the benefits of democratic governance. The goal would be to encourage discussion on the strengths and challenges of different systems, fostering mutual understanding rather than division. Harmonizing with non-democratic countries may also be possible.

Trade Relations

The U.S. has some policies to ensure that imports comply with environmental and labor standards. Still, these are not as comprehensive or uniformly applied as should be. Current U.S. trade strategies include the Green Trade Strategy, which promotes environmentally sustainable trade practices and improves climate resilience in global supply chains. This strategy aims to create incentives for green trade and enforce against environmental bad actors, aligning with broader environmental goals within trade policies.[299]

Additionally, U.S. Customs and Border Protection (CBP) enforces regulations against imports produced with forced labor, ensuring that goods entering the U.S. meet certain ethical standards. This enforcement includes detailed compliance requirements under laws like the Uyghur Forced Labor Prevention Act (UFLPA), which obligates importers to prove their supply chains are free of forced labor through "clear and convincing evidence."[300]

However, while there are mechanisms to address some environmental and labor concerns, a comprehensive policy mandating imports only from countries with equivalent U.S. environmental and labor standards across all sectors is not fully implemented. Such a policy would involve a more extensive and uniform application of these standards and potentially new legislative actions to ensure all imports comply with stringent environmental and fair labor practices.[301]

GOVERNMENT REGULATIONS

Government regulations play a crucial role in fostering economic stability, protecting public welfare, and ensuring fair practices while managing natural resources responsibly. However, balancing effective regulation with economic growth, personal freedoms, and market flexibility remains a topic of debate. Supporters argue that strong regulations prevent abuse and promote long-term stability, while critics warn that overregulation can stifle innovation, burden businesses, and limit individual choices. Ensuring transparency and accountability in regulatory processes is essential for maintaining public trust and economic efficiency.

Freedom of Information Act (FOIA)

While the Freedom of Information Act (FOIA) remains a cornerstone of open government, maintaining the system comes with real costs and challenges. FOIA operations require annual employee training, complex inter-agency coordination, and dedicated personnel to manage requests— resources that are often stretched thin. Many documents requested under FOIA are exempt from disclosure because they are classified, involve national security, or are labeled "pre-decisional," meaning they relate to internal government deliberations. In addition, responding to FOIA requests can create frequent interruptions and burdens on government employees across agencies, pulling them away from their primary duties. There are also legitimate privacy concerns when records contain personal information that must be reviewed and redacted before release. These realities underscore the importance of reforming the FOIA process to balance transparency with operational efficiency and privacy protections.

Have you ever tried to make a FOIA request? If you did, you found the process more complicated than expected, with delays, redactions, bureaucratic hurdles, and often unexpected fees that can make accessing public records both frustrating and costly.

A series of reforms to improve the Freedom of Information Act (FOIA) process and enhance government transparency could be implemented to streamline access and reduce barriers for requesters. Simplifying the FOIA request process through a standardized, user-friendly online submission platform across all federal agencies would make it easier for users to submit accurate requests, thereby reducing initial rejections due to a lack of specificity. Additionally, implementing a clear and consistent fee structure across agencies, with a cap on copying and processing fees, would help ensure that cost is not a barrier. Reduced fees or waivers for educational, journalistic, and non-profit requesters would make the process more accessible and equitable.

Training FOIA officers across agencies would improve the process by ensuring they have efficient information retrieval and customer service skills. With better training, FOIA officers could help requesters refine their submissions and navigate the process more effectively. Another key improvement would be accelerating the digitalization of government records, prioritizing frequently requested documents for quicker access and processing. Proactively disclosing commonly requested information and maintaining regularly updated public databases could reduce the number of individual requests and allow agencies to focus on more complex cases.

For greater transparency and accountability, establishing clear timelines for FOIA request processing, with regular updates to requesters, would create a more predictable system. An online tracking tool where requesters can monitor their submissions would further enhance accessibility. Additionally, an independent review body to handle complaints and disputes could provide a faster, less costly alternative to legal appeals, making it easier to resolve issues.

To promote long-term transparency, periodic reviews of classified information and a 10 to 15-year "sunset clause" for automatic declassification (with national security exceptions) could gradually increase public access to government records. Finally, implementing a feedback system for requesters would provide valuable insights to improve the FOIA process, making it more efficient and responsive to public needs.

While the specifics can vary, here are some general actions and areas of improvement that could enhance open government laws:

1. **Strengthen Freedom of Information Act (FOIA) Enforcement**: This will ensure that government agencies respond to requests promptly and transparently. Penalties for noncompliance should be more substantial to deter uncooperative behavior.

3. **Expand FOIA Scope**: Consider expanding the scope of FOIA to include contractors and subcontractors that perform government functions, in order to prevent the outsourcing of public responsibilities as a means of avoiding transparency and accountability requirements.

4. **Streamline FOIA Processing**: Invest in technology and resources to expedite FOIA processing and reduce

backlog, making it easier for the public to access government information.

5. **Mandatory Transparency Reporting**: Require government agencies to report on their transparency efforts, including the number of FOIA requests received, fulfilled, and denied, as well as the reasons for denials. This information should be readily accessible to the public.

6. **Accessible and Open Data**: Promote the availability of government data in open, machine-readable formats to encourage innovation and public use of government information.

7. **Public Engagement**: Enhance mechanisms for public engagement in policymaking processes, such as soliciting public input on proposed regulations and initiatives and ensuring that public meetings and hearings are accessible.

8. **Protection of Journalists and Press Freedom**: Strengthen legal protections for journalists and safeguard press freedom to ensure investigative journalism can continue to hold the government to account.

Other than in cases involving legitimate national security secrets or sensitive operations, government officials who oppose a well-functioning FOIA process are likely motivated to shield information from public scrutiny due to bureaucratic inefficiencies, political sensitivities, or potential accountability concerns.

Government Efficiency

The DOGE initiative, formally known as the Department of Government Efficiency, was announced as part of former President Trump's administrative strategy, co-led by Elon Musk and Vivek Ramaswamy. The department aims to streamline federal operations, reduce bureaucratic waste, and improve governmental efficiency. Despite its high-profile leadership and ambitious targets of slashing $2 trillion from federal spending, there's skepticism regarding its feasibility. Critics question whether such drastic cuts are practical without compromising essential services or the functionality of the government. The initiative represents a bold attempt at reform as it appears to skirt Congressional approvals. Still, its success and the practical impact of its policies remain to be seen, raising concerns about the potential for oversimplification of complex governmental functions.[298]

Congress should evaluate the potential savings of consolidating all the separate benefits provided to those who work for the government, including health plans, retirement packages, franking privileges, etc. and incorporate them into the general population programs of social security, IRAs, the Affordable Care Act, and such. The same providers should be used for government and civilian workers for greater efficiency.

Unenforced Laws

Unenforced or rarely enforced laws such as the Logan Act of 1799, laws pertaining to treason, and the Alien Enemies Act of 1798 represent a unique category within the U.S. legal system. While still technically active, these laws have fallen out of common use, raising questions about their relevance and application in modern governance and the absence of such laws that may still be needed.

Logan Act

The Logan Act, enacted in 1799, prohibits unauthorized citizens from negotiating with foreign governments in disputes with the United States. The intent was to prevent undermining the government's position. Despite its longstanding presence in law books, the Logan Act has been rarely applied, with no successful prosecutions in its history. This situation raises questions about its practical enforceability and whether it serves any real purpose today.

Treason

Treason, defined strictly in the U.S. Constitution, involves levying war against the United States or aiding its enemies. The definition of "enemies" is not clear. Given its gravity, treason charges are extremely rare and require a high standard of proof, including two witnesses to the overt act or a confession in open court. One of the challenges is the unclear definitions of who is an enemy.

Alien Enemies Act of 1798

The Alien Enemies Act, part of the Alien and Sedition Acts, authorizes the president to apprehend and deport non-citizens from hostile nations during wartime. Although it has been invoked during historical conflicts, such as World War II with the internment of Japanese Americans and Japanese descendants, its compatibility with modern human rights principles and international law is debatable. Illegal immigrants are now being apprehended and deported from non-hostile nations and not during wartime.

Proposed Solutions

Outdated or irrelevant laws should be reviewed and, if necessary, repealed to simplify the legal code and reduce confusion. Laws that remain useful but contain obsolete language should be updated to reflect current legal and geopolitical realities.

Unenforced laws can lead to selective enforcement, creating inconsistency and potential misuse. In a democracy, where laws must be applied equally, legal reforms should prevent such issues.

Raising public awareness about outdated laws can promote informed discussions on their relevance. Encouraging legal scholarship can give lawmakers historical and practical insights for better decision-making. Addressing unenforced laws through legislative action and public discourse helps ensure the legal system stays fair, transparent, and effective.

US Postal Service

The U.S. Constitution requires the establishment of a Post Office, but does that mandate still make sense today? When the Founders included it in Article I, Section 8, the U.S. Post Office was essential for communication, commerce, and national unity. However, its role warrants reexamination in an era of digital communication, social media, and online services.

The decline in first-class mail and the rise of digital communication have already reshaped the Post Office's function. Yet, it remains vital in rural and underserved areas, where private carriers may not operate. Additionally, e-commerce has made package delivery a key part of its operations, keeping it relevant in a changing economy.

One view is that the constitutional requirement for the Post Office is outdated. Removing the mandate could allow for greater flexibility in how future governments address communication and delivery needs, adapting to new technology and societal demands.

Alternatively, the Post Office could retain its constitutional status but modernize its mission. With its vast infrastructure, it could expand into new roles, such as providing digital access, financial services, or supporting secure voting systems. Instead of preserving a historical institution, this approach would repurpose it to meet contemporary needs.

GUN CONTROL– SECOND AMENDMENT

The Constitution grants citizens the right to own guns, allowing them to carry and use firearms for self-defense and other lawful purposes. However, it does not explicitly state that citizens may use them to overthrow the government if it becomes too powerful, though some argue this is implied. The Supreme Court reaffirmed the principle of gun ownership in June 2008 in *District of Columbia v. Heller*, ruling that the right to bear arms is an individual right, rejecting the argument that it applies only as a collective right tied to militia service.[165] The Supreme Court has said that efforts to chisel away at this right are improper according to the original intentions.

Some Americans believe that the Second Amendment is about protecting the right to hunt game. That is only one consideration and not the most important. Guns are not only useful for hunting and self-defense, but they are also a massive deterrent to invasion by a foreign power.

While checking out of a game lodge in Tanzania, a young man at the counter asked whether all Americans owned guns. The question was notable, as he had described himself as a staunch Communist, suggesting his inquiry was less about curiosity and more about assessing the feasibility of a Communist revolution in the United States. When informed that many Americans own firearms, including machine guns, his expression changed, revealing a sudden awareness of the challenge such an effort would face. The exchange underscored how widespread gun ownership can act as a deterrent against both external threats and internal upheaval.

However, mass shootings within the United States necessitates a serious reevaluation of the motivations behind gun ownership. While hunting rights remain a crucial aspect of life in rural communities, they may not constitute the primary justification for the Second Amendment's protection of gun ownership, particularly within urban areas. <u>In any event, Americans must stop shooting Americans!</u>

It is imperative for American citizens to recognize that gun ownership comes with immense responsibility and that resorting to violence against fellow citizens other than in self-defense is unacceptable and contradicts the fundamental principles of a just and peaceful society.

The debate over Second Amendment rights and gun control revolves around differing views on how to balance individual freedoms with public safety. One perspective emphasizes the importance of protecting broad rights to firearm ownership, viewing restrictions as potential infringements on personal liberties. Another perspective supports more comprehensive measures, such as background checks and restrictions on specific types of firearms, arguing that these steps are essential for reducing gun violence and enhancing public safety.

Given the consistent upholding by the Supreme Court of the constitutional right to bear arms, substantial changes to gun laws that restrict access to guns are unlikely, but limitations related to safety may still be considered. Recently, nine states have enacted successful bans on "assault rifles" and high-capacity magazines, with these bans being upheld by the U.S. Supreme Court. Restrictions on "ghost guns," guns assembled with mail-order parts and without serial numbers, are still under review by the federal courts, as are the use of "bump stocks," additions to semi-automatic rifles allowing them to shoot hundreds of rounds per minute.

The Supreme Court recognizes that the right to bear arms is not absolute and can be subject to certain limitations. In cases concerning bans on assault rifles and high-capacity magazines, it may consider whether these restrictions are reasonable and in line with public safety concerns. This approach reflects an effort to reconcile the constitutional right to bear arms with the state's responsibility to protect its citizens, and decisions can vary based on the specifics of each case.

Mass Shootings

The recurring tragedy of mass shootings has become an alarming and distressingly familiar aspect of contemporary society. These horrific events, marked by the indiscriminate targeting of innocent people in public spaces, have fueled intense debates surrounding gun control, mental health, and the role of government in preventing such violence. Beyond the immediate devastation to lives and communities, mass shootings provoke deep questions about the complex intersection of individual rights, public safety, and the urgent need for policies capable of preventing future acts of mass violence. Researchers and law enforcement have identified common traits among individuals who commit these acts, contributing to a broader understanding of the factors that may lead to such tragedies.[122]

1. **Mental Health Issues**: Some mass shooters have a history of mental health problems or psychiatric disorders. They may believe that violence is a solution to their perceived problems or struggles.
2. **Perceived Injustice or Grievance**: In some cases, individuals who commit mass shootings feel wronged, oppressed, or marginalized in some way. They may believe that their violent actions are a way to seek revenge or rectify what they perceive as injustices against them.

3. **Desire for Notoriety**: Some mass shooters seek attention and notoriety through their actions. They may be influenced by previous high-profile shootings and aspire to achieve a similar level of infamy.

4. **Ideological or Extremist Beliefs**: In certain cases, individuals are motivated by extremist political, religious, or racial ideologies. These beliefs can drive them to commit acts of violence as a means of advancing their agendas.

5. **Social Isolation and Alienation**: Feelings of loneliness, social isolation, and alienation from others can contribute to some individuals turning to violence to gain a sense of power, control, or belonging.

6. **Access to Firearms**: The availability of guns can make it easier for individuals with violent intentions to carry out their plans.

7. **Copycat Behavior**: Some mass shooters seek to emulate or exceed the actions of previous perpetrators they have read about in the media or online.

8. **Personal Crisis**: Relationship problems, job loss, financial difficulties, or other life stressors can contribute to individuals resorting to violence.

9. **Lack of Effective Intervention**: In some cases, individuals who exhibit warning signs of violence may not receive adequate mental healthcare or intervention, causing their grievances or mental health issues to escalate.

These contributing factors underscore the argument that the death penalty may not serve as an effective deterrent to mass shootings. Such crimes often arise from mental illness, extremist ideologies, or deeply rooted personal grievances, where the fear of punishment plays a limited role in preventing violent acts. Addressing the complex motivations behind mass shootings remains a persistent challenge for federal and state law enforcement, mental health professionals, and society at large. Tackling this issue requires a comprehensive national dialogue on gun control and public safety.

In December 2023, the "Safer States Initiative" was launched to address gun violence at the state level. The initiative includes two actions. The first provides states with model legislation for safe gun storage, holding individuals legally accountable for the harm caused by unsecured weapons. The second action establishes a model for reporting lost and stolen firearms, enhancing law enforcement's ability to track these weapons. These measures aim to encourage state-level policy improvements in response to recurring mass shootings, particularly given congressional inaction and recent court rulings affirming gun possession rights.[10-01]

A prominent viewpoint in the gun rights debate asserts that the availability of firearms is not the root cause of gun violence; rather, the focus should be on addressing mental health issues, enhancing school safety, and improving bureaucratic processes related to firearm purchases. Advocates of this perspective argue that stricter gun laws would be ineffective in reducing violence and could compromise constitutional rights. They support initiatives to improve mental health services, with some favoring compulsory institutionalization in severe cases, as well as strengthening armed security and safety protocols in schools. This approach emphasizes solutions that target the underlying factors contributing to gun violence while preserving individual rights.[10-02]

Mental Health Services

Expanding mental health facilities for individuals at risk of committing gun violence comes with both benefits and challenges. These facilities could provide early intervention, structured care, and a controlled environment for those in need, potentially reducing the risk of violence. However, concerns include the stigma attached to institutionalization, high costs of operation, inconsistent quality of care, and ethical dilemmas surrounding involuntary treatment. Balancing these factors is crucial to ensuring that any expansion of mental health facilities serves public safety without undermining individual rights or dignity.

Mental Health and Gun Use

If the approach to addressing mass shootings and the misuse of firearms focuses on mental healthcare, such a program would need to include:

1. **Early Detection**: Prioritize early detection of and intervention in mental health issues, particularly among young people. This involves training educators, parents, and community members to recognize warning signs and providing resources for early intervention, such as a way for teachers to refer a student to mandatory counseling.

2. **Accessibility**: Integrate mental health services into community settings, such as schools, workplaces, and healthcare facilities. This makes mental healthcare more accessible and reduces the stigma associated with seeking help.

3. **Destigmatize**: Consider expanding mental health facilities and programs to encourage acceptance of treatment, normalize treatments, and make care more accessible.

Gun Ownership and Use

Just as individuals must learn to drive a car, operate heavy machinery, or fly an airplane — and obtain a license to demonstrate their ability to do so safely and responsibly — every gun buyer should be required to undergo training in firearm use and safety to ensure responsible ownership and awareness of potential risks.

In the United States, firearm-related deaths are primarily attributed to suicides and homicides. According to the Centers for Disease Control and Prevention (CDC), in 2021, approximately 54% of all gun-related deaths were suicides, while about 43% were homicides, many related to domestic abuse. The remaining firearm-related deaths included accidental discharges, incidents involving law enforcement, and cases with undetermined circumstances. The CDC also found that 85% of unintentional firearm deaths among children aged 0–17 occurred in a house or apartment, with 56% happening in the child's own home.

We should find ways to assess gun owners' understanding of gun safety, which may help to prevent accidents that result from improper storage of firearms (which should be secured) and ammunition (which should be kept separate from guns).

We also need to find more effective ways to prevent those with mental health problems from owning guns, for their own safety and for the safety of others.

HEALTH AND WELLNESS

Health and wellness encompass a range of practices and policies vital for maintaining and enhancing quality of American life.

Medicare/Medicaid/Affordable Care

Medicare, Medicaid, and the Affordable Care Act (ACA) are central to the U.S. healthcare system but face ongoing challenges. Medicare and Medicaid, aimed at supporting the elderly and low-income individuals, struggle with sustainability due to rising costs and an aging population. The ACA, designed to expand access and reduce healthcare costs, contends with political disputes jeopardizing its stability. Issues such as fluctuating premiums, inconsistent Medicaid expansions at the state level, and legal challenges undermining key provisions like pre-existing condition protections add to the uncertainty, underscoring the need for comprehensive reform.

The debate around these programs intensifies with the consideration of universal healthcare in the U.S. Proponents believe that universal healthcare could streamline the system, ensure coverage for all, and cut administrative costs. However, concerns about the feasibility of such a system persist, including the costs of implementation, potential tax increases, and possible impacts on service quality due to higher demand. While 27 of 28 developed nations have successfully implemented forms of universal healthcare, the U.S. remains an outlier.[295]

Some people worry that universal healthcare could lower the quality of their medical care, a concern sometimes called "averaging down." They fear that a government-run system might reduce access to specialists, advanced treatments, or shorter wait times that they currently enjoy. Longer wait times, standardized treatments, and overburdened healthcare providers are often cited as potential drawbacks affecting overall quality.

Others argue that universal healthcare does not necessarily eliminate private options and that some countries successfully combine both systems. In many models, those who can afford faster or premium care still have access to private healthcare. The debate comes down to balancing broad access to medical care with maintaining high standards for those used to a more personalized and immediate healthcare experience.

The shift toward a single-payer or similar model raises substantial questions about the role of private insurance and government involvement in healthcare. Single-payer health insurance is a system in which the government funds and administers healthcare coverage for all residents, eliminating the need for private insurers. The healthcare debate reflects contrasting visions for an effective and fair system, each proposing different solutions to improve access, affordability, and quality of care. Smart people should be able to design the best solutions.

Universal Access

One approach emphasizes universal access, advocating for government involvement to ensure healthcare is a fundamental right. This approach for some is based on the premise that "Healthcare should not be a profit-making business." The incentive is considered to be all wrong under a profit-oriented approach. The incentive should be prevention not treatment.

This view advocates for policies that expand coverage, lower costs, and improve quality by making healthcare a shared responsibility among individuals, employers, providers, and the government. It emphasizes consumer protection by prohibiting discrimination based on pre-existing conditions, ensuring continuous coverage despite job changes, and offering subsidies or tax credits to enhance affordability.

Proponents stress preventive care and wellness initiatives, seeking to lower long-term costs by addressing chronic conditions like heart disease and diabetes. Additionally, they call for measures to reduce drug prices, encourage the use of generics, and ensure fair competition within the insurance and pharmaceutical sectors. Partnerships with states, local governments, and tribal entities are essential to addressing healthcare disparities and tailoring solutions to diverse communities.

Market-oriented Approach

In contrast, a market-oriented approach to healthcare calls for minimal government involvement. This approach relies on personal choice, competition, and innovation to boost quality and affordability. It requires deregulation, tax incentives, and health savings accounts to increase options for healthcare and insurance. Proponents believe reducing bureaucracy will empower providers, give families more decision-making freedom, and cut business costs. They also argue that a patient-centered system with fewer government mandates could more effectively address issues such as the rising costs of long-term care, healthcare's impact on jobs and lifestyles, and providers' legal liabilities.

Market forces in U.S. healthcare often fall short of driving competition and efficiency due to inherent industry challenges. Factors such as price opacity, limited consumer choice, and the dominance of large providers and insurers hinder true competition. Additionally, healthcare consumers are rarely in a position to shop based on cost or quality, as urgency, insurance networks, and provider recommendations frequently dictate decisions. While market forces can drive innovation in pharmaceuticals and medical technologies, they struggle to ensure cost efficiency and equitable access in a system heavily influenced by regulation, monopolistic practices, and unequal bargaining power.

Both approaches seek to address Americans' healthcare needs but differ significantly on the role of government in achieving an accessible, affordable, and high-quality healthcare system for all.

As it is, over the past several decades, the cost of medical treatments in the United States has risen significantly, even after adjusting for inflation. Using 2025 dollars, in 1960, national health annual expenditures per capita were approximately $143.[380] by 2003, this figure had escalated to $5,670.[381] Factors contributing to this increase include technological advancements, administrative expenses, and rising prescription drug prices. While these developments have improved patient outcomes and life expectancies, they have also meant higher healthcare spending.[382]

Challenges

The U.S. healthcare system has many problems, both old and new. Insurance companies still have a lot of control, making it harder for some patients to get the necessary treatments. The high cost of medicine is a significant issue, and some drugs have serious side effects, including, in rare cases, death — even for conditions that are not life-threatening. Many people still use emergency rooms for basic medical care, showing that healthcare is not always easy to access or affordable.

Healthcare costs are higher than ever, and patients are paying more out of pocket, which especially affects Hispanic and lower-income communities. There are also not enough doctors and nurses, a problem made worse by the COVID-19 pandemic. Many healthcare workers are burned out, so better working conditions and more support are needed.

AI in Healthcare

Amidst these challenges, the potential of artificial intelligence (AI) in healthcare looms large. AI promises to revolutionize diagnostics, offering faster and more accurate analyses, which could lead to improved treatment plans and patient outcomes. AI may also include more natural treatments reducing the need for prescription drugs. This technological advancement represents hope for a more efficient and effective healthcare system.

Overall

The U.S. healthcare system is renowned for its advanced medical technology, innovation, and specialized care. However, it remains one of the most expensive and inequitable systems globally. While offering cutting-edge treatments and research opportunities, millions of Americans encounter barriers to access due to high costs, lack of universal coverage, and significant disparities in care quality. This juxtaposition of excellence in medical advancements with limited accessibility underscores the system's challenges in providing affordable care for all.

Mental Health

Mental health is crucial for individual well-being, societal stability, and economic productivity. Poor mental health impairs decision-making, relationships, and work performance, driving up healthcare costs, reducing productivity, and increasing crime rates. Conditions like depression and anxiety not only diminish the quality of life but also contribute to chronic diseases, substance abuse, and suicide.

Beyond personal consequences, untreated mental illness burdens healthcare systems, law enforcement, and social services. Investing in mental health care reduces long-term costs, improves public safety, and strengthens the workforce. When mental health is prioritized, individuals thrive, families grow stronger, and communities become more resilient.

Governments at all levels share responsibility for mental health care. Federal agencies, including the Substance Abuse and Mental Health Services Administration (SAMHSA) and the National Institute of Mental Health (NIMH), set policies, conduct research, and fund state and local programs. Laws like the Mental Health Parity and Addiction Equity Act (2008) require insurance companies to cover mental health care at the same level as physical health. Medicaid and Medicare also provide essential funding for vulnerable populations.

State governments implement federal guidelines, regulate licensing, and manage Medicaid programs, state hospitals, and community services. Some states expand coverage through legislation, while others limit funding based on budget priorities.

Local governments deliver direct services through county health departments, schools, and crisis response teams. They also oversee community clinics, suicide prevention programs, and emergency mental health services, often collaborating with nonprofits and private providers to improve accessibility.

Historical Perspective

Mental health has been a concern throughout history, but its understanding and treatment have evolved significantly. In ancient civilizations, mental illness was often attributed to supernatural forces or moral failings, leading to treatments such as exorcisms, religious rituals, and trepanation — drilling holes into the skull to release supposed evil spirits.

By the 18th and 19th centuries, the focus shifted from punishment to institutionalization. Asylums were intended to provide care but often became places of neglect and abuse. The 20th century introduced psychoanalysis, led by Sigmund Freud, alongside advancements in psychiatry and medication, including lithium and antipsychotic drugs. The latter half of the century saw deinstitutionalization efforts, promoting outpatient care and community-based services. Mental health deinstitutionalization in the later 20th century was driven by the development of psychiatric medications that allowed for outpatient treatment, growing awareness of the poor conditions in asylums, and policy shifts favoring community-based care. Government legislation, such as the Community Mental Health Act (1963), replaced large institutions with local mental health services, though inadequate funding and infrastructure often led to gaps in care.

Current Trends

Mental health is now widely recognized as an essential part of overall well-being. Public awareness has grown, helped by high-profile figures openly discussing their struggles. This awareness has reduced stigma and encouraged more people to seek treatment.

Technology is making mental health care more accessible. Teletherapy and mobile apps provide more straightforward ways to get support, while AI-driven tools and digital cognitive behavioral therapy (CBT) offer new treatment options that can reach more people.

At the same time, mental health challenges are increasing. Social media, economic uncertainty, and global events have contributed to rising rates of anxiety and depression, especially among young people. Addressing these issues requires flexible, innovative strategies.

A more holistic view of mental health is gaining attention, emphasizing diet, exercise, and mindfulness. Research shows strong links between gut health, physical activity, and mental well-being, highlighting the need for treatments beyond traditional psychiatry.

Efforts to improve access to mental health care continue, focusing on making services available in underserved areas. Recent reports indicate that mental health services are facing significant challenges due to staffing shortages and funding limitations. In Connecticut, the expiration of federal funding has jeopardized critical mental health programs, affecting access for vulnerable populations.[383] These developments underscore the pressing need for sustained investment and policy attention to ensure that mental health care remains accessible and effective.

The Future of Mental Health

Several key advancements are shaping the future of mental health care. Personalized psychiatry, driven by genetics and neuroscience, aims to improve treatment effectiveness by tailoring medications and therapies to an individual's biological and psychological profile, reducing the trial-and-error approach of current methods.

Psychedelic therapy is emerging as a promising option, with substances like psilocybin, MDMA (Ecstasy), and ketamine showing potential in treating depression, PTSD, and anxiety. While regulatory challenges remain, research suggests these treatments could provide rapid and lasting benefits.

Artificial intelligence is also expected to grow in mental health care. AI-driven tools can detect early warning signs through speech patterns, behaviors, and biometric data, enabling timely interventions through virtual therapists, chatbots, and predictive analytics.

A shift toward proactive mental health care may further improve outcomes by focusing on prevention. Early education, workplace wellness programs, and mental fitness initiatives could help people build resilience, regulate emotions, and manage stress before conditions become severe.

Mental health has evolved from being widely misunderstood to being recognized as essential to overall well-being. Advances in science, technology, and public awareness offer the potential for a future where mental health care is more accessible, effective, and seamlessly integrated into everyday life.

Euthanasia

Medically-assisted dying is now allowed in ten states (Oregon, Washington, Vermont, California, Colorado, Washington, D.C., Hawaii, Maine, New Jersey, and New Mexico). Whether this should be a codified right or determined from state to state is an issue to be decided.

These laws empower individuals to have control over their end-of-life decisions in accordance with their values and beliefs.[104,105]

Public opinion surveys indicate strong support for physician-assisted dying among Democrats. A May 2020 Gallup poll found that 85% of Democrats and Democratic-leaning independents agreed that doctors should be allowed to end a patient's life by some painless means if the patient and their family request it. In contrast, 69% of Republicans and Republican-leaning independents supported the same.[106] This support, however, has not translated into universal enactment of aid-in-dying legislation, partly due to opposition from religious groups and political polarization.

This issue is framed within the context of personal autonomy, compassion for suffering, and ensuring that terminally ill patients can make informed decisions about their end-of-life care with safeguards to ensure patients fully understand their choice and that there is no chance of survival from their illness.[104,105] Of course, a person's religion may and should take precedence over any legislation. The opposition is rooted in their belief in the sanctity of life and a preference for palliative care options that do not hasten death.

Some may argue that individuals have a right to choose when to end their lives—and if a firearm is the only means available, the outcome is not just tragic but also traumatic for others. Gun suicides are often violent, leave loved ones with lasting emotional and physical aftermath, and carry a social stigma not typically associated with medically supervised euthanasia. Expanding access to humane end-of-life options could reduce firearm-related suicides and offer individuals a more dignified alternative. It also raises the broader question of which categories of gun deaths deserve greater attention. For instance, so-called "double suicides"—where one spouse, often the husband, kills a terminally ill partner and then himself—are distressingly common and further complicate the debate over end-of-life choices and firearm use.

Fitness

Conditioning

We need to encourage physical fitness among children as American Adult obesity rates continue to climb. Regular physical activity helps prevent a wide range of diseases, including type 2 diabetes, heart disease, and several forms of cancer. We can mitigate a considerable health crisis affecting our nation by prioritizing fitness.

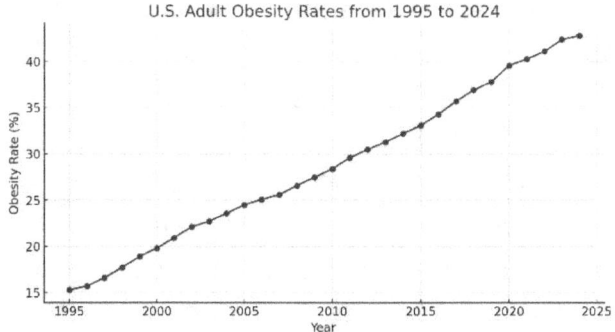

Between 1976 and 1980, the average weight of American adult men was 172.2 pounds, and for women, it was 144.2 pounds. From 2006 to 2014, average weights slightly increased, with men gaining just over a pound and women adding four pounds. In 2023, the average reported weight for men in the U.S. is 199 pounds, while for women it is 164 pounds.[297]

New Weight Control Options

In recent years, the development of weight-loss medications has gained significant attention, particularly with the introduction of GLP-1 receptor agonists like the generic drugs semaglutide and tirzepatide. These drugs have demonstrated substantial efficacy; for instance, patients taking semaglutide (marketed as Wegovy) have experienced an average weight loss of approximately 12% of their body weight, while those on tirzepatide (branded as Zepbound) have reported losses of around 18%.[353] These drugs were developed for diabetes and then found to be "safe and effective" for weight loss.

The market for these medications has expanded rapidly. In 2023, Novo Nordisk's semaglutide-based drugs, including Ozempic, Rybelsus, and Wegovy, achieved a combined sales of about $21.1 billion globally, an 89% increase from the previous year.[352] Similarly, Eli Lilly's tripeptide drug Mounjaro generated nearly $5.2 billion in sales in 2023, its first full year on the market.

Public perception of these treatments is generally favorable. A Gallup poll found that nearly two-thirds of Americans who have used injectable weight-loss drugs consider them effective, with 64% reporting significant weight loss.[351] Older adults (over 65) may experience less benefit from these treatments. Common side effects of weight-loss drugs include nausea, vomiting, diarrhea, constipation, and, in rare cases, pancreatitis or kidney issues. Also, access and affordability remain challenges, as many insurance plans do not cover these medications, leading to high out-of-pocket costs for patients.[354]

Ongoing research and development aim to enhance the drugs' efficacy, safety, and accessibility, potentially benefiting a broader population in the future.

Natural Medicines and Health

Natural health emphasizes using supplements and non-medicinal approaches to manage and enhance well-being, often focusing on prevention and holistic care. There is truth to the slogan, "You are what you eat." Natural Medicine advocates for integrating dietary supplements, such as vitamins, minerals, and herbal products, to correct nutritional deficiencies and support the body's intrinsic healing processes. Additionally, lifestyle practices like a balanced diet, regular physical activity, adequate sleep, and stress management play critical roles in maintaining health. Everyone has heard this advice before, yet it is remarkable how often people ignore what their gut knows is right.

Non-medicinal therapies include acupuncture, massage therapy, chiropractic care, meditation, and yoga, among others, all of which promote mind-body balance. These approaches are valued for their low risk of side effects and ability to complement conventional medical treatments. While medical doctors have traditionally received limited training in natural medicine during their formal education, this may gradually change as integrative approaches gain wider acceptance.

Legalized Addictions

Addictions drain economic and societal resources by reducing productivity, straining families, and driving up healthcare costs. Substance abuse contributes to lost work hours, increased medical expenses, and higher insurance premiums while burdening social services and law enforcement. The consequences extend to public safety, with DUI and DWI offenses leading to traffic accidents, injuries, and fatalities. These incidents not only claim lives but also result in legal costs, emergency medical care, and long-term disabilities, further compounding the financial and emotional toll on society.

Addictions are destructive for America, but the profits involved create strong incentives for industries to market and distribute addictive substances. At the same time, governments benefit from significant tax revenues on alcohol, tobacco, and gambling — often complicating efforts to curb their societal harm.

America needs to intensify efforts to combat "institutionalized addictions." Substances such as alcohol, caffeine, nicotine, and in some states, marijuana are not only legal but are also pervasive and subject to taxes designed to curb their excessive use. However, the widespread availability of these substances in grocery stores suggests that current taxation levels may be inadequate in deterring consumption. Therefore, it seems logical to consider increasing excise taxes to discourage the use of these unhealthy substances more effectively. The taxes on cigarettes significantly reduced tobacco use.

This is a conflict between moral principles and individual liberty. What might be right for people to do is not necessarily what people want the right to do, as the Prohibition era proved.

There is a fundamental conflict of interest when governments rely on tax revenue from addictive substances. Rather than following the Tax Policy Center's (TPC) recommendation to allocate 100% of these "sin" taxes into the general fund, a more balanced approach would direct 40% of these revenues toward healthcare costs related to substance use, including prevention and treatment programs. The TPC, a nonpartisan research organization formed as a joint venture between the Urban Institute and the Brookings Institution, provides independent analysis of tax policies and their economic effects. While its research is widely respected, directing a portion of "sin" tax revenue to healthcare would help mitigate the harm caused by these substances, ensuring that tax dollars are used to address the issues they contribute to. Additionally, this approach would prevent the government from becoming overly reliant on these volatile revenue sources, reducing potential economic risks if consumption patterns decline.

Taste buds play a critical role in human survival and health by acting as a biological mechanism to distinguish between safe and harmful substances. This sensory function enables individuals to enjoy food, consuming nutritionally beneficial items while avoiding potentially toxic ones. This enjoyment is not merely for pleasure but serves as a vital survival mechanism, ensuring that people get the necessary nutrients and avoid dangers. In contrast, the enjoyment derived from substances like alcohol and drugs involves more complex factors, including psychological effects and social contexts. It triggers biochemical reactions in the brain that can lead to dependency or addiction. Unlike the direct health benefits associated with enjoying food through taste, consuming these substances can significantly harm an individual's health and well-being, and potentially shorten their lifespan.

Marijuana

In states that have legalized marijuana, usage rates have increased, along with reports of associated health concerns. Conditions such as cannabis use disorder, psychosis, and cannabinoid hyperemesis syndrome (recurrent severe nausea and vomiting) have been reported more frequently. As with other legal substances, the marijuana industry's business model is often supported by frequent consumers, prompting the development and marketing of high-potency products that may pose increased risks for specific users.

While complete prohibition has drawbacks—such as limiting responsible adult use, encouraging black-market alternatives, and perpetuating enforcement disparities—stricter regulation could offer a more balanced path forward. Proposals like higher taxation to deter overuse and purchase limits to reduce risk have been raised, though they face resistance from an increasingly influential cannabis industry. Like the alcohol sector, it often advocates for lower taxes and minimal regulation despite ongoing concerns about public health impacts.[251]

Legalization has produced measurable economic benefits, with states like Colorado and California each generating over $1 billion in annual marijuana tax revenue.[430-431] The legal industry has also created more than 400,000 jobs nationwide.[432] However, these gains are accompanied by rising public health costs. Studies have documented increases in cannabis-related emergency room visits, traffic incidents, and mental health cases, particularly among adolescents and heavy users. For example, Colorado saw a 54% rise in marijuana-related ER visits in the years following legalization.[433-434] Balancing these fiscal and health outcomes is essential for shaping policies that promote both economic opportunity and public well-being.

Nicotine

Nicotine is addictive and can have harmful effects, including increased heart rate and blood pressure, a heightened risk of heart disease, and potential harm to brain development in adolescents. It can also contribute to the constriction of blood vessels and may affect insulin sensitivity, potentially increasing the risk of type 2 diabetes. However, nicotine is also used in controlled doses in smoking cessation products, such as patches and gums, which can help reduce dependence on more harmful forms of tobacco.

Caffeine

Some of the common problems associated with excessive caffeine intake include insomnia, nervousness, restlessness, stomach irritation, nausea, skin issues, and increased heart rate and blood pressure. Over time, high consumption can lead to dependence and may elevate the risk of heart problems in susceptible individuals. However, moderate caffeine intake is generally considered safe for most adults. It has been linked to potential benefits such as improved alertness, cognitive performance, and reduced risk of certain neurodegenerative diseases.

Sugar

Research suggests that sugar may have addictive-like qualities due to its impact on the brain's reward system. Consumption of sugar triggers the release of dopamine, a neurotransmitter associated with pleasure and motivation, similar to the effects seen with certain addictive substances. Over time, high sugar intake has been linked to behavioral and neurochemical changes—such as cravings and symptoms resembling withdrawal—that can reinforce compulsive eating patterns. Animal studies, in particular, have demonstrated that intermittent access to sugar can produce signs of dependence, including changes in dopamine and opioid receptors. However, while these findings raise significant concerns, there is an ongoing debate among scientists about whether sugar meets the criteria for addiction in humans, as social, behavioral, and metabolic factors also play significant roles in its overconsumption.[338-340]

Gambling

As an Addiction

Gambling addiction poses a significant public health challenge in the United States, impacting approximately 1% of adults with severe issues and another 4 to 6 million with mild to moderate difficulties.[254-255] Specific demographics, such as college students, exhibit higher compulsive gambling rates, around 6%.[256] A 2024 NerdWallet.com survey reported that 62% of Americans gambled within the previous 12 months.[256-01]

Online Gambling

Over the past decade, the shift to online gambling, facilitated by digital and mobile technologies, has contributed to market growth, with the U.S. market projected to reach $25.79 billion by 2030 from $11.68 billion in 2023.[252-253] More than 20% of Americans bet on sports online annually.[256-02] 37% played the lottery.[256-03] Gambling participation rates vary by source. The American Gaming Association reported that 49% of U.S. adults gambled in 2023, while a NerdWallet survey found 72% had done so within the year. The gap may reflect differences in survey methods, definitions, or potential bias tied to the sponsoring organizations. As with any statistic, context and methodology affect interpretation.[256-03]

This growth is driven by advancements in technology such as AI and blockchain, which enhance user experience and transaction security and refine the odds, reducing the instances where bettors might "beat the odds."

Technology in Gambling

While these technological improvements have supposedly increased the fairness and efficiency of gambling, they have also diminished the traditional thrills of gambling — outsmarting bookmakers and exploiting odds inefficiencies — by automating odds setting and using sophisticated technology. This evolution not only changes how gamblers approach betting, often requiring more sophisticated analytical tools, but also reduces the personal interaction and psychological elements, potentially making it feel more clinical and less enjoyable for those who relish its unpredictability and social aspects.

Social Impacts

The broader societal impacts of legalized gambling are profound, including increased addiction, financial strain, and higher crime rates, as well as exacerbating economic disparities and social inequalities.

Lotteries

State-run lotteries in the United States generate substantial revenue, a significant portion of which is transferred from consumers — and what they would have spent that money on — to government funds. In fiscal year 2024, U.S. lottery sales totaled over $113.3 billion.[346] This substantial sum represents funds extracted from consumers and redirected into government budgets like education and infrastructure. For example, a portion of lottery ticket sales in Florida is annually transferred to the Education Enhancement Trust Fund, supporting public education. Similarly, the Louisiana Lottery Corporation contributes over $100 million yearly to the state's Minimum Foundation Program, which funds public education.[343]

However, many states misled citizens by initially promising that lottery revenue would directly boost education funding. Instead of adding to existing budgets, these funds were often used to replace traditional education funding, allowing states to reallocate money to other projects. As a result, overall education spending did not significantly increase. Instead, lottery proceeds created the illusion of more investment in schools while taxpayer dollars were redirected elsewhere.[342]

Fleeting Hope in the Face of Futility

Unfortunately, outright prohibition has drawbacks, such as pushing people towards illegal betting circuits, a balanced approach through stricter regulations could mitigate some of these issues.

Proposals for managing the industry include imposing higher taxes and setting betting limits to curb excessive gambling. Better education about the fruitlessness of gambling might have moderate benefits.

For example, the average percentage return on lottery tickets is about 45%, meaning players, on average, lose 55% of the money they spend. Playing the lottery is an example of the futility of winning for the vast majority of participants, as the odds of winning are astronomically low; approximately 99.9999915% of participants do not win more than they spend on Mega-Million tickets. Therefore, the proportion of lottery losers to winners, considering only prizes that exceed the amount spent, is overwhelmingly high.

The vast majority of players lose more than they win, effectively handing over their money in exchange for fleeting hope. Over time, this habitual spending drains personal finances, while the real winners are the state governments and lottery operators, who collect billions in revenue.

However, these measures often face resistance from a growing and influential gambling industry, similar to the challenges faced in regulating the alcohol and marijuana sectors. This lobbying pressure underscores the complexity of balancing economic benefits against public health and social costs in the regulation of legalized gambling.

Addictions, whether to substances, gambling, technology, or other compulsive behaviors, erode the foundations of a stable society. They strain healthcare systems, fuel crime, weaken families, and diminish productivity. As addiction spreads, it undermines personal responsibility and self-control, replacing purpose and ambition with dependency. A society consumed by addiction loses its ability to function effectively, as individuals prioritize short-term gratification over long-term well-being. Addressing addiction is not just about helping individuals recover — it is about preserving the strength, values, and future of a nation.

INDIVIDUAL FREEDOMS

Throughout U.S. history, the balance between individual freedoms and government authority has shifted in response to changing social, economic, and political conditions. In the 19th century, civil and economic liberty were strongly emphasized, focusing on property rights and minimal government intervention. Over time, perspectives on personal rights and governmental responsibilities have evolved, leading to ongoing debates.

Discussions persist over personal autonomy in health, finances, and life decisions. Should individuals have the right to make harmful choices, or do issues like suicide and abortion fall under the scope of individual liberty? These questions highlight the complexity of defining personal freedom in modern society.

The 20th century brought significant shifts, particularly with the New Deal and civil rights movements, which expanded the government's role in ensuring equal rights and protections, especially for marginalized communities. These changes reinforced civil liberties while increasing governmental responsibility in securing them.

Today, debates continue over the extent of individual freedoms and the government's role in shaping economic and social policies. Clear laws defining rights related to free speech, gun ownership, and privacy are essential, along with guidelines on the government's responsibility in promoting justice and equal protection. A well-defined legal framework would help balance personal freedom with public welfare, ensuring that foundational rights remain relevant while adapting to contemporary needs.

Balancing Rights and Responsibilities

In the U.S., our legal framework protects individual rights while outlining local, state, and federal government roles. It is a complex dance of power and responsibility designed to ensure everyone's voice is heard, from the individual to the entire nation.

At the heart of this system are our fundamental rights — freedom of speech, religion, and fair legal process. These are not just abstract concepts; they are the pillars that support our daily lives. The family, though not explicitly mentioned in our founding documents, is recognized by the courts as having essential rights to privacy and child-rearing. Safeguarded by the First Amendment, religious freedom allows us all to live out our beliefs without government interference, shaping our community's moral backbone.

Local governments handle the day-to-day governance details, staying close to the community's pulse. State governments have their own reserved powers, filling in gaps not covered federally and often acting as laboratories of democracy. The federal government steps in on big-ticket issues that span state lines, making sure our national interests are met.

This system of checks and balances is a living, breathing structure that adapts and responds to our needs, ensuring that no matter how small our voice may seem, it counts in the grand scheme of things. It is about maintaining a balance where personal freedoms are respected, yet collective well-being is protected. Do we still have a voice? More so locally than at the state or federal levels.

Role of Individual Responsibility

People should take responsibility for their choices while having access to systems that provide real opportunities for success. Individuals must actively contribute to their communities, make responsible decisions, and work toward self-sufficiency, particularly in healthcare, education, and employment. At the same time, government and society play a crucial role in building a foundation that enables people to succeed by ensuring access to quality healthcare, education, and economic opportunities. A balanced approach, where individuals take the initiative while society removes unnecessary barriers, creates the conditions for more people to achieve stability and prosperity through their efforts.

How "Free" Should We Be?

If you ask most people whether the government should stay out of their personal affairs, the answer is almost always a resounding yes. This preference for liberty is universal when asked as a simple question.

However, as a society, we often show inconsistency in fully supporting the principle of individual liberty and true freedom of choice. In a framework that genuinely respects absolute personal autonomy, individuals have the right to make decisions about their life, including the right to end it if they choose. This would entail legalizing euthanasia, safeguarded by strict guidelines to ensure it is an informed and voluntary decision.

Under such a framework, decisions on personal safety matters, such as the use of motorcycle helmets, should rest with the individual. Of course, not wearing a helmet, given the statistics, is foolish. In the United States, according to the National Highway Traffic Safety Administration (NHTSA) in 2021, motorcyclists are about 2,400% more likely than people in passenger cars to die in a traffic crash per vehicle mile traveled.[136] Of 100 motorcycle accidents where the rider died, 37 would have been saved if wearing a helmet and 67 of 100 would have avoided brain injuries.[137]

However, the issue becomes more complex when it comes to seat belts. Seat belts reduce the risk of death by 45% and cut the risk of serious injury by 50% among drivers and front-seat passengers. In crashes, people who do not wear seat belts are 3,000% more likely to be ejected from a vehicle, which significantly increases the likelihood of fatal outcomes or severe injuries. And yet, one in seven drivers still do not buckle up.[138] Wearing a seat belt extends beyond individual choice; it significantly impacts overall vehicle safety. In accidents, an unbelted driver can lose control, while unbelted backseat passengers risk being thrown forward, potentially injuring others. Drivers also bear responsibility for ensuring all passengers, especially children, are safely secured. This practice highlights a commitment to collective safety and well-being, transcending personal preference.

This perspective aligns with the broader belief that personal freedom should be balanced with public safety and the rights of others. For example, children have a right to protection from harm, including risks arising from parental or guardian neglect. Thus, while individual freedoms are essential, they come with boundaries shaped by their potential impact on others.

Similarly, personal choice implies that the government should not interfere in health decisions, such as a woman's right to abortion. However, this issue introduces complexity regarding when fertilized cells are considered a person. While doctors routinely remove living cells, such as tumors or moles, these cells are not regarded as separate individuals. Yet, certain religious beliefs consider the fetus a distinct life from conception. That viewpoint asserts that abortion involves not only the woman's autonomy but also the perceived rights of another potential individual.

Liberty as a Right

This brings us to a broader principle: personal liberty should be exercised without harming or infringing on the peace and safety of others. In the case of abortion, this principle becomes intricate, as it involves balancing the rights of the woman (and her mate) with the perceived rights of the fetus. Thus, the debate around abortion embodies both the right to personal choice and the complex interpretation of when and how others' rights — here, those of the fetus — are considered. This complexity lies at the heart of the ongoing discussion, reflecting the challenge of reconciling personal liberty with ethical and moral considerations.

A balanced approach to liberty considers personal autonomy and the broader social framework that ensures equity and respect for all citizens. Policies that support individual choices in healthcare, family, or relationships affirm the value of personal freedom while protecting against discrimination and expanding opportunity. Social values like family and religious expression sustain a diverse society where differing views can coexist. This approach upholds personal responsibility and minimal government oversight while safeguarding essential freedoms.

A core principle of true liberty is that behavior should not be restricted by law unless it causes physical or mental harm to others. This principle includes the freedom to engage in risky activities, such as not wearing a motorcycle helmet, even if society bears some costs like medical care. Such costs are trade-offs for broader personal freedoms and fewer restrictions—but these freedoms must not harm or unduly distress others, especially vulnerable individuals like children.

Freedom of Speech

Views on freedom of speech often intersect with broader societal concerns, such as addressing hate speech and misinformation while ensuring space for diverse voices. Some Americans support policies that balance free expression with protections against harmful or discriminatory rhetoric, particularly on social media and public platforms. This view connects to broader social justice efforts, including healthcare access, climate action, racial equality, and LGBTQ+ rights. Advocates argue that government intervention is needed to safeguard rights and ensure fair opportunity. For example, in cases of online harassment, speech limits may be necessary to protect minors from harm.

Others emphasize minimal restrictions and oppose perceived censorship, especially around controversial or unpopular viewpoints. They argue that broad free speech rights should be upheld, even if the content is offensive, aligning with a philosophy of individual liberty, personal responsibility, and limited government.

Debates over speech often arise through legal challenges. For example, efforts to ban flag desecration in the name of national unity highlight tensions between patriotism and constitutional rights. In *Texas v. Johnson* (1989), the Supreme Court reaffirmed that burning the American flag is protected speech under the First Amendment, illustrating the difficulty of balancing national values with free expression.

These debates reflect a broader question about the limits of personal freedom—where individuals may exercise their rights as long as they do not harm others. The challenge lies in defining harm and proving its consequences, a legal and philosophical issue that continues to shape public policy and opinion.

Freedom of the Press

Freedom of the press is fundamental to a democratic society. It ensures transparency, accountability, and the public's right to be informed. The press plays a key role in holding power accountable and fostering open discourse. Broad support exists for a free and independent press, essential for maintaining checks and balances in governance and promoting diverse societal perspectives.

While preserving press freedom, concerns about misinformation and hate speech — especially on digital platforms — have led to calls for responsible media practices. Some advocate for policies that protect open and equal access to information while limiting the spread of false or harmful content. There is also a push for greater diversity in media representation to reflect a broader range of voices and perspectives.

Others emphasize minimal government interference, arguing that true press freedom means allowing diverse and sometimes controversial views without censorship. This perspective raises concerns about media bias and stresses the importance of a press representing different viewpoints fairly. While supporting open expression, proponents of this approach also recognize the need for responsible reporting and accuracy in journalism.

These differing viewpoints highlight the challenge of balancing press autonomy with modern media realities. Some suggest that media companies should operate as public corporations with no controlling interest, ensuring greater independence and reducing the risk of undue influence. Such an approach could help protect press freedom while fostering a well-informed and balanced public sphere.

Writ of Habeas Corpus

The writ of habeas corpus is a vital constitutional safeguard against unlawful detention, enshrined in Article I, Section 9 of the U.S. Constitution. It ensures that any person held in custody has the right to appear before a judge and challenge the legality of their detention. While the Constitution permits suspension of this right only in cases of rebellion or invasion, it has been tested during moments of national crisis.[427]

One notable example is Ex parte Milligan (1866), a U.S. Supreme Court case in which the Court ruled that the government could not try civilians by military tribunals when civil courts were open and functioning, even during wartime. The Court held that suspending habeas corpus does not eliminate all constitutional protections, reinforcing that civil liberties must be preserved even during emergencies.[428]

More recently, habeas corpus was at the center of Boumediene v. Bush (2008), where the Court ruled that detainees held at Guantanamo Bay had the constitutional right to file habeas corpus petitions in federal Court, striking down parts of the Military Commissions Act of 2006. These rulings affirm that habeas corpus remains a powerful judicial check on executive authority.[429]

Racial and Ethnic Equity

Our society continues to engage in discussions on historical disparities and inclusivity, with different perspectives on how best to address these issues. While most agree on the importance of racial and ethnic equity, the debate centers on the role of government and the most effective means of achieving fairness and opportunity.

One perspective calls for broad policy reforms to address systemic racism and foster inclusivity across American society. Supporters of this view call for criminal justice reform, voting rights protections, and targeted investments in education and healthcare to support historically marginalized communities. They also emphasize the need for diversity in leadership across government and the private sector, believing that proactive measures are necessary to ensure equal opportunities for all.

Another viewpoint prioritizes individual liberty, limited government intervention, and a race-neutral approach to policy. Proponents argue that focusing on racial distinctions could lead to reverse discrimination and prefer solutions that emphasize economic growth, free-market policies, and merit-based opportunities. This perspective often includes skepticism toward affirmative action and a belief that a strong economy benefits all individuals, regardless of background.

Opinions on these issues vary widely, even among individuals within the same political or social groups. While the debate over these approaches continues, the broader goal remains: ensuring a society where all individuals have equal opportunity and fair treatment. The U.S. Constitution guarantees equal protection under the law for all citizens, but disparities in opportunity and treatment persist, partly due to differing societal beliefs about equality.

Equal Rights and Social Justice

Despite significant advancements in civil rights, the U.S. Constitution does not explicitly guarantee equality based on gender, sexual orientation, or identity. The Equal Rights Amendment (ERA), proposed to address this gap, has not been fully ratified, despite Virginia's 2020 ratification bringing the total to 38 states. The amendment's legal status remains uncertain due to expired deadlines and questions over whether prior state withdrawals are valid, keeping the issue tied up in congressional and judicial debate.

While laws such as the Civil Rights Act and court rulings like *Obergefell v. Hodges* have provided protections against discrimination, they do not carry the permanence of a constitutional amendment. Some argue that ratifying the ERA or introducing a new amendment would reinforce the nation's commitment to fairness and equality, aligning with constitutional principles of protecting individual rights. Others believe existing laws already provide sufficient protections and question the necessity of additional amendments. As legal and political discussions continue, the broader debate reflects ongoing efforts to define and secure equal rights under the Constitution.

Right to Privacy

FISA, Search and Seizure, Privacy

Privacy is not explicitly stated as a constitutional right, but the Supreme Court's interpretation of the Fourth Amendment has established legal protections for privacy in various contexts. The Fourth Amendment requires law enforcement to obtain a warrant, supported by probable cause evidence, before conducting searches and seizures of individuals, their homes, and personal property. These legal safeguards significantly influence police conduct and individual privacy rights.

One of the most debated issues in privacy law is the Foreign Intelligence Surveillance Act (FISA), which gained increased attention with the passage of the USA PATRIOT Act 2001 and its subsequent renewals. Before the PATRIOT Act, FISA courts primarily issued surveillance warrants against suspected foreign spies operating within the U.S. However, the law expanded FISA's scope, granting broader counterterrorism surveillance powers and lowering the legal threshold for obtaining warrants. This expansion sparked debates over privacy rights and concerns about potential government overreach and unwarranted surveillance of U.S. citizens. Congress maintains oversight through intelligence and judiciary committees responsible for reviewing FISA-related activity and ensuring compliance with legal standards. However, critics argue that oversight has not always been sufficiently rigorous.

The National Security Agency (NSA) plays a central role in these discussions, monitoring, collecting, and analyzing intelligence for national security purposes. The NSA's scope includes signals intelligence, cybersecurity efforts, cryptographic research, and securing government communications. While these activities are conducted within legal and policy frameworks, concerns about surveillance transparency persist. Edward Snowden's 2013 revelations exposed the extent of NSA surveillance, particularly its ability to intercept Internet communications, raising public awareness about government monitoring practices. Under the PATRIOT Act, surveillance powers were expanded, including access to business and library records and a lower threshold for intelligence agencies to conduct wiretaps.

Recently, calls for greater transparency and accountability in FISA court proceedings have intensified. Critics argue that FISA courts operate without public scrutiny and often make decisions without the knowledge or representation of those being surveilled. Civil liberties advocates worry that this secrecy undermines fundamental privacy rights and increases the risk of potential abuses.

The renewal of key provisions in the PATRIOT Act remains a contentious issue. Some policymakers push for more oversight, stricter evidence standards, and greater transparency in the FISA warrant process to protect civil liberties. Others argue that strong surveillance tools are necessary to safeguard national security, stressing the need to balance privacy rights with preventing security threats.

The debate over privacy and surveillance continues as policymakers and courts seek a middle ground that respects personal freedoms while maintaining national security.

Role of Secrecy

National Security

Government secrecy is essential for specific areas, including national security, diplomatic negotiations, competitive bidding processes, and the protection of classified information. For example, whether true or not, Americans generally expect that the government maintains military capabilities beyond what is publicly disclosed, as was the case with the development of the atomic bomb during WWII. Incidents involving Edward Snowden, Chelsea Manning, and Julian Assange in 2010 and 2013 and the controversy surrounding classified documents at Mar-a-Lago in 2022 have sparked debates over releasing sensitive government information, the need for secrecy, and the limits of government transparency. These cases underscore ongoing concerns about government transparency and national security.

In Politics

In contrast, transparency is fundamental to democratic governance, where openness and public discourse are essential for accountability and trust. Excessive secrecy in political processes can erode public confidence, reduce oversight, and hinder informed decision-making. Recent ethics concerns in the Supreme Court, historical events such as the Watergate scandal and the Iran-Contra Affair, difficulties in enforcing the Freedom of Information Act — including delays and high fees — and ongoing debates over FISA warrant safeguards all highlight the risks associated with the lack of transparency in government.

Making government more open helps people get involved, have good discussions, and ensure leaders do their jobs honestly. Citizens have the right to know what their representatives are doing. Information about how laws are made, where tax money goes, and what policies are being planned should be easy to find. This helps people understand issues, hold leaders accountable, and make better choices when voting.

In Campaign Financing

Transparency should also apply to campaign financing and political contributions. Voters have a right to know who funds political campaigns and to what extent, as this information can expose potential conflicts of interest and outside influence in government decisions. Clear rules on campaign financing help protect the integrity of the democratic process.

While some government actions must remain confidential, citizens deserve insight into political processes that affect their lives. Striking the right balance between necessary secrecy and meaningful transparency is essential for a healthy democracy. Secrecy should be limited to national security, personally identifiable information (PII), confidential business information (CBI), and competitive government processes. On the other hand, transparency should be prioritized in areas that promote public accountability and build trust in institutions.

Improving government openness requires updates to existing laws and practices. Strengthening the enforcement of the Freedom of Information Act (FOIA) would help ensure timely and transparent responses to public information requests, with more substantial penalties for non-compliance. Expanding FOIA to include government contractors and using better technology to reduce backlogs would also improve access. Additional measures, such as stronger whistleblower protections, more transparent campaign finance disclosures, and mandatory transparency reporting by agencies, would further enhance accountability. Ensuring public access to government data, increasing citizen involvement in policy-making, and protecting journalists are critical steps in maintaining a transparent government that serves the public interest.

Property Rights

Property ownership is a fundamental right, but it must coexist with society's broader needs and the role of government. Individuals should be free to use their property as they choose, provided it does not harm neighboring properties, create hazards, or disrupt community stability. Eminent domain, while sometimes necessary, should be applied carefully and not for private commercial gain; private entities should acquire land through voluntary, fair-market purchases for legitimate economic purposes. When eminent domain is used in urban redevelopment or blighted areas, it should avoid displacing residents unnecessarily or without just compensation.

Public-private partnerships (PPPs) often involve government collaboration with private developers, where eminent domain may be used for projects that serve a public benefit. In these cases, the government secures the land, while private developers manage construction or operations, combining public objectives with private sector efficiency. However, PPPs carry risks, including favoritism, lack of transparency, and conflicts of interest that could shift the focus from public welfare to private profit. These partnerships require strict oversight, transparent bidding processes, and regulatory safeguards to prevent corruption and unfair practices,

Balancing property rights with community welfare involves thoughtful land use and zoning regulations. These policies guide urban development, protect environmental health, and promote equitable access to housing, particularly in cities. Preserving agricultural lands and supporting sustainable farming are also priorities in rural areas. Policies that prevent foreclosure and provide crisis assistance for small property owners further ensure that individual ownership remains protected while maintaining broader economic and social stability.

A well-regulated approach is necessary to balance property rights, community needs, and environmental sustainability. Ensuring private ownership and public welfare coexist supports a stable, fair, and functional society.

Reparations

Individual freedoms are foundational to democratic societies, often emphasizing the importance of justice and equality. These principles have led to ongoing discussions about reparations as a means of addressing historical injustices and their lasting impacts.

Reparations, particularly for African Americans affected by the legacy of slavery and persistent racial disparities, remain a complex and contentious issue. Supporters argue that reparations are necessary to redress historical wrongs, reduce economic disparities, and promote national reconciliation. They view reparations as a step toward acknowledging and correcting the long-term harm caused by slavery and segregation, fostering greater racial equity.

Others question the feasibility and fairness of reparations. Critics argue that implementing financial compensation for historical injustices is challenging and may not effectively address current inequalities. Some believe that the best approach is to focus on expanding opportunities for all individuals, ensuring that policies emphasize forward-looking solutions rather than compensation for past grievances.

One perspective contends that reparations should not be imposed on groups or regions that did not directly benefit from slavery, such as those in the North who opposed and fought against it. This viewpoint highlights the difficulty in assigning responsibility across generations and regions, raising ethical concerns about holding present-day individuals financially accountable for past injustices. The challenge of determining collective responsibility further complicates discussions on how historical harms should be addressed.

Another perspective rejects the idea of equity-based policies entirely, arguing that government intervention should focus on ensuring equal opportunity rather than adjusting outcomes based on historical circumstances. Supporters of this viewpoint believe that individual effort, rather than government compensation, should determine economic and social success. They argue that prioritizing equity over equality risks fostering dependency and resentment, ultimately undermining the principles of meritocracy.

The broader implications of reparations extend beyond African American communities. Some argue that recognizing historical injustices in this way could lead to similar claims from other groups, such as Native Americans, whose land was taken and cultures disrupted. Others note that many ethnic and religious groups, such as Irish immigrants in the 1800s or Catholics in early 20th-century America, also faced discrimination, raising questions about how far reparations should extend and which injustices warrant compensation.

The debate over reparations reflects a larger discussion about historical accountability, the definition of justice, and the most effective ways to achieve fairness in modern society. While some see reparations as necessary for achieving racial equity, others advocate for policies that focus on economic growth and expanded opportunity. Still, others challenge the premise of equity itself, emphasizing equal treatment under the law over race-conscious policymaking. This ongoing debate underscores the challenge of acknowledging historical injustices while ensuring that policies remain fair, inclusive, and focused on building a more just future.

JUSTICE AND THE RULE OF LAW

Justice and the rule of law are the foundation of a fair and stable society, ensuring that laws apply equally to all, without bias or political influence. When these principles are upheld, they protect rights, maintain order, and preserve public trust in the legal system.

The Rule of Law

The rule of law is a fundamental principle that keeps our society fair and orderly. It means that laws, not personal opinions, guide decisions. These laws reflect our shared values and include clear rules and consequences. The rule of law applies to everyone equally — citizens, businesses, and the government. It ensures that all laws are applied the same way.

The Constitution serves as the cornerstone of the rule of law in the United States, establishing a framework where laws are supreme and applied equally to all individuals, regardless of status or power. It defines the boundaries of governmental authority, ensuring that no branch exceeds its prescribed limits and enshrines fundamental rights to protect individuals from arbitrary actions.

By providing a system of checks and balances and an independent judiciary, the U.S. Constitution safeguards against abuses of power and upholds legal consistency. The Supreme Court plays a pivotal role in interpreting the Constitution, resolving disputes, and ensuring that governmental actions and laws align with constitutional principles, reinforcing the principle that no one is above the law and guaranteeing justice and stability in society.

Laws set the rules for society and the penalties for breaking them. In civilized countries, a governing body, supported by the people, creates these laws. Our Constitution ensures that laws, not government officials, guide behavior. This is different from undemocratic nations, where dictators make their own rules, as seen in many totalitarian governments today.

Due process, an integral element of the rule of law, mandates that "the government must respect all the legal rights that are owed to a person according to the law of the land." This stance includes adherence to precedent-setting case law, following the guidance of past legal rulings. The rule of law safeguards against arbitrary governance, implying consistency in law application and ensuring that laws are reasonable and "just."[67]

This concept dates to Ancient Greek philosophers like Plato and Aristotle around 350 BC. Plato emphasized the supremacy of law over the government, stating, "Where the law is subject to some other authority and has none of its own, the collapse of the state ... is not far off; but if law is the master of the government and the government is its slave, then the situation is full of promise ..."[67] Aristotle also supported the rule of law, advocating that "law should govern" and those in power should be "servants of the laws."[67] This ideal was further embodied in the Magna Carta in 1215 AD, which subjected English sovereigns and magistrates to the law.[67]

In the United States, the notion that no one is above the law was pivotal during its founding. Thomas Paine, in 1776, expressed in *Common Sense*, "In America, the law is king ... in free countries, the law ought to be king; and there ought to be no other."[69] John Adams, in 1780, sought to establish "a government of laws and not of men" in the Massachusetts Constitution.[70] Thus, the rule of law does not guarantee democracy but is crucial for its existence and the defense of human rights.

Commitment to democratic principles, fairness in law, and an independent judiciary are central to a healthy society. Advocates for transparency and accountability emphasize the need for checks and balances to prevent abuse of power and ensure that government actions remain within legal bounds. Prioritizing civil liberties and human rights, they argue for laws applied equally to all, rejecting discrimination and supporting reforms to address systemic injustices.

On the other hand, strict adherence to constitutional principles and respect for the traditional legal framework are also vital aspects of maintaining order and protecting freedoms. Historically, supporters of a literal interpretation of the Constitution often emphasize limited government intervention, impartial law enforcement, and consistent law application. They focus on public safety and property rights, advocating judicial restraint to prevent overreach and uphold the separation of powers. However, political divisions today have led to inconsistent applications of these principles. Some advocates still push for strict law enforcement, while others selectively interpret constitutional limits based on political interests. The debate over government intervention and judicial power is increasingly shaped by partisan agendas rather than consistent commitment to constitutional principles.

Understanding different views on law and justice helps citizens support a fair and orderly society. However, as the justice system becomes more politicized, its fairness is at risk, weakening public trust. To prevent this, legal experts stress the need for an independent, nonpartisan judiciary to safeguard democracy and equal justice.

Strengthening the Rule of Law

The rule of law is essential to a just society, ensuring equal enforcement, protecting rights, and limiting government overreach. However, political divisions, unequal application of laws, and public distrust have weakened its foundation. When the powerful receive leniency while others face harsher consequences, confidence in justice and social unity erode.

Restoring trust requires impartial enforcement, stronger accountability, and updated laws addressing modern challenges like judicial ethics, digital privacy, and corporate influence. Citizens also have a role — to stay informed, demand fairness, and hold leaders accountable. If both institutions and individuals uphold these principles, the rule of law can continue to protect rights and prevent abuses of power.

Archibald Cox, the Special Prosecutor for the Watergate scandal, reflected on the lessons Americans should have learned from the events surrounding President Richard Nixon's resignation. In a letter dated May 24, 1994, Cox addressed Aaron Leahy, Sherylin Peek, and Nicole Poimiroo, high school students conducting a project commemorating the 20th anniversary of Nixon's resignation. Guided by their teacher, Karl Grubaugh, the students contacted various individuals connected to the scandal, asking for their insights. Cox's response emphasized two critical lessons:

"First, we should be reminded of the corrupt influence of great power, especially when the power is in the hands of someone willing to resort to any tactics, however wrong, to retain and increase his power. Perhaps it is inescapable that modern government vests extraordinary power in the President and puts around him a large circle of men and women whose personal status and satisfaction depend entirely upon pleasing that one man."

"Second, thoughtful Americans should be reminded of our traditional constitutionalism's essential but fragile character — the rule of law inherited from England, which holds that even the highest officials are bound by law. Former President Nixon sought to challenge that rule and was overwhelmed by an aroused public opinion. We should remember that the rule depends upon constant vigilance."

These words remain a powerful reminder of the dangers of unchecked power and the importance of safeguarding constitutional principles through vigilance and public accountability.

Judicial Reforms

Proposed reforms include term limits, rotating judges from lower courts, or expanding the Court to introduce fresh perspectives and ensure broader representation. As discussed earlier, Term Limits could prevent ideological entrenchment while rotating judges and Court expansion would foster a judiciary more responsive to modern challenges.

Rather than being appointed for life, a term limit of 18 years has been suggested as one way to balance the political influence of SCOTUS justices and thereby their findings. However, a certain stability and consistency of rulings supports the concept of lifetime appointment. An age limit does not make sense because it reflects the wisdom that comes with age. However, some non-political mechanism should be created.

Three mechanisms could be implemented to ensure the ongoing fitness of serving justices. First, regular health assessments, including cognitive evaluations conducted by medical professionals, would monitor mental capacity across all federal judges. Second, a peer review process within the judiciary would allow justices to confidentially report any concerns regarding a colleague's mental fitness to an independent expert panel. Finally, if mental capacity concerns arise, the consensus of four jurists could order an independent medical evaluation, with experts assessing whether the justice remains fit to serve.

Crime Victims

Crime victims deserve clear legal protections to ensure their rights are upheld throughout the justice process. While laws exist to support victims, gaps remain — many still are not notified about court proceedings, and some are even barred from attending trials where the accused and their supporters are present.[435-436] Victims of violent crimes, including abused children, domestic violence survivors, and grieving families, should have guaranteed access to case updates, courtrooms, and a voice in the proceedings. Strengthening and enforcing these rights would create a more just and victim-centered legal system.

Campaign Libel

Preserving libel laws during election campaigns is essential to preserving the integrity of the democratic process. These laws help prevent the spread of false and defamatory statements that could unfairly harm a candidate's reputation and mislead voters. While the First Amendment protects free speech, it does not extend to defamatory falsehoods made with actual malice — a standard established by the Supreme Court in *New York Times Co. v. Sullivan (1964)*, which requires that a public figure prove a false statement was made knowingly or with reckless disregard for the truth.

Suspending libel laws during campaigns would risk increased unchecked misinformation, potentially distorting public perception and undermining informed decision-making. However, some critics argue that existing libel laws already place a high burden on public figures seeking legal recourse, making it challenging to hold media or opponents accountable for false claims. Despite this, enforcing libel laws remains essential for ensuring accountability, deterring harmful misinformation, and fostering a fair political environment while protecting legitimate political discourse.

Rights of the Accused

The U.S. justice system is built on key constitutional protections. The Fifth Amendment protects against self-incrimination and double jeopardy. The Sixth Amendment ensures a fair and speedy trial, legal counsel, and the right to face witnesses. The Eighth Amendment bans excessive bail, fines, and cruel or unusual punishment, safeguarding fair treatment under the law.

Debates over criminal justice focus on two main views. Some advocate for tougher law enforcement, harsher sentences, and strict crime control, believing this improves public safety and supports victims. Others emphasize balancing law enforcement with fair treatment, pointing to issues like prison overcrowding, high costs, and the need for rehabilitation over punishment.

Justice should not be about revenge. Sentencing must follow the law, not personal anger, to prevent unfair punishments and maintain integrity. Modern justice focuses on rehabilitation, helping offenders reform instead of repeating crimes. Keeping revenge out of sentencing ensures fairness, protects human rights, and builds trust in the system.

The challenge is finding the right balance — protecting public safety while upholding individual rights and adapting laws to fit society's changing needs.

Policing, Crime, and Punishment

Policing, crime, and punishment remain central issues in governance, with differing perspectives on maintaining public safety while ensuring justice. Some advocate for police reform, emphasizing improved training, accountability measures, and community-based policing strategies to build trust between law enforcement and the communities they serve. Others prioritize stricter sentencing laws and enhanced law enforcement efforts, arguing that tough-on-crime policies serve as effective deterrents and protect public safety.

The debate over criminal justice reform includes discussions on sentencing policies, prison conditions, and rehabilitation efforts. Supporters of reform argue that reducing excessive sentences for nonviolent offenses, expanding mental health and substance abuse programs, and investing in rehabilitation can lower recidivism rates and ease the burden on the prison system. Meanwhile, those in favor of stricter penalties contend that maintaining strong deterrents is essential to preventing crime and ensuring justice for victims.

Balancing public safety with fair and effective law enforcement remains a challenge. Policies that address crime prevention, rehabilitation, and accountability while respecting individuals' rights and the role of law enforcement in protecting communities are required.

Police Force

In 1950 there were approximately 151,300,000 people in the U.S. and about 190,000 police, or one policeperson for every 796 people. In 1970 there were 203.1 million people in the U.S. and 388,000 full-time policepersons, which is 523 people per policeperson. And, in 2021, there were 331,400,000 people in the U.S. and about 697,195 police, or one policeperson for every 475 people. These figures may reflect a need due to higher crime rates or a desire for improved safety.[122]

In recent years, debates over police staffing have intensified, driven by concerns on both sides. Advocates for increasing the number of officers often cite rising crime rates, slower emergency response times, and community demands for greater security and presence in underserved areas. On the other hand, reform advocates push for reducing police budgets or reallocating resources toward social services, mental health support, and community-based programs, arguing that public safety can be improved through prevention and de-escalation rather than enforcement alone. These opposing pressures reflect broader societal questions about the role of policing and how best to achieve safety and justice.

Crime Rates

Discussions about crime often highlight statistics to shape public perception. While crime rates are essential in understanding public safety, isolated incidents or selective data can sometimes create an exaggerated sense of widespread danger. Crime trends fluctuate over time and vary by region, making it essential to rely on comprehensive, long-term data for an accurate picture.

As of 2024, U.S. crime rates continue to show notable improvements. According to the FBI's latest crime reports, both violent and property crimes have generally decreased over the past few years, continuing a long-term decline since the peak levels of the 1990s. In the first half of 2024, preliminary data indicates a further 10.3% reduction in violent crime compared to the same period in 2023, with significant decreases in murder (down 22.7%) and aggravated assault (down 8.1%). Property crimes also fell by 13.1% during this time. These trends align with broader declines observed since the early 2000s, despite temporary increases in specific years, such as 2020 and 2021, due to social and economic disruptions.

While some analysts describe violent crime rates as reaching historic lows, the National Crime Victimization Survey (NCVS), which includes both reported and unreported crimes, has noted fluctuations. In 2022, data suggested a rise in certain offenses, prompting further study into crime patterns and reporting practices. The complexity of accurately measuring crime means that trends should be viewed in context, as they can vary by location and crime type.

Recent declines in crime data from 2023-2024 contribute to a cautiously optimistic outlook, reinforcing the importance of informed policy discussions based on accurate and comprehensive statistics.[218-220]

Perception of more crime

Constant online news about crime and tragedy worldwide can make crime seem worse than it is, even when overall rates are steady or falling. This news emphasis mirrors the tactics of old tabloid newspapers, which used shocking stories to attract readers. Now, with instant updates on crimes and disasters globally, people may perceive crime as rising more than the data supports.

Approaches to criminal justice vary widely. One perspective focuses on preventing crime by addressing its root causes — poverty, addiction, and domestic violence — through education, rehabilitation, and social services. Supporters of this approach emphasize community policing, improved technology for law enforcement, and accountability measures such as body cameras and de-escalation training to build public trust.

Another approach prioritizes strong policing, increased resources for law enforcement, and strict sentencing to deter crime. While this method aims to enhance public safety through firm penalties and a strong police presence, critics argue it may not address deeper causes of crime and could lack sufficient oversight. These differing viewpoints reflect ongoing debates about balancing safety and fairness in the justice system.

Concerns about over-policing and harsh sentencing remain significant. Critics warn that mandatory minimum sentences and aggressive policing can lead to overcrowded prisons and excessive punishment for non-violent offenders, reducing opportunities for rehabilitation. Without proper oversight, a heightened police presence may also increase the risk of misconduct and weaken public trust, particularly in communities with historically strained relationships with law enforcement.

Criminal Punishment

Punishing criminals is a fundamental responsibility of the government. Crime exists for various reasons, including genetics, upbringing, poverty, mental health, and drug use. While these factors contribute to criminal behavior, there will always be individuals who harm others. Governments must establish and enforce laws to protect citizens and ensure that punishment is fair, consistent, and appropriate.

An important consideration in sentencing is the level of danger the offender poses to society—whether the individual is likely to re-offend, escalate their behavior, or endanger others if released. Sentencing should not only reflect the severity of the crime but also consider public safety and the potential need for long-term restraint.

Totalitarian governments maintain control through fear and force, while democracies rely on the rule of law, enforcement, and fair punishment. In the U.S., people have the freedom to make certain harmful choices, such as drug use, whereas Singapore enforces strict penalties, including jail, caning, or even execution for drug trafficking. Singapore also has firm laws against littering, jaywalking, and other offenses, contributing to low crime rates and minimal corruption. While this approach creates a more controlled society, many citizens support these laws and actively assist in crime prevention. Ultimately, it reflects a trade-off — America emphasizes personal freedoms, while Singapore prioritizes strict order and enforcement.

Compared to other Civilized Countries

The severity of criminal punishment in the U.S. differs significantly from many other countries, sparking debates on fairness, justice, and effectiveness. Strict sentencing policies contribute to higher incarceration rates, longer prison terms, and, in some states, the death penalty. This strictness contrasts with nations that prioritize rehabilitation, especially in Western Europe. Norway, for example, emphasizes reintegration, leading to lower recidivism rates and shorter sentences. Life sentences without parole, rare in most European countries, are frequently imposed in the U.S. for severe crimes.

Mandatory minimum sentences, particularly for non-violent offenses, remove judicial discretion and have drawn criticism for imposing rigid penalties. In contrast, Germany and Sweden allow judges to consider factors like an offender's background and capacity for rehabilitation. Capital punishment is another point of contention; while still legal in some U.S. states, most developed nations have abolished it due to concerns over human rights and wrongful convictions.

Reforming the U.S. justice system to emphasize judicial discretion, rehabilitation, and proportional sentencing could create a more balanced approach. Reducing mandatory minimums and expanding rehabilitative programs would allow for fairer sentencing while maintaining public safety. Ultimately, how a society punishes crime reflects its values, and balancing strict penalties with rehabilitation can help shape a more just system.

Death Penalty

In taking an objective look at the death penalty and whether it should continue to exist in the United States, the following may be considered:

Death Penalty Issues

The death penalty remains one of the most debated issues in the criminal justice system, raising questions about justice, deterrence, morality, and fairness. Supporters argue that it serves as a just punishment for the most heinous crimes, deters violent offenses, and provides closure for victims' families. Opponents, however, cite concerns over wrongful convictions, racial and economic disparities in sentencing, and the ethical implications of state-sanctioned executions. With shifting public opinion, legal challenges, and varying state policies, the debate over capital punishment continues to evolve, reflecting broader discussions on crime, punishment, and human rights.

Revenge

One of the underlying premises of having a death penalty appears to be the concept of "an eye for an eye" – payback equal to the crime or, as some might put it, as close to revenge that we can get without appearing to be as barbaric as the criminal. In the United States, we do not take "eye for an eye" literally. We do not take an eye when someone puts out another's eye. We do not torture someone because they tortured someone else, except in extreme cases (e.g., terrorism). We do not use rape as a punishment for rapists. Therefore, justifying the death penalty as punishment for murder based on the "eye for an eye" premise does not follow logically.

Death Penalty Expense

Then why do we have the death penalty? Is it to remove that person from society? Prison already does that. Is it to save money? Nope!

Much to the surprise of many, it turns out that it is cheaper to imprison someone for life than to execute them.[49] In fact, it is almost ten times cheaper! One might ask, "How can that be?"

Every state that has a death penalty also has an intricate system and basis for appeals. These appeals relate to everything from due process claims to equal protection to the cruel and unusual punishment prohibition of the Eighth Amendment to the U.S. Constitution. The result? In California, the slowest state in the Union, the average wait time between conviction and execution for someone sentenced to death is 20 years. The national average is just under nine years.

And, while all this waiting is going on, the process has not ground to a halt. Quite the opposite, in fact. The appeals process consumes hours of labor, not only by court staff, but also by the often court-appointed, taxpayer-funded, and constitutionally-guaranteed public defenders. As a result, some estimate that it costs U.S. taxpayers between $50 million and $90 million dollars more per year (depending on the jurisdiction) to prosecute death penalty cases than life sentences.[49-01]

Of course, the normal response to this fact during a death penalty debate is that we should simply get rid of the appeals. While this would eliminate some of the expenses involved as increased trial and security would still need to be paid for, it would also eliminate fundamental civil rights granted every American. Considering the significant number of individuals exonerated due to DNA evidence unavailable during their initial trials, the provision for multiple appeals seems essential in allowing the development of evidence that could prove the innocence of the accused.

While cost is not the only factor to be considered, the argument that it is cheaper to execute someone than keep them alive in prison for the rest of their lives is entirely wrong.

Different Approaches Across the World

Sentencing guidelines for premeditated murder vary significantly across the world. Some countries, such as the UK, Australia, and Canada, have abolished the death penalty and rely on long-term imprisonment. Others may impose life sentences or have the death penalty on their books. Out of approximately 193 countries worldwide, about 111 have entirely abolished the death penalty for all crimes, while 54 still retain it. The remaining countries have it, but only for special circumstances (e.g., war crimes).

Necessary for Victim Closure?

Seeking retribution in the form of revenge is an emotional response that should have no place in criminal punishment. There is a premise that the death penalty brings "closure" to the family and friends of the victim. One cannot deny that emotional closure for the family or friends is important. However, sentencing the perpetrator to life in prison should provide for the necessary closure without indulging people's primitive urges for revenge.

The death penalty is certainly not the only way to resolve the emotional distress of the victim's families and friends or satisfy an incensed public. Which would be better retribution? Suffering a long, uncomfortable life, reflecting daily on the deed that placed them there, ending in an ignoble death without friend or family present, or dying a quick and painless death?

The Fallacy that Prisoners Live in Ease

Living a life in prison is generally a profoundly harsh experience, marked by a rigid daily routine and limited personal freedoms. Inmates typically reside in small, austere cells with basic amenities, sharing confined spaces in overcrowded facilities. Access to outdoor activities, educational programs, and work opportunities vary, often dependent on the security level of the institution and the inmate's behavior. Social interactions are mostly restricted to fellow inmates and prison staff, with occasional visits from outside, subject to strict regulations. Healthcare can be inconsistent, and the mental strain of facing a lifetime behind bars weighs heavily, affecting mental and emotional well-being. The environment is frequently tense, with the constant presence of strict security measures and the potential for conflict. Overall, life in prison for those serving life sentences is defined by its limitations, monotony, and the ongoing challenge of coping with the reality of a life spent in confinement.

Thou Shall Not Kill?

If someone tries to kill you, you have a right and even an obligation to kill him or her to defend yourself, unless you can incapacitate the attacker in some non-lethal way. Society also has the right and obligation to kill someone who is in the act of attempting to kill one of its members, but it does not NEED to kill that person after the crime has happened, and the perpetrator captured. A person defending against attack cannot avoid being emotionally involved, but society should not run on emotion because that is when mistakes are made.

Deterrent

Another justification for the death penalty is its role as a deterrent to crime. However, some argue that the real deterrent is not the punishment but the likelihood of getting caught. When the risk of apprehension is low, criminal activity often increases, as seen in looting during disasters like Hurricane Katrina. However, the extent to which harsher penalties prevent crime remains unclear.

Evidence suggests that strict penalties in places like Singapore — such as caning or execution for drug offenses and fines for littering — serve as deterrents. However, the deterrent effect is primarily tied to the certainty of enforcement rather than the severity of punishment. Addressing crime requires strict penalties and a high probability of apprehension.

Considering that death row inmates often spend decades awaiting execution, life in prison may not be significantly less of a deterrent. If punishment alone were the primary deterrent, one would expect death row inmates to have little hesitation in attacking guards, yet this is rare. Some may fear the prolonged isolation that follows such actions more than the execution itself, raising the question of whether the death penalty is truly the most feared punishment.

Criminologists often note that capital crimes are frequently committed by individuals under the influence of drugs or alcohol, suffering from mental illness, or acting in extreme emotional states like jealousy or rage. These circumstances suggest that rational deterrence plays a minimal role in preventing such crimes. Even among premeditated cases, executions are rare due to unsolved investigations, legal barriers, or high-powered defense attorneys. The long delays between sentencing and execution further weaken any immediate deterrent effect.

Ultimately, the effectiveness of the death penalty as a deterrent remains debatable. Given that many capital crimes are committed in irrational states of mind or by individuals who do not expect to be caught, the argument that the death penalty prevents most killings is difficult to support.

Unequal Application of the Law

Our Declaration of Independence, Constitution and Bill of Rights established the basis for all laws being applied equally to all citizens. Yet, it is also true that the death penalty is not equally applied. The worst offenders are often not executed (e.g., Ted Kozinski, Terry Nichols, and Andrea Yates). And it depends in which state you are tried. Further, facts show that those who cannot afford to pay for an experienced attorney and require a common public defender are more likely to be sentenced to death than those who can.[161] A public attorney does not have the time or funds to fully investigate the circumstances around their defendant's alleged crimes nor prepare a full and effective defense. For example, an examination of 461 capital cases by *The Dallas Morning News* found that one in four condemned inmates has been represented at trial or on appeal by court-appointed attorneys who have been disciplined for professional misconduct at some point in their careers.[161]

Consequences of Mistakes

It is not just that the poor are misrepresented, but also that the justice system is prone to human error, whether from the investigating detectives and the labs that support them, the defense and prosecution attorneys, or the judges and juries – all are prone to emotions, mistakes, misinterpretations, misperceptions, and even potentially tampering.

Once a death penalty sentence has been imposed, a series of appeals, delays, and technicalities ensue that are prone to more errors. This can lead to retrials. When retried, statistics show 7% of defendants are acquitted – proof of the human error we mentioned. Some of those reversals may even be errors on top of errors (i.e., they really were guilty). The application of the death penalty is inconsistent, sometimes unfair, but more importantly it is irreversible. According to an entry in Wikipedia, as many as 39 people have been executed "in face of compelling evidence of innocence or serious doubt about guilt." Life is not fair, so despite our best efforts we cannot ensure fairness within our justice system. It is not fair to an innocent person who has been found guilty and will be executed. How many times have people serving long sentences or in prison under the threat of execution had those sentences overturned because DNA testing became available which shows that they were never guilty in the first place? (At least 15 since 1992)[162]

A possible exception could be cases where an individual is so dangerous that their imprisonment poses a significant risk to other inmates and prison staff. In such rare instances, carrying out the death penalty might be the only way to ensure safety. However, very few sentenced to death would meet this standard. If such a policy were implemented, clear legal guidelines would be required to prevent misuse. Ensuring these laws are applied fairly and without error would be a major challenge, making their implementation extraordinarily complex, if feasible.

To some religions, life is sacred. If so, then no lives should ever be taken. But most religions recognize that there are times when it is necessary for the protection of society. We take the lives of our enemies in wars and stop violent criminals in the act of committing an offence. But should we take lives once the threat to our safety has been neutralized?

Some argue, "The existence of some systematic problems is no reason to abandon the whole death penalty system."[163] If you were the one innocent person about to be executed, would you agree with this argument? Problems with the judicial system, technicalities that free the guilty, and errors that sometimes convict the innocent are all good reasons why the death penalty should be eliminated. Would it not be better to put all capital criminals in prison for life so we could avoid the risk of taking the life of even one innocent person?

Religious View of Death Penalty

Some arguments for and against the death penalty are grounded in religion. One consideration might be that executing a criminal may deprive that person of their opportunity to repent for their sins before their death. Some on death row find religion and seek forgiveness, but many do not. Some would argue that it is appropriate that criminals deserving of the death penalty should not get the chance to repent; that they deserve to spend eternity in hell. However, religions also teach that we are not the judge, God is. So, it is not for us to decide who should have a chance to repent or whether their request for repentance should be granted.

Also, one could argue that, with the death penalty, the victim's family and friends may lose their opportunity to forgive. One could argue further that if a perpetrator did come to realize the wrongs they committed, then living with that for the rest of their lives could be a punishment worse than death. And, of course, with a death sentence, any chance of correcting a mistake of an innocent person wrongly sentenced, and apologizing for that error, would be long gone as well.

Inconsistency with Religious Principles

Is there a contradiction in the sanctity of life principle? Many religions emphasize the inherent value of human life.

In the case of abortion, this principle is often interpreted as protecting the unborn, whom believers may see as possessing full human dignity and rights from conception. However, when applied to the death penalty, interpretations vary. Some religious traditions argue that capital punishment is a just consequence for the most heinous crimes, upholding justice while still valuing life. Others contend that the sanctity of life should extend to all individuals, including those convicted of serious offenses, making the death penalty morally inconsistent. This divide reflects broader debates on how religious and ethical principles should guide legal and societal decisions.

Rush to Judgment

In the times of the Old West, criminals immediately used to be hanged or summarily executed for common crimes, like cattle rustling, shooting a man in the back, and many times for no crime at all. Sometimes, the perpetrator was subjected to a "kangaroo court" – a hastily gathered court that trades expediency for due process. The worst cases were to justify lynchings during the late 1800s and early 1900s in America – for reasons such as a black man looking at a white woman, fabricated "crimes," enforcing white supremacy, for asserting independence, to intimidate, for wanting to vote, and so on. Lynchings were always perpetrated by hastily assembled groups of white men driven by emotions and mob mentality. In rare cases, mob action might have been justified because it needed to protect remote society from a mad or indiscriminate killer, but the actions against black men were far too often completely unjustified and the consequence of unfettered racial discrimination. Mob action ran on irrational emotion, lacking any system of justice or fair trial to validate the actions taken. As time has progressed, we have become more aware of how fair trials should be managed – and we still get it wrong too often.

On a related note, in early 2025, federal prosecutors are seeking the death penalty for a kidnapping, molestation, and murder case in Vermont where the state has no death penalty law. The federal government is imposing its own penalty at the state level, which appears to be a violation of states' rights and our Constitution.[163-02]

Law Enforcement

Laws are created with the expectation that they will be enforced, as there will always be individuals who believe the rules do not apply to them or engage in antisocial behavior. Ideally, laws should originate from the level of government responsible for their primary enforcement. The U.S. Constitution outlines specific federal responsibilities, primarily concerning national defense, foreign affairs, interstate commerce, and monetary policy. The Tenth Amendment reserves all other powers to the states or the people, reinforcing that law enforcement is primarily a state and local responsibility.

In practical terms this means that laws governing issues like gambling, alcohol, firearms, or drug regulation, despite their potential for taxation, should generally be handled at the state level unless national enforcement is necessary for consistency or to prevent interstate conflicts. Conversely, antitrust laws, securities regulation, telecommunications, and national security concerns fall under federal jurisdiction, as they impact multiple states and require uniform enforcement.

The federal government's role in law enforcement should focus on safeguarding borders, protecting against external threats, and ensuring laws are applied fairly across state lines. However, when addressing crimes and regulations within their own borders, states and local governments are typically better equipped due to their proximity to the communities they serve. Maintaining this division of responsibilities upholds the constitutional principle of federalism while ensuring effective governance.

Justice Free from Political Influence

In a democracy, no one is above the law, and the justice system must operate independently, regardless of political considerations. Legal proceedings should not be halted just because someone is running for office, and the Justice Department must be safeguarded from political intimidation or interference. Similarly, an elected official should not be able to obstruct or shut down ongoing investigations. The Constitution's principles of checks and balances suggest that presidents should not be able to pardon themselves for personal crimes, ensuring accountability remains central to the nation's governance.

Criminal Punishment

With AI we are headed toward a time when we will have automated enforcement of some laws. And conceivably automatic judgement and sentencing. Our laws can be more consistent and fairer. Artificial intelligence should be able to help ensure fair, just, and balanced sentencing.

Many federal and state laws impose significant penalties for assaults that cause bodily injury to law enforcement officers, but sentencing varies widely. While some states have mandatory minimum sentences, others allow judicial discretion or plea deals, leading to inconsistencies. Establishing uniform sentencing guidelines could ensure consistent consequences, though criminal law remains a state matter.

Criminals should generally not be allowed to seek monetary damages for injuries sustained while committing a crime or resisting arrest, except in cases of excessive force beyond what is necessary. While most jurisdictions already limit such claims, more precise and consistent legal standards across states could prevent misuse of the legal system while ensuring accountability in law enforcement practices.

Limits on Facial Recognition

Facial recognition technology has advanced significantly, but it still faces notable limitations. Factors like poor lighting, low-resolution images, and changes in appearance — such as aging, facial hair, or masks — can reduce accuracy. Studies have also found higher error rates in identifying individuals with darker skin tones, raising concerns about racial and gender disparities.

Privacy and security risks remain key issues, as unauthorized surveillance and data breaches can expose sensitive biometric information. Technology also struggles to differentiate between identical twins, and high-quality deepfakes or masks can deceive them. While ongoing improvements aim to enhance accuracy and security, these challenges highlight ethical, legal, and practical concerns that require careful oversight and regulation.

LEADER QUALIFICATIONS

The qualifications for American government leaders have been debated since the country's founding. The Founding Fathers, concerned with creating a stable and just government, believed leaders should possess integrity, wisdom, and a commitment to public service. They envisioned a system where government officials would serve as representatives of the people, though specific qualifications for office were limited to age, citizenship, and residency requirements. Over time, these minimal requirements have persisted, even as the responsibilities and complexities of governance have evolved significantly.

Jefferson's Job Qualifications

Our Founding Fathers were highly intelligent and educated but most had little experience leading large organizations. Government departments were much smaller when Jefferson and Adams served as presidents.

Jefferson received a comprehensive education. He was tutored in various subjects, including mathematics, Latin, Greek, and the classics. His formal education continued at the College of William and Mary, where he studied philosophy, science, and literature and further honed his classical knowledge. Additionally, he studied law under George Wythe, a prominent Virginia attorney and judge.

Jefferson's commitment to learning extended beyond formal education. He was an avid reader and self-learner, amassing a vast personal library that covered history, science, literature, and politics. He was interested in languages and was proficient in Latin, Greek, French, Italian, Spanish, and Anglo-Saxon. His library of 6,500 books was sold to the new Library of Congress in 1815, after the British burned down the original library in 1814. Furthermore, his management skills were honed on his 5,000-acre property, where he conducted agricultural experiments, cultivating crops like tobacco, wheat, corn, and various fruits and vegetables. He also maintained livestock, gardens, orchards, and vineyards on his estate, Monticello.

Adams' Job Qualifications

Adams' qualifications were different but equally impressive. He began his education at a local common school and received guidance from his father and uncle, who were farmers and deacons. Adams pursued a liberal arts education at Harvard, obtaining a bachelor's and a master's degree. His legal career began as an apprentice under James Putnam, a prominent lawyer, where he gained practical experience in the legal profession.

Besides his legal expertise, Adams was known for his avid writing and intellectual contributions. He developed a successful law firm, lived on a small 14-acre farm, Peacefield, and served as a diplomat before entering government. He authored numerous essays, pamphlets, and letters on a wide range of topics, including politics, government, and philosophy.

The point of the above comparison is to emphasize that our Founding Fathers were highly educated, and mostly self-taught, before entering government service. They did not have extensive experience managing large global businesses anywhere near the size of our current government, but then our government and our country at that time were small. They led by their contributions to the structure of the government and by the principles they established. They understood the principles they incorporated in our Constitution.

Current Job Qualifications

Today, our government needs experienced leaders because the population of our country grows exponentially, as does the size and complexity of our government. We need leaders with greater qualifications than spelled out in the Constitution.

In 2024, federal spending is projected to reach a record $6.8 trillion, accounting for roughly 24% of the U.S. GDP of $23.416 trillion. This increase reflects ongoing demands in healthcare, social programs, and national security.

As of March 2025, the federal workforce comprises approximately 2.1 million civilian employees and 2.3 million military personnel, reflecting a reduction from peak levels in the 1960s. This decline is primarily attributed to technological advancements and increased outsourcing.

In recent developments, the Department of Government Efficiency (DOGE), established under President Trump's second administration and led by Elon Musk, is attempting to reduce the federal workforce. In February 2025 alone, 62,530 job cuts (2.9%) were announced across 17 federal agencies to streamline operations and reduce government expenditure. While their objectives may have value, many of our citizens have not widely accepted their methods and the resulting consequences.

The trend of increasing federal expenditures per citizen in the United States has been particularly evident in recent decades. In 1947, the government spent around $2,000 per citizen in 2024 dollars. By 2004, this amount grew to approximately $8,000 (2024 dollars), marking a 400% increase over 57 years. By 2022, federal spending per citizen reached $20,957, (2024 dollars), indicating a continued rise fueled by program expansions, population growth, and increasing administrative demands.[214-216]

Managing this colossal organization and budget now involves addressing increasingly intricate issues, such as a growing federal deficit, international financial dependencies, and reliance on foreign trade, oil, and loans. Consequently, merely being a friend of the president is no longer sufficient to qualify someone for a position as the head of an executive office department. Nor should anyone be elected to a government office without the necessary qualifications just because they have a lot of money.

President

The U.S. Constitution outlines specific qualifications for the nation's highest offices, setting the foundational criteria for those who aspire to lead. For the presidency, Article II, Section 1, Clause 5 requires a candidate to be a natural-born citizen of the United States. This generally means they must be born on U.S. soil or to U.S. citizen parents, even if born abroad. Additionally, they must be at least 35 years old and have resided in the United States for a minimum of 14 years. These requirements reflect the Founders' intent to ensure a president's loyalty to the nation and a level of maturity and experience.

Senate

The qualifications for the Senate, as laid out in Article I, Section 3, Clause 3, include a minimum age of 30, at least nine years of U.S. citizenship, and residency in the state they wish to represent. This age and citizenship threshold reflects the intent to appoint senators with greater life experience and a strong commitment to the states they serve.

House

For the House of Representatives, the qualifications are slightly less stringent. According to Article I, Section 2, Clause 2, candidates must be at least 25 years old, have been U.S. citizens for a minimum of seven years, and reside in the state they represent. This lower age requirement for House members reflects the House's role as the chamber closer to the people, with frequent elections intended to ensure representatives are closely aligned with their constituents. These constitutional qualifications were designed to foster a government that balances experience, loyalty, and representation across federal leadership roles.

Qualification Issues

The qualifications for elected federal offices are outlined in the original text of the U.S. Constitution and have remained unchanged since the nation's founding. However, states may impose additional requirements if they do not conflict with constitutional guidelines.

Today's scope of government vastly differs from when these qualifications were established. Given the complexity of modern governance, candidates should possess a certain level of relevant experience and education. The federal government oversees vast domestic and international responsibilities, requiring leaders with a deep understanding of economics, law, diplomacy, and administration. The president, for instance, manages a workforce of approximately 2.1 million federal civilian employees as of 2023, while Congress oversees more than 40,000 staffers supporting legislative functions.

Some officeholders advocate for significantly downsizing or reconstructing the government due to concerns about its cost and efficiency. However, this perspective must be weighed against the reality of governing a large, complex nation. A more practical approach might be ensuring those elected are qualified to manage such responsibilities effectively.

Beyond basic qualifications, government leadership requires principled and strategic governance—the ability to navigate complex issues with integrity and foresight. While candidates naturally focus on appealing to voters during campaigns, elected officials must prioritize national interests over partisan agendas once in office. The Founding Fathers envisioned a system where representatives serve not just their supporters but the entire nation, making decisions that reflect the broader public good rather than narrow political interests.

Key Government Position Qualifications

High-level business positions typically have clearly defined job descriptions and minimum hiring qualifications. Government leadership roles, including those of elected officials, should have more clearly defined qualifications and experience requirements, provided they do not conflict with the constitutional minimums. Congress can establish such criteria to ensure candidates possess the necessary skills to govern effectively. Additionally, offering competitive compensation for these positions is essential. Ensuring fair salaries would allow highly qualified individuals from diverse economic backgrounds to seek office without requiring personal wealth, thereby fostering a more representative and capable leadership.

MEDIA & FREE SPEECH

What speech is protected?

Why not outlaw or remove lying and misinformation automatically from media? With advancements in AI, it is feasible for every media outlet to conduct fact-checking. However, Meta (formerly Facebook), previously engaged in fact-checking, has recently ceased this practice. The company argues that refraining from fact-checking better supports the principle of Freedom of Speech. Given this context, it raises a critical question: Is our right to Freedom of Speech intended to protect lies, false conspiracy theories, and propaganda? Unfortunately for many, yes.

The Constitution's First Amendment allows individuals to express ideas and opinions freely without government interference. This right is broad but not absolute and has specific legal boundaries. For example, it does not protect speech that incites imminent lawless actions, issues actual threats, or engages in criminal conduct like harassment or defamation.

False statements, including lies, conspiracy theories, and propaganda, generally fall under the protection of the First Amendment, except when they cause harm in specific ways, such as through defamation or false advertising. This protection is grounded in the belief that free speech enables the public to distinguish truth from falsehood in the marketplace of ideas. Truth is a promise kept while trust is what you get back.

However, the First Amendment does not shield speech intended to incite immediate violence or illegal activities. The Supreme Court clarified this in *Brandenburg v. Ohio* (1969), establishing that speech advocating illegal action is not protected if it is directed to inciting or producing imminent lawless action and is likely to succeed in achieving this aim.

Thus, while the First Amendment broadly supports the right to express even unpopular or incorrect opinions, it draws a line at speech that directly causes harm or incites immediate illegal actions.

Media Biases vs. Transparency

Requiring media sources to disclose their biases for transparency is challenging to implement for several reasons. Bias is often subjective; what one person sees as slanted reporting, another may view as balanced. Additionally, media organizations have complex structures, making it hard to pinpoint whether bias originates from individual journalists, editors, corporate owners, or advertisers.

Mandating bias disclosure raises concerns about editorial freedom and potential First Amendment violations. While transparency in media is important, enforcing such a requirement would be legally and practically challenging. Instead, increasing public access to media ownership information and promoting media literacy initiatives could help audiences critically evaluate news sources and recognize biases independently.

MILITARY, WAR & PEACE

In recent years, the U.S. military focus has shifted from wars in Iraq and Afghanistan to broader global challenges, including regional conflicts in Ukraine and the Middle East, climate change, cyber threats, and geopolitical tensions. This shift requires a highly adaptable, technologically advanced military to address traditional and modern security threats. Expanding cyber defense, space operations, and international partnerships have become essential for handling global challenges like pandemics and terrorism. Updating military authorization and operational policies would help ensure transparency, effectiveness, and alignment with today's security needs.

As of late 2024, the United States maintains approximately 2,500 military personnel in Iraq and about 900 in Syria. These forces primarily serve in advisory and training roles, supporting local partners in counterterrorism efforts against groups like ISIS.[224]

In addition to uniformed personnel, the U.S. Department of Defense employs many private military contractors in these regions. As of the second quarter of Fiscal Year 2024, there were approximately 5,455 contractor personnel in Iraq and Syria. Of these, about 48% were U.S. citizens, 47% were third-country nationals, and roughly 1% were local or host-country nationals.[225]

Using private military contractors has long been part of U.S. military operations abroad. These contractors provide services such as logistics, security, and technical support. However, their use has raised concerns about transparency and accountability, particularly when their activities are not fully disclosed to the public, whether for security reasons or due to limited oversight structures that govern their conduct. The involvement of contractors from various nationalities adds complexity to oversight, as monitoring their actions and ensuring compliance with military regulations can be difficult. Additionally, some experts warn that these skilled individuals may later offer their services to other entities, potentially contributing to instability in certain regions. Balancing operational effectiveness with proper oversight remains a key challenge in their continued use.

Building Military Capabilities

The United States must continuously adapt its military capabilities to address conventional and asymmetric threats. Conventional threats typically involve direct military confrontations between nation-states using organized armies, tanks, aircraft, and other traditional forces. In contrast, asymmetric threats come from actors—often non-state groups—who use unconventional strategies to exploit vulnerabilities in more powerful opponents. These may include terrorism, cyberattacks, guerrilla warfare, misinformation campaigns, or the use of low-cost technologies like drones or improvised explosive devices (IEDs). Responding to such diverse challenges requires flexible strategies, technological innovation, and interagency coordination across military and civilian sectors.

Strengthening specialized units — such as special operations forces, civil affairs teams, engineers, and foreign area officers — is essential for effective counter-insurgency operations and stabilization missions. Comprehensive training in foreign languages, cultural awareness, and human intelligence enhances these units' ability to navigate complex environments, build trust with local partners, and contribute to long-term security and stability. Investing in these areas ensures that military operations remain agile, strategic, and effective in an evolving global landscape.

Civilian Capacity and Emergency Response

Military personnel are frequently tasked with non-military duties, including humanitarian aid and infrastructure repair, which can strain resources and divert attention from core defense responsibilities. Our country should consider creating a *National Civilian Assistance Corps* composed of volunteers with specialized skills, such as doctors, engineers, city planners, and agricultural specialists. This civilian corps would rapidly deploy experts during crises, enabling the military to focus on its primary defense missions. Its structure could mirror that of the Peace Corps, offering a civilian-led, organized response system to deploy skilled professionals in times of national or international crisis.

Congress Authorizes Military Action

The last formal declaration of war by the United States Congress was in 1942, during World War II. Since then, the U.S. has engaged in significant military actions — including those in Korea, Vietnam, Iraq, and Afghanistan — without formal war declarations. Instead, Congress has authorized the use of military force through specific resolutions.

While the U.S. Constitution grants Congress the power to declare war, modern practice has evolved to include authorizations that permit military action without formal declarations. Congress could classify these engagements as "armed conflicts" with defined limitations and require periodic reviews of military actions extending beyond a specified timeframe to enhance accountability and uphold democratic principles. Such measures would help ensure that military force use aligns with national security needs and maintains the constitutional balance of power.

The United States Space Force

The establishment of the United States Space Force reflects a strategic shift in national defense as space becomes an increasingly contested domain. Space assets, including satellites for communication, navigation, and national security, are critical to modern infrastructure, and protecting them is essential. The rise of space capabilities among global powers has heightened concerns over potential conflicts and the militarization of space. The Space Force aims to ensure that U.S. space assets remain secure while advancing technological and scientific leadership in this domain. Balancing security and peaceful exploration will be key to shaping space policy in the coming decades.

Cybersecurity as a Threat

Cyber-attacks and military espionage present growing threats that require skilled leadership and proactive defense strategies. New laws should recognize cybersecurity as a national security priority, on par with traditional military defense. Establishing a legal framework for enhanced cybersecurity measures would help ensure effective monitoring and threat prevention while maintaining protections for civil liberties. Balancing security and privacy will be crucial in shaping policies that protect national interests without overreach.

Missile Defense

Initiatives like Ronald Reagan's Strategic Defense Initiative (SDI), which was never deployed in favor of ground-based launch capabilities, and Israel's Iron Dome, which has been 90% successful in the 3-70 km range, support the strategic value of missile defense systems. Both of these systems advanced the technology for intercepting and neutralizing airborne threats.

To defend against longer-range threats, the United States integrates advanced systems such as submarine-launched ballistic missiles (SLBMs) into its layered missile defense strategy, complemented by the Ground-based Midcourse Defense (GMD) and Aegis Ballistic Missile Defense systems for intercepting intercontinental ballistic missiles in space.

Military Budget

The military budget comprises a significant portion of federal spending, highlighting the constitutional importance of national defense. In 2023, defense spending accounted for 13.3% of the total federal budget of the United States and represents around 3.5% to 4.0% of the nation's Gross Domestic Product (GDP).[294] The budget proportion has seen fluctuations over the years, ranging from a high of 27.9% in 1987 to lows of around 11% in recent years.[293]

However, balancing this crucial funding with domestic needs remains a persistent challenge (Guns vs. Butter as described earlier).

Striking a balance between military expenditures and essential domestic priorities — such as healthcare, education, and infrastructure — is vital for Congress, balancing the principle that a powerful nation not only safeguards itself from external threats but also fosters the well-being and prosperity of its people.

Military Depth

The U.S. should conduct a comprehensive inventory of military hardware to assess any reliance on China or any other country for critical components and ensure domestic production capabilities. Given geopolitical uncertainties, reducing dependence on foreign suppliers is essential for national security.

To maintain global defense commitments, the U.S. must enhance its ability to rapidly deploy personnel, equipment, and supplies, particularly in regions vital to national interests and allied security. Expanding robotic warfare capabilities across land, air, and sea — through the large-scale development of autonomous military systems — would improve operational effectiveness while reducing risks to personnel.

Additionally, strengthening coastal defense measures is necessary to address potential threats, such as the presence of foreign submarines near U.S. waters, as observed with a Russian submarine patrolling off the coast in August 2009. Proactive investments in surveillance, naval deterrence, and rapid response capabilities would help secure national borders and deter potential incursions.[181-11]

The U.S. should develop advanced sensors to detect biological and chemical agents in the prevailing westerly air currents off the West Coast. The potential dispersal of harmful agents into these airstreams poses a national security risk, making early detection crucial for rapid response and mitigation.

Additionally, space defense capabilities should be strengthened to address emerging threats, including the removal of dangerous weapons from orbit and the ability to intercept asteroids that could threaten Earth. Investments in space-based defense technology would enhance national and global security.

The extensive use of mercenaries in military operations should be reconsidered due to concerns over accountability and oversight. Relying on private military contractors risks placing critical defense responsibilities in the hands of independent actors who operate outside the structured chain of command. Ensuring that national security operations remain under the direct control of the U.S. military and intelligence agencies is essential for maintaining strategic stability and government oversight.

National Guard

The U.S. president, as commander-in-chief, oversees the military, including the authority to hire private military contractors and deploy National Guard units when necessary. While state governors typically control the National Guard, the president can federalize these forces under Article 1, Section 8, Clause 15 of the U.S. Constitution to enforce federal law, suppress uprisings, and repel invasions. Under Title 32, the National Guard operates within states, often with federal funding for emergency response. Under Title 10, they can be integrated into the regular military for overseas missions. The president's authority over National Guard deployments, both domestically and internationally, remains subject to congressional oversight.

This framework ensures flexibility in military operations while maintaining state control in most situations. However, state governors should not use their National Guard units for personal political purposes. The widespread presence of state militias across 50 states also serves as a deterrent to foreign armed invasion. National Guard soldiers should receive ongoing training to remain as operationally prepared and up-to-date as their active-duty counterparts.

NATO

The North Atlantic Treaty Organization (NATO) was established in 1949 as a military alliance to ensure its member states' collective defense and security. Over time, its role has expanded to address various global security challenges. NATO's core principle remains collective defense, meaning an attack on one member is considered an attack on all. Additionally, NATO engages in crisis management to stabilize conflict zones, fosters international partnerships to combat threats such as terrorism and cyberattacks, and adapts to evolving security concerns, including hybrid warfare and emerging technologies. The alliance also promotes democratic values and cooperates on non-traditional security issues such as climate-related risks and pandemics. While NATO continues to evolve, it remains a key player in maintaining global stability.

Here are the figures:

NATO Expenditures (Exp.) as a % of GDP and Proportion Contribution(% Con.) in $Billions of US Dollars (Bil)				
Country	% GDP	$ GDP (Bil)	$ Exp. (Bil)	% Con.
United States	3.38	$26,000	$ 878.80	64.73%
Germany	2.12	$ 5,000	$ 106.00	7.81%
United Kingdom	2.14	$ 3,200	$ 68.48	5.04%
France	2.06	$ 2,800	$ 57.68	4.25%
Poland	4.12	$ 800	$ 32.96	2.43%
Canada	1.37	$ 2,200	$ 30.14	2.22%
Italy	1.49	$ 2,000	$ 29.80	2.19%
Netherlands	1.85	$ 1,200	$ 22.20	1.64%
Türkiye	2.14	$ 900	$ 19.26	1.42%
Spain	1.28	$ 1,500	$ 19.20	1.41%
Sweden	2.09	$ 700	$ 14.63	1.08%
Norway	2.20	$ 550	$ 12.10	0.89%
Denmark	1.81	$ 450	$ 8.15	0.60%
Belgium	1.30	$ 600	$ 7.80	0.57%
Finland	2.41	$ 300	$ 7.23	0.53%
Greece	3.08	$ 210	$ 6.47	0.48%
Czech Republic	2.10	$ 300	$ 6.30	0.46%
Next 25%[1]	16.40	$ 1,233	$ 25.27	1.86%
Bottom 25%[2]	13.06	$ 316	$ 5.26	0.39%
Total	2.70	$50,259	$ 1,357.73	100.0%

[1] Slovakia, Lithuania, Bulgaria, Estonia, Croatia, Luxembourg, Slovenia, Latvia

[2] Albania, North Macedonia, Montenegro

In the table above, a pessimist might say, "Wow! The U.S. is paying for 68% of NATO." However, an optimist would respond, "Wow! The U.S. has protection across Europe and globally, and others are covering 32% of the cost."

Volunteerism

Volunteerism can be powerful for societal development and personal growth, particularly among young adults. Encouraging individuals aged 18 to 25 to engage in two years of service could foster community, empathy, and responsibility while providing valuable real-world experience. Such a program should include a range of opportunities, from humanitarian and community service to military support roles, allowing participants to choose paths aligned with their skills and interests. While discussions on implementing a structured national service program have occurred since at least 1960, no legislative framework has been established. Expanding voluntary service options could benefit society and participants, strengthening civic engagement and national resilience.

Supporting Veterans

Recognizing the crucial role that veterans and first responders play in national security, it is imperative to provide them with sustained support and resources. This support encompasses comprehensive healthcare, job training, and mental health services to promote their well-being and facilitate reintegration after active service. Providing lifelong services to veterans strengthens recruitment efforts by demonstrating a national commitment to those who serve, an essential foundation for sustaining the all-volunteer force that underpins our country's security.

In fiscal year 2024, the Department of Veterans Affairs (VA) operated with a budget of approximately $407.3 billion, allocated across various services, including medical care, benefits administration, and essential programs for veterans.[384] This funding is critical to maintaining healthcare, housing assistance, and employment support for those who have served.

Over the past year, the VA enrolled 401,006 new veterans into its healthcare system, marking a 30% increase compared to the previous year. This surge reflects the VA's efforts to expand access to medical services for veterans nationwide. Additionally, the VA made significant progress in addressing veteran homelessness, successfully housing 47,925 veterans in 2024, surpassing its annual goal.[385] These achievements demonstrate the commitment to ensuring veterans receive the necessary support for stability and well-being.

Despite these advancements, the VA faced a projected budget shortfall of approximately $15 billion across fiscal years 2024 and 2025. This financial challenge underscores the need for continued funding to maintain and improve essential services. Without adequate resources, programs that benefit veterans, such as housing initiatives and mental health services, could face limitations.

As of 2023, approximately 15.8 million military veterans were in the United States, representing 6.1% of the adult civilian population.[386] Ensuring this diverse group receives proper care and support should remain a national priority. While progress has been made in healthcare expansion and homelessness reduction, sustained financial and policy commitments are necessary to uphold and enhance these critical services.

The U.S. spends an average of $25,800 per veteran annually, though this figure is much higher for those actively receiving VA healthcare, benefits, and support services. While the VA is essential for providing specialized care, such as for PTSD and combat-related injuries, its inefficiencies highlight the need for modernization, better resource management, and potential reforms that could allow veterans more flexibility in choosing their care providers.

Nuclear Weapons

The world must commit to the complete, verifiable, and irreversible elimination of nuclear weapons, ensuring they have no place on Earth or in space. Such a commitment requires enforceable international agreements, robust verification, and universal compliance to prevent stockpiling, secret development, or deployment.

Mutual adherence to the Geneva Conventions is equally essential. These treaties set legally binding standards for humane treatment during armed conflict, including protections for civilians, prisoners of war, and the wounded. They also ban inhumane tactics such as torture, indiscriminate attacks, and biological or chemical warfare.

A global ban on nuclear weapons, coupled with strict observance of the Geneva Conventions, is key to reducing the devastation of war and upholding humanitarian law. Without these commitments, the risk of catastrophic destruction and erosion of global norms will persist. Better yet, the world should stop warring altogether. Our planet is too fragile, and everyone depends on it.

DIGITAL AGE PRIVACY

The Fourth Amendment's protection against unreasonable searches and seizures was established in an era when privacy primarily concerned physical spaces, not data shared online. The Supreme Court has also identified privacy implications in other constitutional amendments, such as the First Amendment's freedom of association, the Third Amendment's prohibition against the quartering of soldiers in private homes, the Fifth Amendment's protection against self-incrimination, and the Fourteenth Amendment's guarantee of personal liberty and restrictions on state action.

With the rise of surveillance, corporate data mining, hacking, and government access to digital communications, the right to privacy in the digital age requires redefinition. New laws may be needed to address personal data collection, storage, and use, ensuring individuals have greater control over their digital presence. It should also protect against corporate and governmental overreach, granting people the right to safeguard their information and manage the communications they receive, as current laws like the CAN-SPAM Act are insufficient.

Technological Change and Regulation

Emerging technologies such as artificial intelligence, genetic engineering, and quantum computing raise unprecedented ethical, societal, and security concerns. These advancements can reshape industries, economies, and even human capabilities, yet the regulatory frameworks governing them are often reactive rather than proactive. As a result, legislation frequently lags behind rapid technological progress, creating regulatory vacuums that can be exploited or lead to unintended consequences.

Legal frameworks must evolve, incorporating multidisciplinary oversight and international cooperation to address these challenges. Safeguarding jobs in the face of automation requires policies that go beyond simple employment protections — such as workforce retraining programs, incentives for human-AI collaboration, and economic models that account for shifting labor markets. Civil liberties in AI-driven decision-making must be protected through transparency requirements, algorithmic accountability, and bias mitigation strategies to prevent discrimination in hiring, law enforcement, and financial services.

Additionally, the ethical oversight of biotechnology must extend beyond current biomedical applications to include concerns like genetic privacy, human enhancement technologies, and potential bioweapon threats. With its potential to break encryption standards, quantum computing demands global cybersecurity measures to prevent economic disruption and digital warfare.

Laws should be dynamic, adjusting as technology grows instead of using strict, one-size-fits-all rules that may quickly become outdated. International agreements may also be necessary to ensure that ethical and security standards for these technologies remain consistent across borders, preventing regulatory arbitrage and misuse.

Internet Security and Privacy

Different perspectives on digital privacy are fueling ongoing debates. Some advocate for strong privacy laws to protect personal data, while others emphasize national security and economic growth, favoring fewer regulations to encourage innovation and free enterprise.

The Internet

The Internet has become a vital platform for political communication, information dissemination, and fundraising, allowing organizations to build digital infrastructures that promote viewpoints, rally support, and counter opposing narratives. As early as the late 1980s, strategists recognized the Internet's potential as a powerful tool for shaping public opinion, comparable to the influence of traditional media, like newspapers and television, in guiding political discourse. The Internet is a tool that, when used wisely, can contribute to fairness and accuracy but is not foolproof against all forms of misrepresentation or bias. It also has created a generation of judgmental users, with many criticizing everything they see or hear online. This judgmentalism has sparked discussions about the need for mandated balance and automated moderation.

In recent years, concerns over content moderation and perceived bias on mainstream platforms like X (formerly Twitter) and Meta (formerly Facebook) have led some groups to seek alternative platforms. These alternatives, such as Bsky.social, Parler.com, Gab.com, and Rumble.com, offer different degrees of moderation and cater to diverse audiences. Meanwhile, Parler, Gab, and Rumble have become popular among users looking for less restrictive content policies, often appealing to conservative viewpoints. Similarly, Bsky.social caters to the liberal viewpoints. These platforms provide a more direct and less filtered line of communication, which can foster community engagement and facilitate grassroots mobilization. However, reduced moderation can also pose challenges, such as the increased spread of misinformation. None of these sites protect the user from lies, propaganda, or conspiracy theories.

This adaptability has allowed various organizations to connect with their respective audiences more authentically and expand their reach.

As digital communication has become integral to public discourse, maintaining a balance between the Internet's openness and legal and ethical standards remains essential.

The Internet, Social Media, and the Erosion of Trust

The rise of the internet, especially social media, has made users significantly more skeptical and distrustful than in previous eras. Constant exposure to conflicting information, clickbait headlines, misinformation, and algorithm-driven outrage has led many to question not just media and institutions but even facts themselves. While healthy skepticism can protect against manipulation and promote independent thinking, the widespread erosion of trust has also fueled cynicism, polarization, and conspiracy thinking. This shift is a double-edged sword: it empowers users to question authority, but it can become socially corrosive and even pathological when taken to extremes.

To address the rise in distrust fueled by the internet and social media, efforts must focus on improving digital literacy, promoting transparency, and rebuilding trust in credible institutions. Education systems can teach critical thinking and media evaluation from an early age, helping users distinguish reliable information from manipulative content. Platforms should be more accountable for spreading misinformation, using clear labeling and context rather than opaque algorithms. Most importantly, institutions—from governments to news outlets—must earn back trust through honesty, consistency, and responsiveness rather than expecting blind faith in an age of justified skepticism.

Internet Rules

In its early days, e-commerce resembled the Wild West — an unregulated space where anything went. Without regulatory oversight, consumer exploitation was common, like highway robbery in the old days. While this environment has gradually changed, further regulation is still needed to protect consumers and businesses in the digital space.

Consumer protection laws, such as the Federal Trade Commission Act, require truthful advertising and clear disclosure of terms to protect buyers from deceptive practices. Data privacy regulations, including the California Consumer Privacy Act (CCPA) of 2020, grant consumers rights over their personal data, such as the ability to access, delete, and opt out of the sale of their information. However, businesses typically have up to 45 days to respond to such requests rather than a strict 14-day requirement. Other emerging privacy laws, such as the Colorado Privacy Act (CPA) and the proposed American Privacy Rights Act (APRA), continue to shape the evolving landscape of consumer data protection.

The Supreme Court's decision in South Dakota v. Wayfair, Inc. (2018) reshaped online sales tax collection by allowing states to require e-commerce businesses to collect and remit sales tax even if they lack a physical presence in the state. This ruling closed a major loophole that had previously given online retailers an unfair advantage over brick-and-mortar stores.

Payment security has been strengthened through compliance with the PCI Security Standards Council's Data Security Standard (PCI DSS) (2024), which governs the secure processing, storage, and transmission of credit and debit card transactions to prevent fraud.

Intellectual property laws combat counterfeit goods and digital piracy, while antitrust regulations ensure fair competition in e-commerce by preventing monopolistic practices. The Americans with Disabilities Act (ADA) (1990/2008) mandates website accessibility for individuals with disabilities, ensuring equal access to digital platforms. International trade laws manage cross-border transactions, addressing customs regulations, tariffs, and trade agreements.

As technology rapidly advances, regulatory bodies are also working to integrate emerging innovations like artificial intelligence into e-commerce while maintaining consumer safety, fair competition, and robust data security. The Consumer Financial Protection Bureau (CFPB) (2011) has proposed stricter rules on data brokers, reflecting growing concerns about the unchecked collection and sale of personal information.

Despite these protections, current measures often lag behind technological advancements. Consumers deserve greater control and transparency over their personal data. While existing laws provide the right to request access, modification, and deletion of personal information, many advocates push for shorter response times and stronger enforcement mechanisms. Future regulations may further refine these standards, ensuring businesses handle consumer data responsibly while empowering individuals with greater oversight of their personal information.

Furthermore, suppose a user replies "STOP" to a text or unsubscribes from an email. In that case, the sending organization should be prohibited from selling, giving, or transferring that phone number or email to any other entity, including for political fundraising or charity purposes. While many laws, such as the Telephone Consumer Protection Act (TCPA) (1991) and the CAN-SPAM Act (2003), regulate opt-out mechanisms, there is currently no universal rule prohibiting the transfer of user contact information after opting out. However, expanding privacy laws to include such restrictions could enhance consumer protections against unwanted solicitations.

Any request to be removed from communications should be honored immediately or within 24 hours to safeguard users from unwanted contact. While laws like CAN-SPAM require honoring opt-out requests within ten business days, current legislation has no strict 24-hour requirement. Implementing faster response times could improve consumer control over their communications, but businesses may face operational challenges in processing high volumes of requests on short notice.

What Could be Better?

Companies should no longer use "no reply" email addresses that prevent communication. Every email a user receives should allow for a reply, enabling individuals to engage directly with the organization as needed. While this is a best practice, no current laws mandate that all emails must accept replies. Regulatory efforts in this area could improve transparency and consumer engagement, but companies may argue that managing direct responses at scale is impractical for certain automated notifications.

Accessible customer support is essential for websites that charge a fee for services. These sites should be required to provide contact options for support via live chat or email, especially to accommodate those who are hard of hearing. Chat responses should be provided within a standard time frame, such as two minutes, while email responses should be answered within 24-48 hours on weekdays and within 48-72 hours on weekends. While accessibility laws such as the Americans with Disabilities Act (ADA) (1990/2008) apply to digital services, there is no current requirement for live chat or specific response times. Setting such standards could improve user experience but may pose financial and logistical challenges for smaller businesses.

Subscription-based sites should offer clear and fair cancellation policies. For sites that utilize auto-renewals, subscribers must receive a 30-day notice before renewal, including a direct link to cancel the subscription. Similarly, any site charging a periodic or annual subscription fee should provide a clear, user-friendly way to cancel at least once per month. For annual fees, early cancellation should come with a pro-rata refund, ensuring users are not penalized for unused services. The Federal Trade Commission (FTC) has proposed new "click-to-cancel" rules requiring easier cancellation processes, but there is no federal mandate yet. Some states, such as California, have stricter cancellation laws under the Automatic Renewal Law (ARL). Expanding such policies could improve consumer fairness but might lead companies to increase upfront pricing to offset cancellation-related losses.

To further protect consumer rights, sites that charge for services should provide a live link (live person chat, telephone number, etc.) allowing users to discuss changes or request immediate refunds. While this would enhance customer service, it is not a legal requirement, and businesses may resist such mandates due to operational costs.

Finally, when users respond to unsolicited text messages with "Report junk and delete," this information should be forwarded to the network provider, allowing them to suspend or block repeat offenders. Currently, carriers do offer spam reporting mechanisms, but there is no automatic forwarding rule requiring action from service providers. A regulatory framework could strengthen enforcement against spam messages, but implementation would require coordination among telecommunications companies, regulatory bodies, and technology providers.

While many of these proposals align with consumer-friendly policies, most are not yet legal requirements. Expanding regulations to include these provisions could enhance consumer protections but also require balancing feasibility, compliance costs, and enforcement mechanisms.

Cybersecurity and Privacy

In our increasingly digital and interconnected world, cybersecurity has become a critical national, economic, and personal concern. Ensuring strong protections against cyber threats while maintaining privacy and civil liberties is essential for public safety and economic stability.

One cybersecurity strategy focuses on strengthening infrastructure through increased government funding and resources to combat cyberattacks. This approach emphasizes stronger public-private partnerships to improve information sharing on cyber threats, vulnerabilities, and incidents. Collaboration between industries and government agencies can enhance early threat detection and response. Additionally, international cooperation through diplomatic channels and multinational agreements plays a key role in addressing global cybercrime and cyberterrorism.

Another perspective prioritizes a market-driven approach, advocating for minimal government regulation and allowing companies to develop their cybersecurity measures. This strategy places a high value on personal privacy and individual rights by limiting government surveillance. It also emphasizes deterrence and retaliation against state-sponsored cyberattacks to safeguard national sovereignty in the digital realm.

Beyond these approaches, securing the Internet from cyber and physical attacks is essential. This initiative could involve building new, independent infrastructure to withstand future threats, including next-generation end-to-end encryption resistant to quantum computing advancements.

By adopting a multi-layered approach that balances regulation, industry innovation, and global cooperation, cybersecurity efforts can better adapt to evolving threats while protecting fundamental freedoms.

Net Neutrality

Net neutrality protects citizen liberty by ensuring equal access to online information and services and preventing internet providers from controlling, slowing, or prioritizing content based on financial or political interests.

Eliminating net neutrality could create new revenue opportunities for internet service providers (ISPs) by allowing them to charge content providers for prioritized access or faster delivery speeds. This shift may lead to higher consumer costs and reduced access to diverse online content. Maintaining net neutrality is crucial for preserving an open internet where all users have equal access to content without preferential treatment. Large corporations could pay ISPs to prioritize their services without these protections, disadvantaging smaller companies and limiting consumer choice. This scenario could stifle competition and innovation, making it more challenging for startups and independent creators to reach audiences.[387]

A neutral internet safeguards fair competition in the online marketplace by ensuring that smaller businesses and emerging platforms are not overshadowed by larger corporations capable of purchasing faster speeds or better access. Without net neutrality, ISPs could create "fast lanes" for those willing to pay more while slowing down or restricting access to competing services. This practice could lead to increased consumer costs, fewer choices, and a decline in the diversity of online content.[388]

Preserving net neutrality upholds the principles of fairness, innovation, and consumer freedom. It ensures that all users, regardless of financial power, can access and share information without interference. By maintaining these protections, we support a competitive and diverse digital landscape where consumers, rather than ISPs, determine which services and information thrive.

Recent legal developments have intensified the debate over net neutrality. In August 2024, the Sixth Circuit Court of Appeals blocked the Federal Communications Commission's (FCC) attempt to reinstate net neutrality rules, stating that broadband providers were likely to succeed in their legal challenge. This decision underscores the ongoing contention surrounding net neutrality and highlights the necessity for explicit legislative action to protect an open and fair internet.[389]

In summary, eliminating net neutrality could benefit ISPs financially but potentially harm consumer choice, fair competition, and innovation. Maintaining net neutrality is essential to ensuring an equitable and dynamic online environment for all stakeholders.

Better Telecommunications Privacy

Phone companies should use the data they collect on high-volume call origins and reported spam numbers to improve fraud prevention while ensuring that updated regulatory frameworks protect user privacy. One existing tool for reducing robocalls and caller ID spoofing is the STIR/SHAKEN framework. STIR (Secure Telephone Identity Revisited) and SHAKEN (Signature-based Handling of Asserted Information Using Tokens) are authentication protocols that verify caller ID information to prevent scammers from using fake numbers. These protocols work by requiring phone carriers to validate calls before they reach consumers, reducing the likelihood of fraudulent calls appearing as legitimate. While STIR/SHAKEN has helped mitigate some types of phone fraud, enforcement gaps, and limitations mean that additional measures may still be necessary.

Improved collaboration between telecom companies and major tech firms such as Apple and Google could enhance data sharing on blocked and spam calls and the IP addresses from which spam emails originate. However, existing privacy laws, such as the General Data Protection Regulation and the California Consumer Privacy Act, impose restrictions on data sharing and require safeguards to prevent misuse. Any expansion of data-sharing agreements would need to comply with these legal frameworks while ensuring consumer privacy is not compromised.

Additionally, implementing a system where businesses face financial penalties for making spam calls or having their calls repeatedly flagged could serve as a deterrent. However, this approach would require strict verification measures to prevent false flags and abuse. Legislative changes would be necessary to ensure due process for businesses and individuals flagged as spammers while holding actual offenders accountable.

While these proposals could help reduce unwanted calls and spam, their success would depend on effective enforcement, clear legal guidelines, and strong consumer protections to prevent overreach or unintended consequences.

Chatbots

A chatbot is an AI program designed to simulate human conversation, providing automated responses to user inquiries. Reliance on chatbots over human customer service can raise concerns about competition. Companies that exclusively use automated systems for customer support might have so much commercial power that they can get away with limiting consumer options or access. It might be appropriate to examine whether such practices reduce consumer alternatives and whether they deserve potential regulatory and antitrust considerations.

SOCIAL ISSUES

Active participation by citizens with diverse perspectives on social issues and human rights is crucial to upholding a democracy that is responsive and represents all views, fostering consensus for a fair and just society.

Role of the Family

A common belief in America is that the family household serves as a cornerstone for education and for instilling moral values and appropriate behavior in children, a role seen as essential to society's structure and health. Through nurturing and guidance, families play a pivotal role in raising individuals who are responsible, well-adjusted, and capable of positively contributing to their communities. This enduring role of the family holds even as societal trends evolve, notably in how and when families are formed. The current trend of marrying later or opting not to marry is altering the traditional timeline of family formation and does not inherently undermine the importance of parenting. However, the romanticized image of the family is not as pervasive as it once was.

Family Composition

As of 2024, the composition of American households continues to evolve. Married-couple households now constitute 47% of all households, down from 71% in 1970.[226]

In contrast, nonfamily households, defined as people living alone or with non-relatives, have increased significantly, making up about 36% of all U.S. households in 2022, compared to just 19% in 1970. This shift reflects broader societal changes, including a rise in single-person and more diverse, nontraditional living arrangements. In 1970, the average number of people per household in the United States was approximately 3.14, highlighting how household structures have grown smaller and more varied over time.[390] This figure has decreased over the decades, with the average household size declining to 2.51 people by 2023. [391] Some might see these facts as a sign of a degrading of society, viewing smaller family sizes and shifting household structures as a decline in traditional values and social cohesion. Others may see it as a natural evolution of society, reflecting greater individual freedom, changing economic realities, and diverse family structures that better align with modern lifestyles.

This trend reflects shifting priorities as individuals delay parenthood to focus on education, careers, and financial readiness, fostering stable environments for children. However, delayed parenting can lead to reduced fertility, contributing to decisions about alternative paths, including abortion. Evolving family norms now accommodate diverse structures and emphasize parenting quality over traditional timelines.

Remote Work

Remote work has changed the way families live and spend time together. It gives people more freedom in where they live and how they care for their children. For parents who don't live with their children full-time, especially after a divorce, working from home makes it easier to stay involved in their kids' lives. It helps with shared custody by making it easier to manage time and travel. When the government supports remote work—by helping with things like internet access, flexible job rules, and tax benefits, it can help families stay strong and balance work with home life. As new technology like artificial intelligence changes the kinds of jobs people do, new policies will be needed to help families adjust and keep up.

At the same time, people still disagree about how much the government should be involved in family life. Some believe the government should help more by offering services like affordable childcare, paid time off for new parents, and help with housing. Others think families should make these choices independently, with less government help or control. These debates also raise questions about what a family should look like since more people live in new ways that don't always follow traditional ideas of marriage or parenting. As society keeps changing, the laws and rules about family life must also change. Finding a balance where families of all kinds are respected and given support can help keep our communities firm and fair.

Abortion

Abortion is one of the most divisive and emotionally charged topics in American discourse, involving complex ethical, moral, religious, and legal questions that center on personal autonomy, individual rights, liberty, and societal values. For expecting mothers, the decision is deeply personal, requiring consideration of challenges such as potential neglect or poverty, moral principles like the sanctity of life, and alternative options including adoption. Understanding the diverse perspectives on this issue is crucial, as each viewpoint highlights unique considerations about individual choice, constitutional rights, societal responsibilities, and deeply held beliefs.

Government's Role

The government's role in abortion policy is particularly challenging. Some argue that the government should define when life begins and actively protect it, while others believe it should allow individuals to make personal decisions about their bodies. This debate raises broader questions about balancing the government's constitutional duty to protect life, liberty, and the pursuit of happiness with the need to avoid overreach into citizens' private choices. The Founding Fathers often emphasized limited government interference in individual actions, making this issue even more complex in modern governance.

The question of government intervention in defining when life begins touches on moral, religious, and constitutional dimensions. Critics argue that government involvement risks imposing a singular perspective in a pluralistic society, potentially infringing on individual freedoms. Supporters, however, point to the Fourteenth Amendment as a basis for extending legal protections to life at all developmental stages, including the unborn. The U.S. Supreme Court has not affirmed this interpretation, leaving the extent of fetal legal protections a matter of ongoing legal and political debate.

Background Facts

Laws restricting abortion do not eliminate abortions but push most of them into unsafe and illegal operations, as history has shown. Before *Roe v. Wade* was overturned in the *Dobbs* ruling, 81% of abortions occurred within six weeks of gestation, and only 7% were performed at 14 weeks or later.[238]

Since the *Dobbs* decision, the number of abortions has increased by 11%, reaching over one million annually, according to the Guttmacher Institute.[239] This rise reflects heightened interstate travel to permissive states, expanded access to medication abortions, and improved reporting. The Guttmacher Institute's research, while clear in its policy positions, is widely regarded as rigorous and methodologically sound, cited by both proponents and critics of abortion rights.

Ethical and Scientific Views

Proponents of abortion restrictions argue that life begins at conception, making abortion the termination of an innocent human life. Science identifies the biological beginning of life at fertilization, but this life's moral and legal status is debated. Viability, typically occurring around 22 to 24 weeks of gestation with modern medical support, is often a milestone in determining when life can be considered sustainable outside the womb.

Moral, Religious, and Societal Views

Religious and philosophical beliefs vary widely regarding when a soul forms if one exists. Traditions like Catholicism teach that the soul is present at conception, while Islam suggests it enters at around 120 days. Secular perspectives often focus on consciousness and brain development rather than the concept of a soul.

Abortion, comparing it to plastic surgery, involves altering one's body — whether to address a physical or emotional need — raising questions about the balance between exercising personal choice and reconciling with the natural or spiritual outcomes of one's circumstances.

These divergent views reflect the complex interplay of morality, religion, and cultural values in abortion debates.

Women's Rights

Does a woman have the right to make decisions about her own body? Advocates for personal autonomy argue that individuals have a fundamental right to private medical choices, including abortion, consistent with the Founding Fathers' emphasis on inherent rights to life, liberty, and the pursuit of happiness.

Policy and Solutions

Both sides of the abortion debate should be able to agree that reducing the number of abortions is a shared goal. Therefore, the discussion should focus on how much the practice can be safely reduced. Those who oppose abortion must acknowledge that making it illegal will not eliminate the practice but will instead endanger lives by pushing it underground. A more constructive approach lies in establishing reasonable standards, such as limiting abortions to within 14 weeks of pregnancy, except in cases of medical emergencies. However, the exact limit is a matter of legal, medical, and ethical debate, and any policy must consider medical expertise and individual circumstances. Additionally, all involved should agree that unbiased counseling should be made available to ensure that individuals are fully informed and supported in their decision-making process.

Achieving national unity on abortion requires a balanced policy that reflects a broad consensus. Efforts to reduce unwanted pregnancies should prioritize accessible birth control, emergency contraception, and comprehensive sex education. Such measures can help address the issue at its roots while respecting differing views on abortion.

Birth control has proven essential for women's health, autonomy, and societal advancement. It has allowed women to control their reproductive lives, pursue education and careers, and reduce poverty by preventing unintended pregnancies. Historically, opponents argued that birth control could lead to societal decay, weaken traditional family structures, and undermine moral and ethical values. Some have claimed that opposition to birth control was rooted in efforts to maintain traditional gender roles and limit women's independence. Others might argue that greater access to birth control has contributed to a more permissive society, which they see as either progress or decline, depending on perspective.

If you prioritize liberty and minimal government interference in personal decisions over external influences, then allowing abortion as an individual choice, particularly in cases of medical necessity, aligns with those principles. Optional counseling could provide additional support for those seeking guidance, especially in cases of repeat procedures.

For equity, health insurance providers could ensure access to abortion coverage, particularly for low-income women, to prevent financial barriers from determining medical decisions. However, policies on abortion coverage vary widely, with some states restricting funding for the procedure, especially under public insurance programs like Medicaid. Establishing a national standard could reduce inconsistencies across states, providing a more uniform approach. However, such a policy would need to balance individual rights, societal values, and the concerns of those who oppose public or private funding for abortion on moral or religious grounds.

Current Status

Since *Dobbs v. Jackson Women's Health Organization* overturned *Roe v. Wade* in 2022, abortion laws across the U.S. have become a patchwork of restrictions and protections. Some states, such as Texas and Alabama, have enacted near-total bans, while others, including California and New York, have expanded access. This evolving legal landscape underscores the dynamic nature of abortion rights in America and complicates the lives of many.

Abortion Pill Regimen

Any criteria would need to include the prescription and use of the abortion pill regimen (mifepristone and misoprostol) which is medically approved for use during early pregnancy and can be safely used up to 70 days (10 weeks) from the first day of the last menstrual period (LMP). In some cases, healthcare providers may extend their use to 77 days (11 weeks) with additional monitoring, though the effectiveness decreases slightly as pregnancy advances.

Where to Start

Everyone should be able to agree on three foundational principles. First, we all should want to reduce the number of abortions. Second, the reality is that no law will stop abortions. Third, for abortions that cannot be avoided, it is better that they occur in clean, safe environments by trained medical professionals. With these three principles, what remains is to define parameters around the criteria and timeframe within which abortions should be permitted. I believe everyone would agree that abortions after the point of viability should not be allowed. Everyone should agree on the need for greater focus on and availability of contraceptives, including morning-after pills (Plan B and Ella), which function before conception by preventing or delaying ovulation and do not affect implantation or an existing pregnancy. Additionally, more education and unbiased mental health counseling should be prioritized.

Religious Freedom

Religious freedom, a cornerstone of American democracy, influences various aspects of national life, including education, law, and public policy, reflecting the diverse religious landscape of the United States.

The Constitution defines religious freedom as balancing individual rights and societal harmony. It emphasizes the separation of church and state, fostering a pluralistic society where the government remains neutral on religious matters and respects all beliefs. This approach protects the rights of individuals, including those of minority religions and non-religious people, while preventing policies that enable discrimination under the guise of religious freedom.

An alternative interpretation views the Constitution's religious freedom provisions as protecting the right of individuals and institutions to act according to their beliefs, both privately and publicly, including in commercial settings. This perspective supports religious values in public life, such as education and community activities, and argues that religious expression should be safeguarded within government boundaries.

Religion in Government

Many Americans recognize the central role of faith in personal and community life, echoing the Founders' belief that the nation is strengthened by acts of justice and mercy inspired by faith. This perspective values grassroots change and acknowledges the unique influence of faith-based communities — churches, synagogues, temples, and mosques — in serving the public.

Supporters of faith-based service organizations argue that these institutions can align with constitutional principles when public funds are used responsibly, avoiding proselytizing or discriminatory practices. They highlight the constitutional guarantee of religious freedom, affirming citizens' rights to apply their values to public life. This perspective supports faith-based organizations' participation in public programs without requiring them to compromise their symbols or beliefs. It also views public displays of religious symbols, such as the Ten Commandments, as honoring the historical influence of Judeo-Christian values in the U.S. However, critics contend that religious influences in government programs or decisions may challenge the separation of church and state. They emphasize the need for constitutional neutrality to balance religious freedom with governmental impartiality.

The religious landscape in the U.S. has shifted significantly. According to a 2023 report by the Public Religion Research Institute (PRRI), nearly one-quarter of Americans (24%) attend religious services, either virtually or in person, at least once a week, a 7-percentage-point decline from 31% in 2013. Similarly, around two in ten Americans (21%) say they attend church services once or twice a month or a few times a year in 2023, a decline of four percentage points from 25% in 2013.[392]

Despite this trend, active participants in religious communities report high satisfaction, with over 80% expressing optimism about their congregations' future. The COVID-19 pandemic has further influenced attendance patterns, with some fluctuations observed in participation rates.[393]

Over the past five decades, the percentage of U.S. adults identifying as atheist or agnostic has gradually increased. In 1991, approximately 2% identified as atheists and 4% as agnostics. By 2014, these figures rose to 3.1% for atheists and 5% for agnostics. Recent data from 2023 indicates that 5% of Americans identify as atheists and another 5% as agnostics. This trend reflects a steady, though modest, growth in the proportion of individuals who identify as atheist or agnostic in the United States over the past several decades.[394-395]

Globally, religion offers solace, unity, and moral guidance but has also been a source of conflict. The Arab-Israeli conflict and intra-religious tensions, such as those between Shia and Sunni Muslims, illustrate the complex interplay of religion and geopolitics. Cases of intolerance, including hostility toward minority faiths in some regions, highlight the consequences of ignorance and distrust. Despite these challenges, many religions aim to promote peace, compassion, and cooperation.

Addressing the root causes of religious conflict is crucial for fostering global harmony and requires understanding of diverse beliefs, historical tensions, and religion's socio-political role. The separation between religion and state helps prevent conflicts from influencing government decisions and ensures equal treatment for all citizens, regardless of faith.

Holy Scriptures

The Bible and the Quran, the sacred scriptures of Christianity and Islam, respectively, have profoundly shaped the belief systems and worldviews of billions. However, interpretations of these texts vary widely and can sometimes lead to misinformation or conflict.

Some interpretations of the Bible conflict with scientific theories like evolution. However, many religious individuals and scholars reconcile their faith with science by interpreting biblical texts allegorically or metaphorically rather than literally. Numerous denominations and religious scientists embrace scientific principles, finding no inherent contradiction between faith and science.

Similarly, interpretations of the Quran range widely. While some verses have been interpreted as promoting violence, scholars emphasize that these references are tied to specific historical contexts of conflict and are not general directives. The Quran also contains numerous passages advocating peace, compassion, and justice. According to Pew Research, 75% to 80% of Muslims reject extremist interpretations and actively promote peace and interfaith dialogue. With approximately 2.3 billion Christians and 2 billion Muslims worldwide, these scriptures influence nearly half the global population.

Does the Quran instruct Muslims to kill non-believers, as some Americans believe? Verses addressing non-believers often pertain to historical conflicts and are not universal instructions. Many passages, such as Quran 60:8-9, emphasize peaceful coexistence, encouraging kindness and justice toward those who are not hostile. Islam, widely recognized as a religion of peace, promotes compassion and prohibits hatred. Muslims are encouraged to form friendships with non-Muslims, reflecting the inclusive spirit of the faith. The Ahmadiyya Muslim Community's motto, "Love for all, hatred for none," encapsulates these values.

Prophet Muhammad exemplified tolerance and kindness toward non-Muslims, engaging amicably with others through acts like visiting the sick, exchanging gifts, and respectful dialogue. His interactions with Christian delegations and other religious groups set a standard of inclusivity and compassion that his followers embraced.

Islamic teachings strongly emphasize justice, mercy, and compassion While interpretations and practices have varied throughout history, Islam's core message focuses on peace, mutual respect, and understanding among people of all faiths. As Abrahamic religions, Islamic teachings share significant commonalities with Judeo-Christian teachings, including monotheism, moral principles, and reverence for shared figures like Abraham and Moses, despite theological differences.

Religious Leaders

Islam has no single leader, making it harder to unite different religions. Leadership is local and varies by region, with imams or sheiks leading prayers and teaching in their communities.

Islam teaches justice, kindness, and mercy, values found in the Quran and the life of Prophet Muhammad. These ideas are practiced in many ways, but the message of peace and respect for others stays the same.

Religion can be both good and bad. It can bring people together and guide them to do good, but it can also be used to spread hate or cause harm. How people follow their faith depends on their culture and life experiences.

Some think a world without religion might have less conflict, but such a world still needs ways to teach right and wrong. A world with only one religion might be more peaceful but could also limit freedom and differences. If major religions like Islam, Christianity, and Judaism worked together, it might help unity—but might also reduce cultural variety.

As the world becomes more connected, cultural differences may slowly fade due to shared ideas and new technology.

Role of God, Morals, and Religious Freedom

Laws should not be biased towards the beliefs of any specific religion or group of religions at the expense of the freedoms of other religions or non-religious citizens. Laws, in their nature, represent certain moral points of view. Laws based on specific morals may be reasonable as long as those morals are not shaped by the agenda of any organized religion and are universally relevant and widely accepted by all citizens.

Founding Fathers' Views on Religion

In the opinion of our Founding Fathers, organized religion has no place in influencing the creation or interpretation of laws – laws must be based on unbiased reasoned judgment of people with no personal or organizational agenda. Jefferson wrote a letter to the Danbury Baptist Association in 1802 to answer a letter from them written in October 1801.

Jefferson's Letter to the Danbury Baptist Association in 1802
(Bold for emphasis)

To messers Nehemiah Dodge, Ephraim Robbins, & Stephen S. Nelson a committee of the Danbury Baptist association in the state of Connecticut.

Gentlemen,

The affectionate sentiments of esteem & approbation which you are so good as to express towards me, on behalf of the Danbury Baptist association, give me the highest satisfaction. my duties dictate a faithful & zealous pursuit of the interests of my constituents, and in proportion as they are persuaded of my fidelity to those duties, the discharge of them becomes more & more pleasing.

Believing with you that religion is a matter which lies solely between man & his god, that he owes account to none other for his faith or his worship, that the legitimate powers of government reach actions only, and not opinions, I contemplate with sovereign reverence that act of the whole American people which declared that their legislature should make no law respecting an establishment of religion, or prohibiting the free exercise thereof, thus building a wall of separation between church and state. [Congress thus inhibited from acts respecting religion, and the Executive authorized only to execute their acts, I have refrained from presenting even occasional performances of devotion presented indeed legally where an Executive is the legal head of a national church, but subject here, as religious exercises only to the voluntary regulations and discipline of each respective sect.] Adhering to this expression of the supreme will of the nation in behalf of the rights of conscience, I shall see with sincere satisfaction the progress of those sentiments which tend to restore to man all his natural rights, convinced he has no natural right in opposition to his social duties.

I reciprocate your kind prayers for the protection and blessing of the common Father and creator of man, and tender you for yourselves and your religious association, assurances of my high respect & esteem.

(signed) Thomas Jefferson on Jan.1.1802.[181-09]

"Thomas Jefferson was a man of deep religious conviction – his conviction was that religion was a very personal matter, one which the government had no business getting involved in."[181-09]

Religion per our Constitution

A balanced approach to religious freedom emphasizes the right of every individual to practice their faith without government interference. It supports a pluralistic society where diverse religious and secular values coexist in an atmosphere of mutual respect.

A core principle of religious freedom is the separation of church and state, which ensures that religious institutions and individuals can practice their beliefs openly while honoring the nation's varied moral landscape. This approach includes upholding individuals' rights to follow their moral and religious convictions in personal life, as long as these practices do not infringe on the rights and freedoms of others.

At the same time, religious expression in public life, including in schools and community spaces, remains essential to this freedom, highlighting the positive role that religious values can play in the nation's ethical foundation. Respect for traditional values, family, and moral principles can contribute to public policy in a way that enhances societal well-being without overstepping boundaries. This framework reflects the belief that the nation's prosperity is deeply connected to its commitment to religious and moral principles, affirming religious freedom as a cornerstone of American democracy.

Cultural History

Perspectives on cultural history — especially on contentious topics like Confederate symbolism, cultural revisionism, and the renaming of public places — reflect the nation's complex historical narrative, which is deeply interwoven with race, heritage, and national identity themes.

One perspective advocates for the reevaluation and, in some cases, revision of cultural history, supporting the removal of Confederate statues and renaming public spaces associated with Confederate figures. This view emphasizes confronting and rectifying historical injustices to create a more inclusive narrative that acknowledges the darker chapters of American history, such as slavery and racial discrimination. Proponents see these acts of revision as essential steps toward healing, progress, and social justice, believing that an honest reflection on history fosters a society committed to equality.

An opposing viewpoint upholds the preservation of traditional historical symbols, including Confederate monuments, as part of the nation's heritage. This perspective emphasizes that retaining these symbols contributes to historical continuity and provides opportunities to learn from the past rather than revise it. Advocates believe that traditional narratives and values form the foundation of the nation's identity and continuity, arguing that preserving these symbols reflects respect for history and the lessons it imparts.

Examining these perspectives makes it clear that American society is deeply divided over cultural and social issues. Topics such as LGBTQ+ rights, gender identity, abortion, religious freedom, legal and illegal immigration, and cultural history are not merely political but reflect the evolving dynamics and diverse values within the nation. However, regardless of a person's proclivities or beliefs, we are all citizens of this country, sharing its rights, responsibilities, and future.

For unity to be achievable, finding common ground and engaging in compromise is essential. Through negotiation and mutual respect, Americans can strive toward a more cohesive society, preventing the nation from remaining unsettled and its citizens at odds. Absolutism will never result in peace and calm in our society.

LGBTQ+ Rights And Gender Roles

As of 2024, approximately 7.6% of U.S. adults identify as LGBTQ+, a figure that has steadily risen over the past decade, showing distinct generational differences. In the early 1990s, estimates showed only around 3-4% of U.S. adults identified as LGBTQ+. The level reported has risen steadily, particularly over the past two decades.[228]

Among Generation Z (born 1997–2012), 22.3% identify as LGBTQ+, reflecting a marked increase compared to previous generations. Millennials (born 1981–1996) follow with 9.8%, while Generation X (born 1965–1980) has 4.5%. Baby Boomers (born 1946–1964) show a lower percentage at 2.3%, and the Silent Generation (born 1945 or earlier) has the smallest percentage, with only 1.1% identifying as LGBTQ+. These figures may not reflect a rise in LGBTQ+ population so much as a greater willingness to acknowledge identities and orientations that have always existed openly.

Issues surrounding rights and gender roles in America highlight deep philosophical divides, often influencing the debate over the Equal Rights Amendment (ERA). Different ideological foundations shape viewpoints on how society should address personal rights, identity, and traditional values. Concerns about gender identity may sometimes arise from discomfort with differences or a lack of understanding about the diversity of identities and orientations within the LGBTQ+ community.

Debates over societal roles reflect contrasting views. One perspective supports expansive rights and protections, emphasizing inclusivity, equal opportunities, and discrimination protections. Another defends traditional norms, emphasizing stability and the established roles within family and societal structures.

Similarly, discussions on gender roles divide between promoting flexibility and inclusivity, such as equal pay and parental leave, and upholding traditional roles as beneficial to social stability. Both approaches highlight differing priorities in addressing evolving social dynamics.

Research consistently indicates that sexual orientation is inherent in an individual's identity and not subject to voluntary change. The American Psychological Association (APA) conducted a systematic review and concluded that efforts to change sexual orientation are unlikely to be successful and involve some risk of harm.[320]

Additionally, a review by the UK Government found no robust evidence that conversion therapy can achieve its stated aim of changing sexual orientation or gender identity.[321] The conclusive perspective might be to allow individuals to live as authentically as they choose. This view aligns with the constitutional right to liberty.

Lastly, Christian beliefs center on the teachings of love, compassion, and acceptance, as demonstrated by Jesus Christ. The commandment to "love your neighbor as yourself" (Mark 12:31) calls Christians to embrace all individuals, regardless of their gender identity or sexual orientation. Supporting LGBTQ+ individuals is consistent with the Christian principle of treating others with dignity and respect, recognizing that every person is created in the image of God (Genesis 1:27). By affirming the inherent worth and diversity of all people, Christians can reflect Christ's unconditional love and foster a more inclusive and compassionate community.

TAXES

Thomas Jefferson wrote about the taxation system, emphasizing the importance of selecting a basis for taxation that reaches every member of society and draws an equal proportion of public contributions from them. He warned against double taxation, where the same income is taxed multiple times, and stressed the duty of the government to provide equal and impartial justice to all citizens. He also mentioned concern about overgrown wealth threatening the state.

Thomas Jefferson's view on taxation emphasized fairness and consistency in applying taxes across different bases. He outlined three primary foundations for taxation: capital, income, and consumption, noting that "consumption being generally equal to income, and income the annual profit of capital." He argued that a government could choose any of these bases for its tax system and should apply it uniformly to ensure each citizen contributes their fair share to public expenses. However, Jefferson warned against "double taxation," when the government taxes an item more than once by crossing these categories. For example, if a person's income has already been taxed, imposing an additional tax on goods purchased with that income, such as "broadcloth or homespun, wine or whiskey, a coach or a wagon," would unfairly tax the same resources twice. According to Jefferson, this practice goes against the government's duty to ensure "equal and impartial justice to all its citizens." This is the basis for sales tax being deductible from income for Federal tax purposes.

He acknowledged that there could be reasons for temporarily taxing specific items — such as promoting domestic manufacturing or discouraging goods harmful to health or morals — but considered these exceptional cases.

Jefferson also addressed what should be taxed: whether it should be property alone, the surplus after essential needs are met, or the annual earnings from one's labor and skills. Regardless of the choice, he believed the principle should be applied equally. Taking more from those who have accumulated more incredible wealth through their own or their ancestors' industry to benefit those with less, he argued, violates the "first principle of association, the guarantee to everyone of a free exercise of his industry, and the fruits acquired by it." If large individual fortunes threaten the state, he suggested that the "law of equal inheritance to all in equal degree" (vs. leaving the whole estate to the eldest son) was a natural corrective, unlike extra taxation, which he saw as contrary to nature's laws. [02-c]

Jefferson, in his autobiography in 1821, expressed dislike of wealth-driven aristocracy, writing, "An aristocracy of wealth [is] of more harm and danger than benefit to society."[180-02-b]

He added later, in a letter to John Adams, "Enough wealthy men will find their way into every branch of the legislature to protect themselves."[181-02]

John Adams also said, "Government is instituted for the Common Good; for the protection, safety, prosperity, and happiness of the people; and not for the profit, honor, or private interest of any man, family, or class of men: Therefore, the people alone have an incontestable, unalienable, and indefeasible right to institute government; and to reform, alter, or totally change the same when their protection, safety, prosperity, and happiness require it."[313]

The Role of Greed

Sadly, the cosmic secret of our civilization has been described as this: We have built a society entirely dependent on money, where its flow dictates every decision and priority. Those with the most wealth often find themselves trapped in a relentless cycle of greed, their insatiable pursuit self-perpetuating and self-justifying. Worse still, this relentless chase comes at any cost, with many of those at the top perfectly willing to accept — or even perpetuate — disastrous consequences for those economically beneath them. Whether it is environmental collapse, systemic exploitation, or even mass deaths, nothing is considered sacred if it stands in the way of accumulating more money. This grim reality exposes a profound flaw in our collective design: a system where human value and survival are secondary to wealth accumulation.[229] This reality is why we must provide a basic level of safety nets for the neediest and redistribution of great wealth.

The assertion that American economics are fundamentally driven by greed has been a longstanding topic of debate. A prominent Wall Street trader, Ivan Boesky, was convicted of insider trading in 1986. Earlier that year, on May 18, during a commencement address at the University of California, Berkeley's School of Business Administration, he infamously stated, "Greed is all right, by the way. I want you to know that. Greed is healthy. You can be greedy and still feel good about yourself." This remark suggested that embracing greed could benefit the economy and markets.[396]

Proponents argue that greed is intricately tied to economic growth, fostering higher salaries and job creation. The premise is that growth creates opportunities for satisfying personal ambition, while greed, in turn, fuels economic expansion by reinvesting profits. How would our economy function if growth ends?

However, while greed can motivate economic activity as a natural human trait, this view also brings up ethical issues. The pursuit of more and more profits, particularly when it involves what many perceive as speculative practices or manipulation of others' financial resources, brings forth questions about fairness and moral boundaries. It suggests that unchecked greed, especially when it leaks into market manipulation, fraud, monopolistic or exploitative practices, may warrant regulatory intervention or higher taxation to curb potentially harmful behavior.

In this context, self-interest and profit-seeking are not inherently immoral as long as they operate within fair governance and do not exploit others through deception or unethical practices. Actions such as fraud, misleading tactics, speculative excess, market manipulation, monopolistic behavior, and unfair fees can undermine trust and fairness in the economy. While ambition and self-interest contribute to economic growth and innovation, maintaining ethical standards and fairness helps sustain market integrity and public confidence.

Wealth Redistribution through Taxes

Balancing Wealth and Opportunity

Some wealth redistribution is necessary to reduce economic inequality, which benefits society in several ways. It strengthens social cohesion by preventing extreme disparities that can lead to unrest and even rebellion. It also promotes fairness, ensuring everyone has access to basic needs and opportunities, which supports a stable democracy.

Economically, reducing inequality boosts consumer demand by increasing the purchasing power of lower- and middle-income groups, driving sustainable growth. It also helps fund essential public services like education and healthcare, improving overall productivity and quality of life. By preventing extreme poverty, redistribution reduces social and personal costs, leading to a healthier, more productive society.

However, wealth should only be redistributed as needed to help those struggling through no fault of their own and to mitigate the concentration of power. No one should go hungry, children should not suffer for their parents' shortcomings, and everyone should have the opportunity to learn, work, and prosper.

What is the proper distribution of wealth? Make everyone equal? Have one king, a few knights or earls, and the rest serfs? Or have a wide range of wealth levels like in the U.S.?

Even in Communist countries, which ideologically promote a classless society, a wealthy and elite class exists. This group typically includes high-ranking government officials, party leaders, military officers, and individuals close to the ruling regime who enjoy privileges far beyond those available to the general population. For example, from 1922 to 1991, in the old Soviet Union, Communist Party leaders had access to exclusive stores, housing, education, and healthcare. In contemporary Russia, while the Soviet Union's formal system of privileges for Communist Party members has been dismantled, there are still significant disparities in access to resources based on wealth, power, and political connections. Elite groups in Russia, which often include government officials, high-ranking businesspeople (oligarchs), and others with political connections, access a higher standard of living. This privileged access includes exclusive residential areas, private healthcare, prestigious education, and luxury goods and services.

Similarly, a wealthy elite has emerged in modern China, including politically connected families and influential business leaders. North Korea presents another stark example, where the ruling Kim family and their inner circle live in luxury while much of the population faces severe poverty. These disparities often arise from the concentration of power within government and party structures, enabling corruption, favoritism, and nepotism to flourish despite the professed ideals of equality.

What would society look like with a nearly perfect wealth distribution system, or if there were no clear "haves and have-nots"? It seems that government structures tend toward a powerful elite with the rest, as homogenized as possible.

While no system is flawless, the ideal distribution of wealth would include fairness, ensuring wealth aligns with justice and equity; efficiency, maximizing productivity without waste; and equality, minimizing disparities that hinder social mobility or cause unrest. Other critical factors expected in America are social mobility, allowing individuals to advance based on merit rather than birth, and ensuring basic needs like food, housing, and healthcare are universally met.

An ideal system would balance incentives for innovation with stability and sustainability. It would prevent billionaires from consolidating power through financial influence with legislators, thus avoiding power imbalances and promoting long-term well-being balance.

The following analysis aims to put into perspective the breadth and depth of the wealth held by the world's billionaires, revealing the scale of their financial power and its potential impact on the global economy and society.

As of 2024, the combined wealth of the world's billionaires has reached approximately $14 trillion, according to the UBS Billionaire Ambitions Report. This growth reflects a significant increase from \$6.3 trillion in 2015, a compound annual growth rate of 9.28%.[397-398]

In contrast, the total value of U.S. farmland has also seen growth. The United States Department of Agriculture (USDA) reported that the average value of U.S. farm real estate was \$4,170 per acre in 2024, a 5% increase from the previous year.[399]

While comprehensive data on the total value of all U.S. land (including residential, commercial, and agricultural) is not readily available for 2024, previous estimates valued U.S. commercial real estate at \$22.5 trillion as of the fourth quarter of 2023.[400-401]

Assuming billionaire wealth continues to grow at an annual rate of 9.28 percent, it would double approximately every 7.8 years. Conversely, if the total value of U.S. land appreciates at a more conservative rate of 3 percent annually, it would double roughly every 23.4 years. These differing growth rates suggest that billionaire wealth could outpace the total value of U.S. land at an accelerating rate, assuming no significant economic shifts or policy changes alter these trends. Based on these growth rates, projections suggest that the combined wealth of the world's billionaires could surpass the total value of U.S. land within the next 15 to 20 years.

These projections depend on various economic factors, including market performance, policy changes, and global economic conditions. Nonetheless, they highlight the rapid wealth accumulation among billionaires compared to the appreciation of physical assets like land. If these trends continue, billionaire wealth could grow to a level where, hypothetically, they could afford to purchase all the land in the United States. While such a scenario remains theoretical, it is a striking point of comparison, emphasizing the scale of wealth concentration and its potential implications for investment and economic power.

While financial incentives are significant motivators for work, many individuals are driven by intrinsic factors such as personal fulfillment, a sense of purpose, and the joy of creation. These internal motivators often rival material rewards, including mastering a skill or achieving recognition. People seek meaningful engagement and challenges even when basic needs are met, as human nature thrives on purpose rather than idleness. This concept aligns with Maslow's Hierarchy of Needs. This psychological theory arranges human needs into a five-tier model: physiological necessities, safety, love and belonging, esteem, and self-actualization at the peak. According to this model, higher needs can only be pursued once foundational ones are satisfied.

As Franklin D. Roosevelt stated in 1933, "Happiness lies not in the mere possession of money; it lies in the joy of achievement, in the thrill of creative effort." This sentiment is often reflected in professions like farming, where individuals can directly observe and take pride in the tangible results of their labor.

Equality and Wealth Distribution

Achieving absolute equality in wealth is impractical due to differences in talents, physical capabilities, choices, and circumstances. Therefore, the focus typically shifts toward ensuring a minimum standard of living and addressing severe inequalities while allowing opportunities for individual aspirations, achievements, and rewards.

An optimal environment is where the economic "pie" grows over time, benefiting everyone. Economic growth can be achieved by encouraging innovation, productivity, and trade. Ensuring this growth is inclusive is crucial, as it creates more opportunities and enhances upward mobility for a broader segment of society. However, the portion of economic growth driven by population increases — both in the U.S. and globally — is slowing. The aging baby boomer generation continues contributing to the economy, temporarily offsetting this decline. Once this generation significantly diminishes, the population-driven component of economic growth may effectively end unless birth rates rise or immigration increases.

Brian Czech, founder of the Center for the Advancement of the Steady State Economy (CASSE), has an alternative view where he advocates for a steady state economy as a sustainable alternative to perpetual economic growth. He argues that continuous development is incompatible with ecological limits and contributes to environmental degradation and social inequality. In his book *Supply Shock: Economic Growth at the Crossroads and the Steady State Solution*, Czech emphasizes the need to transition to an economy that maintains a stable size, focusing on equitable distribution of wealth and resources rather than expansion. This model balances human needs with environmental sustainability, promoting long-term societal well-being over short-term economic gains. While Czech's model promotes fairness through sustainable economic structures, it also raises important questions about how equality should be understood and pursued in practice.

The principle of "equal opportunity but not necessarily equal results" acknowledges that individuals will achieve varying levels of success. This principle does not imply that the rewards of the more successful should be arbitrarily redistributed to the less successful.

Reflecting on Thomas Jefferson's views on wealth redistribution, there is a perspective that individuals who do not utilize their opportunities due to a lack of effort or responsibility should not benefit from the successes of those who have achieved through hard work and preparation.

Impact of Cash Transfer Programs

Critics argue that simple redistribution could discourage industriousness and encourage dependency. However, research does not conclusively support this. Studies on cash transfer programs, such as those conducted by the World Bank, have shown that these programs do not lead to a reduced work ethic or increased dependency. For instance, evaluations of conditional cash transfer programs have found that while these transfers have raised consumption levels and reduced poverty, there have been relatively modest reductions in labor market participation among beneficiaries. This evaluation suggests that providing financial assistance does not necessarily discourage work. Additionally, a broader examination of the effects of welfare programs reveals that they often support rather than discourage the working poor. For example, U.S. Census Bureau data shows a significant disparity in poverty rates between working and nonworking individuals, indicating that work remains a key factor in escaping poverty despite the availability of social benefits.

Expanding this idea, the concept of a guaranteed minimum income, or more commonly, a guaranteed minimum wage, has been proposed to ensure that all full-time workers earn enough to meet basic living needs. Countries such as France, Australia, and Canada have implemented national minimum wage policies that reduce poverty and support economic stability by stimulating consumer demand. In the United States, cities like Seattle and San Francisco have experimented with higher local minimum wages, showing mixed but generally positive effects on earnings and employment, especially among low-wage workers. These efforts reflect a broader understanding that economic assistance and wage guarantees, rather than reducing motivation, can provide a secure foundation from which individuals are better able to pursue stable employment and upward mobility.[308]

Why Not Handle Poverty Through Charity?

The notion of "self-propelled generosity" suggests that the most successful individuals should also be the most generous based on cultural and psychological values. However, this is not always the case. Unlike individual generosity, which can be unpredictable and uneven, government assistance is often seen as more stable and equitable. Philanthropists face challenges in effectively distributing funds while navigating complex legal, ethical, and cultural factors to create lasting positive impacts.

Government Assistance

As the government has grown more complex, ideas about taxes and social support have changed. Overlapping taxes can make the system harder to manage and may not always help those in need. Many now believe that giving people tools like job training and a safety net is a better way to help. The debate continues over providing support while encouraging people to be responsible and productive.

Finally, you cannot discuss wealth distribution without considering tax systems.

Tax Framework

A modestly progressive tax structure ensures high earners contribute a fair share without being subjected to excessively burdensome rates. This approach ensures that successful individuals are not disincentivized from further wealth creation and investment, which are vital for economic dynamism and job creation. Simultaneously, this taxation model supports essential public services and social welfare programs, helping to bridge income inequality gaps. The objective is to strike a balance between rewarding success and ensuring social equity, fostering an environment where individual ambition and collective well-being can thrive. The taxation framework for those on higher incomes should continue to align with the principles of prioritizing economic growth and innovation while addressing social responsibilities.

Flat Tax?

A flat income tax, where all individuals pay the same percentage regardless of how much they earn, is often praised for its simplicity and transparency. Supporters argue that it eliminates loopholes, reduces administrative costs, and creates a fairer system by treating all taxpayers equally under the law. It can also encourage investment and economic growth by lowering tax rates for high earners and reducing the disincentive to work or expand businesses.

However, critics argue that a flat tax is inherently regressive, placing a heavier burden on lower-income individuals who spend a larger share of their income on basic needs. Taxing the rich and poor at the same rate may worsen income inequality and reduce the government's ability to fund essential public services. The debate ultimately centers on whether fairness means equal treatment or an adjustment based on ability to pay.

Taxes and a Balanced Budget

Taxes and a balanced budget are central to a nation's fiscal health. Taxes provide the primary revenue needed to fund government services and programs. At the same time, a balanced budget ensures that spending does not exceed revenue, reducing the need for borrowing and promoting long-term economic stability. The primary issue with operating at a deficit isn't just the total amount of debt but the cost of servicing this debt, particularly the interest payments on bonds issued to fund the deficit. These interest payments need to be made from annual tax revenues, which can constrain the budget and restrict spending on essential public services.

Healthy debt-to-GDP ratios can vary significantly by country and economic context, but a common fiscal sustainability benchmark is keeping the ratio below 100%. For the United States, as of the third quarter of 2024, the debt-to-GDP ratio was approximately 120.73%.[312]

This high ratio indicates a challenging fiscal environment, where interest costs can substantially affect government spending flexibility and economic health.

Historically, economists have considered lower ratios healthier, with thresholds often discussed around 60% for developed economies and 40% for developing nations, according to guidelines set by the International Monetary Fund for fiscal sustainability. However, the tolerance for higher debt levels can depend on factors like the country's ability to generate economic growth, the stability of its revenue streams, and investors' confidence in its fiscal management.

A well-structured tax system that encourages economic activity while generating sufficient revenue is key to maintaining fiscal balance.

Governments face budget deficits when tax revenues fall short of expenditures, leading to increased borrowing and higher debt servicing costs. Conversely, a surplus budget, achieved through adequate taxation and prudent spending, can allow for debt reduction, public investments, or even tax cuts. However, economic cycles complicate this relationship

— recessions can shrink tax revenues and increase deficits. At the same time, booms can generate surpluses, though these are often offset by political pressures to expand spending or reduce taxes.

A balanced budget and effective tax policies mutually reinforce each other. Responsible tax strategies promote steady revenues, enable balanced budgets, stabilize fiscal policy, and reduce the need for abrupt tax or spending changes. Achieving this equilibrium requires careful planning to balance short-term economic needs with long-term fiscal sustainability.

One way to manage tax escalation is to implement a cap on all forms of taxes at each level of government — federal, state, and local — excluding fees for specific services like passport issuance. This would create a more stable tax structure. For instance, a maximum tax rate of, say, 35% could be set across all tax categories combined.

Budget and Expenses

How many of the top government budgetary expenditures can you name? If you think government spending should be reduced, which of these budgets would you cut and what would be the impact on your fellow Americans if you did? Here they are:

The U.S. government's largest expenditures reflect its commitments to social support, defense, and essential public services.

1. **Social Security ($1.1 trillion)** is funded by payroll taxes designated specifically for this purpose, distinct from regular income taxes. It supports retirement, disability, and survivor benefits through the Social Security Trust Fund, which comprises the Old-Age and Survivors Insurance (OASI) and Disability

Insurance (DI) Trust Funds. The Trust Fund, which accumulates surplus payroll tax revenues, was intended to ensure there are adequate funds for future benefits and invests these in special U.S. Treasury securities to generate interest and increase the fund's value over time. However, the disproportionately aging population has increased demand for withdrawals faster than the growth of the fund. (More later on the specifics).

2. **Medicare and Medicaid ($1.3 trillion)** are major healthcare programs that address the needs of seniors, low-income families, and people with disabilities. Funded by payroll taxes, Medicare provides health coverage primarily for those over 65, while Medicaid, jointly funded by federal and state governments, extends healthcare to low-income individuals. Together, these programs play a vital role in ensuring healthcare access nationwide. Similarly, individuals often consider these programs pre-funded through contributions made during their working years.

3. **Defense spending ($1.3 trillion)** funds military branches, research, and procurement to maintain national security. Rooted in U.S. history since its founding, it remains a significant federal budget component, reflecting long-standing priorities in military readiness.

4. **Interest on the national debt ($305 billion)** is another considerable expenditure. As the government has borrowed for more than a century to fund programs, with the bulk of the debt accumulating since the 1980s, interest payments have become a substantial and growing cost, driven

by both the total amount borrowed and prevailing interest rates.

5. **The Supplemental Nutrition Assistance Program (SNAP) ($85 billion)**, or food stamps, assists low-income individuals in purchasing food, bolstering food security and poverty alleviation. Initially introduced in 1964, it has adapted to meet evolving economic needs.

6. **Income security programs ($622 billion)** support those facing economic hardship. Unemployment Insurance provides temporary assistance for jobless workers, while Supplemental Security Income (SSI) aids elderly, blind, and disabled individuals. Programs like Temporary Assistance for Needy Families (TANF) promote work and financial stability for low-income families.

7. **Veterans' benefits and services ($216 billion)** honor military service by providing healthcare, disability compensation, home loan guarantees, burials, mental health services, education benefits, and more. With a history dating back to the Revolutionary War, these programs expanded with the GI Bill in 1944, affirming a commitment to veterans' well-being.

8. **Transportation funding ($92 billion)** supports infrastructure development, from highways to transit systems. Federal initiatives like the Interstate Highway System underscore the importance of transportation to economic growth and national connectivity.

9. **Education funding ($68 billion)** provides resources for student grants, K-12 support, and higher education assistance. Landmark legislation like the Elementary and Secondary Education Act (ESEA) and the Higher Education Act (HEA) have promoted equal educational access and made education a priority in the federal budget.

Further down the list is foreign aid, which only amounts to about 1% of the federal budget. This includes a wide range of programs and initiatives to promote U.S. interests abroad, support international development, and address global challenges such as poverty, health crises, and humanitarian emergencies. These programs include economic help, humanitarian aid, security assistance, and contributions to international organizations. Some expenditure helps to protect our importing of certain critical raw materials, such as oil, platinum, and palladium.

Should governmental expenditure be cut? How, and who will be affected? Your grandmother who lives on your grandfather's social security? Those receiving social security who have been contributing along with their employers their whole working lives? Where would be the justice in that? Would you end pensions for future generations so that the many people who fail to save and live hand to mouth become a burden on society when they reach old age? This would be kicking the proverbial can down the road. We must think about both the intended and possible unintended consequences when proposing changes. Many highly intelligent senators and congresspersons were involved in crafting these programs; hopefully, any subsequent changes will be as carefully thought through.

Sweeteners Tax

One way to help balance the budget and a major source of potential tax revenue is the untaxed commodity of Sugar and other sweeteners.

We could implement an excise tax on all sweeteners, including natural and sugar equivalents such as high-fructose corn syrup (HFCS), corn syrup, dextrose, fructose, glucose, sucrose, maltose, lactose, cane juice, evaporated cane juice, sugar alcohols, sugar polyols and fruit juice concentrate. A flat rate per ounce for all forms of added sweeteners could raise hundreds of millions in federal revenue and have a positive impact on the health of all Americans. This tax could be applied at the point of sale to food processors. Other than failed efforts by California, Arizona, and Washington State to tax Sugary Sweet beverages, this commodity remains untaxed and has great positive potential.

Sugar

The U.S. taxes legally-available addictive substances such as alcohol and cigarettes, and, likely soon, marijuana upon national legalization, but not one of the most addictive substances of all: sugar. Excessive sugar consumption is associated with numerous health issues, including obesity, type 2 diabetes, heart disease, and dental problems. High sugar intake not only contributes to obesity but also elevates insulin levels, which can potentially increase the risk of developing certain types of cancer. And yet it has escaped the taxman.

U.S. sugar production (cane and beet) expanded from an average of 6 million short tons raw value (STRV) in the early 1980s, which is 12 billion pounds, to an average of 8.6 million STRV (17.2 billion pounds) since 2005/06. This increase in production is due to demand and investments in new processing equipment, improved crop varieties, and expanded acreage.[59-01] It basically means that sugar consumption has increased 43% in the last 40 to 50 years.

Sugar and Cancer

In recent years, researchers and health organizations have examined the potential relationship between sugar intake and cancer development, producing a range of findings. A 2016 article in the National Institutes of Health database reviews both preclinical and clinical studies that suggest a possible link between sugar consumption and cancer. Although the evidence remains inconclusive, some studies have shown associations between sugar intake and certain types of cancer, even when weight and BMI are accounted for. Similarly, the MD Anderson Cancer Center highlights that while sugar itself has not yet been shown to directly cause cancer, it contributes to obesity — a well-established risk factor for several cancers.

They also point out studies indicating that high blood sugar levels may foster an environment conducive to cancer growth. A 2023 article from Cancer Research UK provides further clarity by noting that while sugar is not a carcinogen, there is a strong connection between high sugar consumption, weight gain, and increased cancer risk. Specifically, obesity linked to excessive sugar intake is associated with thirteen different types of cancer. Additionally, an article from Australia's Cancer Council underscores that although cancer cells use sugar as a fuel source, sugar is not a direct cause of cancer. That analysis references a review by the National Health and Medical Research Council, which found no definitive evidence linking sugar consumption to specific cancers such as pancreatic, bowel, breast, or bladder cancer. These perspectives collectively suggest that while sugar may not be directly responsible for causing cancer, its role in contributing to obesity and potentially high blood sugar levels highlights its indirect influence on cancer risk. 59-02,03,04,05

Perspective on Sugar as a Tax Target

Taxing sugar as a public health strategy brings complexity and political considerations. Sugar is already subject to state and local sales taxes, but these vary significantly by region. While some states exempt essential food items, including sugar, from sales tax, many treat it similarly to essential food products despite its lack of nutritional necessity. This inconsistent approach underscores the challenges of viewing sugar through a taxation lens aimed at public health.

Implementing a federal tax on sugar would bring further complications. Establishing a comprehensive tax system would require clear definitions, tax rates, and a collection mechanism similar to existing federal taxes on alcohol, gasoline, and nicotine. Though these precedents suggest that managing such a system is feasible, it would nonetheless demand substantial regulatory and administrative efforts to navigate the complexities unique to sugar.

Sugar Lobby

Moreover, the industry's significant lobbying power heavily influences the political landscape surrounding sugar taxation. The sugar industry, encompassing producers, processors, and refiners of sugar cane and beet, has a longstanding and formidable presence in Congress. This sector has consistently protected its interests through subsidies, import quotas, and price supports, bolstering its profitability and competitive edge. Given this history of political clout and influence over legislative decisions, any proposal to introduce a federal sugar tax would likely face strong resistance.

While a federal tax on sugar could theoretically mirror existing taxes on other consumable goods, the multifaceted challenges — ranging from administrative complexity to significant lobbying pose substantial hurdles. This reinforces the current reliance on state and local initiatives to address the public health implications of sugar consumption.

A sugar tax could raise $435 million per year per 1% tax based on retail sugar prices.[402] This tax would increase annual federal revenues by 0.001% per 1%-point tax at retail prices. However, the primary benefit would come from health improvements.

Policy Reform: Efficiency and Equity

Taxation could be simplified by restricting tax credits for social engineering purposes, except when justified by public health concerns. This approach aligns with constitutional principles that limit government interference in personal choices while recognizing public health as a legitimate governmental responsibility.

Governments are critical in protecting public health, ensuring economic stability, and promoting social well-being. They are uniquely positioned to legislate, coordinate resources, and manage health services — functions essential for preventing and responding to public health crises.

When tax credits are necessary, they should focus on capital investments rather than modifying individual behavior. Incentivizing business expansion, technological advancements, and infrastructure improvements foster economic growth and job creation, producing broader and more sustainable benefits.

Additionally, a comprehensive review of federal excise taxes should be undertaken to simplify the tax structure, reduce rates where feasible, and ensure stability for businesses and consumers.

The tax exemption on unrealized capital gains for non-profit organizations should also be reevaluated, particularly for institutions with substantial assets not actively used for charitable purposes. Ensuring that tax-exempt entities fulfill their intended public service role will promote fairness and accountability within the tax system.

Finally, limiting lobbying influence on tax legislation could help ensure that the tax code serves the public equitably rather than disproportionately benefiting specific industries or economic classes.

Church Taxes

The debate over whether to tax churches and other religious institutions is long-standing and contentious, primarily concerning the principles of church-state separation and the economic roles these organizations play in society. Historically, religious institutions in the United States have been exempt from federal, state, and local taxes, a practice rooted in the First Amendment's provisions to prevent governmental interference in religious practices.

However, taxation proponents contend that many religious organizations should be held to the same fiscal responsibilities as other economic entities when they engage in commercial activities that generate significant revenue and sometimes attempt to influence government policies. They contend that such taxation could provide substantial public revenue to enhance community services and infrastructure. A progressive tax on churches would help curb the economic influence of mega-churches, much like taxing billionaires aims to reduce wealth concentration.

On the other hand, opponents argue that taxing religious organizations could infringe on constitutional rights and allow governmental control over religious practices, harming religious freedom. They also point out that many religious groups offer essential community services — like food banks and homeless shelters — that might be at risk if these institutions were burdened with taxes. This complex issue involves balancing legal rights, financial equity, and the broader societal values related to the role of religion in public life.

One option might be to tax churches based on "excess liquidity." This approach aims to establish a fair taxation method that aligns with religious organizations' financial activities, ensuring they maintain their essential non-profit functions while potentially contributing to public revenues if their financial reserves exceed what is necessary for their operations. This approach would define "excess liquidity" as the volume of liquid assets, such as cash and easily liquidated investments, surpassing what is necessary for a church's religious, charitable, and administrative operations. Regular financial audits could be mandated to maintain transparency in financial activities, coupled with a graduated tax scale that increases with the level of excess liquidity to implement this concept. This system allows for fairness, focusing on organizations with substantial surplus funds while safeguarding smaller entities from undue financial strain. Churches do use the same services individuals use, such as fire, police, and emergency services.

Another option that ensures fairness in religious taxation could be to require churches and other religious organizations that engage in lobbying or political advocacy to forfeit their tax-exempt status and pay taxes on all their revenue or assets. This approach would align with the principle that tax exemptions are granted to organizations primarily focused on charitable, educational, or religious missions rather than political influence. Such a policy would ensure that religious institutions engaging in lobbying are subject to the same tax obligations as other advocacy groups, reinforcing the separation of church and state while preserving tax-exempt status for those that remain non-political.

However, the proposal also presents challenges such as regulatory complexity in determining necessary reserves, potential privacy concerns with and the costs of frequent audits, and the risk of disproportionately affecting smaller or financially unstable churches. Careful consideration is needed to set clear financial benchmarks, like operational thresholds and revenue-to-expense ratios, to delineate necessary versus excess reserves. Any such taxation policy would require a transparent, consistent approach that respects the financial diversity and religious missions across different faith communities, ensuring that any tax structure is fair and sensitive to varying economic capabilities.

Farm Taxes

An old saw: "When a farmer won a $1 million lottery and was asked what he would do with the windfall, he answered, "Farm for another year." In 2024, the median total household income for U.S. family farms is projected to be $99,683, with most of this income derived from off-farm sources.[403]

Breaking this down, using 2023 figures, small family farms with a gross cash farm income (GCFI) under $350,000 had a median total household income of $97,984, but their median farm income was negative at -$900. Midsize family farms, with a GCFI between $350,000 and $999,999, reported a median total household income of $62,014, while their median farm income stood at -$1,974. Large-scale family farms, with a GCFI of \$1,000,000 or more, had a significantly higher median total household income of \$253,496, with a median farm income of \$167,550. Across all farm sizes, off-farm employment plays a major role in household income, particularly for small and midsize family farms.[404]

We must protect both the quality and quantity of our food production while ensuring the ongoing training and development of new and replacement farmers. Agriculture was one of our founding industries, and we remain heavily dependent on having enough families with the specialized skills needed to operate farms. We also must protect the condition of the ground in which our food is grown.

Making small family farms tax-exempt could provide financial relief by eliminating income taxes on farm profits and reducing property taxes, freeing up resources for reinvestment and offsetting volatility. However, since many small farms operate at a loss due to high expenses and low revenues, tax exemptions alone may not resolve their financial challenges. Broader measures, such as direct subsidies, market access, and cost-saving technologies, are necessary to address systemic issues and improve long-term viability. Tax relief could be a helpful component of a comprehensive strategy to support small farms, but it must be paired with efforts to reduce costs and boost profitability.

How To Stabilize Taxation

U.S. Federal Budget and Spending Analysis

In fiscal year 2024, which ended on September 30, 2024, the U.S. federal budget was approximately \$6.752 trillion, with a total revenue of \$4.919 trillion. This resulted in a deficit of \$1.833 trillion. Here is the breakdown of revenue sources and their respective proportions of revenue and spending:

- Individual Income Taxes: $2.426 trillion (49.3% of revenue, 35.9% of spending). This may decrease some in 2025.
- Social Insurance and Retirement Contributions: $1.710 trillion (39.9% of revenue, 25.3% of spending)
- Corporate Income Taxes: $530 billion (12.4% of revenue, 7.9% of spending). This may change in 2025.
- Excise Taxes, Customs Duties, Estate and Gift Taxes, Miscellaneous Receipts: $253 billion (5.9% of revenue, 3.7% of spending). This is projected to increase substantially in 2025.

Comparison to National Personal Income

The total personal income of Americans in 2024 was estimated at $14.7 trillion. Using this figure:

- Income Taxes as a Percentage of Personal Income: Individual income taxes accounted for approximately 16.7% of personal income. This figure represents the effective average tax rate on individuals.
- Government Spending as a Percentage of Personal Income:
  - Current Spending: $6.752 trillion equates to 45.9% of total personal income.
  - Spending Without Deficit: If spending matched revenue ($4.919 trillion), it would represent 33.5% of total personal income.

Suggested Spending Limit

To solidify fiscal responsibility, a spending limit tied to a fixed percentage of national personal income is worth considering. Setting such a limit at approximately 33.5% of personal income would align federal spending with revenues, effectively eliminating deficits, and establish a predictable and monitorable framework for government spending. It would allow businesses to plan with greater consistency.

To avoid economic shocks, transitioning to this spending limit should occur gradually over several fiscal years. This phased approach would allow federal programs and agencies to adjust while minimizing disruptions to essential services and economic growth.

Adopting a spending limit based on a percentage of personal income could ensure fiscal sustainability while maintaining fairness and accountability in tax obligations. This framework would tie government spending more closely to the nation's economic output, fostering long-term stability.

Minimum Wage

Minimum wage laws exist in many countries to set a baseline for worker compensation, aiming to balance economic sustainability with fair labor standards. These laws are subject to ongoing debates regarding their appropriate levels and effectiveness. A key concern is how minimum wages impact both workers and businesses, with differing views on their economic consequences.[405]

Another concept, a balanced wage system with both minimum and maximum wage limits, has been proposed as a way to address income disparities while maintaining economic competitiveness.

However, regional cost-of-living differences present challenges in implementing such a national system. For example, the cost of living in New York City is 87% higher than in Ames, Iowa.[410] A flexible framework with regionally adjusted wage limits could address these disparities, but careful planning is needed to avoid unintended consequences such as inflation or stifled business growth.[406]

Economists remain divided on the effects of minimum wage increases. Some argue that raising the minimum wage boosts the income of the lowest-paid workers, thereby reducing income inequality and increasing consumer spending, which can stimulate economic growth. This perspective is supported by studies showing that higher minimum wages have led to wage gains for low-income workers while having minimal effects on employment in specific labor markets.[407]

However, critics contend that such increases can lead to job losses, particularly in industries that rely on low-wage labor, such as retail and hospitality. They argue that higher wages increase labor costs for employers, which might lead them to reduce their workforce, cut hours, or raise prices to maintain profitability, potentially contributing to inflation. Additionally, there is concern that higher minimum wages could accelerate automation as businesses invest in technology to reduce reliance on human labor, potentially decreasing entry-level job opportunities.[408]

One proposed method to address these issues is to index the minimum wage to local housing costs. For instance, the minimum wage should be set so that two full-time workers can afford the median rent for a two-bedroom apartment without spending more than 30% of their income on housing. This approach ensures wages align with living costs in different areas, providing a more tailored solution to wage setting. This idea builds on existing practices. Government jobs already provide "locality pay," and many businesses offer cost-of-living adjustments, suggesting that location-based wage policies are practical and precedented.

Implementing such policies requires careful consideration of regional economic conditions and potential impacts on workers and businesses. Balancing fair compensation with economic viability is crucial to fostering a healthy economy that benefits all members of society.

Homelessness

Can you imagine yourself being homeless? At a minimum, our economy should ensure that everyone, especially the homeless, hungry children, and those in extreme poverty, has access to basic necessities. Everyone needs a place to be, and if they are not welcome there, legal or non-legal provisions should ensure access to a safe and viable alternative.

Government-sponsored work programs provide opportunities for individuals to contribute and feel productive while receiving support. Linking essential services such as food, healthcare, and housing to these programs ensures that basic needs are met while fostering personal responsibility and self-sufficiency. This approach upholds individual dignity by encouraging active participation in society and reducing long-term reliance on government aid.

Additionally, strong support systems play a crucial role in strengthening community and familial bonds, fostering a sense of belonging that extends beyond economic aid. Investing in these services now can prevent more significant future costs related to crime, emergency healthcare, and social instability, demonstrating fiscal responsibility and a commitment to public well-being.

Ultimately, this comprehensive approach reflects a moral obligation to assist those in need, aligning with shared values of compassion and integrity across the political spectrum.

Corporate Personhood

Corporations in the United States are treated like individuals regarding certain legal rights. This treatment is based on the legal concept of corporate personhood. Corporate personhood means that a corporation, as a legal entity, can enter into contracts, sue and be sued, own assets, and pay taxes. This concept has been part of U.S. law since the 19th century but gained significant attention from the Supreme Court's 2010 decision in Citizens United v. Federal Election Commission (2010). In that case, the Court ruled that corporations have a First Amendment right to free speech, which includes the right to spend money on political campaigning. This decision affirmed the idea that corporations can exercise some of the same legal rights as individuals, particularly regarding political speech. This decision thereby legitimizes corporate lobbying which overwhelms citizens' access to their representatives.

While corporations in the United States are granted certain rights similar to individuals, they do not possess all the rights that natural persons do. For instance, corporations cannot vote in elections, register for social security, obtain driver's licenses, or serve in the military. Their privacy rights are also more limited; business premises may be subject to regulatory inspections without the stringent requirements that protect individuals' homes from searches. Regarding the Fifth Amendment, protections against self-incrimination apply differently to corporations, particularly concerning business records, which cannot be shielded under self-incrimination claims. Furthermore, some constitutional freedoms that are deeply personal, such as protection against self-incrimination and degrading treatment, do not extend to corporations since these entities cannot experience humiliation, pain, or imprisonment like humans. Therefore, corporations are not entirely equivalent to individuals.

The Citizens United decision has led to debates over whether corporations should have the same political speech rights as individuals, especially given the disparities in rights and responsibilities between corporations and natural persons.

Truth About Corporate Taxes

Corporations pay less tax than individuals. Recent data highlights an advantage for large, profitable U.S. corporations, which have seen a significant reduction in their effective tax rates following the Tax Cuts and Jobs Act (TCJA) (2017). While individuals continue to face consistent tax burdens, these corporations' average effective tax rate plummeted from 22% to approximately 12.8%, underscoring tax treatment favoring corporate entities over individual taxpayers.

Multiple analyses, including those from the Institute on Taxation and Economic Policy (ITEP), confirm a trend of reduced effective tax rates for corporations. These reports indicate that many profitable companies now pay an effective tax rate of less than 10%, with some even paying less than 5%. In certain cases, the effective tax rate can be as low as 0% to 10%, starkly contrasting with the average effective tax rate of 14% for middle-income individuals.[257-259]

Corporate Tax Trickle Down

The argument for low corporation taxes is called "supply-side economics" or the "trickle-down" economic theory. Advocates argue that lower corporate taxes allow businesses to reinvest their earnings into innovation, new products, and more efficient equipment, potentially expanding their operations and workforce and increasing wages and bonuses. Despite these claims, evidence shows that the benefits have predominantly favored the wealthy, intensifying wealth concentration rather than broad economic improvement. Studies, including one from the London School of Economics, demonstrate that decades of tax cuts for the rich have not significantly boosted job or income levels for the average person but have instead exacerbated income inequality.[317]

Further, a study by economist Owen Zidar showed that tax cuts for the wealthy also had minimal effects on employment growth compared to more substantial positive impacts when lower-income groups received tax cuts. [318]

The Economic Policy Institute also reported that the post-TCJA investment levels did not substantiate claims that cutting corporate taxes boosted private investment.[319]

These findings indicate that wealth accumulated by corporations and high-income individuals under trickle-down tax policies is more likely to be directed towards increasing retained earnings, higher dividends and executive pay, rather than being used to significantly increase job creation or raise wages for the average worker.

Scaled Corporate Tax Rates

Implementing a graduated tax system for businesses could be one approach to addressing disparities in earning capacity. Under this model, sometimes called a progressive tax system, larger corporations would pay taxes at a higher rate relative to their earnings. At the same time, smaller businesses might receive tax relief or incentives to support entrepreneurship and economic growth. Proponents argue that this structure could help balance the competitive landscape by easing the financial burden on smaller enterprises while ensuring that highly profitable corporations contribute proportionally. At the same time, business and personal taxation must be structured to adequately fund government operations.

Businesses, individuals, and our government must expect an annual inflation rate of around 3% which aligns with some economic theories that suggest moderate inflation can be beneficial. Three percent is also the average over the last 75 years.[59-31] This rate reflects the natural growth in economic productivity and efficiency and can help avoid the pitfalls of deflation.

Thomas Jefferson wrote in a letter to J. W. Eppes in Sep. 1813, "The public contributions should be as uniform as practicable from year to year, that our habits of industry and of expense may become adapted to them; and that they may be duly digested and incorporated with our annual economy."[02] His statement suggests that keeping the tax structure stable over time allows businesses and individuals to incorporate its effects into prices and wages, eliminating the need for continual adjustments.

Taxation Today

The government runs on money; taxpayer money. The economy runs on taxpayer money too, specifically what citizens have left over for spending after the government taxes them.

A larger government requires more funding from taxpayers, which means withdrawing more money from the economy. Conversely, downsizing the government and lowering taxes should result in more money circulating in the economy.

Similarly, stimulus payments are like tax cuts, putting money into the economy, but they are rare. Our country began with no income tax, and Jefferson spoke against having income taxes, believing a consumption tax would be better. A pure consumption tax could replace income tax, but it would require a high sales tax or a Value Added Tax (VAT) rate (explained later) of 30% or more and strong safeguards to avoid overburdening lower-income individuals. A hybrid system (such as reducing income tax while increasing consumption taxes) might be more practical in today's economy.

A pure consumption tax is not really needed, but tax reform could be beneficial, such as lowering income tax and broadening the tax base. Corporations pay higher taxes in other countries but those often pass through to the consumer anyway. A complete switch would be a massive economic shift that could bring unintended consequences.

Tax Rates

In 2020, according to the most recent data as of early 2025, those earning below $42,184 paid an average income tax rate of 3.1%, while the top 1% of earners paid an average of 26% and accounted for 42.3% of all federal income taxes paid.[50]

Individual tax Rates have been relatively stable since 1988.

Historical Tax Rates – 1862 to 2023[56]		
Era	Bottom Rate	Top Rate
Early Days (1862-1913)	0%	7%
World Wars (1914-1964)	1% to 14%	94%
Great Society (1965-1987)	11% to 14%	70%
Modern (1988-present)	12%	37%

Jefferson on Taxation

Jefferson said in a letter to General Washington in 1787, "Wealth acquired by speculation and plunder is fugacious in its nature and fills society with the spirit of gambling."[02-a]

About taxation, Thomas Jefferson wrote to James Madison in December 1784, "The simplest system of taxation yet adopted is that of levying on the land and the laborer. But it would be better to levy the same sums on the produce of that labor when collected in the barn of the farmer; because then if through the badness of the year he made little, he would pay little. It would be better yet to levy taxes only on the surplus of this product above his own wants. It would be better, too, to levy it not in his hands, but in those of the merchant purchaser; because though the farmer would in fact pay it, as the merchant purchaser would deduct it from the original price of his produce, the farmer would not be sensible that he paid it. This idea would no doubt meet its difficulties and objections when it should be reduced to practice; yet I suspect it would be practical and expedient. ... What a comfort to the farmer to be allowed to supply his own wants before he should."

Thomas Jefferson was proposing a tax system he felt was fairer where farmers would be taxed based on the surplus produce, they could sell, reducing their burden in lean years. Of course, that would make the government budget vary too.

In a letter to James Madison in 1789, Jefferson wrote, "Let taxes be few, non-enumerate, and variable only with the indispensable necessities of government." He advocated for a predictable, reliable tax system that enables individuals to plan effectively. A stable tax rate supports economic equilibrium and consistent pricing, though exceptions should be allowed, when necessary, despite the risk of disrupting stability and predictability.

Taxes Reduce Production

Thomas Jefferson felt that too much tax takes away from production. He said, "To equalize and moderate the public contributions, that while the requisite services are invited by due remuneration, nothing beyond this may exist to attract the attention of our citizens from the pursuits of useful industry, nor unjustly to burthen those who continue in those pursuits ... [is one of the] functions of the General Government on which you have a right to call."[172-02]

He went on to say, "I thought at first that the power of taxation [given in the new federal Constitution] might have been limited. A little reflection soon convinced me it ought not to be."[173-02]

Jefferson also believed that taxation should reflect the will of the people as much as possible. He said, "Taxation is the most difficult function of government, and that against which their citizens are most apt to be refractory [upsetting]. The general aim is, therefore, to adopt the mode most consonant with the circumstances and sentiments of the country."[174-02]

He also did not believe we should tax citizens for wars until needed. He said, "Sound principles will not justify our taxing the industry of our fellow citizens for wars to happen we know not when, and which might not perhaps happen but from temptations offered by that treasure."[175-02]

Jefferson also made an especially crucial point about the consistency of taxes, "Taxes on consumption like those on capital or income, to be just, must be uniform."[176-02]

He also made clear that taxes should not exceed necessities, "No tax should ever be yielded for a longer term than that of the Congress wanting it, except when pledged for the reimbursement of a loan."[177-02]

He also did not think taxes should place a burden on our citizens, "To impose on our citizens no unnecessary burden ... [is one of] the landmarks by which we are to guide ourselves in all our proceedings."[178-02]

Income Taxes and Expenditures

Like any organization or household, a government has sources of income and necessary expenses. Primary sources of government revenue include income taxes (both personal and corporate), tariffs (taxes imposed on imported goods ideally to maintain fair competition for domestic producers), and service fees (such as passport issuance costs). Additionally, individuals and corporations contribute to Social Security, Medicare, Medicaid, and other public healthcare programs, which form another significant revenue stream.

In fiscal year 2023, the U.S. federal government received tax filings from 161,781,457 individual taxpayers and 8,269,075 corporations. These filings resulted in significant revenue from individual income taxes amounting to $2,176.5 billion on $12.7 trillion in income , and corporate income taxes totaling $419.6 billion on income of $3.1 trillion (14.7%).[271-272] Additionally, smaller revenue streams from fees and charges, like passport issuance and national park entry fees, brought in about $703 million, while other business and miscellaneous revenues amounted to approximately $510 million.[270]

On the expenditure side, government spending typically includes operating costs (overhead), military funding, entitlements (like social security, Medicare, Medicaid, and potentially more comprehensive healthcare programs), and aid for foreign and domestic needs.

In fiscal year 2023, the U.S. government spent $6.16 trillion on public programs, exceeding the revenue it generated of $4.47 trillion. This spending and revenue gap contributed to a federal deficit of approximately $1.69 trillion for the year.[273-274]

Imports and Tariffs

Tariffs are intended to protect skilled jobs within the country and maintain competitiveness against foreign industries that benefit from government subsidies or other forms of support. When foreign corporations receive financial aid, tax breaks, or other advantages from their governments — practices that constitute unfair trade tactics — it is reasonable to counterbalance these inequities. This counterbalance can be achieved by imposing tariffs on their products or providing matching subsidies to domestic industries, ensuring a level playing field for local businesses and workers.

Most would agree that raising the living standards of lower- and middle-income populations in other countries at the expense of America's middle class would be unpopular—particularly when such changes happen too quickly, as critics say occurred under certain trade agreements. For example, some argue that the North American Free Trade Agreement (NAFTA) encouraged outsourcing U.S. manufacturing jobs to Mexico, benefiting foreign workers while contributing to job losses and wage stagnation in American industrial regions. Others contend that NAFTA helped improve environmental standards, stabilize trade balances, and create employment abroad, reducing pressures for illegal immigration.

Also, placing tariffs on essential imports has the dangerous upside of fueling inflation. As examples, In 2009, tariffs of up to 35% on Chinese tire imports intended to protect U.S. jobs increased tire prices for American consumers, contributing to inflationary pressures.[59-27] In

2017-2018, 25% tariffs on imported steel and 10% on aluminum, intended to support domestic production, led to increased manufacturing costs and higher prices for various consumer goods, contributing to inflation.[59-28] Additionally, tariffs of up to 24% on Canadian softwood lumber escalated construction expenses, raising new housing costs in the U.S.[59-29]

Tariffs should be used selectively to protect American jobs from unfair competition, but they should be avoided for high-demand consumer products to prevent inflationary effects. Additionally, tariffs are not a practical solution for equalizing the Balance of Payments, as they often lead to retaliatory tariffs, reducing their effectiveness and potentially harming international trade relations.

The current administration has proposed the creation of an External Revenue Service (ERS), a new agency intended to collect tariffs, duties, and other revenues from foreign sources. The goal behind this proposal is to shift a portion of the federal revenue burden away from domestic income taxes and toward international trade-related income. While the ERS has been publicly discussed, it had not been formally established at the time of this writing and would likely require legislative action to be fully implemented. In a related development, the administration issued an executive order to establish the Department of Government Efficiency (DOGE), tasked with streamlining federal operations by cutting waste, reducing unnecessary spending, and restructuring agencies. DOGE's mission overlaps in part with the existing responsibilities of the Office of Management and Budget (OMB), which already plays a central role in preparing the federal budget, monitoring agency performance, and evaluating the effectiveness of federal programs. Whether DOGE becomes a lasting institution or a short-term initiative remains to be seen, but its creation signals a renewed focus on operational efficiency within the federal government.

However, proponents of a new department argue that DOGE would bring a more focused mandate on cutting waste, restructuring agencies, or implementing specific efficiency reforms, while the OMB's responsibilities are broader and primarily budget-centric. Critics could see this as bureaucratic redundancy, adding another layer of government rather than streamlining it, but, yet to be determined, it could also result in creating some new efficiencies with the risk of unintended consequences of disrupting essential government functions that citizens and constituents rely on.

Simplified Income Tax Structure

For the last couple of decades, there has been consistent discussion about tax code reform, with many arguing that it is overly complex and filled with special interest loopholes and tax shelters. While simplifying the tax code and closing corporate loopholes are widely supported ideas, efforts to implement these changes often face resistance due to lobbying and established financial interests.

Proposals generally focus on making the tax system fairer, with some advocating reducing the burden on lower — and middle-income households while increasing contributions from higher-income individuals and corporations. However, others caution that raising corporate taxes too aggressively could impact business investment and economic growth.

Despite differing views on specific policies, most taxpayers agree that the tax reporting process is unnecessarily complicated and could benefit from streamlining and simplification.

A simplified tax structure would likely involve eliminating deductions to reduce government bureaucracy and administrative costs. However, such a shift would require careful planning to ensure that changes do not disproportionately impact certain taxpayers.

Simplest Tax Structure

One approach for a simplified income tax structure would be a minimal framework with a few fixed tax tiers based on income range, adjusted annually for inflation. This system would eliminate all deductions, aiming to reduce government bureaucracy and administrative costs. It could also be automated online, streamlining the filing process and reducing compliance burdens.

This more straightforward system could lower administrative costs and increase transparency in tax obligations. However, it would also remove incentives designed to influence economic behavior, such as mortgage interest deductions that encourage homeownership by making it more affordable earlier in life. Critics argue that eliminating these incentives could have unintended consequences, such as reduced homebuying activity or decreased charitable donations, if deductions for these contributions were also removed.

Behavior Control Deductions

Tax deductions are an important policy tool for our government to control citizen behaviors.

Policy Control

The original principles of America, as laid out by the Founding Fathers, did not precisely anticipate or make provisions for manipulating behavior through taxes. There was significant debate in the nation's early years about the imposition of taxes, with a consensus that they should be limited to funding common defense and the administration of the government. Some argue that the Founding Fathers did not intend taxes to be used to steer citizen behaviors in specific directions.

The U.S. government began using tax deductions to influence taxpayer behavior, notably in the early 20th century. The Revenue Act of 1913, which reintroduced the federal income tax following the ratification of the 16th Amendment, included various deductions aimed at encouraging specific economic activities and providing relief for certain expenses.

Over time, Congress expanded these deductions to promote behaviors such as homeownership and charitable giving. For instance, the mortgage interest deduction has been a longstanding feature of the tax code, incentivizing individuals to purchase homes by allowing them to deduct mortgage interest payments from their taxable income. Similarly, deductions for charitable contributions encourage taxpayers to donate to nonprofit organizations. These policy tools have guided economic and social behaviors by making certain activities more financially attractive through tax incentives.

The federal government extensively uses tax deductions, tax credits, and excise taxes to encourage or discourage various behaviors. These tools incentivize homeownership, support education, and promote energy efficiency, serving broader social, economic, and environmental goals. While the Constitution does not explicitly preclude using taxes for social and economic engineering, tax credits add complexity to tax reporting. The evolving use of tax policies allows the government to adapt to contemporary challenges, with excise taxes being one of the most common methods. If tax incentives are deemed necessary, they could be structured as simple tax credits that fit within a one-page tax return, eliminating the need for itemization and reducing complexity in the filing process.

Excise Taxes

Excise taxes are imposed on specific goods, services, or activities, such as gasoline, alcohol, and tobacco. Unlike broader income or sales taxes, excise taxes are applied at the point of manufacture or import, often as a fixed amount per unit (e.g., cents per gallon) rather than a percentage of value. While these taxes generate revenue, they are also designed to influence consumer behavior and discourage using certain products due to health or environmental concerns. Additionally, excise tax revenue is often earmarked for related public expenditures — for example, tobacco taxes funding healthcare initiatives or gasoline taxes supporting road maintenance — creating a direct link between taxation and policy goals.

Despite their intended benefits, excise taxes face criticism, particularly for their regressive nature, economic impact, and potential unintended consequences. Since excise taxes impose a fixed cost per unit, they disproportionately affect lower-income individuals, who spend a larger share of their income on taxed goods. For instance, tobacco or fuel taxes can create a heavier financial burden on low earners than wealthier individuals, raising equity concerns in tax policy.

Excise taxes can also distort market dynamics by making certain goods more expensive, reducing demand. While this can be desirable for harmful products like tobacco, it can have adverse effects on essential goods by discouraging production and potentially leading to job losses in affected industries. High excise taxes may also encourage black markets, resulting in revenue losses and increased criminal activity. In cases such as gasoline taxation, the economic effects can ripple across industries dependent on transportation, further amplifying financial pressures.

Despite these concerns, excise taxes are often justified to promote public health by reducing harmful behaviors and pollution, reflecting the government's interest in creating a healthier society. Common Products with Federal Excise Taxes include[59-07]

1. Alcoholic Beverages: Including beer, wine, and distilled spirits. The tax rate can vary based on the type and alcohol content. Federal beer taxes range from $0.11 to $0.581 per gallon, depending on production, location, and quantity. The tax rate for most wines is $1.07 per gallon, and for distilled spirits is $13.50. State taxes on distilled spirits are up to $36.55 per proof gallon at volume (Washington). State-level beer taxes vary from $0.02 per gallon (Wyoming) to $1.29 (Tennessee).

2. Tobacco Products: These include cigarettes, cigars, snuff, chewing tobacco, and pipe tobacco from $1.01 per pack plus state excise tax of $0.17 (Missouri) to $4.35 (Connecticut and New York) per pack.

3. Fuel: This includes gasoline, diesel, and other types of motor fuels. Aviation fuel is also taxed (from $0.184 to $0.244 per gallon).

4. Firearms and Ammunition: Generally, these are taxed at the point of manufacture (10% on handguns and 11% on other firearms and ammunition).

5. Air Transportation: Taxes on passenger tickets (7.54%), freight, and aviation fuel.

6. Health-Related Products: This includes taxes on certain types of medical devices and pharmaceuticals (was 2.3% but was repealed).

7. Communication Services: Excise taxes can be levied on telephone and other communication services (3% as part of the overall 30% taxes).
8. Tanning Services: A tax on services provided by indoor tanning salons (10%).
9. Gambling: This includes wagers, certain types of betting, and gaming (0.25% plus $50 for each employee involved).
10. Insurance Policies: Certain types are subject to an excise tax (~1%). Excise taxes on insurance can apply to high-cost health plans, various premium insurances like life and automobile, and surplus lines, varying by jurisdiction.
11. Heavy Trucks and Trailers: The sale of particular trucks, trailers, and tractors, like vehicles over 55,000 pounds and 75,000 pounds, can be subject to an excise tax (12%).
12. Environmental: Including taxes related to the sale or use of ozone-depleting chemicals, coal, and other chemicals (For example, the petroleum Superfund tax rate was $0.164 per barrel in 2023).

In fiscal year 2024, the federal government of the United States collected approximately $5.1 trillion in total tax revenue.[59-32] Of this, excise tax revenues accounted for less than 2% of federal receipts, continuing a historical decline from 18% in 1946.[59-33]

Excise taxes are primarily levied on specific goods and services, including motor fuel sales, airline tickets, tobacco, alcohol, and health-related goods and services. In 2024, the federal government is estimated to have collected approximately $112.5 billion in excise tax revenue. Alcohol excise taxes contributed around $11.8 billion (10.5% of total excise tax revenue), while tobacco excise taxes accounted for approximately $15.4 billion (13.7% of total excise tax revenue). These figures reflect the continued significance of alcohol and tobacco taxes in federal revenue generation, maintaining similar proportions to previous years despite overall fluctuations in tax collections and economic conditions.[59]

If tax incentives are deemed necessary, they could be limited to simple tax credits that fit within a one-page tax return, eliminating the need for itemization. Excise taxes should also be applied as a percentage (e.g., 1%) rather than a fixed amount per unit (e.g., 5 cents per gallon) so that revenue keeps pace with inflation and never requires revision.

Federal Taxes on Addictive Substances

Taxing addictive substances, such as alcohol, tobacco, and, increasingly, cannabis, is an issue that governments worldwide grapple with. These substances are often subject to special taxes, sometimes referred to as "sin taxes" (included in the excise taxes above) due to the potentially negative impact of their consumption on individuals and society at large. The primary objectives of taxing addictive substances are to generate revenue, discourage consumption, and offset some of the societal costs which arise from their use.

Higher taxes can act as a deterrent by increasing the price of these products and making them less affordable. For example, research has shown that a 10% increase in the price of cigarettes led to a 4% reduction in cigarette consumption in the United States.[59-13]. Similarly, in Canada, studies have found that a 10% increase in the price of alcohol leads to a 5.7% reduction in alcohol consumption.[59-14]

Additionally, these taxes provide governments with a dedicated revenue stream that can be earmarked for specific purposes. For instance, in the United States, federal and state excise taxes on alcohol and tobacco generated in 2019 approximately \$12.5 billion and \$10.0 billion in revenue, respectively.[59-15,16] These funds can be used to treat addiction and for prevention programs, which are essential for mitigating the public health impacts of substance misuse.

However, the taxation of addictive substances is not without its challenges. The existence of an illegal market or illicit production of addictive substances can undermine the effectiveness of taxation efforts. In the case of cannabis, for example, states in the U.S. which have legalized recreational use have implemented taxes ranging from 10% to 37%, aiming to strike a balance between generating revenue and competing with illicit markets.[131-135]

As far as marijuana is concerned, its sales are indirectly taxed at the federal level. Under section 280E of the Internal Revenue Code, businesses involved in controlled substances, a category that includes marijuana, are barred from deducting typical business expenses when calculating federal income tax. This results in marijuana businesses, even in states where they operate legally, facing higher federal tax burdens due to the inability to deduct expenses like rent, utilities, and wages. This could all be simplified by legalizing the substance and placing a clear excise tax on sales. Furthermore, states and local governments where marijuana is legal often levy taxes on its sale, significantly boosting their revenues. If legalized everywhere, more jobs will be created, the taxation approach would be simplified, and there will be no need to police its production, distribution, and use.

VAT Alternative

Income taxes could be phased out entirely and replaced with a national tax on consumption, as Thomas Jefferson preferred. This tax would be a Federal Sales Tax or Value-Added Tax (VAT). As of 2024, 175 countries have implemented a Value Added Tax (VAT) or Goods and Services Tax (GST).[275] Often VAT systems have exemptions for foreign visitors who can request a rebate on their way out of the country.

This widespread adoption reflects VAT's revenue collection efficiency and lower economic distortions. The United States remains one of the few countries without a VAT, instead relying on varied state-level sales taxes—an approach consistent with its constitutional structure as a democratic republic. A federal sales tax could supplement or replace income taxes.

Such a shift would tax spending rather than earnings, potentially encouraging saving and investment. However, consumption taxes can burden lower-income individuals, who spend more on essentials. To offset this, exemptions or rebates for necessities like food, housing, and fuel could reduce the impact on those least able to afford it.

WOMEN'S RIGHTS

Women

Many assume that women's rights are no longer a major issue in the United States. After all, women can vote, pursue careers, and hold political office. But when you look at real-life experiences, it is clear that challenges remain. Whether it is earning a fair paycheck, feeling safe in public spaces, or accessing quality healthcare, these issues affect millions of women across all walks of life.

Take pay equality. The law says men and women must be paid the same for the same work, but the reality is different. On average, women earn about 82 cents for every dollar men make. Over a lifetime, that gap can mean hundreds of thousands of dollars lost — money that could help support a family, buy a home, or secure retirement. The problem is even worse for women of color, who often make even less. Imagine working just as hard as your coworkers but always being behind simply because of your gender. That is not just unfair — it holds back families and communities.

Then there's violence against women, a reality too many face. Domestic violence, sexual harassment, and assault continue to be serious issues. Women who report abuse often struggle to get justice, facing skepticism, legal obstacles, or fear of retaliation. Laws like the Violence Against Women Act help, but legal protections only work if they are properly enforced, and if survivors feel safe coming forward.

Healthcare access disparities persist, with women often facing higher medical expenses than men, particularly in areas such as maternity care, mental health services, and chronic condition management. Women aged 18 to 44 incur healthcare costs that are 84% higher than men in the same age group.[415] Historically, gender-based pricing in insurance plans led to higher premiums for women. While reforms like the Affordable Care Act have prohibited these pricing differences, significant out-of-pocket costs remain challenging. Additionally, women are disproportionately affected by chronic conditions, which further increases their healthcare spending.[416] Many also experience higher rates of misdiagnoses and delays in treatment, compounding financial and medical burdens.[417] These disparities highlight the ongoing need for policies that ensure equitable healthcare access and affordability.

Women are making strides in politics but are still underrepresented in elected office. While they make up over half of the population, they hold far fewer leadership positions in government. When lawmakers do not reflect the diversity of the people they represent, policies may not fully address the realities of working mothers and caregivers or women's unique health and safety concerns.

Economic independence is another area of inequality. Women are less likely to have access to financial resources, investment opportunities, and business funding. This concern is not just about fairness — it is about economic growth. When women succeed, entire communities benefit. Countries with greater economic opportunities for women tend to have stronger economies, yet barriers still exist that limit women's ability to build wealth.

Education and career opportunities have improved, but disparities persist in science, technology, and high-paying trades. Encouraging young women to enter these industries and ensuring they have the same chances for advancement as men can help close the earnings gap over time.

Even in family law, women often face hurdles in securing fair divorce settlements, child support, and custody arrangements. Legal systems should ensure that both parents share responsibilities and that women are not unfairly disadvantaged in these cases.

Finally, social and cultural expectations still shape what women can and cannot do. In many workplaces, women feel pressured to choose between career and family. At home, caregiving responsibilities often fall disproportionately on women, even when both partners work full-time. Meanwhile, issues like sexual harassment, gender stereotyping, and unrealistic beauty standards continue to influence how women navigate daily life.

Despite progress toward gender equality, some men still do not believe women should have equal status, whether due to cultural traditions, personal biases, personal insecurities, or ingrained societal norms. In some cases, this manifests as opposition to women's leadership, wage equality, or autonomy, reflecting deeply held beliefs rather than rational arguments.

So why does all of this still matter? Because these are not just policy debates — they are questions of constitutional principle and personal liberty. The right to liberty enshrined in the Constitution demands that every individual, regardless of gender, has an equal opportunity to live freely and fully. Women's rights are not a separate category of concerns; they are central to fulfilling the Constitution's promise of liberty and justice.

While the United States has made progress, these challenges do not resolve themselves. Advancing liberty requires persistent legal reforms, policy improvements, and cultural change to remove barriers restricting equal participation. Yes, women in the U.S. enjoy more freedom than in many parts of the world — but that does not mean the work is finished. True equality does not mean special treatment; it means living in a nation where no one is held back from exercising their full rights as a free citizen.

Men vs Women

Historically, some have claimed men are better suited for leadership based on outdated gender stereotypes. Many men believe this; most women know better.

Research shows men are still more likely to be seen as leaders. A University at Buffalo study found both men and women often view leadership roles as more fitting for men, helping to explain the ongoing gender gap.[411]

Additionally, studies have found that men frequently devalue female leaders, which can impact women's advancement in professional environments. This devaluation is linked to deep-seated biases and stereotypes that associate leadership qualities more closely with men than women.[412]

However, it is important to note that these perceptions do not reflect actual differences in capability. Research has shown that women are equally competent, if not more so, than men in various professional domains.[413]

The persistence of outdated stereotypes continues to influence perceptions, but empirical evidence does not support the notion of male superiority in important jobs.

Historical and cultural narratives have long reinforced the idea that men are naturally better suited for certain professions, but modern research disproves this notion. Studies consistently show that any gaps in leadership or professional achievement are driven by societal biases, not inherent differences in ability. As outdated stereotypes fade and opportunities become more equitable, the evidence overwhelmingly supports that men and women are equally capable of excelling in high-level roles.

VOTING

Rights

The right to vote has two dimensions.

Who is Eligible to Vote?

In the U.S. it was any citizen aged 21 and above until 1971, when the legal age for voting was lowered to 18 in recognition of the age of our soldiers with the ratification of the 26th Amendment to the U.S. Constitution. Only citizens can vote, a concept fundamental to the principle of national sovereignty.

On What Are They Permitted to Vote?

Typical subjects for voting are initiatives, referendums, and elections. In America, naturalized citizens are NOT permitted to vote on federal initiatives (i.e., federal laws) and, in most cases, individual citizens do not vote directly on state laws. Even amendments to the Constitution are not voted on by individual citizens, only by state representatives. This is common for democracies.

Voting Depends On Trust

When election cheating is exposed, it can erode trust across the entire electoral system. There are a variety of circumstances that must be handled to maintain the integrity and accessibility of elections. Supporting early and absentee voting options for a broader range of voters, including ex-patriot voters, house-bound individuals, first responders on duty, military personnel, and voters in remote areas, is crucial. Additionally, practical assistance should be provided to those who need it, such as voters with disabilities, older people needing transportation, and non-English speakers requiring language support. These measures encourage broader participation and help restore confidence in the voting process.

Voting in a Democratic Republic

Because our democracy is a Democratic Republic, the States are given the power to define and manage voting processes, including overseeing their Electoral College votes.

Voting Processes

There are several voting process alternatives, each designed to address specific issues such as voter access, election security, representation, or administrative efficiency. These methods vary widely in approach and impact, from ranked-choice voting and mail-in ballots to same-day registration and proportional representation systems.

Direct Voting

There are those who echo the wishes of some of our Founding Fathers that we move away from party politics in electing public officials and voting on new laws. One approach would be direct voting.

In a direct voting system, citizens typically participate in decision-making through referendums, plebiscites, or initiatives. Here is a brief explanation of each option:

1. Referendum: This is a direct vote in which an entire electorate votes on a particular proposal. This approach can lead to adopting a new law, changing an existing law, or deciding on a specific governmental policy. The

concept of majority rule is fundamental to democratic systems, where decisions are made based on the preferences of the majority of voters. However, this approach can also expose the system to the dangers of mob psychology and mob rule. Mob psychology refers to how individual decision-making can be heavily influenced by the emotions and desires of a group when people are part of a large crowd. This phenomenon can lead to irrational behavior, as personal judgment is often overwhelmed by the collective mood and impulses of the crowd.

Mob psychology can manifest when widespread sentiments, whether driven by misinformation, intense emotions, or popular leaders, sway the majority to make decisions that may not necessarily be in their best interest or reflective of reasoned deliberation. This emotional wave can lead to "mob rule," where decisions are made impulsively without thoroughly considering their long-term effects or the rights and opinions of the minority. Such scenarios can undermine the principles of fair and balanced governance that protect all citizens' interests, highlighting the need for safeguards in democratic systems to prevent the tyranny of the majority and ensure comprehensive deliberation in decision-making processes.

2. Plebiscite: Like a referendum, a plebiscite is a method of direct democracy that gauges public opinion on a specific issue. The critical difference is that plebiscites are often non-binding, meaning the results are used as a guide rather than a mandate.

3. Initiative: This process allows citizens to propose or initiate a statute or constitutional amendment. Initiatives may be direct or indirect. With a direct initiative, a measure is put directly to a vote after enough signatures are collected. To amend the State Constitution in Florida,

a petition must be signed by a number of citizens equal to 8% of the votes cast in the most recent presidential election, amounting to approximately 900,000 signatures. These signatures must be collected from at least 14 of the state's 28 congressional districts, with each contributing a minimum of 8% of its voter turnout to the petition. With an indirect initiative, the proposal is first submitted to the legislature, which can approve it or submit it to the voters for a decision.

Direct voting has pros and cons. It can boost civic engagement, reduce polarization by focusing on issues over parties, and increase accountability. However, it may overwhelm voters, raise practical challenges, and risk ignoring minority rights. Shifting to direct voting would require significant changes to the current system and Constitution.

National Referendums

One option is to use national referendums to enact all but the most urgent laws, thereby reducing the frequency and volume of legislation. Requiring a 60% or 66% approval threshold could further slow the rate at which new laws are passed, ensuring that only widely supported measures are enacted.

Universal Ratification

A radical idea is requiring all voters to approve or reject every law. This concept could reduce the number of laws, improve clarity, and promote stability through public buy-in. However, decisions should not rely on a simple majority—approval or veto should require 60% or more to ensure strong consensus.

Overview of Electoral Reforms

In the United States, two key electoral reforms — Open Primaries and Ranked Choice Voting (RCV) — have been designed to make elections more inclusive and representative.

Open Primaries

Open primaries allow all registered voters, regardless of party affiliation, to vote for any candidate, with the top two vote-getters advancing to the general election, even if they are from the same party. This system aligns with a trend toward more open electoral processes.

Ranked Choice Voting

Similarly, Ranked Choice Voting (RCV) enhances electoral inclusivity by allowing voters to rank candidates in order of preference. If no candidate secures a majority of first-place votes initially, the candidate with the fewest votes is eliminated, and those votes are redistributed to the following choices indicated on the voters' ballots. This process repeats until a candidate achieves a majority, ensuring the elected official reflects a broader consensus.

However, despite their benefits, various states, including Arizona, Colorado, Missouri, Montana, Nevada, Oregon, and South Dakota, which vary widely in political leanings, have rejected changes to implement either open primaries or RCV. These rejections reflect regional resistance to modifying traditional voting systems and highlight the complexities of pushing electoral reform across diverse political landscapes.

The Voting Law

Initially, the U.S. Constitution did not define voter eligibility, leaving it to states. Article I, Sections 2 and 4, and Article II, Section 1, allowed states to set voting qualifications and election processes, creating diverse and restrictive practices, often limiting voting to <u>white male property owners</u>. Later amendments – the 15th, 19th, 24th, and 26th – explicitly expanded and protected voting rights across race, gender, and age:

- 15th Amendment (1870): Prohibits the denial of the right to vote based on race, color, or previous condition of servitude. This amendment was crucial in ensuring African Americans, particularly former slaves, had the right to vote.
- 19th Amendment (1920): Grants women the right to vote, a landmark change in extending suffrage to half the population.
- 24th Amendment (1964): Eliminates poll taxes in federal elections. Poll taxes had been used in some states to prevent low-income individuals, particularly African Americans, from voting.
- 26th Amendment (1971): Lowers the voting age from 21 to 18, a response to arguments that those old enough to be drafted for military service should also have the right to vote.

These amendments collectively expanded voting by addressing discrimination and removing barriers to voting.

Further laws could enhance accessible voting practices nationwide, including automatic registration, early voting, and mail-in ballots. These provisions would aim to ensure that all eligible citizens have a fair opportunity to vote while maintaining election integrity. Accommodations for disabled voters, non-English speakers, and overseas Americans could help broaden participation, while resources to reduce wait times and protections against improper voter roll purges would support a more efficient and reliable voting process.

At the same time, policies could reinforce election security by establishing clear and reasonable voter identification requirements and mandating regular, fair updates to voter rolls. Ensuring voting machines produce paper ballots and expanding in-person early voting access would help strengthen both transparency and public confidence in elections.

Redistricting laws could also be structured to promote impartial standards that minimize gerrymandering. By ensuring district boundaries reflect population and community interests rather than partisan objectives, such measures would support fair representation and uphold the integrity of elections, ensuring that every vote carries equal weight.

Additionally, policies that reveal funding sources could improve campaign finance transparency, safeguard free speech, and balance political influence with public awareness. A commitment to secure, transparent, and fair elections from all political perspectives would help build trust in the electoral process and strengthen democracy at every level of government.

Redistricting and Gerrymandering

The term "gerrymandering" originated in 1812 when Vice President Elbridge Gerry signed a bill that redistricted Massachusetts, creating a district resembling a salamander. This practice has since evolved into a powerful tool for manipulating electoral boundaries to favor specific political parties or groups. By altering the demographic composition of voters in each district, gerrymandering distorts representation, allowing parties to win disproportionate seats relative to their vote share. Tactics like "packing," which concentrates opposition voters into a few districts, and "cracking," which spreads them thinly across many districts, dilute voter influence, undermine the principle of equal representation, and often target racial and political minorities, suppressing their voting power.

Advances in computer technology have made gerrymandering more precise, allowing for highly detailed manipulation of district lines to influence elections. As a result, it has contributed to political polarization by creating 'safe seats,' where candidates are more likely to focus on securing primary victories by appealing to their party's base rather than building broad electoral support. Additionally, it has reduced accountability by insulating incumbents from challenges, making elections less responsive to public opinion.

While the Supreme Court has ruled that partisan gerrymandering may conflict with democratic principles, it is not inherently unconstitutional unless it violates specific protections, such as those against racial discrimination. As a result, decisions about redistricting practices are often left to state legislatures and courts.

Various solutions have been proposed to address gerrymandering. Independent or bipartisan redistricting commissions are seen as a way to reduce political bias and ensure district lines reflect community interests. Legal protections under the Voting Rights Act and nonpartisan criteria for drawing districts are also advocated to promote fair representation and restore trust in the electoral process. A bipartisan-approved mathematical algorithm applied uniformly across states could define fair districts based on geography rather than political influence. By implementing these reforms, gerrymandering can be curtailed, fostering a more equitable and transparent redistricting process that upholds electoral integrity and strengthens democracy.

A nonpartisan or independent commission, possibly combined with public oversight or judicial review, is more likely to be the approach to ensure fair and objective redistricting.

The Electoral College

The U.S. Electoral College, the process used to elect the President, has been a subject of debate since our Constitution was written. Established by the framers of the Constitution as a compromise between direct popular election and selection by the Congress, it was designed to balance the interests of small and large states and prevent the possibility of uninformed or impulsive voting.

Electoral Processes

The electoral process only partially standardizes how states run their elections and how they appoint electors to represent them in national elections. Congresspeople cannot serve as an elector for their state.

The process was originally intended to keep a check on the tyranny of popular voting. As Hillsdale College Professor Kevin Portteus described in his video, "The Electoral College Explained," our Forefathers tried out using the popular vote first in their origin country (U.K.) and then here in the United States, between the signing of the Declaration of Independence and our Constitution, and found it created chaos and unfairness.

The concept of the Electoral College is discussed in Federalist Paper #68, written by Alexander Hamilton. In this paper, Hamilton describes the purpose of the Electoral College as a method to ensure that the office of President will never fall to the lot of any man who is not in an eminent degree endowed with the requisite qualifications. It mentions the importance of having an "intermediate body" to elect the President, which would be composed of members possessing the information and discernment requisite to such complicated investigations. This aligns with the idea of selecting a president based on "ability and virtue."

The electoral process began evolving with the emergence of political parties and states began binding the electors to vote according to the outcome of the state's election. This resulted in most states requiring their electors to vote as a "block." This created a "winner-take-all" system where in some cases a candidate could win all the electoral votes even though they garnered less than 50% of the vote in the case where there were more than two candidates. Nebraska and Maine are exceptions because they tie their electoral votes to the distribution of popular votes.

As Professor Portteus observes, while the Electoral College no longer functions exactly as originally intended, it still acts as a check on majority rule, promoting moderation to address the needs of citizens nationwide. It compels national candidates to travel across the country, engaging with regional issues and presenting their platform to each state, rather than relying solely on mass media to appeal to densely populated urban centers. Without the Electoral College, Direct Voting would shift the focus almost entirely to urban issues, leaving much of the country underrepresented.

One of the primary critiques of the Electoral College is that it gives disproportionate power to smaller population states. While technically true, the impact is minimal because each state gets electors based on the number of its representatives and senators, smaller states end up with slightly more electoral votes per capita than larger states. This means that the votes of individuals in less populous states carry slightly more weight than those in states with larger populations.

In most states, where the Electoral College operates on a winner-take-all basis, this system can result in a candidate winning the presidency without securing the majority of the popular vote, as has happened in several elections, most notably in 2000 and 2016. This disconnect, between the popular vote and the Electoral College outcome, can leave voters in heavily partisan states feeling disenfranchised, as their votes have little impact on the selection of Electors and the overall result.

Because the Electoral College centers attention on a handful of battleground states, voter turnout in "safe" states — where one party has a clear majority — tends to be lower. In these states, voters may feel that their votes do not matter since the outcome is all but predetermined. This can discourage participation and engagement in the democratic process, as many citizens believe their votes have little impact on the national outcome.

The current system can exclude large portions of the electorate. For example, a candidate who loses a state by a small margin still receives no electoral votes from that state. This means that millions of voters, particularly those in the minority party within their state, have no representation in the Electoral College. A popular vote system, in contrast, would ensure that every vote counts equally, no matter where the voter lives, and that the candidate who wins the most votes nationwide becomes the President.

A Better Way?

As the importance of electoral integrity becomes more pronounced, there is increasing discussion about whether laws are needed to standardize the appointment and management of electors across all fifty states. Why?

1. Inconsistent Rules Across States: Currently, each state has the authority to establish its own methods for appointing electors, which has led to significant variation in processes. Some states appoint electors through political party conventions, while others have different mechanisms. This patchwork of rules can create confusion and make it more difficult to ensure the fairness and transparency of the system. National laws to standardize these procedures could help create a more uniform and equitable process, reducing the potential for discrepancies and irregularities that could undermine confidence in the system.

2. Electors Using Their Personal Judgment: State rules governing the selection of Electoral College electors have evolved to prioritize party loyalty and adherence to the outcome of the state's popular vote, often requiring electors to pledge their votes in advance. This requirement removes their ability to exercise personal judgment, a key element of the original intent outlined in Federalist No. 68. The Founders envisioned electors as independent, deliberative individuals who would ensure the presidency was awarded only to those eminently qualified. Modern state laws, however, reduce electors to ceremonial roles, effectively preventing them from acting as safeguards against unfit candidates.

3. The Role of Faithless Electors: One of the most controversial issues in the Electoral College is the phenomenon of "faithless electors," or electors who do not vote for the candidate to whom they are

pledged. While the vast majority of electors cast their votes according to the popular vote in their state, there have been instances where electors have deviated from their assigned role. Some states have laws requiring electors to vote according to the popular vote, while others allow for more discretion. The 2020 Supreme Court ruling in Chiafalo v. Washington upheld states' rights to penalize or replace faithless electors, but there is no uniform national standard. Federal laws could mandate that all electors must cast their votes according to their state's popular vote results, thereby removing any ambiguity and ensuring the system reflects the will of the voters. But this also takes away the intended discretion to ensure that the elected President has "in an eminent degree the requisite qualifications."

4. Safeguarding Against Electoral Manipulation: Without standardized laws, there is a risk that electors could become targets for manipulation or coercion, particularly in closely contested elections. In some cases, the lack of strict guidelines leaves room for political parties or interest groups to influence electors. Before the general election, political parties in each state nominate their slates of electors. These nominees are often party loyalists, including party leaders, activists, or other prominent supporters. The method of nomination varies by party and state, ranging from decisions by party committees to votes at state party conventions. Implementing national standards for the appointment and conduct of electors could protect against these kinds of interference. Laws could be enacted to clearly define the responsibilities of electors, establish penalties for misconduct, and

ensure that the process is free from external pressures or corruption.

5. Clarity in the Event of Disputes: Another concern is the lack of standardized procedures for resolving disputes over electors or electoral votes. In contested elections, where the margin of victory is slim, disagreements over how electors are appointed or how their votes are counted can create a constitutional crisis. By implementing national laws that clearly define how electors are chosen, how disputes are resolved, and how states must certify electoral results, the U.S. can prevent the chaos and confusion that sometimes accompany contested elections. Standardized rules would provide a clear framework for addressing any issues that arise, ensuring a fair and transparent process.

6. Ensuring Public Confidence: The Electoral College is often criticized for being an opaque and outdated system, and the current lack of uniformity in the appointment and management of electors only exacerbates these concerns. Public trust in the electoral process is essential for the health of democracy, and inconsistent rules can lead to skepticism or a sense of unfairness. By enacting federal laws to standardize the appointment and management of electors, the government could enhance transparency, reduce the risk of disputes, and restore confidence in the Electoral College process.

7. The Case for State Autonomy: While national laws would bring consistency, there are those who argue that states should retain control over their own

electors as part of the federalist system. Proponents of state autonomy believe that allowing states to manage their own electoral processes helps preserve their unique political cultures and protects against federal overreach. However, this state-level control has led to the inconsistencies and vulnerabilities currently present. Any effort to standardize the management of electors would need to carefully balance state autonomy with the need for a coherent and uniform electoral process that serves the interests of the nation as a whole.

The Supreme Court has not yet directly ruled on the constitutionality of the winner-take-all process for assigning electors.

Another possibility

One proposal suggests that a state's Electoral College votes be distributed proportionally based on the popular vote within that state. This approach means each presidential candidate would receive a share of the state's electoral votes corresponding to their percentage of the state's popular vote (No winner-take-all). For example, if a candidate secures 60% of the popular vote in a state with ten electoral votes, they would be allocated six electoral votes. This method aims to more accurately reflect the preferences of the state's voters compared to the current winner-take-all system used by most states. This is a variation on the method used by Maine and Nebraska.

Maine and Nebraska use a district system to allocate their Electoral College votes, differing from the winner-take-all approach used by most states. In this system, each congressional district awards one electoral vote to the candidate who wins the popular vote in that district, while the remaining two electoral votes, representing the state's U.S. Senate seats, are awarded to the candidate who wins the statewide popular vote. This method, adopted by Maine in 1972 and Nebraska in 1996, is not a fully proportional allocation. Instead, it reflects the winners of individual districts and the statewide vote, meaning electoral votes are distributed based on localized and statewide outcomes rather than a strict percentage of the popular vote.

Electoral College Inconsistencies

The current decentralized approach to the appointment and management of electors has led to inconsistencies, vulnerabilities, and potential risks to the integrity of the electoral process. Federal laws that standardize the selection, conduct, and responsibilities of electors could reduce confusion, prevent manipulation, and enhance public confidence in presidential elections. While some may argue for state autonomy, the need for a fair, transparent, and consistent process across all states makes a strong case for enacting national standards to govern the Electoral College system.

While the Electoral College was initially designed to balance competing interests and protect the union's stability, its relevance in today's democratic landscape is increasingly questioned. The system's potential to deliver a President who did not win the popular vote, its emphasis on swing states, and its discouragement of voter turnout raise significant concerns about fairness and representation. Reforming or replacing the Electoral College with a more direct method of election, such as the popular vote, could better reflect the will of the people and restore faith in the electoral process. However, any such change would require careful consideration of the impact on smaller states and the broader balance of regional interests in the union.

Proportional representation, ranked-choice voting, and independent commissions to address gerrymandering represent significant steps that could be taken toward creating a more equitable and functional electoral system. These reforms could help ensure that elections more accurately reflect the will of the people, encourage broader participation, and reduce the political manipulation that undermines trust in the democratic process. By adopting these reforms, the U.S. could move closer to a system that values fairness, inclusivity, and true representation for all citizens.

Framework for Automated Voting

As elections grow in scale and complexity, efficiency, accuracy, and security of the voting process become increasingly important. Automated voting systems offer a potential solution by streamlining ballot counting, reducing human error, and improving accessibility for all voters. By leveraging technology, these systems can enhance election transparency, expedite results, and minimize the logistical challenges of manual vote audits. Why is automated voting important?

Election Security

A common approach to election security emphasizes integrity, accessibility, and transparency throughout the election process. This approach includes implementing strong measures against cybersecurity threats and foreign interference, supporting federal funding from the U.S. Election Assistance Commission (EAC), which is the primary federal agency that assists states with voting processes. Established by the Help America Vote Act (HAVA) of 2002, the EAC provides guidance, resources, and support to states to improve election administration to upgrade election infrastructure and enhance security protocols. It also involves advocating for policies that protect voter access and prevent suppression, ensuring equal access to the ballot box for all eligible voters. Transparency and oversight in election administration are also prioritized, with recommendations for paper ballot backups and post-election audits to verify the accuracy and integrity of election results. This approach underscores the importance of a secure, reliable voting process that guards against interference and supports paper ballots for dependable audits. However, paper ballots have challenges.

Difficulty in an Election Audit

For perspective on a voting audit, manually auditing 1,000,000 ballots at two minutes per ballot would require 50 people working full-time for over 83 days. With machine assistance, this process could be completed in about 50 days. Since the average state had over 3,000,000 ballots in 2024, conducting a full manual audit would require significant time and resources. For example, Florida processed 11.0 million ballots, California 17.8 million, and Texas 11.3 million, making large-scale audits a substantial logistical challenge. This potential work effort highlights the importance of having a secure and reliable voting system from the outset.

Given the immense scale of complete manual audits, statistical sampling offers a highly efficient and scientifically sound alternative. By randomly selecting a representative subset of ballots for detailed examination, officials can detect anomalies or verify outcomes with a high degree of confidence—often with only a fraction of the time and labor required for a full audit. When properly designed, a statistical audit can identify errors or fraud at levels far below what would be needed to alter election results. This method allows states to balance transparency, accuracy, and resource constraints while maintaining public trust in the electoral process.[437]

Better Option

Clearer standards can be developed to specify which new laws and legal changes must be voted on by a state's citizens, and more proposed laws should require citizen approval than is currently the case.

Investment should be made in automation so we can vote on every issue securely from the comfort of our homes over the Internet or cell phones. This functionality ensures that our vote will be counted and remain unaltered, with an audit trail for each ballot so that recounts become unnecessary. It could also allow voters to correct any voting mistakes up to a given deadline. The outcome would not be revealed until reaching a specific deadline for everyone in that state. So, "projecting" winners would no longer be needed.

CLOSING COMMENTS

Dear fellow citizens,

Today, our democracy stands at a crossroads — a time when our rights, our voices, and our future are more precious than ever. We have inherited a legacy of freedom, courage, liberty, and unity, and it is now our duty to defend these values with unwavering resolve. Let us stand together, not in anger or violence, but in peaceful determination and collective action. Every vote cast, every voice raised, and every step taken in protest when needed is a testament to our belief in a society where justice and equality flourish.

In these challenging moments, remember: the strength of our nation lies in the power of its people. Let us unite, engage, and protect our democracy, ensuring that our future remains bright and free. The time to act is now — rise up and let your voice be heard for the sake of our shared destiny.

Thank you.

Charles Patton
American Citizen

APPENDICES

Copy and Paste the following links for the details of:

I.   THE CONSITUTION OF THE UNITED STATES:
https://charlespattonbooks.com/Constitution.php

II.   THE DECLARATION OF THE RIGHTS OF MAN –
1789:
https://charlespattonbooks.com/RightsofMan.php

III.   THE U.N.'S DECLARATION OF HUMAN RIGHTS
https://charlespattonbooks.com/HumanRights.php

REFERENCES

01.   U.S. Census Bureau. *U.S. and World Population Clock*. U.S. Department of Commerce, https://www.census.gov/popclock/. Accessed 31 Dec. 2023.

01-01. The University of Chicago, Harris School of Public Policy. "The Overlooked Power of Moderate Voters in the Era of Polarization." New research led by Professor Anthony Fowler makes an empirical case for renewed attention to the middle of the political spectrum. 14 February 2022, by Mike Pilarz, harris.uchicago.edu/news-events/news/overlooked-power-moderate-voters-era-polarization.

01-02. "The Politics Watcher. "Congress: Finding the Middle Ground: Understanding Moderate Political Views." The Politics Watcher, published on Friday, June 16, 2023, at 8:22 PM EST, thepoliticswatcher.com/pages/articles/congress/2023/6/17/finding-middle-ground-understanding-moderate-political-views.

01-03. Gallup. "U.S. Political Ideology Steady; Conservatives, Moderates Tie." POLITICS, 17 Jan. 2022, BY LYDIA SAAD, news.gallup.com/poll/388988/political-ideology-steady-conservatives-moderates-tie.aspx.

01-04. "Google." Google Search, "350 Years: The History of the Jews in America." Submitted by Suzanne Sobczak. Copyright © 2005, Weaver Family Foundation. www.WeaverFoundation.org. Page 1 of 9. Available at: https://www.boulderjcc.org/clientuploads/Lesson%20Plans/1JewishHistoryandCulture_6-8.pdf.

01-05. WeChronicle. 'How Colonialism Created a Rigid Social Hierarchy in America.' WeChronicle, 2023, https://wechronicle.com/colonial-america/examining-the-impact-of-colonial-social-hierarchies-on-american-class-structure/.

02. Jeffersonian Cyclopedia. http://etext.virginia.edu/toc/modeng/public/JefCycl.html.

02-a. Washington Edition, vol. II, p. 252.

02-b. Washington Edition, vol. I, p. 36; Ford Edition, vol. I, p. 49.

02-c. Note in Destutt Tracy's Political Economy. Washington Edition, vol. VI, p. 573. 1816.

03. The Adams-Jefferson Letters, Edited by Lester J. Cappon, Volumes I and II, Published for The Institute of Early American History and Culture at Williamsburg, Virginia by The University of North Caroline Press, Chapel Hill, printed by Van Ress Press, New York, NY 1959

04. Thomas Jefferson to A. Coray, 1823, The Writings of Thomas Jefferson, Memorial Edition (Lipscomb and Bergh, editors), 20 Vols., Washington, D.C., 1903-04. 15:488 (http://etext.virginia.edu/jefferson/quotations/jeff1000.htm)

05. Thomas Jefferson to Samuel Kercheval, 1816. ME 15: (http://etext.virginia.edu/jefferson/quotations/jeff1000.htm)

06. OpenAI. "ChatGPT." October 2023.

10. "Criminal Law of Singapore." Wikipedia, Wikimedia Foundation, August 2023.

10-01. Ward, Myah. "White House Announces New State-Based Gun Violence Initiative." POLITICO, 13 Dec. 2023, www.politico.com/news/2023/12/13/white-house-gun-violence-00131473.

10-02. Leonard, Kimberly. "The Politics of Mass Shootings in the Gunshine State." POLITICO, 27 Oct. 2023, www.politico.com/newsletters/florida-playbook/2023/10/27/the-politics-of-mass-shootings-in-the-gunshine-state-00123930.

11. Naegeli, Phyllis. "The History of Political Parties in the United States." EdHelper, August 2023. http://www.edhelper.com/ReadingComprehension_34_26.html. Page 4.

12. "Sunday Morning." CBS, 18 Oct. 2009.

13. " UNAFEI. August 2023. http://www.unafei.or.jp/english/pdf/PDF_rms/no56/56-12.pdf.

14. "Lobbying." Wikipedia, Wikimedia Foundation, August 2023. http://en.wikipedia.org/wiki/Lobbying.

15. The Washington Post. 21 June 2005, http://www.washingtonpost.com/wp-dyn/content/article/2005/06/21/AR2005062101632.html.

16. "Federal Employment Statistics." U.S. Office of Personnel Management, August 2023. http://www.opm.gov/feddata/HistoricalTables/TotalGovernmentSince1962.asp.

17. Garrett, Thomas A., and Russell M. Rhine. "On the Size and Growth of Government." Federal Reserve Bank of St. Louis Review, Jan./Feb. 2006, http://research.stlouisfed.org/publications/review/06/01/GarrettRhine.pdf.
18. "Article 11 of the Treaty of Tripoli." Ratified by the U.S. Senate. The treaty was ratified by the U.S. Senate and is considered a historical document affirming the secular nature of the United States government.

19-01. Jefferson, Thomas. "The Writings of Thomas Jefferson." Edited by Andrew A. Lipscomb and Albert Ellery Bergh, vol. 16, 1907, p. 113.

19-02. Madison, James. "A Memorial and Remonstrance Against Religious Assessments." 1785. Madison and other members of the Virginia General Assembly wrote this document. It argued against a bill that would have established a state church in Virginia. The document contains a passage that is similar to this quote:
"Who does not see that the same authority which can establish Christianity, in exclusion of all other Religions, may establish with the same ease any particular sect of Christians, in exclusion of all other Sects? That the same authority which can force a citizen to contribute three pence only of his property for the support of any one establishment may force him hereafter to contribute three pounds. And that in time the same authority which can force him to pay three pounds, may force him to pay whole hundreds, or thousands?"

19-03. Paine, Thomas. "The Age of Reason; Being an Investigation of True and Fabulous Theology." 1794.

1. "Roman Law." Wikipedia, Wikimedia Foundation, August 2023.
http://en.wikipedia.org/wiki/Roman_Law.

22. Kelly, Kevin. "The New Socialism." Wikipedia, Wikimedia Foundation, Aug. 2023, en.wikipedia.org/wiki/The_New_Socialism, p. 23.

23. Dahl, Robert A., and Seymour Martin Lipset. Who Governs? August 2023, p. 29. https://en.wikipedia.org/wiki/Who_Governs%3F.

24. Naegeli, Phyllis. "The History of Political Parties in the United States." EdHelper, August 2023. http://www.edhelper.com/ReadingComprehension_34_26 .html.

25. Münsterberg, Hugo. American Traits from the Point of View of a German. Houghton Mifflin, 1901. 240 pgs. http://www.questia.com/read/54118835.

26. "Natural Justice." Wikipedia, Wikimedia Foundation, October 2023. http://en.wikipedia.org/wiki/Natural_justice.

27. Wikipedia contributors. "Social Contract - John Locke's Second Treatise of Government (1689)." Wikipedia, The Free Encyclopedia, Oct. 2023, en.wikipedia.org/wiki/Social_contract#John_Locke.27s_S econd_Treatise_of_Government_.281689.29.

28. New World Encyclopedia contributors. "Socrates." New World Encyclopedia, Sept. 2023, www.newworldencyclopedia.org/entry/Socrates.

29. Wikipedia contributors. "Direct Democracy." Wikipedia, The Free Encyclopedia, Sept. 2023, en.wikipedia.org/wiki/Direct_democracy.

29-01. OpenAI. ChatGPT Version 3.5. 2023. Accessed Sept. 2023, openai.com/chatGPT.

30. Wikipedia contributors. "Socialism." Wikipedia, The Free Encyclopedia, Sept. 2023, en.wikipedia.org/wiki/Socialism.

30-01. "Democratization." Britannica, Encyclopædia Britannica, Inc., www.britannica.com/topic/democratization.

31.   Taylor, Bayard. A Visit to China in the Year 1853. G.P. Putnam, 1860, p. 448.

32. "Democracy." Wikipedia, Wikimedia Foundation, Sept. 2023, en.wikipedia.org/wiki/Democracy.

33. "Pluralism (Political Philosophy)." Wikipedia, Wikimedia Foundation, Sept. 2023, en.wikipedia.org/wiki/Pluralism_(political_philosophy).

34. "Right to Petition." Wikipedia, Wikimedia Foundation, 1 Feb. 2010, en.wikipedia.org/wiki/Right_to_petition.

34-02. "Founding Fathers." Memoria Press, 1 Feb. 2010, www.memoriapress.com/articles/founding-fathers.html. Accessed Sept. 2023.

35. "Civil and Political Rights." Wikipedia, Wikimedia Foundation, Sept. 2023, en.wikipedia.org/wiki/Civil_and_political_rights.

36. "Democracy." Wikipedia, Wikimedia Foundation, Sept. 2023, en.wikipedia.org/wiki/Democracy.

37. "Individualism." Wikipedia, Wikimedia Foundation, Sept. 2023, en.wikipedia.org/wiki/Individualism. Sept. 2023.

38. "Separation of Powers." Wikipedia, Wikimedia Foundation, Sept. 2023, en.wikipedia.org/wiki/Separation_of_powers.

39. Global Citizen Solutions. "The Sixteen Best Citizenship by Investment Programs in 2024." Global Citizen Solutions, 26 Jan. 2024, www.globalcitizensolutions.com/best-citizenship-by-investment-programs/.

39-01. "Origin of Communism and Marxism." The 7th Fire, Sept. 2023, www.the7thfire.com/new_world_order/final_warning/origin_of_communism_and_marxism.htm.

39-02. Marx, Karl. "Critique of the Gotha Program." Marxists Internet Archive, 1 Feb. 2010, www.marxists.org/archive/marx/works/1875/gotha/index.htm.

39-03. Acton, Lord. Letter to Bishop Mandell Creighton. 1887.

39-04. Oxford Reference Dictionary, 2023, https://www.oxfordreference.com/display/10.1093/oi/authority.20110803100349558. Accessed Dec. 2023.

39-05. OpenAI. "ChatGPT." Dec. 2023.

39-06. "Why the US and EU are at odds over tech regulation." New Statesman. 25 February 2021. https://www.newstatesman.com/science-tech/2021/02/why-us-and-eu-are-odds-over-tech-regulation.

39-07. Skroejer, Morten, and Nicole Lawler. "Can the US and EU Rein in Big Tech with Diverging Approaches?" Atlantic Council, 20 Jan. 2022, www.atlanticcouncil.org.

39-08. Lawless, J. "The Right to Protest Is Under Threat in Britain, Undermining a Pillar of Democracy." AP World News, 26 Dec. 2023. and
"Managing Borders and Migration: Earned Citizenship." UK Border Agency, Sept. 2023, www.ukba.homeoffice.gov.uk/managingborders/managing migration/earned-citizenship/.

39-09. von Thun, Max. "After Years of Leading the Charge Against Big Tech Dominance, is the EU Falling Behind?" TechPolicy.Press, 1 Mar. 2023, techpolicy.press/after-years-of-leading-the-charge-against-big-tech-dominance-is-the-eu-falling-behind/.

39-10. Whitener, M. "The Future of Antitrust: Ideology, Alternative Facts, and the Rule of Law." Georgetown University, n.d., https://georgetown.app.box.com/s/qocakylth08s3xz2p87ot bi973ucz87a.

39-11. Sisco, J. "Here's How Biden May Cement His Antitrust Legacy in 2024." Politico, 30 Dec. 2023, www.politico.com/news/2023/12/30/heres-how-biden-may-cement-his-antitrust-legacy-in-2024-00132756.39-12.

Werden, G. J., and Froeb, L. M. "Don't Panic: A Guide to Claims of Increasing Concentration." Antitrust, vol. 74, Fall 2018.

39-13. Neuro, Benzinga. "Former Microsoft CEO Steve Ballmer To Pocket $1B Annually In Dividends." Benzinga, 26 Dec. 2023, www.msn.com/en-us/money/other/former-microsoft-ceo-steve-ballmer-t.

39-14. "Alexis de Tocqueville on the Tyranny of the Majority." Edsitement, National Endowment for the Humanities, 2023, https://edsitement.neh.gov/curricula/alexis-de-tocqueville-tyranny-majority.

39-15. Camia, Catalina. "More than 300 Republicans Ask Supreme Court to Back Gay Marriage." UsaToday, ONPOLITICS, 6 Mar. 2015, www.usatoday.com/story/news/politics/onpolitics/2015/03/06/gay-marriage-supreme-court-republicans/81556582/.

39-16. "Whatever Happened To Equality Of Opportunity?" Hoover Institution. Accessed 16 June 2023. Hoover Institution.

40-02. "Founding Fathers" Memoria Press, Feb. 1, 2010. http://www.memoriapress.com/articles/founding-fathers.html.

41 "Whig Party (United States)." Wikipedia, Wikimedia Foundation. Sep. 2023. en.wikipedia.org/wiki/Whig_Party_(United_States).

41-01. "Democratic-Republican Party." Wikipedia, Wikimedia Foundation, [September 2023].

http://en.wikipedia.org/wiki/Democratic-Republican_Party.

42. "Whig Party (United States)." Wikipedia, Wikimedia Foundation, [September 2023]. http://en.wikipedia.org/wiki/Whig_Party_(United_States).

43. Jefferson, Thomas. "Thomas Jefferson's First Inaugural Address." Wikisource, [September 2023]. http://en.wikisource.org/wiki/Thomas_Jefferson's_First_Inaugural_Address.

44. "Capitalism." *Investopedia*, edited by Adam Hayes, 6 Oct. 2023, www.investopedia.com/terms/c/capitalism.asp.

45. OpenAI. "ChatGPT." [September 2023].

46. Bard query. [September 2023].

47. Federal Bureau of Investigation. "Uniform Crime Reporting [United States], 1930-2022." ICPSR, 23 Nov. 2023. https://doi.org/10.3886/ICPSR03666.v1 and United States Department of Justice. Federal Bureau of Investigation. "Uniform Crime Reports [United States], 1930-1959." Inter-university Consortium for Political and Social Research [distributor], 19 Jun. 2003. https://doi.org/10.3886/ICPSR03666.v1.

48. Pew Research Center. "The Changing Face of Congress in 8 Charts: Race, Ethnicity, Gender, Generation, Immigrant Status, Education and More." 19 Feb. 2019. Retrieved on 26 Nov. 2023, from https://thelawmakers.org/find-representatives.
49. "Which is Cheaper: Execution or Life in Prison Without Parole?" HG.org Legal Articles. [September 2023].

https://www.hg.org/legal-articles/which-is-cheaper-execution-or-life-in-prison-without-parole-31614.

50. York, Erica. "Summary of the Latest Federal Income Tax Data, 2020 Update." Tax Foundation, 25 Feb. 2020, https://taxfoundation.org/data/all/federal/summary-of-the-latest-federal-income-tax-data-2020-update/.

51. Madison, James. "Federalist Paper #10." The Federalist Papers.

52. Wikipedia contributors. "John Emerich Edward Dalberg-Acton." Wikipedia, The Free Encyclopedia. Wikipedia, The Free Encyclopedia, [September 2023]. http://en.wikipedia.org/wiki/John_Emerich_Edward_Dalberg-Acton.

53. "Crime: Total Crimes Per Capita." NationMaster. [September 2023]. http://www.nationmaster.com/graph/cri_tot_cri_percap-crime-total-crimes-per-capita.

54. "Proceedings and Debates of the 111th Congress, Second Session." Congressional Record, vol. 156, pt. 15, U.S. Government Publishing Office, 2010, p. 10169.

55. Boesky, Ivan F. "Greed is all right, by the way." Speech, Haas School of Business, University of California, Berkeley, 1986.The exact wording of the statement is disputed, but it is generally agreed that Boesky expressed a positive view of greed and its role in the economy.

56. BARD. [September 2023]

57. "National Debt by Year Compared to GDP and Major Events." The Balance Money. [September 2023]. https://www.thebalancemoney.com/national-debt-by-year-compared-to-gdp-and-major-events-3306287.

58. Idea 1: Stricter Regulation of High-Frequency Trading (HFT)

    Hendershott, T., Kissell, R., & Menkveld, A. J. "High-frequency trading and market microstructure." Journal of Financial Economics, vol. 100, no. 2, 2011, pp. 405-429.

    Menkveld, A. J. "The high-frequency trading paradox." Journal of Financial Markets, vol. 16, no. 1, 2013, pp. 1-5.

U.S. Securities and Exchange Commission. "The flash crash: A review of the Securities and Exchange Commission's findings and recommendations." 2014.

Idea 2: Enhanced Transparency in Derivatives Trading

    Financial Stability Board. "The role of transparency in derivatives markets." 2011.

    Bank for International Settlements. "Derivatives markets and financial stability." 2012.

    International Organization of Securities Commissions. "Transparency in the over-the-counter derivatives market: A regulatory perspective." 2013.

Idea 3: Reforming the Credit Rating System

    Financial Stability Board. "The credit rating agency conundrum." 2012.

    U.S. House Committee on Financial Services. "Reforming the credit rating agencies." 2010.

    European Commission. "Credit rating agencies: A new European framework." 2016.

Idea 4: Reinforcing the Separation Between Investment and Commercial Banking

Sanders, B. "The return of Glass-Steagall: Why we need to revive the separation of commercial and investment banking." The American Prospect, vol. 41, no. 2, 2010, pp. 32-37.

Stiglitz, J. E., & Wolf, M. "Glass-Steagall in the 21st century." Foreign Affairs, vol. 89, no. 3, 2010, pp. 135-147.

Volcker, P. A. "Restoring financial stability: Why we need to revive Glass-Steagall." Speech, Brookings Institution, Washington, DC, 2010.

59. Tax Policy Center. "What Are the Major Federal Excise Taxes, and How Much Money Do They Raise?" Urban Institute & Brookings Institution, https://www.taxpolicycenter.org/briefing-book/what-are-major-federal-excise-taxes-and-how-much-money-do-they-raise. Accessed 1/2/2023.

59-01. "Economic Research Service." U.S. Department of Agriculture, https://www.ers.usda.gov/topics/crops/sugar-and-sweeteners/. Accessed 1/2/2024.

59-02. Gibson, Suzanne A., et al. "Understanding the Link between Sugar and Cancer: An Examination of the Preclinical and Clinical Evidence." NIH Public Access Author Manuscript, National Institutes of Health, 4 Sept. 2016, ncbi.nlm.nih.gov/pmc/articles/PMC5546054/.

59-03. MD Anderson Cancer Center. "Does Sugar Cause Cancer?" MD Anderson Cancer Center, 2023, www.mdanderson.org/cancerwise/does-sugar-cause-cancer.h00-159354754.html.

59-04. Cancer Research UK. "Sugar and Cancer – What You Need to Know." Cancer News, Cancer Research UK, 15 Dec. 2023, www.cancerresearchuk.org/about-cancer/causes-of-cancer/diet-and-cancer/does-sugar-cause-cancer.

59-05. Cancer Council. "Does Sugar Cause Cancer?" Cancer Council Australia, 2023, cancercouncil.org.au/cancer-information/causes-and-prevention/diet-and-exercise/does-sugar-cause-cancer/.

59-06. Pandey, Ashutosh. "Airbus-Boeing WTO Dispute: What You Need to Know." DW, 13 Oct. 2020, www.dw.com/en/airbus-boeing-wto-dispute-what-you-need-to-know/a-49442616. Accessed 1/3/2024.

59-07. "Alcohol Tax Modernization: ABV Tax and other Drink Tax Reforms." Tax Foundation, Tax Foundation, taxfoundation.org/alcohol-tax-modernization/.

59-08. Arendt, Hannah. The Origins of Totalitarianism. Harcourt, Brace, Jovanovich, 1973.

59-09. U.S. Department of State. "Human Rights and Democracy." United States Department of State, www.state.gov. Accessed 9 Feb. 2024.

59-10. McCain Institute. "Advancing Freedom Promotes U.S. Interests." McCain Institute for International Leadership, www.mccaininstitute.org. Accessed 9 Feb. 2024.

59-11. Thomas, Virginia. "Solitude in a Social World." Psychology Today, Sussex Publishers, 30 Mar. 2022, www.psychologytoday.com/us/blog/solitude-in-a-social-world/202203/is-your-solitude-authentic.

59-12. Zhang, Jia Wei, and Thuy-Vy T. Nguyen. "Balance between Solitude and Socializing: Everyday Solitude Time Both Benefits and Harms Well-Being." Scientific Reports, vol. 11, no. 1, Dec. 2021, www.nature.com/articles/s41598-021-94858-0.

59-13. Centers for Disease Control and Prevention (CDC). "Health Topics - Tobacco." POLARIS, https://www.cdc.gov/policy/polaris/healthtopics/tobacco/index.html.

59-14. DiNardo, John, and Thomas Lemieux. "Alcohol, Marijuana, and American Youth: The Unintended Consequences of Government Regulation." Journal of Health Economics, vol. 20, no. 11, 2001, pp. 991-1010, https://www.nber.org/papers/w4212.

59-15. United States, Department of the Treasury. Alcohol and Tobacco Tax and Trade Bureau Congressional Budget Justification and Annual Performance Plan and Report FY 2023. "In FY 2021, TTB collected approximately $20.3 billion in excise taxes from the alcohol, tobacco, firearms, and ammunition industries." 2023, https://home.treasury.gov/system/files/266/14.-TTB-FY-2023-CJ.pdf.

59-16. "Key Elements of the U.S. Tax System." Tax Policy Center Briefing Book, Tax Policy Center, https://www.taxpolicycenter.org/briefing-book/what-are-major-federal-excise-taxes-and-how-much-money-do-they-raise.

59-17. Fiscal year 2022 deficit: "Joint Statement of Janet L. Yellen, Secretary of the Treasury, and Shalanda D. Young, Director of the Office of Management and Budget, on Budget Results for Fiscal Year 2022." U.S. Department of the Treasury, 21 Oct. 2022, www.home.treasury.gov/news/press-releases/jy0919.

59-18. Fiscal year 2021 deficit details: "Joint Statement by Secretary of the Treasury Janet L. Yellen and Acting Director of the Office of Management and Budget Shalanda D. Young on Budget Results for Fiscal Year 2021." U.S. Department of the Treasury, 22 Oct. 2021, www.home.treasury.gov/news/press-releases/jy0387.

59-19. Fiscal year 2022 budget deficit halving: Lawder, David. "U.S. 2022 Budget Deficit Halves to $1.375 Trillion Despite Student Loan Costs." Reuters, 21 Oct. 2022, www.reuters.com/article/us-usa-budget/u-s-2022-budget-deficit-halves-to-1-375-trillion-despite-student-loan-costs-idUSKBN2HG2L0.

59-20. 2023 deficit projection: "The 2023 Deficit Is Projected To Total $1.5 Trillion. Here's Why It Could Be Even Higher." Peter G. Peterson Foundation, 20 June 2023, www.pgpf.org/blog/2023/06/the-2023-deficit-is-projected-to-total-15-trillion-heres-why-it-could-be-even-higher.

59-21. Macrotrends. "U.S. Life Expectancy 1950-2024." https://www.macrotrends.net/countries/USA/united-states/life-expectancy#:~:text=Chart%20and%20table%20of%20U.S.,a%200.08%25%20increase%20from%202022.

59-22. Shmerling, Robert H., MD. "Why Life Expectancy in the US Is Falling: COVID-19 and Drug Overdoses Are the Biggest Contributors." Harvard Health Publishing, Harvard Medical School, 20 Oct. 2022, www.health.harvard.edu/blog/why-life-expectancy-in-the-us-is-falling-202210202835.

59-23. Democracy Index 2022: Stagnation, War and No Post-COVID Revival." Democracy Without Borders, 10 Feb. 2023.

59-24. "Authority in Religious Traditions." Encyclopedia.com, www.encyclopedia.com/religion/encyclopedias-almanacs-transcripts-and-maps/authority-religious-traditions.

59-25. Nieuwsma, Alexandra. "The American Nation-State, Cosmopolitanism, and Identity Politics in the Millennial Imagination." Providence, providencemag.com/2021/american-nation-state-cosmopolitanism-identity-politics-millennial-imagination.

59-26. Funk, Josh. "Annual letter: Warren Buffett says to ignore Wall Street pundits." AP News, 24 Feb. 2024, apnews.com.

59-27. American Enterprise Institute - AEI. "2009 Tire Tariffs Cost US Consumers $926K per Job Saved and Led to the Loss of 3 Retail Jobs per Factory Job Saved." AEI, www.aei.org.

59-28. Amadeo, Kimberly. "Trump's Steel and Aluminum Tariffs." The Balance, 2020, www.thebalance.com.

59-29. Lumber Coalition. "U.S. Department of Commerce Issues Final Antidumping and Countervailing Duty Determinations on Canadian Softwood Lumber Imports." Lumber Coalition, 2017, www.lumbercoalition.org.

59-30. Federal Reserve History. "The Second Bank of the United States." Federal Reserve History, Federal Reserve Bank of San Francisco, www.federalreservehistory.org/essays/second_bank_of_the_united_states.

59-31. United States Inflation Rate, 1946-2021." MacroTrends, www.macrotrends.net/countries/USA/united-states/inflation-rate-cpi. Accessed 2 Mar. 2024.

59-32. Internal Revenue Service. *IRS Publishes 2024 Financial Report, Resolves Longstanding Significant Deficiency.* U.S. Department of the Treasury, 2024, https://www.irs.gov/newsroom/irs-publishes-2024-financial-report-resolves-longstanding-significant-deficiency. Accessed 20 Feb. 2025.

59-33. Congressional Research Service. *Federal Excise Taxes: Overview and Economic Effects.* U.S. Congress, 2024, https://crsreports.congress.gov/product/pdf/R/R48313. Accessed 20 Feb. 2025.

61. Münsterberg, Hugo. American Traits from the Point of View of a German. Houghton Mifflin, 1901.

62. "American Traits from the Point of View of a German." Questia. [September 2023]. http://www.questia.com/read/54118835.

63. "Universal Declaration of Human Rights." United Nations, [September 2023].
http://www.un.org/en/documents/udhr/.
64. "Totalitarianism." Wikipedia, Wikimedia Foundation, [September 2023].
http://en.wikipedia.org/wiki/Totalitarianism.

65. "Marxism." Wikipedia, Wikimedia Foundation, [September 2023]. http://en.wikipedia.org/wiki/Marxism.

66. "Capitalism." Wikipedia, Wikimedia Foundation, [September 2023].
http://en.wikipedia.org/wiki/Capitalism.

67. "Rule of Law." Wikipedia, Wikimedia Foundation, [September 2023].
http://en.wikipedia.org/wiki/Rule_of_Law.

68. "Magna Carta." Wikipedia, Wikimedia Foundation, [September 2023].
http://en.wikipedia.org/wiki/Magna_Carta.

69. "Common Sense (Pamphlet)." Wikipedia, Wikimedia Foundation, [September 2023].
http://en.wikipedia.org/wiki/Common_Sense_(pamphlet).

69-01. "'Incompetent dumpster fire: Michigan GOP rocked by financial turmoil and infighting.," Curt Devine, Audrey Ash, Allison Gordon, Daniel Strauss, and Jason Carroll, CNN,
https://www.cnn.com/2023/12/20/politics/michigan-gop-financial-turmoil-infighting-invs?cid=ios_app.

69-02. Note from Author. I wrote the paragraph during Obama's term, not Trump's.

69-03. Schoffstall, Joe. "427 Former Members of Congress Moved to Lobbying or Similar Work." Washington Free Beacon, 22 Sept. 2015, https://freebeacon.com/issues/427-former-members-of-congress-moved-to-lobbying-or-similar-work/.

69-04. Nadler, Judy, and Miriam Schulman. "Lobbying Ethics." Markkula Center for Applied Ethics, Santa Clara University, www.scu.edu/ethics/focus-areas/government-ethics/resources/lobbying-ethics/.

69-05. Hong, Ki. "Lobbying regulation: a global phenomenon." Reuters, 23 Oct. 2015, www.reuters.com/article/us-lobbying-regulation-idUSKCN0SH2L120151023. 2015, https://freebeacon.com/issues/427-former-members-of-congress-moved-to-lobbying-or-similar-work/.

69-07. American Bar Association. 'How Venezuela Lost the Rule of Law.' American Bar Association, www.americanbar.org. Accessed [date you accessed the site].

69-08. General Social Survey, conducted by NORC at the University of Chicago in 2006. Results discussed in 'The General Social Survey' by Demo Memo, 29 May 2008, demomemo.blogspot.com/2008/05/.

69-09. https://gemini.google.com/app/25a99b1451db4661. Accessed 2/9/2024. Which listed the following as partial sources from which it compiled this list:

☐ The US Census Bureau's website, which provides statistics on population demographics and diversity: https://www.census.gov/topics/population.html.

☐ Pew Research Center reports on immigration and religious diversity: https://www.pewresearch.org/.

☐ "American Pragmatism" movement and its influence on US culture: https://www.philosophytalk.org/shows/american-pragmatism.

☐ The Global Entrepreneurship Monitor (GEM): https://www.gemconsortium.org/.

☐ Gallup offers polls on career aspirations and work ethic in the US: https://www.gallup.com/topic/employee-engagement.aspx.

☐ The "American Dream" concept and its historical context: https://www.bushcenter.org/catalyst/state-of-the-american-dream/churchwell-history-of-the-american-dream.

☐ Michael Novak's "The Spirit of Democratic Capitalism" exploring self-reliance in American culture: https://www.amazon.com/Spirit-Democratic-Capitalism-Michael-Novak/dp/0819178233.

☐ The Pew Research Center study on personal debt: https://www.pewresearch.org/.

☐ Giving USA: https://givingusa.org/.

☐ Volunteerism statistics from organizations like the Bureau of Labor Statistics: https://www.bls.gov/news.release/volun.toc.htm.

☐ Polls on patriotism conducted by institutions like Pew Research Center or Gallup.

☐ Historical studies on American national identity, like David Hackett Fischer's "Albion's Seed": https://www.amazon.com/Albions-Seed-British-Folkways-cultural-ebook/dp/B000SEKM9C.

☐ Pew Research Center's reports on religious demographics and trends in the US.

☐ Pew Research Center studies on technology adoption and internet usage in the US.

☐ Isaac Asimov's "Innovation and Opportunity": https://www.aboutamazon.com/news/innovation-at-amazon.

☐ Pew Research Center studies on political polarization and public opinion.

☐ Major news articles or reports analyzing the current political climate in the US.

☐ Milton's "Areopagitica": http://www.gutenberg.org/ebooks/608.

☐ Studies on debate culture and its place in American society.

69-10. U.S. Bureau of Labor Statistics. "All Employees, Federal [CES9091000001]." FRED, Federal Reserve Bank of St. Louis, 2 Feb. 2024, fred.stlouisfed.org/series/CES9091000001.

69-11. chatGPT v3.5, accessed 2/13/24. Response was: In 1960, the federal civilian and military personnel breakdown was: Federal civilian personnel: Approximately 2.2 million and Military personnel: Approximately 1.3 million. These numbers are approximate and may vary slightly depending on the specific source and methodology used for calculation.

69-12. "Sources: Statistical Abstract of the United States. U.S. Census Bureau, "Historical Statistics of the United States, Colonial Times to 1970. And:

U.S. Census Bureau. "Historical Population Estimates."

U.S. Census Bureau, www.census.gov/data/tables/time-series/demo/popest/pre-1980-national.html.

U.S. Bureau of Economic Analysis (BEA). "National Income and Product Accounts Tables."
U.S. Office of Management and Budget (OMB). "Budget of the United States Government: Historical Tables."

U.S. Department of Commerce, www.bea.gov/data/national/national-accounts.

U.S. Government Publishing Office, www.govinfo.gov/app/collection/budget/2023/.

69-13. Guzman, Gloria, and Melissa Kollar. Income in the United States: 2022. U.S. Census Bureau, Report Number P60-279, 12 Sept. 2023, www.census.gov/library/publications/2023/demo/p60-279.html.

69-14. Wong, Belle, J.D. "Average Salary By State In 2024." Forbes Advisor, Forbes, 23 Aug. 2023, www.forbes.com/advisor/business/average-salary-by-state/.

69-15. Statista Research Department. "U.S. Total Number of Lobbyists 2000-2022." Statista, 3 Nov. 2023, www.statista.com/statistics/257340/number-of-lobbyists-in-the-us/.

70. "John Adams." Wikiquote, Wikimedia Foundation, [September 2023]. http://en.wikiquote.org/wiki/John_Adams.

71. "U.S. Constitution." [Adapted from]. [September 2023]. http://www.usConstitution.net.

71-01. "Ten All-American Traits." New Strategist, 29 May 2008. http://www.newstrategist.com/store/index.cfm/feature/30 _15/ten-all-american-traits.cfm.

71-02. "Poll: Gallup Evolution Survey." Pollster. [September 2023]. http://www.pollster.com/blogs/poll_gallup_evolution_sur vey.php.

72, Birnbaum, Jeffrey H. "The Road to Riches Is Called K Street, Lobbying Firms Hire More, Pay More, Charge More to Influence Government." The Washington Post, 22 June 2005. http://www.washingtonpost.com/wp-dyn/content/article/2005/06/21/AR2005062101632.html.

72-01 Author [Charles Patton] enhanced with added traits.

73. "Federal Election Campaign Act." Answers.com. [September 2023]. http://www.answers.com/topic/federal-election-campaign-act.

74. "Politics of Venezuela." Wikipedia, Wikimedia Foundation, [September 2023]. http://en.wikipedia.org/wiki/Politics_of_Venezuela.

75. "Spain–United States Relations." Wikipedia, Wikimedia Foundation, [September 2023]. http://en.wikipedia.org/wiki/Spain–United_States_relations.

76a. U.S. Energy Information Administration. "Annual Energy Outlook 2023." [September 2023]. https://www.eia.gov/outlooks/aeo/.

76b. International Energy Agency. "Oil 2023." [September 2023]. https://www.iea.org/reports/oil-2023.

76c. "World Energy Outlook 2022: Executive Summary." International Energy Agency. [September 2023]. https://www.iea.org/reports/world-energy-outlook-2022/executive-summary.

77. U.S. Environmental Protection Agency. "Greenhouse Gas Emissions from a Typical Passenger Vehicle." 2018. https://19january2021snapshot.epa.gov/greenvehicles/greenhouse-gas-emissions-typical-passenger-vehicle_.html.

78. Auffhammer, M., Park, J., and Stavins, R. N. "The Economic and Environmental Impacts of a Carbon Tax and Cap-and-Trade System in the United States." Columbia University Center on Global Energy Policy, July 2021.

79. US Retail Gas Price." YCharts, YCharts, Inc., Accessed 16 February 2024, https://ycharts.com/indicators/us_gas_price.

79-01. Xu, Conglin, and Laura Bell-Hammer. "Global Oil and Natural Gas Reserves Both Increase." Oil & Gas Journal, 4 Dec. 2023, www.ogj.com/general-interest/economics-markets/article/14302481/global-oil-and-natural-gas-reserves-both-increase.

79-02. "Average Vehicle Occupancy Remains Unchanged From 2009 to 2017." Department of Energy, U.S. Department of Energy, 30 July 2018, www.energy.gov/eere/vehicles/articles/fotw-1040-july-30-2018-average-vehicle-occupancy-remains-unchanged-2009-2017.

79-03. Friedrich, Johannes, et al. "This Interactive Chart Shows Changes in the World's Top 10 Emitters." World Resources Institute, 2 Mar. 2023, www.wri.org.

79-04. "Global Greenhouse Gas Emissions Data." U.S. Environmental Protection Agency, www.epa.gov.

79-05. "Executive Orders and the Supreme Court." JURIST - Legal News & Commentary, www.jurist.org/archives/feature/executive-orders-and-the-supreme-court.

79-06. "Executive Orders 101: What Are They and How Do Presidents Use Them?" National Constitution Center, 23 Jan. 2017, constitutioncenter.org/blog/executive-orders-101-what-are-they-and-how-do-presidents-use-them.

81. White House Office of Public Engagement. "The Open Government Initiative." 2009. https://www.whitehouse.gov/ope/.

82. Obama, Barack. "The Open Government Memorandum." 2009. https://obamawhitehouse.archives.gov/the-press-office/transparency-and-open-government.

83. Sunlight Foundation. "The Sunlight Foundation Open Government Principles." 2009. https://sunlightfoundation.com/.

84. Center for Responsive Politics. "The Center for Responsive Politics Open Government Principles." 2009. https://www.opensecrets.org/.

85. "The Freedom of Information Act." 1967.
https://www.law.cornell.edu/uscode/text/5/552.
86. Government Accountability Office. "Government
Accountability Office: Status of Federal Programs." 2019.
https://www.gao.gov/.

87. National Academies of Sciences, Engineering, and
Medicine. "Early Childhood Education and Care." 2017.
https://nap.nationalacademies.org/.

88. Government Accountability Office. "Government
Accountability Office: Workforce Development Programs."
2016. https://www.gao.gov/.

89. National Low Income Housing Coalition. "The Outlook
for Fair Housing: Examining the Role of Federal Programs."
2015. https://nlihc.org/annual-housing-policy-conference.

89-01. Republican National Committee. "Republican
Platform." 2008.
https://www.presidency.ucsb.edu/documents/2008-
republican-party-platform.

89-02 Schneider, M. (2023, December 28). World
population up 75 million this year, standing at 8 billion on
Jan. 1. AP World News. Retrieved from
https://apnews.com/article/world-population-census-
bureau-growth-b2a32ff77b9f3ae977c943014fe2b853.

89-03. "Most Expensive Ever: 2020 Election Cost $14.4
Billion." OpenSecrets, Center for Responsive Politics,
https://www.opensecrets.org/news/2021/02/2020-cycle-
cost-14p4-billion-doubling-2016.

91. "Progressivism." Wikipedia, Wikimedia Foundation, October 2023. http://en.wikipedia.org/wiki/Progressivism.

92. "Glenn Beck Show." Fox Television. 18 Jan. 2010.

93. "Progressivism." ProgressiveLiving.org. October 2023. http://www.progressiveliving.org/progressivism_1.htm.

94. "Contribution Limits." Federal Election Commission, October 2023. https://www.fec.gov/help-candidates-and-committees/candidate-taking-receipts/contribution-limits/.

95. OpenAI. "ChatGPT." October 2023.

96. Raw Story, "A 'prophetic' Alexander Hamilton note described Trump almost to a T", Matthew Chapman. *Raw Story,* November 3rd, 2023. Bias warning: Publication has been called Left-wing and Independent.

97. "Minimum Wage." U.S. Department of Labor, U.S. Department of Labor, www.dol.gov/agencies/whd/minimum-wage. Accessed 16 Feb. 2024.

98. McCann, Adam. "Average Credit Card Interest Rates." WalletHub, 26 Feb. 2024, wallethub.com/edu/cc/average-credit-card-interest-rate/50841. Fact checked by Alina Comoreanu.

101. "Historical Debt Outstanding." TreasuryDirect, http://www.treasurydirect.gov/govt/reports/pd/histdebt/histdebt.htm. and
"U.S. National Debt by Year." Infoplease, http://www.infoplease.com/ipa/A0104753.html. and
"Historical Statistics." U.S. Census Bureau, http://www.census.gov/compendia/statab/hist_stats.html.

102. Democratic National Committee. "Health Care." Democrats.org, 2023. https://democrats.org/where-we-stand/the-issues/health-care/.

103. Physicians for a National Health Program. "Republican and Democratic platforms on health care." 2023. https://pnhp.org/news/republican-and-democratic-platforms-on-health-care/.

104. "Why Democrats Should Become the Party of Medically Assisted Dying." Washington Monthly. February 12, 2022. https://www.washingtonmonthly.com/.

105. "Democrats platform and policy on Euthanasia." iSideWith. October 2023. https://www.isidewith.com/.

106. "Americans' Strong Support for Euthanasia Persists." Gallup, 2018. https://www.gallup.com/.

111. "Republican Platform 2008." The American Presidency Project. http://www.presidency.ucsb.edu/ws/index.php?pid=7854.

112. "Democratic Platform 2008." The American Presidency Project. http://www.presidency.ucsb.edu/ws/index.php?pid=7828.

113. "Constitution Party Platform 2008." Constitution Party. http://www.Constitutionparty.com/party_platform.php.

114. "Green Party Platform 2008." Green Party of the United States. http://green.gpus.org/platform/2000/2002summary.html.

115. "Libertarian Platform 2008." Libertarian Party. http://www.lp.org/platform.

116. "Origin of Public Education in the U.S." The Agonist. http://www.agonist.org/Learning-Center/education/originofpubliceducationintheus.html.

120. Wikipedia contributors. "Immigration to the United States." Wikipedia, The Free Encyclopedia. Wikipedia, The Free Encyclopedia, October 2023. http://en.wikipedia.org/wiki/Immigration_to_the_United_States. And Motomura, Hiroshi. Americans in Waiting: The Lost Story of Immigration and Citizenship in the United States. Oxford University Press, 2006.

121. The Presidents of The United States of America, Frank Freidel, White House Historical Association in cooperation with the National Geographic Society, 5026 New Executive Office Building, 726 Jackson Place, N.W., Washington, D.C. 20506, sixth edition, second printing, 1974.

122. chatGPT OpenAI. "ChatGPT." October 2023.

123. The White House. "Build Back Better: Investing in America." 2 Nov. 2023. https://www.whitehouse.gov/briefing-room/statements-releases/2021/10/28/president-biden-announces-the-build-back-better-framework/.

124. Heritage Foundation. "The Case for Private Sector Disaster Relief." Dec. 2017. https://heritage-foundation.org/donations/help-in-natural-disasters/.

125. Republican Party. "Republican Party Platform."
https://prod-cdn-
static.gop.com/docs/Resolution_Platform_2020.pdf.

126. The Heritage Foundation. "Commentary." 12 Dec.
2010.

127. Obama, Barack. "Remarks at Cooper Union in New
York City." 27 Mar. 2008.

128. Clinton, Hillary. Speech at Georgetown University,
2009.

129. "Historical Oil Prices Chart." InflationData.com.
October 2023. https://inflationdata.com/articles/inflation-
adjusted-prices/historical-oil-prices-chart/.

129-02. "U.S. Petroleum Net Imports." U.S. Energy
Information Administration.
https://www.eia.gov/dnav/pet/hist/LeafHandler.ashx?n=p
et&s=mttntus2&f=m. and
"Petroleum Products Net Imports." U.S. Energy
Information Administration.
https://www.eia.gov/dnav/pet/hist/LeafHandler.ashx?n=p
et&s=mttntus2&f=m. and
"FAQ: How much petroleum does the United States import
and export?" American Geosciences Institute.
https://www.americangeosciences.org/critical-
issues/faq/how-much-oil-does-us-export-and-import.

129-03. Republican National Committee. "2016 Republican
Party Platform." Republican National Convention,
Cleveland, OH, 18-21 July 2016.

129-04. "Social Security Trust Fund depletion date is 2034 without action." Financial Planning. October 2023. https://www.financial-planning.com. and "Social Security's Financial Outlook: The 2023 Update in Perspective." Center for Retirement Research at Boston College, 2023. https://crr.bc.edu. and "The Ratio of Workers to Social Security Beneficiaries Is at a Low and Projected to Decline Further." Peter G. Peterson Foundation. October 2023. https://www.pgpf.org.

129-05. Democratic National Committee. "Creating a 21st Century Immigration System." Democrats.org. October 2023 https://democrats.org/where-we-stand/the-issues/immigration-reform/.

129-06 Democratic Platform. "Where we stand on Immigration." Democrats.org. https://democrats.org/where-we-stand/the-issues/immigration-reform/

129-07. "Republicans and Democrats Have Different Top Priorities for U.S. Immigration Policy." Pew Research Center. October 2023. https://www.pewresearch.org/short-reads/2022/09/08/republicans-and-democrats-have-different-top-priorities-for-u-s-immigration-policy/.

129-08. "Republican and Democratic Party Platforms Reflect Parallel Universes on Immigration Policy." Migration Policy Institute. October 2023. https://www.migrationpolicy.org/article/republican-and-democratic-party-platforms-reflect-parallel-universes-immigration-policy.

129-09. "Republicans' Perspectives on Immigration." Politicsphere.com. October 2023.

https://www.politicsphere.com/republicans-perspectives-on-immigration/.

131. Centers for Disease Control and Prevention (CDC). "Economic Facts about U.S. Tobacco Production and Use." 2020. https://www.cdc.gov/tobacco/data_statistics/fact_sheets/economics/econ_facts/index.htm.

132. Centers for Disease Control and Prevention. "Economic Facts about U.S. Tobacco Production and Use." 2020. Centers for Disease Control and Prevention, https://www.cdc.gov/tobacco/data_statistics/fact_sheets/economics/econ_facts/index.htm.

133. DiNardo, J., and Lemieux, T. "Alcohol, Marijuana, and American Youth: The Unintended Consequences of Government Regulation." Journal of Health Economics, vol. 20, no. 6, 2001, pp. 991-1010.

134. U.S. Department of the Treasury. "Alcohol and Tobacco Tax and Trade Bureau (TTB) Statistical Release." 2021. https://www.ttb.gov/statistics/stat-release.shtml.

135. Tax Foundation. "How High Are Marijuana Taxes in Your State?" 2021. https://taxfoundation.org/marijuana-taxes-state-2021/.

136. National Highway Traffic Safety Administration. Motorcycle Safety. 2023. https://www.nhtsa.gov/road-safety/motorcycles.

137. Liu, BC, et al. "Helmets for Preventing Injury in Motorcycle Riders." Cochrane Database of Systematic Reviews, 23 Jan. 2008,

www.cochrane.org/CD004333/INJ_helmets-are-shown-to-reduce-motorcyclist-head-injury-and-death.

138. "Policy Impact: Seat Belts." Centers for Disease Control and Prevention, National Center for Injury Prevention and Control, 3 Jan. 2011, www.cdc.gov/motorvehiclesafety/seatbeltbrief/index.html.

139. "Pew Research Center." Republicans and Democrats Move Further Apart in Views of Voting Access, 22 Apr. 2021, www.pewresearch.org/politics/2021/04/22/republicans-and-democrats-move-further-apart-in-views-of-voting-access/. Accessed 7 Jan. 2

139-01: Pew Research Center. "Views on Voting by Mail." Pew Research Center, 13 Oct. 2020, www.pewresearch.org/politics/2020/10/13/views-on-voting-by-mail/.

139-02. Texas v. Johnson, 491 U.S. 397. Supreme Court of the United States. 21 June 1989.

161. "Death Penalty Representation." Death Penalty Information Center. October 2023. http://www.deathpenaltyinfo.org/death-penalty-representation.

162. "Capital Punishment." Wikipedia, Wikimedia Foundation. October 2023. http://en.wikipedia.org/wiki/Capital_punishment.

163. "About the Arguments." Death Penalty Curriculum for Teachers. October 2023.

http://deathpenaltycurriculum.org/teacher/c/about/argum ents/argument4b.htm.

163-02. Fox News. [October 2023].

164. Becker, [Author's First Name Unk]. "Antitrust Chronology." St. Olaf College. October 2023. http://www.stolaf.edu/people/becker/antitrust/by_date.ht ml.

165. NPR. [October 2023].

166. Environmental Defense Fund. October 2023.

167. "Car Emissions Fact Sheet." Environmental Defense Fund. October 2023. http://www.edf.org/documents/2209_CarEmissionsFactS heet.pdf.
168. "Europe Charges Microsoft with Abuse." Network World. October 2023. http://www.networkworld.com/news/2009/011709-europe-charges-microsoft-with-abuse.html.

169-01. OpenAI. "ChatGPT." October 2023.

171. "Republican Issues and Suggestions." Republican Policies. http://republicanpolicies.com/.
Author Note: For the Jeffersonian Cyclopedia entries, since specific URLs for each entry are not provided, I will format them as references to a print source. See Jeffersonian Cyclopedia at http://etext.virginia.edu/etcbin/foleyx-browse?id=Taxation,%20Basis%20of.
172-02. Jefferson, Thomas. "Reply to Vermont Address." Washington ed., vol. 4, p. 418. Washington, 1801.

173-02. Jefferson, Thomas. "To F. Hopkinson." Washington ed., vol. 2, p. 586; Ford ed., vol. 5, p. 76. Paris, Mar. 1789.

174-02. TITLE: Preface to Tracy's Political Economy, EDITION: Washington ed. Vi, 570, PLACE: [none given], DATE: 1816

175-02. Jefferson, Thomas. "First Annual Message." Washington ed., vol. 8, p. 9; Ford ed., vol. 8, p. 119.

176-02. Jefferson, Thomas. "To Samuel Smith." Washington ed., vol. 7, p. 285; Ford ed., vol. 10, p. 252. Monticello, 1823.

177-02. Jefferson, Thomas. "To J. W. Eppes." Washington ed., vol. 6, p. 195; Ford ed., vol. 9, p. 395. Poplar Forest, Va., Sep. 1813.

178-02. Jefferson, Thomas. "Second Annual Message." Washington ed., vol. 8, p. 21; Ford ed., vol. 8, p. 187. Dec. 1802.EDITION: Ford ed., viii, 187, DATE: Dec. 1802

179. "Capitalism." Wikipedia, Wikimedia Foundation, October 2023. http://en.wikipedia.org/wiki/Capitalism. 180-02-b. Jefferson, Thomas. "Autobiography." Washington ed., vol. 1, p. 36; Ford ed., vol. 1, p. 49. 1821.

181. Gillet, [Author's First Name unk.]. CIRANO, [November 2023].

181-02. Jefferson, Thomas. "To John Adams." Washington ed., vol. 6, p. 224; Ford ed., vol. 9, p. 426. Monticello, 1813.

181-03. "Andrew Jackson." Wikipedia, Wikimedia Foundation, October 2023. http://en.wikipedia.org/wiki/Andrew_Jackson.

181-04. "End the Fed." The Foundation for Rational Economics and Education, Inc. (FREE), Grand Central Publishing, Hachette Book Group, 2009.

181-05. "Independent Treasury System." Wikipedia, Wikimedia Foundation, October 2023. http://en.wikipedia.org/wiki/Independent_Treasury_System.

181-06. "Calculate Carbon Footprint." The Carbon Company. October 2023. http://www.carboncompany.com/calculate-carbon-footprint.

181-07. "Passenger Vehicles in the United States." Wikipedia, Wikimedia Foundation, October 2023. http://en.wikipedia.org/wiki/Passenger_vehicles_in_the_United_States.

181-08. "What is the total number of lawyers in the US?" WikiAnswers. October 2023. http://wiki.answers.com/Q/What_is_the_total_number_of_lawyers_in_the_US.

181-09. "Jefferson's Wall of Separation Letter." U.S. Constitution Online. October 2023. http://www.usConstitution.net/jeffwall.html.

181-10. Google Answers. October 2023.
181-11. "Russian Submarines." CNN. [August 2009]. http://www.cnn.com/2009/US/08/05/russian.submarines/index.html.

182. Princeton Weekly Bulletin, [November 2023].

183. "Title of the Bill." GovTrack.us, [November 2023]. http://www.govtrack.us/congress/bill.xpd?bill=h110-984.

184. "Current Numbers." Center for Immigration Studies, [November 2023]. http://www.cis.org/CurrentNumbers.

185. "U.S. Immigration Policy Likely to Boost Population." YaleGlobal Online, [November 2023]. http://yaleglobal.yale.edu/content/us-immigration-policy-likely-boost-population.

186. Seabrook, Andrea. "2009 Was The Most Partisan Year Ever." NPR Radio News, 5:30 PM, 11 Jan. 2010.

190. Minnesota State University, Mankato founded in 1868, known then as Mankato Normal School. https://www.mnsu.edu/Constitution-day/the-Constitution/Constitutional-amendments-summary/.

191. Greene, Brian. "The Fabric of the Cosmos: Space, Time, and the Texture of Reality." New York: Vintage Books, 2004. Print.

20-21. Pew Research Center. "Attendance at Religious Services - Religion in America: U.S. Religious Data, Demographics and Statistics." 2023. Pew Research Center. https://www.pewresearch.org/.

20-22. Public Religion Research Institute. "The State of American Churches." 2023. PRRI. https://www.prri.org/.

20-23. Gallup. "U.S. Church Attendance Still Lower Than Pre-Pandemic." 2023. https://www.gallup.com/.

20-24. IslamReligion.com. "Rights of Non-Muslims in Islam (Part 1 of 13)." [n.d.]. https://www.islamreligion.com/articles/394/rights-of-non-muslims-in-islam-part-11/.

20-25. AlIslam.org. "Does Islam Teach Muslims to Hate Non-Believers?" [n.d.]. https://www.alislam.org/articles/does-islam-teach-muslims-to-hate-non-believers/.

20-26. IslamReligion.com. "Rights of Non-Muslims in Islam (Part 1 of 13)." [n.d.]. https://www.islamreligion.com/articles/394/rights-of-non-muslims-in-islam-part-11/.

20-27. Pew Research Center. "Muslim Publics Share Concerns about Extremist Groups." 10 Sep. 2013. https://www.pewresearch.org/global/2013/09/10/muslim-publics-share-concerns-about-extremist-groups/.

20-28. Guttmacher Institute. "About Half of U.S. Abortion Patients Report Using Contraception in the Month They Became Pregnant." Guttmacher Institute, 11 Jan. 2018, www.guttmacher.org/news-release/2018/about-half-us-abortion-patients-report-using-contraception-month-they-became.

20-29. Bradley, Sarah. "When can my baby survive outside the womb?" BabyCenter, 15 Sept. 2022, www.babycenter.com/health/premature-babies/fetal-viability-by-week-what-age-is-the-age-of-viability_40005764.

211. Department of Homeland Security. Legal Immigration and Adjustment of Status Report for FY 2022. Department of Homeland Security, 2022.

212. "Highway Beautification Act." Environmental Working Group, December 2023, https://www.ewg.org/research/highway-beautification-act.

213. Trend & Tradition, The Magazine of Colonial Williamsburg, Autumn 2024, page 3.

214. USAFacts. "How Has the Federal Budget Changed Over Time?" *USAFacts*, 1 Aug. 2024, www.usafacts.org/articles/how-has-the-federal-budget-changed-over-time/.

215. National Taxpayers Union. "Government Spending in Historical Context." *National Taxpayers Union Foundation*, www.ntu.org/foundation/detail/government-spending-in-historical-context.

216. USAFacts. "Current State of the Union: US Federal Budget." *USAFacts*, 2024, www.usafacts.org.

217. *Youngstown Sheet & Tube Co. v. Sawyer*, 343 U.S. 579. Supreme Court of the United States. 1952.

218. Federal Bureau of Investigation. "FBI Releases 2024 Quarterly Crime Report and Use-of-Force Data Update." *FBI Crime Data Explorer*, 30 Sept. 2024, www.fbi.gov. Accessed 28 Oct. 2024.

219. Federal Bureau of Investigation. "FBI Releases 2023 Crime in the Nation Statistics." *Uniform Crime Reporting (UCR) Program*, 23 Sept. 2024, www.fbi.gov. Accessed 28 Oct. 2024.

220. Snopes. "Biden Administration Claimed Crime Rate Is at 50-Year Low. Is It?" *Snopes*, 28 Oct. 2023, www.snopes.com. Accessed 28 Oct. 2024.

220. "U.S. Budget Deficit Tops $1.8 Trillion in Fiscal 2024, Third Largest on Record." *Reuters*, 18 Oct. 2024, www.reuters.com/markets/us/us-budget-deficit-tops-18-trillion-fiscal-2024-third-largest-record-2024-10-18/. Accessed 1 Nov. 2024.

221. Budiman, Abby. "U.S. Immigrant Population in 2023 Saw Largest Increase in More Than 20 Years." *Pew Research Center*, 27 Sept. 2024, www.pewresearch.org/short-reads/2024/09/27/u-s-immigrant-population-in-2023-saw-largest-increase-in-more-than-20-years/.

222. Passel, Jeffrey S., and D'Vera Cohn. "U.S. Population Projections: 2005-2050." *Pew Research Center*, 11 Feb. 2008, www.pewresearch.org/social-trends/2008/02/11/us-population-projections-2005-2050/.

223. Spagat, Elliot. "US Sees Largest Immigration Surge in 23 Years with 1.6 Million New Immigrants in 2023." *Associated Press News*, 8 Oct. 2024, apnews.com/article/9d468330973502761647c961162917c5?utm_source=chatgpt.com.

224. "US Troops in Iraq and Syria Fight Against ISIS." *Stars and Stripes*, 27 Sept. 2024, https://www.stripes.com/theaters/middle_east/2024-09-27/us-troops-iraq-syria-isis-coalition-15324087.html.

225. "Department of Defense Contractor Personnel in Iraq and Syria." *Congressional Research Service Reports*,

Congressional Research Service, 2024, https://crsreports.congress.gov/product/pdf/IF/IF10600.

226. United States Census Bureau. "Families and Living Arrangements: Married-Couple Households." *U.S. Census Bureau*, 2024, www.census.gov/newsroom/press-releases/2024/families-living-arrangements.html. Accessed 13 Nov. 2024.

227. Statista. "Average Number of People per Family in the United States from 1960 to 2022." *Statista*, 2023, www.statista.com/topics/1484/families/. Accessed 13 Nov. 2024.

228. Jones, Jeffrey M. "LGBT Identification in U.S. Ticks Up to 7.1%." *Gallup*, 17 Feb. 2022, https://news.gallup.com/poll/389792/lgbt-identification-ticks-up.aspx.

229. Ms Robot. "Governed by Idiots." *BlueSky*, 26 Nov. 2024, trudi.bsky.social. Expanded content.

230. Jefferson, Thomas. "Letter to Joseph Milligan, 6 April 1816." *Founders Online*, National Archives, https://founders.archives.gov/documents/Jefferson/03-09-02-0346.

231. Nye, Joseph S. *The Future of Power*. PublicAffairs, 2011.

232. Pew Research Center. "How the World Views America and Americans." *Pew Research Center*, 29 Jan. 2020, www.pewresearch.org/fact-tank/2020/01/29/how-the-world-views-america-and-americans/.

233. Jefferson, Thomas. *Letter to Edward Rutledge*. 18 June 1790. *The Writings of Thomas Jefferson*, edited by Andrew A. Lipscomb and Albert Ellery Bergh, vol. 5, Thomas Jefferson Memorial Association, 1905, pp. 238-239.

234. "List of United States Federal Legislation." *Wikipedia*, Wikimedia Foundation, https://en.wikipedia.org/wiki/List_of_United_States_federal_legislation. Accessed 30 Nov. 2024.

235. Gorsuch, Neil. "America Has Too Many Laws." *The Atlantic*, The Atlantic Monthly Group, Aug. 2024, https://www.theatlantic.com/ideas/archive/2024/08/america-has-too-many-laws-neil-gorsuch/679237/. Accessed 30 Nov. 2024.

236. Owen, Taylor. "The Merger of State and Tech Power Is a Fundamental Challenge to Democratic Governance in the Digital Age." *Tech Policy Press*, 12/1/2024,https://www.techpolicy.press/on-the-coming-merger-of-tech-and-state-power/.

237. "United States Gross National Product (GNP)." *Trading Economics*, Trading Economics, 2024, https://tradingeconomics.com/united-states/gross-national-product. Accessed 3 Dec. 2024.

238. Centers for Disease Control and Prevention. *Abortion Surveillance — United States, 2022*. November 2024, www.cdc.gov/mmwr/volumes/73/ss/ss7307a1.htm. Accessed 5 Dec. 2024.

239. Guttmacher Institute. "Despite Bans, the Number of Abortions in the United States Increased in 2023."

Guttmacher Institute, 2024, www.guttmacher.org/article/2024/03/despite-bans-number-abortions-united-states-increased-2023. Accessed 5 Dec. 2024.

240. National Abortion Federation. *Who Decides? A State-by-State Review of Abortion Rights in the United States*. National Abortion Federation, www.prochoice.org/wp-content/uploads/women_who_have_abortions.pdf. Accessed 5 Dec. 2024.

241. "Doveryai, no proveryai." Russian Proverb. Quoted by Ronald Reagan during arms control negotiations, 1980s. Reagan, Ronald. *An American Life: The Autobiography*. Simon & Schuster, 1990.

242. "Presidential Campaign Costs Over the Last Century." *OpenSecrets*, Center for Responsive Politics, adjusted to 2024 dollars. Accessed 15 Dec. 2024. https://www.opensecrets.org/elections-overview/cost-of-election.

243. "Electricity – Renewables 2023 – Analysis." *IEA*, International Energy Agency, 2023, www.iea.org/reports/renewables-2023/electricity.

244. "Massive Expansion of Renewable Power Opens Door to Achieving Global Tripling Goal Set at COP28." *IEA News*, International Energy Agency, 11 Jan. 2024, www.iea.org/news/massive-expansion-of-renewable-power-opens-door-to-achieving-global-tripling-goal-set-at-cop28.

245. "Clean Energy Infrastructure Program and Funding Announcements." *Department of Energy*, U.S. Department

of Energy, www.energy.gov/eere/femp/clean-energy-infrastructure-program-and-funding-announcements.

246. "Biden-Harris Administration Makes Historic, $11 Billion Investment to Advance Clean Energy Across Rural America Through Investing in America Agenda." *Rural Development*, U.S. Department of Agriculture, 16 May 2023, www.rd.usda.gov/newsroom/biden-harris-administration-makes-historic-11-billion-investment-advance-clean-energy-across-rural-america-through.

247. Fernández, Lucía. "Renewable Energy Investments in the U.S. 2013-2023." *Statista*, 23 Aug. 2024, www.statista.com/statistics/718742/renewable-energy-investment-in-the-us/.

248. "U.S. State Carbon Pricing Policies." *Center for Climate and Energy Solutions*, Center for Climate and Energy Solutions, www.c2es.org/document/us-state-carbon-pricing-policies/.

249. Gray, Jason, et al. "Cap and Trade Heats Up — For Better or Worse." *Legal Planet*, 15 Mar. 2023, legal-planet.org/2023/03/15/cap-and-trade-heats-up-for-better-or-worse/.

250. "Reform for Cap & Trade." *The Climate Center*, 5 Oct. 2023, www.theclimatecenter.org/reform-for-cap-and-trade/.

251. Lopez, German. "Legal Vice." *The New York Times, The Morning*, 20 Dec. 2024.

252. "U.S. Online Gambling Market Size | Industry Report, 2030." *Grand View Research*,

www.grandviewresearch.com/industry-analysis/us-online-gambling-market. Accessed 20 Dec. 2024.

253. "Online Gambling Market Size & Trends Analysis Report, 2030." *Grand View Research*, www.grandviewresearch.com/industry-analysis/online-gambling-market. Accessed 20 Dec. 2024.

254. "National Council on Problem Gambling: NGAGE 2.0 National Detailed Report." *NCPGsurvey.org*, www.ncpgsurvey.org. Accessed 20 Dec. 2024.

255. "Gambling Addiction Statistics - Right Choice Recovery NJ." *Right Choice Recovery NJ*, rightchoicerecoverynj.com. Accessed 20 Dec. 2024.

256. "A Public Health Approach to Problem Gambling - Health Resources in Action." *Health Resources in Action (HRiA)*, www.hria.org. Accessed 20 Dec. 2024.

256-01. Marder, Andrew. "Survey: 62% of Americans Say They Gambled in the Last 12 Months." *NerdWallet*, 2024, www.nerdwallet.com/article/investing/2024-gambling-survey.

256-02. Gramlich, John. "As More States Legalize the Practice, 19% of U.S. Adults Say They Have Bet Money on Sports in the Past Year." *Pew Research Center*, 14 Sept. 2022, www.pewresearch.org/short-reads/2022/09/14/as-more-states-legalize-the-practice-19-of-u-s-adults-say-they-have-bet-money-on-sports-in-the-past-year/.

256-03. American Gaming Association. "Leading Types of Gambling in the U.S. 2021-2023." *Statista*, 10 Sept. 2023, www.statista.com/statistics/1313317/top-types-of-gambling-us/.

257. Institute on Taxation and Economic Policy (ITEP). "Corporate Taxes Before and After the Trump Tax Law." ITEP, 26 May 2024, www.itep.org/corporate-taxes-before-and-after-the-trump-tax-law.

258. Johnson, Jake. "Tax Rates for Big Corporations Fell by Nearly Half After Trump Cuts." Common Dreams, 2 May 2024, www.commondreams.org/news/2024-05-02/tax-rates-big-corporations-fell-nearly-half-after-trump-cuts.

259. Owen, Tess. "Taxes for Big Companies Fell by 50% After Trump Cuts." Portside, 4 May 2024, www.portside.org/2024-05-04/taxes-big-companies-fell-50-after-trump-cuts.

270. "Government Revenue Details: Federal State Local for 2023 - Charts." *USGovernmentRevenue.com*, www.usgovernmentrevenue.com. Accessed 10 December 2023.

271. Internal Revenue Service. "SOI Tax Stats - Number of Returns Filed, by Type of Return and State and Fiscal Year - IRS Data Book Table 3." *Internal Revenue Service*, 2023, www.irs.gov/statistics/soi-tax-stats-number-of-returns-filed-by-type-of-return-and-state-and-fiscal-year-irs-data-book-table-3.

272. U.S. Treasury Department. "Final 2023 CS Charts." *U.S. Treasury*, 2023, www.fiscal.treasury.gov/files/reports-statements/combined-statement/cs2023/receipt.pdf.

273. "The Federal Budget: An Overview." *USAFacts*, 1 Aug. 2024, usafacts.org/articles/the-federal-budget-an-overview/.

274. "2024 Current State of the Union: US Federal Budget." *USAFacts*, usafacts.org.

275. "How Many Countries Have VAT or GST?" *VATCalc*, August 2024, www.vatcalc.com/global/how-many-countries-have-vat-or-gst-174/.

276. Ithaca DSA | Grassroots Economic Organizing. https://geo.coop/people/ithaca-dsa.

277. Board of Governors of the Federal Reserve System. "Distribution of Household Wealth in the U.S. since 1989." Federal Reserve, www.federalreserve.gov/econres/scfindex.htm. Accessed 28 Dec. 2024.

278. "How has wealth distribution in the US changed over time?" USAFacts, 13 Nov. 2023, www.usafacts.org/articles/wealth-distribution-in-the-us-changed-over-time. Accessed 28 Dec. 2024.

279. "Wealth Inequality in America over Time: Key Statistics." St. Louis Federal Reserve, www.stlouisfed.org/publications/regional-economist/fourth-quarter-2021/wealth-inequality-america-over-time-key-statistics. Accessed 28 Dec. 2024.

280. "National Center for Education Statistics." *NCES*, U.S. Department of Education, 21 Aug. 2024, www.nces.ed.gov.

281. Muste, A.J. "The two decisive powers of the government with respect to war are the power to conscript and the power to tax." *Everyday Peacebuilding*. https://www.everydaypeacebuilding.com. Accessed 28 Dec. 2024.

282. Gilbert, Gustave. "Naturally the common people don't want war... but after all it is the leaders of a country who determine policy, and it is always a simple matter to drag the people along..." *A-Z Quotes*. https://www.azquotes.com/quote/441928. Accessed 28 Dec. 2024.

283. Washington, George. "Farewell Address." 1796. *The Avalon Project*, Lillian Goldman Law Library, Yale Law School, 2023. avalon.law.yale.edu/18th_century/washing.asp. Accessed 30 Dec. 2023.

284. 2023." *National Priorities Project*, https://www.nationalpriorities.org/interactive-data/taxday/average/2023/receipt/. Accessed 2 Jan. 2025.

285. Pew Research Center. "Americans' Deepening Mistrust of Institutions." *The Pew Charitable Trusts*, 2024, www.pewtrusts.org/en/research-and-analysis/blogs/stateline/2024/americans-deepening-mistrust-of-institutions.

286. No Kid Hungry. "How Many Kids in the United States Live With Hunger?" *No Kid Hungry*, 5 Sept. 2024, www.nokidhungry.org.

287. Himmelstein, David U., et al. "Medical Bankruptcy: Still Common Despite the Affordable Care Act." *American*

Journal of Public Health, vol. 109, no. 3, Mar. 2019, pp. 431-433. *AJPH*, doi:10.2105/AJPH.2018.304901.

288. Tocqueville, Alexis de. *Democracy in America.* Translated by Henry Reeve, corrected by Francis Bowen, edited by Phillips Bradley, vol. 1, Vintage Books, 1945.

289. Reuters. "Global Billionaire Wealth Leaps, Fueled by US Gains, UBS Says." *Reuters*, 5 Dec. 2024, www.reuters.com/business/global-billionaire-wealth-leaps-fueled-by-us-gains-ubs-says-2024-12-05/.

290. USDA Economic Research Service. "Farm Real Estate Values." *United States Department of Agriculture*, 2023, www.ers.usda.gov/topics/farm-economy/land-use-land-value-tenure/.

291. RER. "Commercial Real Estate Value 2022." *Real Estate Roundtable*, 2022, www.rer.org/wp-content/uploads/CRE-By-The-Numbers.pdf.

292. Zillow. "Total Market Value of U.S. Housing Stock." *Zillow Research*, 2023, www.zillow.com/research/total-market-value-2023-33031/.

293. "Military Budget of the United States." *Wikipedia*, Wikimedia Foundation, 2023, en.wikipedia.org/wiki/Military_budget_of_the_United_States.

294. "Budget Basics: National Defense." *Peter G. Peterson Foundation*, 2 May 2024, www.pgpf.org/budget-basics/national-defense.

295. Ashcroft, Bryony. "Which Countries Offer Universal Healthcare?" *The Insiders' Guide to Expatriate Health*, 9 May 2012, expathealth.org/healthcare/which-countries-offer-universal-healthcare/.

296. Centers for Disease Control and Prevention. "Physical Activity and Health." *CDC*, U.S. Department of Health & Human Services, 4 June 2021, www.cdc.gov/physicalactivity/basics/pa-health/index.htm.

297. "Average Weight of Men and Women Since the 1970's." *24/7 Wall St.*, 24/7 Wall St, 20 Nov. 2018, www.247wallst.com/special-report/2018/11/20/average-weight-of-men-and-women-since-the-1970s.

298. "Trump Announces 'DOGE' Initiative with Elon Musk and Vivek Ramaswamy to Overhaul Government Efficiency." *Business Insider*, Business Insider, 8 Jan. 2025, www.businessinsider.com/trump-elon-musk-vivek-ramaswamy-doge-initiative-government-efficiency-2025-1. Accessed 9 Jan. 2025.

299. "Green Trade Strategy." *U.S. Customs and Border Protection*, U.S. Customs and Border Protection, www.cbp.gov/trade/priority-issues/green-trade-strategy. Accessed 9 Jan. 2025.

300. "Supply Chain Compliance with Human Rights and Environmental Obligations." *White & Case LLP*, www.whitecase.com/publications/alert/supply-chain-compliance-human-rights-and-environmental-obligations. Accessed 9 Jan. 2025.

301. "The Complete Guide to Trade Policy in Import and Export Data." *The Trade Vision*, The Trade Vision, 31 Jul. 2024, www.thetradevision.com/blogs/the-complete-guide-to-trade-policy-in-import-and-export-data. Accessed 9 Jan. 2025.

302. "Current Population of Canada." *Worldometer*, www.worldometers.info/world-population/canada-population/. Accessed 10 Jan. 2025.

303. "Canadian Opinion on U.S. Election." *GlobalNews.ca*, 10 Jan. 2025, www.globalnews.ca/canadian-opinion-us-election-2025. Accessed 10 Jan. 2025.

305. Brandeis, Louis D. Quoted in Lonergan, Raymond. *Mr. Justice Brandeis, Great American*. Van Rees Press, 1941, p. 42.

306. Twain, Mark. *Following the Equator: A Journey Around the World*. American Publishing Company, 1897, p. 156.

307. World Economic Forum. "The Truth Behind Welfare Dependency." World Economic Forum, www.weforum.org/agenda/2017/06/this-is-the-truth-about-welfare-dependency. Accessed 11 Jan. 2025.

308. Brookings Institution. "Redistribution through Work." Brookings, www.brookings.edu/articles/redistribution-through-work. Accessed 11 Jan. 2025.

309. "The 2024 OASDI Trustees Report." Social Security Administration, 2024, www.ssa.gov/OACT/TR/2024/. Accessed 11 Jan. 2025.

310. "Summary: Actuarial Status of the Social Security Trust Funds." Social Security Administration, May 2024, www.ssa.gov/OACT/TRSUM/index.html. Accessed 11 Jan. 2025.

311. "Social Security: Selected Findings of the 2024 Annual Report." Congressional Research Service, 2024, crsreports.congress.gov/product/pdf/R/R46745. Accessed 11 Jan. 2025.

312. U.S. Office of Management and Budget and Federal Reserve Bank of St. Louis. "Federal Debt: Total Public Debt as Percent of Gross Domestic Product." *FRED, Federal Reserve Bank of St. Louis*, 2024, https://fred.stlouisfed.org/series/GFDEGDQ188S. Accessed 11 Jan. 2025.

313. "Massachusetts Declaration of Rights – Article 7." *Mass.gov*, www.mass.gov/info-details/massachusetts-constitution. Accessed 11 Jan. 2025.

314. "Breaking Down the U.S. Government's 2024 Fiscal Year." *Visual Capitalist*. Accessed 12 January 2025, https://www.visualcapitalist.com/breaking-down-the-u-s-governments-2024-fiscal-year.

315. CBO estimates $1.8 trillion US deficit for fiscal 2024, largest after COVID. *Reuters*, 8 October 2024. Accessed 12 January 2025, https://www.reuters.com/world/us/cbo-estimates-18-trillion-us-deficit-fiscal-2024-largest-after-covid-2024-10-08.

316. "Federal Deficit Hit $1.8 Trillion for 2024, CBO Says." *The Wall Street Journal*. Accessed 12 January 2025,

https://www.wsj.com/politics/policy/budget-deficit-national-debt-2024-079d8d13.

317. Limberg, Julian, et al. "50 Years of Tax Cuts for the Rich Have Failed to Trickle Down." *The London Economic*, 10 Nov. 2024, www.thelondoneconomic.com/news/50-years-of-tax-cuts-for-the-rich-have-failed-to-trickle-down-192664/.

318. Zidar, Owen. "Arguments and Evidence Against Trickle-Down Economics." *Profolus*, www.profolus.com/topics/arguments-and-evidence-against-trickle-down-economics/.

319. "It's Not Trickling Down: New Data Provides No Evidence That the TCJA Is Working as Its Proponents Claimed It Would." *Economic Policy Institute*, www.epi.org/publication/its-not-trickling-down-new-data-provides-no-evidence-that-the-tcja-is-working-as-its-proponents-claimed-it-would/.

320. American Psychological Association. *Report of the Task Force on Appropriate Therapeutic Responses to Sexual Orientation.* 2009. apa.org.

321. United Kingdom Government Equalities Office. *An Assessment of the Evidence on Conversion Therapy for Sexual Orientation and Gender Identity.* 2021. gov.uk.

322. Kelly, Jason. "Saving Democracy." *The University of Chicago Magazine*, Spring 2019, pp. 24–25.

323. "U.S. Cities Factsheet." *Center for Sustainable Systems, University of Michigan*, 2020,

611

https://css.umich.edu/publications/factsheets/built-environment/us-cities-factsheet.

324. "U.S. Cities Factsheet." *Center for Sustainable Systems, University of Michigan*, 2023, https://css.umich.edu/publications/factsheets/built-environment/us-cities-factsheet.

325. Wallace, Henry A. "The Danger of American Fascism." *The New York Times*, 9 Apr. 1944, https://alba-valb.org/wp-content/uploads/2020/06/Wallace.pdf.

326. Cicero, Marcus Tullius. *De Legibus*, Book I, Section 6. Translated by Clinton Walker Keyes, Harvard University Press, 1928.

327.Cicero, Marcus Tullius. *De Legibus*, Book I, Section 10. Translated by Clinton Walker Keyes, Harvard University Press, 1928.

328.Cicero, Marcus Tullius. *De Legibus*, Book III, Section 19. Translated by Clinton Walker Keyes, Harvard University Press, 1928.

329. Statista. "Global CO_2 Emissions from Fossil Fuels and Industry from 1750 to 2024." Statista, https://www.statista.com/statistics/276629/global-co2-emissions/. Accessed 19 Jan. 2025.

330. World Economic Forum. "Visualizing Changes in Carbon Dioxide Emissions Since 1900." World Economic Forum, https://www.weforum.org/stories/2022/11/visualizing-changes-carbon-dioxide-emissions-since-1900/. Accessed 19 Jan. 2025.

331. International Energy Agency (IEA). "Global Energy Review 2021." IEA, https://www.iea.org/reports/global-energy-review-2021. Accessed 19 Jan. 2025.

332. Food and Agriculture Organization (FAO). "Tackling Climate Change Through Livestock: A Global Assessment of Emissions and Mitigation Opportunities.", 2013, https://www.fao.org/3/i3437e/i3437e.pdf. Accessed 19 Jan. 2025.

333. International Water Management Institute (IWMI). "Water for Food, Water for Life: A Comprehensive Assessment of Water Management in Agriculture." IWMI, 2007, https://www.iwmi.cgiar.org/Publications/CABI_Publications/CA_CABI_Series/Comprehensive_Assessment/index.htm. Accessed 19 Jan. 2025.

334. Environmental Protection Agency (EPA). "Sources of Greenhouse Gas Emissions: Agriculture Sector Emissions." EPA, https://www.epa.gov/ghgemissions/sources-greenhouse-gas-emissions. Accessed 19 Jan. 2025.

335. World Resources Institute (WRI). "Reducing Food Loss and Waste: Setting a Global Action Agenda." WRI, 2019, https://www.wri.org/research/reducing-food-loss-and-waste-setting-global-action-agenda. Accessed 19 Jan. 2025.

336. United Nations Environment Programme (UNEP). "Food Waste Index Report 2021." UNEP, 2021, https://www.unep.org/resources/report/unep-food-waste-index-report-2021. Accessed 19 Jan. 2025.

337. Worldometers. "World Population Growth." *Worldometers*, https://www.worldometers.info/world-population/. Accessed 21 Jan. 2025.

338. Avena, Nicole M., Pedro Rada, and Bartley G. Hoebel. "Evidence for Sugar Addiction: Behavioral and Neurochemical Effects of Intermittent, Excessive Sugar Intake." *Neuroscience & Biobehavioral Reviews*, vol. 32, no. 1, 2008, pp. 20–39.

339. Rada, Pedro, Nicole M. Avena, and Bartley G. Hoebel. "Daily Bingeing on Sugar Repeatedly Releases Dopamine in the Accumbens Shell." *Neuroscience*, vol. 134, no. 3, 2005, pp. 737–744.

340. Westwater, Margaret L., Hisham Ziauddeen, and Paul C. Fletcher. "Sugar Addiction: The State of the Science." *European Journal of Nutrition*, vol. 55, no. 1, 2016, pp. 55–69.

341. "Lotteries and State Fiscal Policy." *Tax Foundation*, 2004, https://taxfoundation.org/research/all/state/lotteries-and-state-fiscal-policy/.

342"Florida Lottery Program Summary." *Florida Office of Program Policy Analysis and Government Accountability*, https://oppaga.fl.gov/ProgramSummary/ProgramDetail?programNumber=2090.

343. "Louisiana Lottery Corporation." *Wikipedia*, https://en.wikipedia.org/wiki/Louisiana_Lottery_Corporation.

344. "Powerball Prize Chart." *Powerball Official Website*, https://www.powerball.com/powerball-prize-chart.

345. "Mega Millions Lottery Winner Becomes Instant Millionaire After Buying Ticket at Texas Gas Station." *The Sun*, https://www.the-sun.com/money/12080102/mega-millions-lottery-winner-millionaire-texas-gas-station/.

346. North American Association of State and Provincial Lotteries (NASPL). "Lottery Industry FAQ." *NASPL*, https://www.naspl.org/faq.

347. Pew Research Center. *Public Trust in Government: 1958-2024*. 24 June 2024, https://www.pewresearch.org/politics/2024/06/24/public-trust-in-government-1958-2024. Accessed 3 Feb. 2025.

348. Bloomberg. *A History of Government Trust in the U.S.* 2024, https://www.bloomberg.com/graphics/2024-opinion-history-government-trust. Accessed 3 Feb. 2025.

349. Schwabish, Jonathan, and Megan Curran. *Challenges and Opportunities of Providing Free School Meals for All.* Center for American Progress, 24 Jan. 2023, www.americanprogress.org/article/challenges-and-opportunities-of-providing-free-school-meals-for-all/. Accessed 4 Feb. 2025.

350. Acton, John Emerich Edward Dalberg. *Essays on Freedom and Power*. Edited by Gertrude Himmelfarb, The Free Press, 1948, p. 364.

351. Gallup, Inc. "Injectable Weight-Loss Drugs: Uses and Effectiveness." *Gallup News*, 2024, news.gallup.com.

352. Pew Research Center. "As Obesity Rates Rise in the U.S. and Worldwide, New Weight-Loss Drugs Surge in Popularity." *Pew Research*, 21 Mar. 2024, www.pewresearch.org.

353. UCSF Magazine. "Weight-Loss Drugs: Too Good to Be True?" *University of California, San Francisco Magazine*, 2024, magazine.ucsf.edu.

354. VCU Health. "Weight-Loss Drugs 101: Benefits and Risks You Need to Know Before Picking Up a Prescription." *VCU Health News*, 2024, www.vcuhealth.org.

355. Southern Poverty Law Center. *Year in Hate & Extremism 2023: Decoding the Far Right's Plan to Undo Democracy*. SPLC, 2023, https://www.splcenter.org/presscenter/splc-releases-annual-year-hate-extremism-report-decodes-far-rights-plan-undo-democracy. Accessed 10 Feb. 2025.

356. States United Democracy Center. *Americans' Views on Political Violence*. States United, 2022, https://statesunited.org/resources/americans-views-political-violence. Accessed 10 Feb. 2025.

357. OpenSecrets. "Where the Money Came From." *OpenSecrets*, Center for Responsive Politics, https://www.opensecrets.org/elections-overview/where-the-money-came-from. Accessed 11 Feb. 2025.

358. Brennan Center for Justice. "Billionaires Provided 15 Percent of Funding for the Midterms." *Brennan Center for Justice*, 8 Dec. 2022, https://www.brennancenter.org/our-work/analysis-opinion/billionaires-provided-15-percent-funding-midterms. Accessed 11 Feb. 2025.

359. Cybersecurity Ventures. "Cybersecurity Almanac 2024." *Cybersecurity Ventures*, 2024, https://cybersecurityventures.com/cybersecurity-almanac-2024.

360. Spacelift. "Phishing Statistics: The 2024 Ultimate List." *Spacelift Blog*, 2024, https://spacelift.io/blog/phishing-statistics.

361. Varonis. "2024 Cybersecurity Statistics, Trends & Facts." *Varonis Blog*, 2024, https://www.varonis.com/blog/cybersecurity-statistics.

362. Congressional Budget Office. *The Budget and Economic Outlook: 2024 to 2034.* 12 Feb. 2024, www.cbo.gov/publication/60843. Accessed 12 Feb. 2025.

363. Social Security Administration. *Annual Report of the Social Security Trust Funds, 2024.* Social Security Administration, 2024, www.ssa.gov/OACT/FACTS. Accessed 12 Feb. 2025.

364. Social Security Administration. *The 2024 Annual Report of the Board of Trustees of the Federal Old-Age and Survivors Insurance and Federal Disability Insurance Trust Funds.* Social Security Administration, 2024, www.ssa.gov/oact/TR/2024/II_A_highlights.html. Accessed 12 Feb. 2025.

365. Centers for Medicare & Medicaid Services. *Medicaid and CHIP Enrollment Data Highlights.* U.S. Department of Health & Human Services, Oct. 2024, www.medicaid.gov/medicaid/program-

information/medicaid-and-chip-enrollment-data/report-highlights/index.html. Accessed 12 Feb. 2025.

366. Centers for Medicare & Medicaid Services. *National Health Expenditure Fact Sheet.* U.S. Department of Health & Human Services, 2024, www.cms.gov/data-research/statistics-trends-and-reports/national-health-expenditure-data/nhe-fact-sheet. Accessed 12 Feb. 2025.

367. Assistant Secretary for Planning and Evaluation (ASPE). *ACA-Related Enrollment as of February 2024.* U.S. Department of Health & Human Services, Feb. 2024, www.aspe.hhs.gov/reports/aca-related-enrollment-february-2024. Accessed 12 Feb. 2025.

368. Centers for Medicare & Medicaid Services (CMS). *Historic 21.3 Million People Choose ACA Marketplace Coverage.* U.S. Department of Health & Human Services, 24 Jan. 2024, www.cms.gov/newsroom/press-releases/historic-213-million-people-choose-aca-marketplace-coverage. Accessed 12 Feb. 2025.

369. Investopedia. *Health Insurance Costs Will Soar If Republicans Let Subsidies Expire.* Dotdash Meredith, 2024, www.investopedia.com/say-goodbye-to-savings-health-insurance-costs-will-soar-if-republicans-let-subsidies-die-8748723. Accessed 12 Feb. 2025.

370. "Head Start Program Facts: Fiscal Year 2022." *Head Start ECLKC,* U.S. Department of Health and Human Services, 2022, https://eclkc.ohs.acf.hhs.gov/sites/default/files/pdf/hs-program-fact-sheet-2022.pdf.

371. Heckman, James J., et al. "A New Cost-Benefit and Rate of Return Analysis for the Perry Preschool Program: A Summary." *National Bureau of Economic Research*, Working Paper No. 16180, July 2010, https://www.nber.org/papers/w16180.

372. "Head Start Policy Agenda (2023-2024)." *National Head Start Association*, 2023, https://nhsa.org/wp-content/uploads/2023/03/Head-Start-Federal-Policy-Agenda-2022-23.pdf.

373. "Head Start Program Annual Fact Sheets." *Head Start ECLKC*, U.S. Department of Health and Human Services, https://eclkc.ohs.acf.hhs.gov/about-us/article/head-start-program-fact-sheets.

374. "Early Childhood: High Return on Investment." *Pennsylvania Early Learning Investment Commission*, https://www.impact.upenn.edu/early-childhood-toolkit/why-invest/what-is-the-return-on-investment/.

375. Ludlow Cub Editorial Board. *The Decline of Arts in Schools: A Call to Action for LHS Community.* Ludlow Cub, 7 June 2024, www.ludlowcub.com/opinion/2024/06/07/the-decline-of-arts in-schools-a-call-to-action-for-lhs-community. Accessed 12 Feb. 2025.

376. Truthout. *Schools Are Divesting from Arts Education as COVID-Era Federal Funds Evaporate.* Truthout, 2024, truthout.org/articles/schools-are-divesting-from-arts-education-as-covid-era-federal-funds-evaporate. Accessed 12 Feb. 2025.

377. Internal Revenue Service. *Restriction of Political Campaign Intervention by Section 501(c)(3) Tax-Exempt Organizations.* U.S. Department of the Treasury, 2024, www.irs.gov/charities-non-profits/charitable-organizations/restriction-of-political-campaign-intervention-by-section-501c3-tax-exempt-organizations. Accessed 12 Feb. 2025.

378. Platoff, Emma. *Some Churches Are Ignoring Law That Bars Them from Endorsing Political Candidates.* The Texas Tribune, 30 Oct. 2022, www.texastribune.org/2022/10/30/johnson-amendment-elections-irs. Accessed 12 Feb. 2025.

379. Reuters. *U.S. Power Use to Reach Record Highs in 2025-2026, EIA Says.* Reuters, 11 Feb. 2025, www.reuters.com/business/energy/us-power-use-reach-record-highs-2025-2026-eia-says-2025-02-11. Accessed 14 Feb. 2025.

380. Centers for Medicare & Medicaid Services. "National Health Expenditure Data: Historical." *CMS.gov*, 2023, www.cms.gov/data-research/statistics-trends-and-reports/national-health-expenditure-data/historical.

381. Kamal, Rabah, et al. "How has U.S. spending on healthcare changed over time?" *Peterson-KFF Health System Tracker*, 2023, www.healthsystemtracker.org/chart-collection/u-s-spending-healthcare-changed-time/.

382. Hartman, Micah, et al. "National Health Spending In 2022: Growth Rate Accelerated While Underlying Factors Changed." *Health Affairs*, vol. 42, no. 1, 2023, pp. 10-20.

383. Keating, Christopher. "Mental Health and Homeless Services at Risk in Connecticut as Funds Run Out."

CTInsider, 15 Feb. 2025,
www.ctinsider.com/politics/article/ct-lamont-arpa-budget-homelessness-mental-health-20158678.php.

384. Department of Veterans Affairs. *FY 2024 Budget in Brief.* U.S. Department of Veterans Affairs, 2023, https://www.usaspending.gov/agency/department-of-veterans-affairs.

385. U.S. Bureau of Labor Statistics. "Employment Situation of Veterans – 2023." *U.S. Department of Labor*, 2024, https://www.bls.gov/news.release/pdf/vet.pdf.

386. House Committee on Veterans' Affairs. "Chairman Bost Presses VA on Budget Shortfall, Impact on Veterans." *U.S. House of Representatives*, 17 July 2024, https://veterans.house.gov/news/documentsingle.aspx?DocumentID=6511.

387. Masaar Network. "Net Neutrality: What Is It? How Does It Affect Us?" *Masaar*, https://masaar.net/en/net-neutrality-what-is-it-how-does-it-affect-us/. Accessed 20 Feb. 2025.

388. Reuters. "U.S. Court Blocks Biden Administration Net Neutrality Rules." *Reuters*, 1 Aug. 2024, https://www.reuters.com/legal/us-court-blocks-biden-administration-net-neutrality-rules-2024-08-01/. Accessed 20 Feb. 2025.

389. Walden University. "The Impact of Net Neutrality on Internet Service Providers and Consumers." *Walden University ScholarWorks*, https://scholarworks.waldenu.edu/cgi/viewcontent.cgi?article=16556&context=dissertations. Accessed 20 Feb. 2025.

390. U.S. Census Bureau. "Historical Household and Family Data." U.S. Census Bureau, https://www.census.gov/content/dam/Census/library/visualizations/time-series/demo/families-and-households/hh-6.pdf. Accessed 20 Feb. 2025.

391. Statista. "Average Size of Households in the U.S. from 1960 to 2023." *Statista*, https://www.statista.com/statistics/183648/average-size-of-households-in-the-us/. Accessed 20 Feb. 2025.

392. Public Religion Research Institute. *The State of Religion in the U.S.: Shifts in Religious Affiliation and Practice.* PRRI, Mar. 2024, https://www.prri.org/wp-content/uploads/2024/03/PRRI-March-2024-Religious-Change.pdf. Accessed 20 Feb. 2025.

393. Pew Research Center. *How the COVID-19 Pandemic Affected U.S. Religious Life.* Pew Research, 12 Feb. 2025, https://www.pewresearch.org/2025/02/12/how-the-covid-19-pandemic-affected-u-s-religious-life/. Accessed 20 Feb. 2025.

394. Hout, Michael, and Tom W. Smith. "Fewer Americans Affiliate with Organized Religions, Belief and Practice Unchanged: Key Findings from the 2014 General Social Survey." NORC, Mar. 2015.

395. Pew Research Center. "About Three-in-Ten U.S. Adults Are Now Religiously Unaffiliated." *Pew Research Center*, 14 Dec. 2021, https://www.pewresearch.org/religion/2021/12/14/about-three-in-ten-u-s-adults-are-now-religiously-unaffiliated/. Accessed 20 Feb. 2025.

396. RealClearPublicAffairs. *Great American Stories: What Boesky Said.* RealClearPublicAffairs, 18 May 2021, https://www.realclearpublicaffairs.com/articles/2021/05/1 8/great_american_stories_what_boesky_said_777701.htm l. Accessed 20 Feb. 2025.

397. Reuters. "Global Billionaire Wealth Leaps, Fueled by U.S. Gains, UBS Says." *Reuters,* 5 Dec. 2024, https://www.reuters.com/business/global-billionaire-wealth-leaps-fueled-by-us-gains-ubs-says-2024-12-05/. Accessed 20 Feb. 2025.

398. Fortune. "Billionaires' Wealth Has More Than Doubled to $14 Trillion, UBS Report Finds." *Fortune,* 6 Dec. 2024, https://fortune.com/europe/2024/12/06/billionaires-wealth-doubled-14-trillion-ubs/. Accessed 20 Feb. 2025.

399. United States Department of Agriculture. *Land Values 2024 Summary.* National Agricultural Statistics Service, 2024, https://www.nass.usda.gov/Publications/Todays_Reports/reports/land0824.pdf. Accessed 20 Feb. 2025.

400. Federal Reserve Bank of St. Louis. "Commercial Real Estate in Focus: Trends and Market Dynamics." *Federal Reserve Bank of St. Louis,* May 2024, https://www.stlouisfed.org/on-the-economy/2024/may/commercial-real-estate-in-focus. Accessed 20 Feb. 2025.

401. Bureau of Economic Analysis. *New Estimates of Value of Land in the United States.* U.S. Department of Commerce, 2015,

https://www.bea.gov/research/papers/2015/new-estimates-value-land-united-states. Accessed 20 Feb. 2025.

402. Federal Reserve Bank of St. Louis. "Average Price: Sugar, White, All Sizes (APU0000715211)." *FRED Economic Data*, U.S. Bureau of Labor Statistics, Jan. 2025, https://fred.stlouisfed.org/series/APU0000715211. Accessed 20 Feb. 2025.

403. Congressional Research Service. *U.S. Farm Income Outlook: 2023 Forecast and 2024 Projections*. U.S. Congress, 2024, https://crsreports.congress.gov/product/pdf/R/R48278/4. Accessed 20 Feb. 2025.

404. U.S. Department of Agriculture, Economic Research Service. *Farm Household Income Estimates*. USDA, 2024, https://www.ers.usda.gov/topics/farm-economy/farm-household-well-being/farm-household-income-estimates. Accessed 20 Feb. 2025.

405. Bureau of Labor Statistics. *The Effects of Minimum Wage Increases on Employment*. U.S. Department of Labor, 2023, https://www.bls.gov/opub/mlr/2023/article/the-effects-of-minimum-wage-increases-on-employment.htm. Accessed 20 Feb. 2025.

406. Brookings Institution. *How Minimum Wages Impact Employment and Economic Growth*. Brookings, 2024, https://www.brookings.edu/research/how-minimum-wages-impact-employment-and-economic-growth/. Accessed 20 Feb. 2025.

407. World Bank. *Minimum Wages and Their Effects on Labor Markets*. World Bank Group, 2024,

https://www.worldbank.org/en/topic/jobs/publication/minimum-wages-and-their-effects-on-labor-markets. Accessed 20 Feb. 2025.

408. National Bureau of Economic Research. *The Impact of Minimum Wage Increases on Employment and Automation.* NBER Working Paper No. 30042, 2024, https://www.nber.org/papers/w30042. Accessed 20 Feb. 2025.

409. Brookings Institution. *Housing Affordability and Minimum Wages.* Brookings, 2024, https://www.brookings.edu/research/housing-affordability-and-minimum-wages/. Accessed 20 Feb. 2025.

410. BestPlaces. *Cost of Living Comparison: Ames, IA vs. New York, NY.* BestPlaces, 2024, https://www.bestplaces.net/cost-of-living/ames-ia/new-york-ny/160000. Accessed 20 Feb. 2025.

411. University at Buffalo. *Men Still More Likely Than Women to Be Perceived as Leaders, Study Finds.* University at Buffalo News, 2024, https://www.buffalo.edu/news/news-releases.host.html/content/shared/mgt/news/men-still-more-likely-than-women-perceived-leaders-study-finds.detail.html. Accessed 20 Feb. 2025.

412. American Psychological Association. *Women Are Now Seen as Equally — If Not More — Competent Than Men.* APA News, 2019, https://www.apa.org/news/press/releases/2019/07/women-equally-more-competent. Accessed 20 Feb. 2025.

413. National Institutes of Health. *Men Frequently Devalue Female Leaders: Gender Bias in Professional Environments.* PMC, 2024, https://pmc.ncbi.nlm.nih.gov/articles/PMC9912935. Accessed 20 Feb. 2025.

414. U.S. Geological Survey. "U.S. Borders and Coastline Lengths." *U.S. Department of the Interior,* https://www.usgs.gov. Accessed 2 Mar. 2025.

415. Wikipedia contributors. *"Gender-Based Price Discrimination in the United States."* Wikipedia, Wikimedia Foundation, https://en.wikipedia.org/wiki/Gender-based_price_discrimination_in_the_United_States. Accessed 9 Mar. 2025.

416. Davey, Melissa. *"Alyse's Chronic Health Conditions Have Cost Her $400,000: Doctors Say the System Unfairly Penalizes Women." The Guardian,* 12 Nov. 2024, https://www.theguardian.com/australia-news/2024/nov/12/alyses-chronic-health-conditions-have-cost-her-400000-doctors-say-the-system-unfairly-penalises-women.

417. Park, Alice. *"The Next Frontiers of Women's Health." Time,* 2024, https://time.com/7018231/womens-leadership-forum-next-frontiers-of-womens-health.

418. PMC. *"Microplastic Pollution and Its Impact on Marine Life." National Library of Medicine,* https://pmc.ncbi.nlm.nih.gov/articles/PMC9920460/. Accessed 10 Mar. 2025.

419. World Economic Forum. *"How Microplastics Get into the Food Chain." WEF*, https://www.weforum.org/stories/2025/02/how-microplastics-get-into-the-food-chain/. Accessed 10 Mar. 2025.

420. PMC. *"Health Risks of Microplastic Contamination in the Food Chain." National Library of Medicine*, https://pmc.ncbi.nlm.nih.gov/articles/PMC8704590/. Accessed 10 Mar. 2025.

421. Wikipedia contributors. *"Biodegradable Plastic." Wikipedia*, Wikimedia Foundation, https://en.wikipedia.org/wiki/Biodegradable_plastic. Accessed 10 Mar. 2025.

422. Scola, Nancy. "Foreign-Owned Corporations Put Millions into U.S. Elections." *OpenSecrets News*, Center for Responsive Politics, 14 Mar. 2019, www.opensecrets.org/news/2019/03/citizens-united-foreign-owned-corporations-put-millions-in-us-elections/.

423. King, Martin Luther, Jr. *Letter from Birmingham Jail*. Penguin Books, 2018.

424. Council on Foreign Relations. *China's Massive Belt and Road Initiative*. 2 Feb. 2023, https://www.cfr.org/backgrounder/chinas-massive-belt-and-road-initiative. Accessed 22 Apr. 2025.

425. Westat. *Evaluation of the Accuracy of E-Verify Findings*. U.S. Citizenship and Immigration Services, 2012. https://www.e-verify.gov/sites/default/files/everify/data/FindingsEVerifyAccuracyEval2012.pdf.

426. U.S. Citizenship and Immigration Services. *Naturalization Through Military Service*. U.S. Department of Homeland Security, 2024, www.uscis.gov/military/naturalization-through-military-service.

427. U.S. Constitution. *Article I, Section 9, Clause 2*. Legal Information Institute, Cornell Law School, www.law.cornell.edu/constitution/articlei#section9.

428. *Ex parte Milligan*, 71 U.S. 2 (1866). Supreme Court of the United States. https://supreme.justia.com/cases/federal/us/71/2/

429. *Boumediene v. Bush*, 553 U.S. 723 (2008). Supreme Court of the United States. https://supreme.justia.com/cases/federal/us/553/723/

430. Marijuana Policy Project. "Cannabis Tax Revenue in States that Regulate Cannabis for Adult Use." *MPP*, 2023, https://www.mpp.org/issues/legalization/cannabis-tax-revenue-states-regulate-cannabis-adult-use/.

431. Angell, Tom. "Colorado Has Generated Over $1 Billion in Marijuana Revenue, State Announces." *Forbes*, 12 June 2019, https://www.forbes.com/sites/tomangell/2019/06/12/colorado-has-generated-over-1-billion-in-marijuana-revenue-state-announces/.

432. Marijuana Moment. "The Legal Marijuana Industry Now Supports More Than 440,000 Full-Time Jobs, Up 5% From Last Year, Report Finds." *Marijuana Moment*, 2024, https://www.marijuanamoment.net/the-legal-marijuana-industry-

now-supports-more-than-440000-full-time-jobs-up-5-from-last-year-report-finds/.

433. Monte, Alex A., et al. "The Implications of Marijuana Legalization in Colorado Emergency Departments." *Journal of Medical Toxicology*, vol. 11, no. 4, 2015, pp. 347–349. https://pmc.ncbi.nlm.nih.gov/articles/PMC6625695/.

434. CentraCare. "How Does the Legalization of Marijuana Affect Our Health?" *CentraCare*, 2023, https://www.centracare.com/articles-stories/legalization-of-marijuana-affect/.

435. Cassell, Paul G. "In Defense of Victim Impact Statements." *Ohio State Journal of Criminal Law*, vol. 6, no. 2, 2009, pp. 611–630. https://moritzlaw.osu.edu/students/groups/osjcl/files/2012/05/Cassell-FinalPDF.pdf.

436. U.S. Department of Justice. *Victims and Witnesses: Understanding Your Rights and the Federal Court System*. 2019, www.justice.gov/usao-ak/page/file/1442866/download.

437. National Academies of Sciences, Engineering, and Medicine. *Securing the Vote: Protecting American Democracy*. The National Academies Press, 2018. https://doi.org/10.17226/25150.

INDEX

For other books by Charles Patton see
www.charlespattonbooks.com